The
American Literary History
Reader

Edited by
Gordon Hutner

New York   Oxford
OXFORD UNIVERSITY PRESS
1995

To My Teachers,
David Levin and Ralph Cohen

Oxford University Press

Oxford   New York
Athens Auckland Bangkok Bombay
Calcutta Cape Town Dar es Salaam Delhi
Florence Hong Kong Istanbul Karachi
Kuala Lumpur Madras Madrid Melbourne
Mexico City Nairobi Paris Singapore
Taipei Tokyo Toronto

and associated companies in
Berlin   Ibadan

Published by Oxford University Press, Inc.,
200 Madison Avenue, New York, New York 10016

Library of Congress Cataloging-in-Publication Data
The American literary history reader /
edited by Gordon Hutner.

ISBN 0-19-509504-9
1. American literature—History and criticism—Theory, etc.
2. American literature—History and criticism.
I. Hutner, Gordon.
PS25.A44 1995 810.9—dc20 94-39554

9 8 7 6 5 4 3 2 1

Printed in the United States of America
on acid-free paper

Contents

Contents

Introduction

When the idea for a new journal in American literary studies first came to my mind, I imagined a quarterly that would bring together the various critical approaches to the diversity of American literature. Several journals continued to serve the Americanist community, but missing was a scholarly periodical that made the method and politics of critical practice its subject and that took as its linchpin the conviction that critical assumptions had changed. The paradigms governing the humanities were everywhere under serious and scrupulous revision, and a journal was needed, I believed, to help redefine the issues constellating American literary history.

I wanted this new quarterly to focus on the broadest range of discussion, because American critical practices, in the spring of 1987, seemed more embroiled than they were to become. By the time *American Literary History* was announced, new historical criticism had begun to establish itself and, having learned some key practices from deconstruction, had already begun to supplant it as an orthodoxy. Yet it would be misleading to suppose that the shift toward history was so straightforward. Ever since the New Criticism called itself "new," critical history has conceived of change with a sense of progress that exaggerates succession. Archetypalism may follow 1950s formalism, but to say so only satisifies our hunger for narrative, not our understanding of the way criticism responds to a prevailing wisdom as well as to cultural stimuli. Any critical history useful to the student of the subject ought to suggest that while one set of normative features is crystallizing into a hegemony, another one is in the process of breaking apart, while another is in its initial stages of articulation, while several competing others are testing the legitimacy or power of any paradigm in the making. Perhaps future generations will see the concatenation of approaches in our era as an uninterrupted march from structuralism to reader-response to deconstruction to New Historicism to Cultural Studies, and onward, even as we know how these models were—and are—debated in reaction to the felt urgencies of our time.

ALH set out to become a forum for debates about the theory, method, and subject of a new American literary history. American literary history had begun to seem static, perhaps the result of the Americanist establishment's reluctance to welcome the new theoretical work being disseminated through the 1970s. Although the movement toward a new American literary history progressed so slowly through the fifties, sixties, and into the seventies that, at times, there was no need for a journal to mark its development, the new history did gain an added impetus in the several struggles of African-American and ethnic studies, feminist theory, and gay/lesbian studies, and other forms of ideological criticism to achieve respectability and a measure of centrality. By the early 1980s, the cumulative effect of these efforts was exceptionally strong and coincided very well with the restlessness that deconstruction had unleashed.

For many, the urgent need for a new critical consciousness revealed a generational split. American literary history had for too long been written, it seemed, in the hand of the elders, though it is easy to forget that the arguments to open the canon had been going on at least since the 1950s. Still, the formulation of critical values, the reputations of authors, the claims of genres, and the priority of the American literary historiography written in the 1950s now might be undone or changed. To a significant extent, the criticism of the 1980s has been a liberal reaction to a stalwart conservatism, and one of the most vitalizing sources of contemporary criticism has been the reconsideration of the era of consensus politics that held sway after World War II, when the institutionalization of American literary studies had become so entrenched, the profession perhaps even more bourgeoisified than it already was. That era's value for democratic humanism, according to a new radical critique of a liberally constructed history, was seen to be in collusion with socially and politically repressive forces. One way of recalculating that legacy was to be found in the several new books devoted to once powerful precursors—Lionel Trilling and F. O. Matthiessen most often—or in the number of books, like Russell Reising's *The Unusable Past* or Sacvan Bercovitch's *Reconstructing American Literary History* that specifically call for new attention to the way previous generations had construed the subject of literary history.

Perhaps no single book embodied this overturning spirit more spiritedly than a collection of essays called *The American Renaissance Reconsidered* (edited by Walter Michaels and Donald Pease), nearly all of whose contents reappeared as significant chapters in some of the most influential books of the 1980s—Jane Tompkins' *Sensational Designs*, Michaels' *The Gold Standard and the Logic of Naturalism*, and Pease's

Visionary Compacts. The several compelling arguments in that book bade us perform a literary history that saw its goal as crystallizing forces beyond the author and as questioning cultural formations, such as the social preoccupations, political anxieties, and the gendered and racial shaping of interpretative frameworks. This variety of contexts, and their combination, became more the subject of critics' inquiries than the texts ostensibly under examination. To that end, Alan Trachtenberg's *Incorporation of America* (1982) and *American Realism: New Essays* (1982), including editor Eric Sundquist's commanding introduction, were harbingers of a new engagement with history and of how literary history might be written during the decade.

The relative ease with which this new historical studies earned its purchase (at the expense of deconstruction, feminism and reader-response criticism, among other strategies it more or less subsumed) on the academic establishment comes from the relief it offered from the formalism that seemed altogether too abstruse or too desiccated to win converts either in the classroom or in the credentialing vehicles that academic quarterlies had become since World War II. The formalism of the 1970s seemed to have widened the gap between scholars and literary critics—an appellation falling into disuse—while more and more critics, as the 1980s progressed, saw the object of their inquiry as culture, not literature. Rather than explain the operations or significance of great or forgotten or underappreciated works, the critic's job was to "interrogate," "problematize," and "valorize" how history, discourse, and society were entangled. Professors in English departments began to call themselves cultural critics, perhaps because the title more forthrightly signified to them a renewed sense of their public function, for instance, to descry the political and social constructions of meaning, particularly those that reveal the pressures of race, class, and gender.

Whereas literary historians once saw the study of literature as a good insofar as it led to the broader purpose of humanizing future generations, cultural critics saw literary works as participating in a conversation with several discourses—popular, economic, social, material, etc.—that could more or less bring the complex moment of a novel or poem more closely into view. To a generation of critics raised on the gruel that New Criticism had become through the 1950s and 1960s, history seemed not only more intellectually sustaining, but also more politically satisfying. History has fascinated Americanist critics since the 1980s, perhaps because the society on which they looked out seemed increasingly to deny or disguise it. A humanities professoriate could thus find redress, in New Historicism and Cultural Studies, against the accusations of ivory-towered isolation. These newer critics emphatically did not want to be removed from the general reading public. If anything they wanted most of all to address both the citizenry and its objects of consumption. While American literature professors have always eyed nervously the nation's reading habits, the state of literacy, the value of tradition, and the healthiness of art, many now attacked such concerns as passe or problematic. Others, especially those committed to pedagogy reform or those who specifically saw criticism as an ethical engagement, tried to reimagine the place of the humanities.

Thus the way for *ALH* was cleared even before our first issue in the spring of 1989. In drawing plans, I knew well enough from my previous reading and in working as an editorial assistant on *New Literary History* that the foremost reason for any journal's success was its defining editorial vision. I came to see, very quickly, that the vitality of this new journal could not depend on committing it to any one methodology or institution, or even to a circle of critics, such as typified august publications as diverse as the *Partisan* or the *Kenyon Review*s in the past, or, in the present, *Critical Inquiry*, *Raritan*, or *Representations*. Instead, these last five years, *American Literary History* has served to mediate the ongoing discussions among literary scholars and cultural critics, and it has done so by assembling as many good articles as it could from viewpoints as various as possible. I have tried to make the journal into the venue in which people who never consulted one kind of criticism would find it side by side with the kind they did read, because I believed that readers wanted to find things that they meant to take up or that they too seldom encountered or that they even distrusted, articles that would keep the study of American literature energetic and rich. Casting *ALH* according to one school or interest meant that other excellent provocative, instructive pieces of different critical stripes would never come to us, and I saw the mission of the journal as bringing together as many lively, well-written, and informative articles as possible. With the approval of the editorial board, we printed articles that represented views at odds with my own or at odds with some of our judges', but that gave evidence of the substantial work that always goes on, whatever the fashion. My hope is that *ALH* will continue to circulate the decisive, most learned, and innovative critical studies.

I believe that the seventeen essays reprinted here are among the most distinguished representatives both of our contents and of contemporary criticism. They have been chosen, out of so many equally good candidates, through an unsatisfying process of balancing sets of competing needs. Even as I wished most of all to give a vivid sense of the journal's many interests and diversity of contributors, I have emphasized essays from our first two or three years. In addition, it would have been impossible to include a fair sampling of our wide-ranging essay-reviews, the article-length meditations on one book or some combination and the issues to which several recent studies give rise—which from the beginning were conceived not as a static supplement to our scholarly papers, but as the dynamic complement to the journal's ongoing redefinition of the three words of our title. Nor could we find room here to include any of the interviews or literary documents we like to publish.

This five-year compilation represents as complete an array as possible of the cultural, social, and pedagogical issues facing American literary studies. Appearing in our premier issue was Lauren Berlant's study of *The Blithedale Romance*, which we featured for the model it creates of how historical scholarship and cultural theory could be brought explicitly together. In the next issue, Richard Brodhead's "Veiled Ladies" masterfully explores the relation between midcentury fiction and public entertainment, an essay that signaled the journal's commitment to studying cultural discourse. It appeared, as it does again here, alongside Hertha Wong's study of Indian pictographs and the language of selfhood they inscribe. Later, in the first year, we published Nina Baym's authoritative analysis of the early historiographies of American literature, as part of our first special issue, which was devoted to the tradition of American literary study as cultural critique. Lora Romero's study of the discourse of domesticity encoded in *Uncle Tom's Cabin* was also a crucial essay from the first year, for its intervention in debates about sentimental fiction.

The following volumes were no less various and exciting. In the next two years, we printed an essay by Giles Gunn on the premises of American critical practice, while we continued to present work concentrating on single texts that exemplified the changes American cultural studies was witnessing, such as Myra Jehlen's study of race and sex in *Pudd'nhead Wilson*. No essay more fully embodied our critical reassessment of current values than Walter Michaels' study of Willa Cather's *The Professor's House* and the historicizing of identification. José David Saldívar's critique of ethnographers' incursions into the specificities of identity and region, "The Limits of Cultural Studies," proposed a new direction for ethnic studies, while David L. Smith's article on the Black Arts Movement carefully articulated the historical context of such issues. "Reassembling Daisy Miller," by Lynn Wardley, directed attention to gender politics, as did David Leverenz in "The Last Real Man in America," which pursued the idea of "representative man" in new ways while registering *ALH*'s interest in popular culture studies.

Henry Louis Gates, Jr., addressed some of the journal's key concerns in a forum devoted to his arguments concerning the role and character of the new pluralism, the expectations we should still hold forth and limits we must face. The journal met this challenge in the fourth and fifth year by continuing to explore the boundaries of our title. In her discussion of Dickinson and class, Betsy Erkkila raised issues about how to read this poet from a social perspective, a perspective Americanists are sometimes least ready to acknowledge. Lawrence Buell further challenged readers to see American literature in its postcolonial aspect, in a special issue of Volume 4 on the possibilities of an inter-American literary studies. Ramón Saldívar analyzes the literature of the border to complicate the terms for constructing nationhood. Our essays in the fifth-year special issue on eighteenth-century American cultural studies might be typified in Nancy Ruttenberg's new historical study of Christian fervor and the formation of "democratic personality." As if to complete our first five years, Charles Bernstein's "What's Art Got to Do with It?" imaginatively meditates on current critical practices.

Perhaps the major contribution of this five-year volume is to recreate the forum for the critical exchange of paradigms for studying American literature and culture. So I see this volume as representing the larger debate that has occurred in the pages of *ALH*, not the "greatest hits" of literary criticism, but representative voices of the most significant claims in the argument over literature's importance. The imperative followed here is to be found in the way our articles have created a dialogue with others in our pages, sometimes explicitly, to give readers of all critical orientations a new chance to ascertain their relation to the critical debates of their day, and thus to vivify their practice, refine their theories, and inform their teaching.

The whole first year or two was full of surprises, and it delights me to recall how much fun it was, how gracious and patient people were as I learned the job, how so many professors so generously helped to assess the articles that so many scholars were willing to submit. *ALH* always aimed to be of uniform quality, however diverse the essays in any issue, so that every contribution counted. I need first of all to thank the dozens of contributors I have had to leave out. Beyond the academic community, I am grateful to my tireless colleagues at Oxford University Press. The biggest debt is surely to Susan Keiser, formerly the Journals Director, who believed that an assistant professor with an idea should get the kind of chance I was given. As much as any one person, she is the most responsible for the journal's founding. Nor would this volume have been possible without Liz Maguire's encouragement and backing. Throughout the years, the Oxford Journals Division met every request with the good-humored commitment to making *ALH* succeed: Mathew Bedell and Joe Fodor never let me down; and every contributor since 1990 has had a pleasure I've come to prize—working with our production editor, the incomparable Bob Milks.

At Wisconsin, I must thank the Graduate School and the College of Letters and Science for their contribution, along with several graduate students who have assisted me, especially Colleen Hamilton, Kari Kalve, Joan Parks, and, most of all, Mary Marchand. I am also very grateful to Bill Cain and Ross Posnock for their faithful support and excellent advice. Art Casciato, the book review editor for the first three years, collaborated with me in all plans and decisions. His efforts were prodigious, and his imprint on the journal is more enduring than he knows. Finally, I owe more than I can say to Dale Bauer whose expertise and counsel, instruction and suggestions, and guidance and love have led me to clarify, time and again, what *ALH* should be. She has shared in the journal's challenges without ever getting the recognition she deserves.

The
American Literary History
Reader

Fantasies of Utopia in *The Blithedale Romance*

Lauren Berlant

For instance, if my Reader will count how many letters there are in this one word, Nummatchekodtantamooonganunnon-ash, *when he has done, for his reward, I'll tell him it signifies no more in English than,* our lusts; *and if I were to translate,* our loves, *it must be nothing shorter than* Noowomantam-mooonkanunonnash.

Cotton Mather, The Life of the Renowned John Eliot

From its publication, *The Blithedale Romance* has been read as a commentary on the project of utopian socialism as executed in George Ripley's Brook Farm experiment. But Brook Farm/Blithedale is not the only site of utopian theory—and failure—in the novel. A fantasy of communion informs the love plots of *Blithedale* as fully as it does the story of collective life. The perfect knowledge that will accompany perfect social relations is also sought through the body; the "subject" constructed within collective identity is also defined sexually. *Blithedale* stages the relationship between collective and subjective desire not simply as a similitude—where love and community become simultaneous ends of utopian practice and projection—but also as a site of tension. Specifically, the novel plays what Jacques Ehrmann has called the tragic and the utopian directions of history against each other; the narrative poses the double articulation of individual and collective identity as a *problem* in history and for the narratives and persons that operate within its sphere.

Ehrmann writes that in reading the correlation between the tragic and the utopian, we encounter "the combined union of two forms of temporal sequence: the individual, which bears the mark of temporality; and the collective, which bears the mark of historicity." These modes of experience, these two forms of "destiny" and thought, are not lived simultaneously, but "alternately," along a "double perspective." The mode of the individual, in which "his" (sic) own origin becomes the meaning of his present, his end, is called the "tragic" mode, because it is "marked by the individual birth and death"; the mode of the "utopian," in which the end is the "true origin" of the past, is read as "collective destiny . . . marked by the origin and the end of humanity" (16).

These "spatio-temporal" modes of thought, and their narration in literature and history, require the suspension of the present: the subject is always in exile from whatever privileged space and time he desires, and is always in a search for love and knowledge, "the two answers which our civilization has invented to the problem, posed by death, or, in other words, the problem of *desire*" (27). The utopian mode of representing this exile, "framed within" the tragic figuration, sees exile as the very possibility of completion (24); the tragic voyager, who experiences the nowhere of exile as a fate always already played out, can only experience time as a "lag," a "dis-location" and fragmentation of consciousness (24).

The Blithedale Romance presents us with a special instance of national utopian fantasy. Miles Coverdale's particular obsession is a topographical one, of how to map out the personal and the transpersonal stories of birth and death that constitute the tragic and the utopian content of his life, and of the Blithedale experiment. But, in Coverdale's view, the project is haunted by the fear that such a mapping, describing only surface relations, is itself a utopian delusion. "Altogether, by projecting our minds outward, we had imparted a show of novelty to existence, and contemplated it as hopefully as if the soil, beneath our feet, had not been fathom-deep with the dust of deluded generations, on every one of which, as on ourselves, the world had imposed itself as a hitherto unwedded bride" (III: 128). This passage lays out—but paradoxically, with a false clarity—the field of collective and individual subjectivity on which history takes place. On this field it is possible to construct a collective "we" that knows itself because it holds a common fantasy of a perfected future. This "people," according to Coverdale, sees the present moment as a hopeful fore-gleam of a future luminescence. But the scene of utopian fantasy is founded on the repression of histories that would, presumably, challenge the "fact" of our present existence: Coverdale notes that his fellow workers act as if they are the land's first tillers and, by association, the nation's first utopians. But the community's historical amnesia with respect to the utopian projects that have preceded it reveals that American history has never been written or even thought. It has only been repressed, buried by new "dirt," new stories. America, in this view, is always distinctively post-utopian, but has never "known" it.

But knowledge has its dark side for Coverdale. Along with his recognition that "the dust of deluded generations" requires an archaeological operation on contemporary and past collective history, comes a strange analogy: the "world," in the act of erasing our memory, imposes itself on "us" as "a hitherto unwedded bride." It is perhaps here, in the text's deployment of the bride, that we find one suturing figure between the fields of collective and individual utopian fantasy—the hymen.[1] Zenobia's virginity and/or hidden sexual history, Coverdale's bachelorhood, Priscilla's virgin strength, Hollingsworth's aggressively sexual "availability" to Zenobia, Priscilla, and Coverdale: each of these is a local instance of the "unwedded bride," who seems by definition to herald historical change, as she is always "hitherto unwedded" at the moment she forces herself on "us."[2]

In *Blithedale* the virgin's untouched hymen is the only barrier that protects "us" from the death of our own utopian desires. The "virgin" mind, mirroring the virgin body in its lack of "knowledge," can project itself purely into the future without limits. But when historical and sexual knowledge comes, when "the world had imposed itself" upon us, we lose the clarity of utopian, libidinal perfection. The postvirginal bride who weds her demystifying knowledge to us is simultaneously the source of our historical consciousness, our historical amnesia, and our personal nostalgia for those moments before her "knowledge" atomized our whole bodies and destroyed our utopian collective dreams.

Coverdale's critical analysis is riddled with ambivalence toward demystification. On the one hand, until someone like Coverdale (or Hawthorne) "fathoms" the lost material beneath the fantasy, we will be shocked by each failure of the collective utopian project and compelled to repeat the repression of its existence. Revealed knowledge, in this context, is good, because it "grounds" us in history, and reveals to us our motives. But knowledge also heralds the death of desire, and is set up here as an antithesis of love. The figure and agent of the disappointments of utopian community is a bride: the institution whose repetition repeats the national and socialist pattern of utopian fantasy and tragic knowledge is, implicitly, a marriage.

This essay will attempt to unravel the associations of this postnuptial metaphor, and the love plots to which it alludes—the plots of "storied love" (III: 56) that constitute the main interest of Coverdale's narrative. To Coverdale, love, "a true and available mode of life that might be struck out . . . between theory and practice" (III: 63), contains the potential for the mutual utopian transformation of the subject and her/his context, as well as the seeds of its death, in knowledge. Love acts as a thread that travels through the various elements that constitute the manifest and buried historical sites on which individuals negotiate their lives, in this narrative: ultimately the novel questions the language of love itself, exposing love's inability truly to mediate, to merge, to illuminate, to provide a clarifying model of anything, whether utopian or tragic, with which it comes in contact.[3]

To find a way into the conjunction of these material and buried sites I will look at something limited: Coverdale's sexuality. I say that this is limited because Coverdale is a bachelor and probably a virgin, which means that the sexual for him exists only in the realm of "hope or fear" — that is, a realm of theory where speculation is a kind of practice.[4] Coverdale's sexuality is central to the question of history in *The Blithedale Romance* because sexual discourse provides for him a stimulating and yet comforting structure within which he theorizes about himself, his partners at Blithedale, and the Blithedale project itself. Sexuality provides for him an epistemology, a conventional and stabilizing structure of interpretation. It spans his young, promising bachelorhood and the paralyzing bachelorhood of middle age; it provides a name for relations that are otherwise awkward, unstable, and undefined in "our new arrangement of the world" (III: 13).

Indeed, Coverdale's own "character" embodies the activity of translation and mediation that marks his sexual discourse, although he doesn't "know" it. The namesake of Miles Coverdale, the sixteenth-century Englishman who was the first translator of the Bible into English (and a close friend of Thomas More), he also may be the namesake of Miles Standish, whose military and amorous mediations between Native American and colonial culture are legend.[5]

These allusions suggest his special positioning as a Pandarus figure in *The Blithedale Romance*: sexual discourse enables him to justify his failures on the battlefields of personal and political desire by showing that individual, tragic destiny and collective, utopian projects are mutually constituted and contained in each other, and therefore must share each other's fate. For example, I will suggest that when Coverdale addresses—and undresses—women, he focuses on the tragedy of individual history to explain their way of inhabiting utopian, public life. When he addresses men, especially Hollingsworth, he invokes the history of collective-utopian practice—in particular, via the French uto-

Love acts as a thread that travels through the various elements that constitute the manifest and buried historical sites on which individuals negotiate their lives, in this narrative: ultimately the novel questions the language of love itself, exposing love's inability truly to mediate, to merge, to illuminate, to provide a clarifying model of anything, whether utopian or tragic.

pian theorist Charles Fourier, and via the Puritan "Apostle" John Eliot, whose utopian plan also included the translation of the Bible (from English to the Algonquin language)—to unveil and critique masculine libidinal will to power. Finally, I will ask just how eccentric Coverdale's consciousness really is. For his fellow and sister characters too rely on a discourse of love to define the language and the experience of political and personal history, the relation that generates the analogy between the "unwedded bride" and the archaeological mandate of American history.

1. *"Ara nudus, sere nudus"*: Coverdale's Vulgar Reading

Coverdale's translation to Blithedale not only provides for him a new way of life, but also gives him a new body (it serves this function for Priscilla as well). He describes himself as he has lived in the city as solitary, immobile, and effeminate; on his move to Blithedale he goes through an illness that looks a lot like birth, but which he describes as a kind of death: "My fit of illness had been an avenue between two existences; the low-arched and darksome doorway, through which I crept out of a life of old conventionalisms, on my hands and knees, as it were, and gained admittance into the freer region that lay beyond" (III: 61). As a result of his physical conversion experience—an experience, as I will discuss, that converts Coverdale's consciousness as well—life on the farm makes him in "literal and physical truth . . . quite another man" (III: 61). Everyone notices this; it even fascinates Coverdale. Silas Foster comments that his "shoulders have broadened, a matter of six inches" and that his "lungs have the play of a pair of blacksmith's bellows" (III: 137, 138). His fist is so rough that Hollingsworth cannot imagine him writing ballads; he is so much larger that he imagines himself for future generations an enormously powerful mythical figure, painted "in my shirt-sleeves, and with the sleeves rolled up, to show my muscular development" (III: 129).

The physical insistence of his new masculine body, demonstrated by his self-characterization as Bacchus (one among many mythical and literary potentates with whom he identifies), does not translate into a newly developed sexual consciousness; indeed, Coverdale's sexual immaturity is only highlighted by the new physical manifestation of his desire (Schroeder; Murray). A minor but symptomatic example may be found in his Carlylean discussion of the chaos of inappropriate clothing at Blithedale: "So we gradually flung them all aside, and took to

honest homespun and linsey-woolsey, as preferable, on the
whole, to the plan recommended, I think, by Virgil—'*Ara nudus, sere nudus*'—which, as Silas Foster remarked when I translated the maxim, would be apt to astonish the women-folks"
(III: 64). This phrase is indeed from Virgil's *Georgics*.[6] In major
nineteenth-century translations this phrase is translated more
decorously: Coverdale, a vulgar reader, clearly and typically
translates "nudus" literally—as "nude."[7]

Both in his eyes and his imagination, and even in his translations, Coverdale undresses the women at Blithedale: Zenobia—or should I say Zenobia's body—is the main recipient of
the narrative gaze of heterosexual desire. Initially Coverdale,
who smiles and blushes, "no doubt, with excess of pleasure"
(III: 14) at her compliments to him, cannot get over how much
life Zenobia's body has. Yet, paradoxically, he disempowers
Zenobia by fully sexualizing her: "Pertinaciously the thought—
'Zenobia is a wife! Zenobia has lived, and loved! There is no
folded petal, no latent dew-drop, in this perfectly developed
rose!' . . . drove out all other conclusions, as often as my mind
reverted to the subject" (III: 47). His attraction to her turns
sour when he "discovers," through his intuition, that she is no
virgin: he fears that Zenobia will offer herself as "a free woman,
with no mortgage on her affections nor claimant to her hand,
but fully at liberty to surrender both, in exchange for the heart
and hand which she apparently expected to receive" (III: 127).
Having reduced Zenobia from a politically and sexually complex person to a sex effect, Coverdale takes on a mission to
"know" her body in any way he can; he will be "satisfied" only
when he can construct a full narration of Zenobia's definitive
"history."

It is immediately after Coverdale's speculation about both
Zenobia's virginity and the veracity of her self-representation
that he ruminates about the false history on which utopian
projects like his own are based, in the passage I have quoted—
a falseness attested to by the way the world always thrusts itself
on utopians "like a hitherto unwedded bride." Clearly, in this
passage, he has Zenobia on his mind. The bride, in this metaphor, ought to be the most transparent of signifiers, as she is
a virgin, "hitherto unwedded." But Zenobia gives the lie to the
meaning of virginity, because she can "pass." Her crime, in
Coverdale's view, is that she represents herself to Hollingsworth
as unwedded, thereby forcing him to pledge himself unawares
not to building a new life on new land (the American utopia),
but to one based on used property, tilled land, a life of broken

ideals. Here Zenobia is the "world," disillusioning knowledge, the sign that the visionary man can never be sure that what he sees is the whole story. She imposes herself on "us" by the materiality of her presence, and yet it is this very materiality that deceives. While "woman" in the abstract is the perfected image of desire, woman's presence becomes, in Coverdale's logic, the point of resistance to desire's fulfillment, the sign of its impending death (this doubleness generates Zenobia's association with images of unbearable beauty in life and of monstrous hideousness in death), and in retrospect comes to figure the inevitable failure of collective, utopian desire as well.

Coverdale's ambivalence toward female sexuality, which is played out in the hymenal, utopian space between individual and collective history, refers to more than his interest in Zenobia. For if Zenobia is behind the image of the deceptively unwedded bride who has lived and known her one "event," then Hollingsworth is here associated with the utopian experiment; indeed, it is Hollingsworth's happiness that Coverdale is concerned with in this chapter, "The Crisis."[8] Why should the potential disappointment of Hollingsworth—in love, in utopian fantasy—mean anything to Coverdale? As with Zenobia, Coverdale is attracted to Hollingsworth, and repulsed by his own attraction: while he is in part bitterly suspicious of Hollingsworth's use of personal magnetism to forward his philanthropic schemes, Coverdale also desires Hollingsworth, even to the point of including himself in his list of "proselytes" (III: 68).

The erotic relationship between Coverdale and Hollingsworth suggests that Coverdale's real "secret," the one that "possibly may have had something to do with these inactive years of meridian manhood, with my bachelorship" (III: 247) is that he—he himself—was in love—with—Hollingsworth. But rather than look merely for the sexual, passional "roots" of this relation—this would typically be Coverdale's mistake—we must read the homoerotic bonds at Blithedale as *relays,* signifying complexly motivated relations among men. The operation of homosociality in *Blithedale* is politically multivalent—describing relations between philosophy and the desiring subject, as these conjoin in the utopian project; between men competing, patriarchally, for women and other profitable resources; as well as between men who desire each other sexually and emotionally.[9]

For surely there is a specifically sexual component to this relation. To begin with, Coverdale observes that the "Golden Age" represented by the Blithedale experiment "seemed to authorize any individual, of either sex, to fall in love with any other, regardless of what would elsewhere be judged suitable and prudent" (III: 72). Coverdale implies that in the real world men fall in love exclusively with women, and vice versa. Blithedale makes possible alternative forms like polygamy, extramarital sex, and homosexuality, and in this it is symptomatic of contemporary historical movements as well as of Coverdale's own eccentric discourse of love. Thus despite his vehement insistence on the unnaturalness of Hollingsworth's philosophical commitment and utopian vision, Coverdale's very attraction to Hollingsworth is made possible and fully authorized by the sexual *politics* of Blithedale itself. This means that this homoerotic love plot too, as with all of Coverdale's others, is his attempt to forge or imagine a utopian experience whose implications will extend farther than the limits of the dyad—personal utopia and communion would be proof of the possibility that every utopia might not only be thought, but lived, in unheard-of combinations.

The Hollingsworth love plot begins during Coverdale's illness. Released from his own worldly "effeminacy" (III: 145), Coverdale finds Hollingsworth's "more than brotherly attendance" inspiring, heartwarming (III: 41); it is Hollingsworth's example that reveals to Coverdale just how distasteful he finds conventional masculinity. This repulsion constitutes much of Coverdale's "feminism." He says, for example, that he would much prefer to be ruled by women than by men, for "I hate to be ruled by my own sex. . . . It is the iron sway of bodily force, which abases us, in our compelled submission" (III: 121). Christianity or the influence of woman might ameliorate man's basic violence, but at root, "young or old, in play or in earnest, man is prone to be a brute" (III: 73). He reveals his own distaste for "this ugly characteristic of our sex": that men—a group in which Coverdale explicitly includes himself—cannot show the tenderness of love (III: 41).

"But there was something of the woman moulded into the great, stalwart frame of Hollingsworth; nor was he ashamed of it" (III: 42). Hollingsworth's generous nurturance of Coverdale reveals to him the utopian possibility of redeeming manhood itself, making it beautiful internally as well as externally: in *Blithedale,* handsome men—of whom the only two are Westervelt, "the handsomest man in the whole world," and Coverdale (III: 110; 227)—are under great suspicion because their beauty, like woman's beauty, hides their "ugly characteristics." In contrast, Hollingsworth, massive like a bear, displays "a tenderness in his voice, eyes, mouth, in his gesture, and in every indescribable manifestation, which few men could resist, and no woman" (III: 28).

Paradoxically, Coverdale also abhors Hollingsworth's version of masculinity. Hollingsworth's polemic against the independence of women and for phallic supremacy, in which he "boldly uttered what he, and millions of despots like him, really felt . . . the well-spring of all these troubled waters," repels Coverdale, who in turn aligns himself with women and feminism (III: 123). But this speech takes place, at Eliot's Pulpit, in the context of a rhetorical competition between the two men for the women's affection. Thus when women are present, Coverdale competes with and denigrates Hollingsworth's sexual ideology. When women are absent, however, when Hollingsworth is alone with his feminine soul, or with Coverdale, Coverdale covets Hollingsworth, imagining them growing old together, two patriarchs of the "Phalanstery."

Twice they speak of making a bond using language that, between a man and a woman, would sound like marriage talk: "'Dear friend,' said I, once, to Hollingsworth . . . 'I heartily wish that I could make your schemes my schemes, because it would be so great a happiness to find myself treading the same path with you.'" (III: 56); "'Coverdale,' he murmured, 'there is not the man in this wide world, whom I can love as I could you. Do not forsake me!'" (III: 133). Like Damon and Pythias they would tread the same path; they would "love" each other (in more guarded moments Hollingsworth uses the conventional language of "brotherhood" rather than love), and this bond would carry them through the joint project of their life. This bond would save them from the intrusion of the "hitherto unwedded bride" of false representation and disillusionment that plagues ideal institutions. But of course they refer to no real marriage; just the language they use makes the stakes that high. Instead, they speak of Coverdale's possible conversion to Hollingsworth's philanthropic scheme: while sexual discourse is Coverdale's comfortable mode of speech, social philosophy is Hollingsworth's—although from Coverdale's point of view, it is Hollingsworth's discourse that really aims to seduce.

2. Hollingsworth, Coverdale, Fourier:
Le Nouveau Monde Amoureux

Coverdale, like many a Hawthornean narrator, despises theory. Even before they meet, Coverdale decides that Hollingsworth will be intolerable because he is a philanthropist; as he does with Zenobia's feminism, Coverdale demonstrates his ability to strike to the heart of a political issue by insisting that Hollingsworth's theories should be tested empirically—either by the members of Blithedale or by Hollingsworth himself, who "ought to have commenced his investigation of the project by perpetrating some huge sin, in his proper person, and examining the condition of his higher instincts, afterwards" (III: 36). Coverdale does not believe that reason or logic can test a theory: more extremely, he implies a connection between theorizing and criminality. The evidence of Hollingsworth's own sinfulness *is* his theorizing; the "peccadillo" he perpetrates is in imposing his theories on the lives of others (III: 22).

Yet during the illness he produces at the outset of his stay at the community, Coverdale undergoes a conversion experience. Somehow he has managed to make it to Blithedale, to the vanguard of social theory, without actually having read any. He comes to Blithedale not knowing the theory that informs his own practices: he is not self-conscious, while nonetheless full of self. So he becomes modern. He reads Transcendentalist theory in Emerson and *The Dial,* romantic philosophy in George Sand, and utopian cultural theory in Charles Fourier.[10] Coverdale converts to/is seduced by Fourier—this kind of submission is the danger of reading theory, no doubt. He comes to use Fourier in his own philosophical discourse of seduction: "I talked about Fourier to Hollingsworth, and translated, for his benefit, some of the passages that chiefly impressed me" (III: 53). Parodically, Coverdale reports on Fourier's fantasy of the utopian production of *limonade à cèdre* (III: 53–54); here, as well as in Coverdale's previous translation of Virgil, we see that this Miles Coverdale translates literally, vulgarly, whatever "bible" he reads.

But what substantive material does he find in Fourier, and how does his dissemination of that material enter into the discourses of love and power he adopts and then, violently, repudiates? Coverdale enjoys the obvious analogy between Fourier's system and that of Blithedale, yet the two theories differ, he says, "as widely as the zenith from the nadir, in their main principles" (III: 53). The main principles to which he refers address the relative place of the passions and man's "higher instincts" in the utopian schemes. Hollingsworth, as many critics have noted, is a conventional Transcendentalist in his assertion that the reformation of man must come primarily from the "inside" (Johnson; Sherbo). Cultivating that which is best and strongest in himself, the subject subordinates the claims of his social environment as well as his physical body.

It is not surprising that Hollingsworth is disgusted, then,

by what he understands to be Fourier's philosophy: for, via Coverdale's translation, he understands that Fourier

> has committed the Unpardonable Sin! For what more monstrous iniquity could the Devil himself contrive, than to choose the selfish principle—the principle of all human wrong, the very blackness of man's heart, the portion of ourselves which we shudder at, and which it is the whole aim of spiritual discipline to eradicate—to choose it as the master-workman of his system? . . . And his consummated Paradise, as he pictures it, would be worthy of the agency which he counts upon for establishing it. (III: 53–54)

The "zenith" is Hollingsworth's domain: the spirit, the heart. The "nadir" of Fourier engages what Coverdale calls "the promised delights of his system": the erogenous zones treated by Fourier's theory of the passions (III: 54). The paradigm of the passions becomes the touchstone for what Coverdale feels would be truly ideal for Blithedale: while Coverdale closes this scene with a joke about Fourier's fantastic lemonade, he in fact seems to desire the fruition of the literal delights of the system, which bases its structure on fulfillment of the principles of attraction in both work and play, in industrial and sexual armies.

Coverdale's reading of Fourier's plan is closest to that of Roland Barthes. In Barthes's view, "The motive behind all Fourierist construction . . . is not justice, equality, liberty, etc., it is pleasure. . . . 'amorous freedom, good food, insouciance, and the other delights that the Civilized do not even dream of coveting because philosophy has taught them to treat the desire for true pleasures as vice' " (Barthes 80–81). As if he had read *Le Nouveau Monde Amoureux* (Fourier's development of his early theories of sexual perfection, which was not published until 1967), Coverdale instinctively understands that a literal extension of the Fourierist plan to harness the passions to improve both love and play, an achievement made by breaking down the traditional philosophical primacy of reason and of conventional juridical and moral law, would be to provide not only a "social" minimum for the members of the Phalanx, but also a "sexual minimum."[11] The utopian state's commitment to the production of pleasure would liberate both women and men from monogamy.

The germ of Fourier's late conceptualization of passionate freedom as the root of social improvement is planted in his early work, *Théorie des Quatre Mouvements,* in which he asserted that "The degree of emancipation of women is the natural measure of general emancipation."[12] Ultimately, love would be the principle of all relations in the association; this love would be both physical and spiritual, since in Fourier's view one without the other is deformed and deforming.[13] Coverdale, clearly excited by the idea of a utopia run on a principle of love that would not only include but require the fulfillment of sexual desire, seems to read Fourier as if he does not mention the spirit at all. This misreading would be consistent with Coverdale's statement to Hollingsworth that Fourier does not rely on God to authorize his project; in fact, much of his and his followers' work relies on his reading of God's intentions. Brisbane, for example, writes that "Attraction is, in the hands of God, a magic wand, which enables him to secure from love and pleasure the performance of work, which man can alone obtain by constraint or violence" (459). In retrospect, when Coverdale muses over the reasons why the community died the death it "well deserved," he blames its "lapsing into Fourierism" (III: 246), which might also be what Zenobia describes when she alludes to "such Arcadian freedom of falling in love as we have lately enjoyed" (III: 170).

While the Coverdale who narrates the novel has moved beyond having any "hope or fear" about his life—which is thus over, in the narrative sense—the young Coverdale was essentially given a new body, a sense of feeling and hope by Fourierism, with its plan of government by love. Coverdale is so enthusiastic about this configuration of utopia that belief in its perfection becomes crucial to his belief in himself, and in the future. Indeed, Hollingsworth's rejection of Fourier provokes the first break between them: "I began to discern that he had come among us, actuated by no real sympathy with our feelings and our hopes . . ." (III: 54–55).

Read in light of Fourier, the Perfectionist movement might also be said to construct the physical and spiritual utopia of individual redemption through the language of love. Coverdale's vulgar reading of contemporary philosophy provides the "theory" for his fatal insistence that the life of the body equals the life of the mind and spirit (Johnson). His conversion experience to Fourierism, which takes place during his intense illness (and which is later undone when he leaves his utopian body behind and resumes the "effeminacy of past days" (III: 145)), alters his desire, and makes him "another" man, the one who wants to speak the discourse of love and philosophy to Hollingsworth, who nonetheless repudiates what he hears.

For Hollingsworth's discourse is not explicitly about love,

especially a love that authorizes and valorizes the body's passions. Moreover, the project the philanthropist imagines is not constructed for the new world comfort of the privileged classes; it does not seek to ameliorate the condition of all mankind, as Blithedale does, and it does not incorporate the principle or the language of love to make its scheme palatable to the soft hearts of the sympathetic public. Rather, "he purposed to devote himself and a few disciples to the reform and mental culture of our criminal brethren" (III: 56). Stoehr suggests that for Hawthorne Hollingsworth's project of criminal reform is "some ultimate philanthropy, a summation of all the do-good projects and salvation sciences of the times" (227); he, along with Baym, insists that the purpose of such a characterization is to satirize and debunk philanthropic movements whose high seriousness and earnestness merely mask a vile will to power.

But more than a satire and repudiation of contemporary social reform is struck out in the blacksmith's characterization. Hollingsworth is also the reformer in history, an embodiment not only of the contemporaneous project of American utopianism, but also of the utopianism that since the Puritans has constituted the mythos and the politics of American national identity. Hollingsworth's characterization by Coverdale hinges on his inheritance of the voice of the utopian past. Eliot's Pulpit, where Hollingsworth "preaches" to his own brethren two centuries after John Eliot preached to some Native Americans, is thus simultaneously a gloss on the history and politics of missionary/philanthropic activity in America and an evaluation of the crisis of national-utopian politics contemporary to the Blithedale experiment. At no time is Eliot's Pulpit characterized by the kind of democratic love ethos characteristic of radical nineteenth-century social theories—although, as I will suggest, nineteenth-century interpretations of Eliot insist on his exemplary treatment of the Indians. Instead, this utopian heritage is distinguished by the enlightened man's covenantal duty to educate and convert the "proselytes," or natives.

3. The "dust of deluded generations" and "Apostle Eliot's Pulpit"

However much legitimacy one gives to Zenobia and Coverdale's claim that Hollingsworth is a moral monster, it must also be said that Coverdale recognizes a greatness of spirit in Hollingsworth as well. Through the thin walls of the common house, Coverdale hears Hollingsworth fervently pouring out his soul to God: a man this pious, in Coverdale's eyes, is "marked out by a light of transfiguration, shed upon him in the divine interview from which he passes into his daily life" (III: 40). Hollingsworth's transfiguration is clearly not physical—as Coverdale's has been, through his illness and subsequent muscular development—it is spiritual, otherworldly, the biblical veil that hides nothing but signifies the man's relation to heavenly spirit. It is in this holy light that Hollingsworth first assumes the form of Apostle Eliot.[14]

John Eliot does not figure actively in this narrative—not in the way, for example, Reverend Wilson does in *The Scarlet Letter*—and the characters' collective consciousness of him seems limited to "a tradition that the venerable Apostle Eliot had preached" at "a certain rock," "two centuries gone by, to an Indian auditory" (III: 118). But the Apostle is active in Coverdale's fantasy life. Seated at Eliot's Pulpit, Coverdale "sees" the Apostle: "I used to see the holy Apostle of the Indians, with the sunlight flickering down upon him through the leaves, and glorifying his figure as with the half-perceptible glow of a transfiguration" (III: 119). Eliot's Pulpit is to *Blithedale* what the scaffold is to *The Scarlet Letter*: the place of sexual, juridical, and theological confrontation.[15] It is also Coverdale's personal touchstone. Both during his tenure at Blithedale and after he leaves, he returns in memory and refers to this rock, anointing it the omphalos of his experience, the place that contains the tangle of memory and desire his narration attempts to unravel (or reconstruct).

Hollingsworth becomes Eliot there, and Priscilla, Zenobia, and Coverdale by analogy become Eliot's Indians, neophytes who try to learn the language of the spirit and the necessity of commitment. But Hollingsworth's exhortations are valuable less for what they contain—Coverdale never reports their content to us—than for what they sound like. As with Dimmesdale, Hollingsworth's seductive pulpit moves listeners not by the light of reason but by the attraction of emotions transmitted by rhetoric—even while Hollingsworth is emphatically against theories of the passional basis of social reform.

> . . . Hollingsworth, at our solicitation, often ascended Eliot's pulpit, and—not exactly preached—but talked to us, his few disciples, in a strain that rose and fell as naturally as the wind's breath among the leaves of the birch-tree. No other speech of man has ever moved me like some of these discourses. It seemed most pitiful—a positive calamity to

the world—that a treasury of golden thoughts should thus be scattered, by the liberal handful, down among us three, when a thousand hearers might have been the richer for them; and Hollingsworth the richer, likewise, by the sympathy of multitudes. (III: 119)

Coverdale here expresses the values of sentimental religion. Hollingsworth ought to become "rich" by "enriching" the masses with his "golden thoughts": rather than take to heart what Hollingsworth says (it is the following chapter, "The Crisis," where Hollingsworth proposes to and is rejected by Coverdale), Coverdale covets his *discourse,* his style, his golden "language." In this respect Coverdale is very much like an Indian listening to John Eliot: he may or may not actually comprehend the content of what he hears, but he thinks he knows the *sense* of the language itself, and thinks he knows that the act of translation from one system (English; Hollingsworth's philosophy) to another (Indian; the proselytes' combined ignorance and resistance) is an act of love. But aside from structural analogies perfectly clear to Coverdale, what does it mean—to *The Blithedale Romance*—that Hollingsworth repeats Eliot?

Coverdale brings the collective and the individual together by giving priority to individual history: he cannot see Blithedale as a significant mass of people, but can only see the psychodrama of a limited few on the dramatic stage of his own consciousness. Elevating the fulfillment of the individual's passions to the place of the utopian principle, he sees Hollingsworth as a monster because he acknowledges no body, and sees his philanthropy as a deformed and distorted approach to the human subject, because Hollingsworth is committed to reclaiming a group of nameless and placeless people, people so marginalized that they are unimaginable within the complacent and class-divided system of Blithedale.

The ideational split between these two men suggests that, in *The Blithedale Romance,* a philosopher's relation to his libidinal desire can be predicted by the centrality to his social theory of the individual subject. Coverdale's Blithedale works on the star system; Hollingsworth's vision, influenced largely by his own working-class background, assumes a postlapsarian inevitability to the criminality he wants to reform in others. Coverdale valorizes his own passions, and so his social theory relies on a collective egotism, a mass commitment to subjectivity. Hollingsworth is a more complex case. For him, the libidinal impulses of the self must be subordinated to the regulation of social behavior, and so he attempts to reformulate the criminal subject by transforming the sphere of the social.

Yet Hollingsworth, according to Coverdale, also wants to use the force of his individual will to redeem the collectivity. Hollingsworth's system is insidious because the anonymity of his potential subjects contrasts with his personal power so much that his personality (the key to the project) looks like the monstrous egotism of which he has been justly accused by characters and critics alike. This distortion of personality may be a failure on Hollingsworth's part. But it may also signify a symptomatic contradiction for a certain kind of utopian thinker; it is this contradiction that informs Apostle John Eliot's place in the text.

The project of historical archaeology that takes us from Blithedale to Natick, Eliot's first missionary settlement, suggests that Eliot's function as a pre-text for Hollingsworth extends to the way his missionary work precedes Blithedale. Eliot is the originary American reformer, and his "praying towns" are among the originary American utopian experiments. One can see in the fate of that movement some kind of analogy to the present case. The Apostle "transfigures" Hollingsworth in two ways. First, Eliot's approach to social reform anticipates Hollingsworth's own theories about how to reform a particular marginal group (Indians, criminals) by seeing them as individuals to be reformed but also as functions in an ongoing social economy. They do not want to transform the world—both are conservatives, in that sense—but to transform problematic individuals in it. Second, both Eliot and Hollingsworth are said to project powerful personalities that rouse suspicions about the motives behind their visionary social schemes. The cultural reception of this kind of utopian thinker turns out often to substitute for a rigorous analysis of his project; that this is so, and why this is so, not only figures heavily in the historical status of Eliot, but also translates into Coverdale's representation of Hollingsworth as well.

"We had a tradition among us, 'That the country could never perish so long as Eliot was alive'," writes Cotton Mather (I: 578). Writing a biography of Eliot, then, would be coterminous with writing the life of America, and so too the "meaning" of John Eliot would also, somehow, provide a meaning for his country. Mather's *Life of Eliot* is, like many of Mather's major biographies, careful to establish a particular paradigm for his subject that would contain at once the history of the man, its effect on the formation of America, and its place in

Puritan eschatology: "The world would now count me very absurd, if, after this, I should say that I had found the SEPULCHRE of MOSES in America: but I have certainly here found Moses himself; we have had among us one appearing in the Spirit of a Moses; and it is not the *grave*, but the *life* of such a Moses, that we value ourselves upon being the owners of" (I: 528).

Mather identifies John Eliot as Moses not because he led his people on an exodus into exile, but because through his missionary work he brought the Algonquin Indians of New England from their spiritual exile into a new regenerate community. This interpretation of Eliot's work is complicated by the fact that the English immigrants to New England were simultaneously pushing the Indians off of their tribal property. But for those who, sympathetic to the Puritan cause, believed in the missionary project that was an original motivation for the Massachusetts Bay Colony—the seal of the colony contains in its center a picture of an Indian saying "Come over and help us" (Jennings 229)—the displacement of the Indians reveals "a law of human progress, that civilization must overtop and displace uncivilized man."[16]

Eliot is typologically Moses because he institutes a civil and ecclesiastical government for the Indians according to the rules laid out in Exodus 18; he does this by envisioning and then actually instituting "praying towns" for willing tribes of Indians.[17] These towns, instituted in 1650 and growing to twelve in number, sprung from Eliot's assumption that a change in the spirit of an Indian would be insufficient conversion; rather, a full conversion to the ways of civility was needed in order to assure that the Indians' feelings of regeneration would be accompanied by appropriate practice (Francis 161). Eliot himself purchased the land at Natick; he also purchased the materials the Indians would need to become self-governing and self-sufficient in these regenerate towns.

The parallels between Eliot's and Hollingsworth's utopian plans are clear: Hollingsworth's criminal, the nineteenth-century version of Eliot's Indian—whose practice of Indian religious ritual was actually outlawed on pain of death in 1646—would be set up in a community with other criminals, and only a few outsiders would participate in the material and spiritual self-improvement of the participants (Jennings 241). Each enterprise has as its goal the eventual assimilation of its members into mainstream society. In this sense utopian thought is being employed for local, not millennial ends—although, as James

Holstun points out, Puritan consciousness demonstrated a strong tendency to confuse or to obliterate the distinction between the two. Moreover, each enterprise claims pure motives for its philanthropy, because the missionary apparently gets nothing but good feeling from his efforts: repeatedly in Eliot's own representations of his project as well as others' redactions of it, Eliot's labor of "love" manifests itself not in wages he earns, but in his "love" for the Indians as brethren under the skin, so that "love" becomes both the motivating factor of the difficult labor and the payment-in-kind the labor generates.[18]

This unambivalent interpretation of Eliot's mode of utopian thought and practice is evident in many histories of Hawthorne's day, especially that of Convers Francis.[19] In the tradition of many of Eliot's contemporaries, and reinforced by Cotton Mather's hagiographic biography of Eliot, Hawthorne himself, in *Grandfather's Chair,* a history book for children, fashions Eliot's humanitarian and visionary benevolence as an ideal type of American social consciousness and practice.[20] "Grandfather," who "was a great admirer of the Apostle Eliot" (VI: 45), distinguishes Eliot from the mass of Puritan magistrates and ministers because he had faith in the reformability of the Indians: "[The Puritan rulers] felt no faith in the success of any such attempts, because they had no love for the poor Indians. Now Eliot was full of love for them, and therefore so full of faith and hope, that he spent the labor of a lifetime in their behalf" (VI: 43). Eliot, Grandfather says, viewed the Indians as "his brethren"; he "persuaded" them "to leave off their idle and wandering habits," and to live like the English: building houses, farming, going to school, praying (VI: 44). The Indian Bible was perhaps Eliot's greatest achievement, says Grandfather, because Eliot, like Grandfather himself, gave the Indians (who were the "long lost descendants of the ten tribes of Israel," according to some theories) access to "the history of their forefathers" (VI: 48).

But young Laurence, who identifies mightily with the spirit of the Apostle, brings a dark cloud to Grandfather's proceedings: he wonders whether Eliot's labors were for naught, since there are no Indians left to read the language of which Eliot's work is now a "relic." The moral of the story, says Grandfather, is not that utopian gestures such as Eliot's fail, but that "man is capable of disinterested zeal for his brother's good" so that "if you should ever feel your own self-interest pressing upon your heart too closely, then think of Eliot's Indian Bible. It is good for the world that such a man has lived, and left this emblem of his life" (VI: 49).

Grandfather, in contrast to Hawthorne, identifies himself as a Harvard man (VI: 32), and this locates him squarely within liberal, Unitarian ideology and tells us something about the purpose of Grandfather's storytelling: to reproduce American history in its full and inevitable providential glory, and to reveal along the way the "capability" of (especially American) man to perform truly and purely good acts. We must read this strain of thought into Hawthorne's reading of Eliot, and into Coverdale's idolization of the Apostle in *Blithedale*. Hollingsworth and Eliot are both characterized as central to the reproduction of the American utopian project: each embodies the national commitment to reading human nature as capable of thinking utopian thoughts and of trying to enact them in good faith.

But Eliot, like Hollingsworth, was also subject to much criticism for these same acts.[21] The missionary was criticized for being both hypocritical and obstinate in his opinions; at once ascetic and yet luxuriantly egocentric in his practice (Francis; Bancroft; Mather). In addition, "Great opposition was made to the collection [of funds for missionary work with the Indians] in England; and the conversion of the Indians was represented as a mere pretence to draw money from men of pious minds" (Hutchinson I: 141). Francis Jennings writes that some of the money Eliot received disappeared; moreover, he documents that Eliot took credit for missionary work done by others, especially Thomas Mayhew, Jr., "the man who had worked in lonely isolation with never a penny of encouragement from Massachusetts" (245). Like Hollingsworth, Eliot was accused of accumulating capital (and sacrificing people) for the advancement of his own cause—some people thought that his cause was himself.

What do these various charges of corruption say about the mutual glossing of Eliot and Hollingsworth? That visionary thinkers are, as Hollingsworth says, "by necessity" obstinate and egocentric. But this is not because every act hides a secret will to power (although this might always be the case) but because it takes power to articulate and hold a theoretical position, and even more (in the logic of this novel) to resist the encroachments of the "world," the "hitherto unwedded bride," who would distract you from or annihilate your theory and your practice in the name of the claim of that which already is. Both of these thinkers operated on a principle of "love" with respect to the objects of their philanthropy, but their love fuels a private, personal commitment that preexists the implementation of their project as well as its public expression.

Thus both men are "transfigured" by their theoretical and

practical zeal, because they do not need to think personal and collective history "alternately," but instead try to think them together, as one. This very act of will (the force that most frightens Coverdale and attracts the women) makes the utopian theorist look like a monster of self, a master totalizer who refuses to honor the differences between the individual and the collective, public and private, spirit and politics. The "world's" fundamental lack of sympathy with the utopian thinker is masked by a cult of personality that forms in homage to the thinker's personal power; along with it grows the "tragic" trajectory of history that relies fully on the personal story; the utopian as a category of possible political and philosophical thought is then entirely repudiated as too frightening and *self*-consuming a project.

The "deluded generations," whose histories would be otherwise articulated by the utopian course of history, are buried under the "dust" of nationalist-romantic historiography. If Coverdale is any example, the clichés of Puritan history are a part of our national consciousness and our individual personalities—we all can *identify with* the Pilgrims, as the Blithedalers do, but we cannot *identify* John Winthrop's "city on a hill" speech when Hollingsworth gives his version of it—but much about the Puritan settlers (both events and ideology) is buried under this dust; and along with those are buried generations of Indians whose histories are entirely unknown to us.[22] In Hawthorne's romances too, Native Americans are always at the farthest margins of representation—of the crowd (in *The Scarlet Letter*), of property (land and the map in *Seven Gables*), and in parentheses, in *Blithedale*: ". . . it was still as wild a tract of woodland as the great-great-great-great grandson of one of Eliot's Indians (had any such posterity been in existence) could have desired, for the site and shelter of his wigwam" (III: 118).

Eliot's project of constructing villages in which the Indians would learn to live exemplary lives was crushed by King Philip's War (1673–75). The "praying Indians" were annihilated, because they were caught between the interests of the white population (who did not entirely trust them) and the hostile Indian population (who felt that their conversion to Christianity signified their allegiance to the Englishmen). The history of these utopian experiments therefore cannot be usefully integrated into American self-mythologizing; instead, the one figure whose life might in part redeem our national treatment of the Indians, John Eliot, is valorized and apotheosized.

Thus the burial of Indian history beneath the dust of other American delusions is both enacted and alluded to in this novel by an allusion to one man, Apostle Eliot. Instead of a truly collective history, one that would take into account the complete story of American culture, Coverdale symptomatically provides for us a romance of history marked by great figures; character, rendered allusively, parodically, or stereotypically substitutes for the exposition and explanation of plot, and also for the social configurations on which the plotting hinges.

Characters in his *Blithedale* are the site of history's burial: the "unwedded bride" is the analogy for that which we do not know, and—given Coverdale's particular feelings about Zenobia—that which we, as readers and citizens, do not want to know. The veil is a powerful object because, as Zenobia's story of Theodore and "The Silver Veil" tells us, it hides that which we do not want to uncover, just as the hymen (a figure of history, here) is a fetish because it signifies a mystery that, for all its attractions, is better off left mysterious.

To write the complete American history on its utopian trajectory would be to write the history of scandal (mass killing) and to read a series of failures; thus what we get instead is a record of the obsessions of a failed (his) storyteller and a bachelor to boot (Coverdale), who writes about a failed world-historical figure (Hollingsworth), a dead "unwedded bride" (Zenobia), and a pallid and yet self-satisfied audience (Priscilla), the single-minded reader who gets what she wants—a "great man" whose authority she never questions.

4. The Ends of Love

Hollingsworth's philosophy is motivated by a certain kind of love—it is philanthropy. We can see this in his use of the term "love" to express his own desire to couple with Coverdale, to merge their wills in the cause of redeeming the criminal's soul. And yet in his prime he refuses to acknowledge the heterosexual love plot imagined for him by Coverdale, and desired for him by both Zenobia and Priscilla, both of whom are too "womanly," too silent, to impose it on him explicitly. Any sign of his erotic interest in either of the women must be attributed to his need for money—he instrumentalizes the personal motives he deplores in order to further his project. Like Apostle Eliot, Hollingsworth only valorizes passions that are not of the body. However monomaniacal these reformers might be in their obsessive commitment to the criminal or Indian, however much private pleasure they might generate in their incessant planning for not one, but many houses of "storied love," their political choices require them to deny the claims of simply "personal" designs. At the end Hollingsworth surprises himself by loving Priscilla, for his admission of love for her (as he well knows) is simultaneously the admission of his own political defeat: "It was the abased and tremulous tone of a man, whose faith in himself was shaken, and who sought, at last, to lean on an affection. Yes; the strong man bowed himself, and rested on this poor Priscilla" (III: 219).

Coverdale, in contrast, is entirely self-consistent in his commitment to love: he finds in Fourier a philosophical position that acknowledges and reinforces his urgent need to make love and to make others love. He enforces his desire first by insisting that Zenobia, Priscilla, and Hollingsworth (and to a lesser extent, Westervelt and Old Moodie) are all living within a love plot; he desires to effect that plot either through his personal involvement in love or by the women's recognition that he is the ideal witness and judge of the crimes committed in the name of love. Failing that, he tells a story, *The Blithedale Romance,* in which the only possible motive is love—only love counts for anything; love becomes the site of a totalizing theoretical discourse, the occasion of that too incessant fiddling on one string that Coverdale so despises in theorists like Hollingsworth.

Thus in Coverdale's translation, utopia is a totalitarian state; we hear the cries "of anger or words of grief" (III: 135) rising in the collective throats not just of women (III: 103–04), but of everyone, as they are variously silenced and killed off by the love he imagines. He misreads his own *Blithedale* narrative in thinking that its appropriate telos lies in the revelation of his truest love; the minute attention he gives to the progress of his body as he ages—as he has also given to his "strenuous aspirations," the heavy breathing which dies out "with his youthful fervor" (III: 3)—suggests that he never relinquishes his commitment to it and to the desire he feels in his "earnest" bones (III: 68), even as their decay means more and more that since he cannot live by love he will, like Zenobia, die for it. Here he speaks nostalgically of his desire, and of the disastrous consequences his analytic mode—in which the will to know the "truth" of love paradoxically resulted in tragic, vulgar mistranslations— has had for his own happiness:

> It is a matter which you do not see, but feel, and which, when you try to analyze it, seems to lose its very existence, and resolve itself into a sickly humor of your own. Your understanding, possibly, may put faith in this denial. But

your heart will not so easily rest satisfied. It incessantly remonstrates, though, most of the time, in a bass-note, which you do not separately distinguish; but now-and-then, with a sharp cry . . . 'Things are not as they were!' — it keeps saying — 'You shall not impose on me! I will never be quiet! I will throb painfully! I will be heavy, and desolate, and shiver with cold! For I, your deep heart, know when to be miserable, as once I knew when to be happy! All is changed for us! You are beloved no more!' And, were my life to be spent over again, I would invariably lend my ear to this Cassandra of the inward depths, however clamorous the music and the merriment of a more superficial region. (III: 139)

Coverdale sees that love is "engrossing" (III: 220), for it gives the lover a body; giving the lover a body, it gives life (constituted not by "superficial music and merriment," but by a deep and repetitive death knell) as well as death, the tragic trajectory of individual history. He is able only to speculate about and to gaze at the lovers (who, he momentarily admits, might also be haters), whose intensity of passions "puts them into a sphere of their own, [and gives] them the exclusive property of the soil and atmosphere" (III: 213–14). Coverdale longs to experience the full tragedy of individual love, its life and its death, but because he operates according to a regime of will-to-knowledge — repressing the woman in him, the Cassandra, who operates not by way of truth but via dissimulation — he ends up suspended in the death-in-life of narrative, an endless well-ordered love plot about his own eternal lovelessness.

In this misreading of love, Coverdale's experience is, though eccentric, symptomatic of a more generalized social practice: first, because the aborted love plot between himself and Hollingsworth, whose narrative specter is raised and destroyed, is repeated in the stories of Zenobia and Priscilla. (Old Moodie and Coverdale constantly ask: does Zenobia love Priscilla? Does Priscilla love Zenobia? And Coverdale always wants to know: whom, if not each other, do the women really love?) Second, they all live in an "epoch" when love itself is the named principle of history: even a simple act like eating a communal supper reminds them that they are making progress towards "the millennium of love" (III: 24); it is the utopian spirit of "love and free-heartedness" (III: 29) that brings them together, that determines first their political condition and then provides for them a model of emotional attachment.

As in *The Scarlet Letter,* political love in *Blithedale* slips into personal, physical love (although for quite different reasons); and it is this slippage that results, always in Hawthorne, in the tragic meaning of (utopian) history. We see political institutions that represent themselves as nonpolitical because operating on the principle of love (a love that is nonideological; one that is neither carnal nor inscribed in systems of earthly power); we see political discourse that uses the representational and social conventions of love to insist that the violent excesses and exclusionary tactics of power can be brought under control by the principle of love; in Hawthorne's work love usually, but not always, provides the comfort of personal origins, personalities, and characters, and ultimately denies the potential strength in thinking through collective history (in America, a utopian concept), collective experience, collective consciousness.

Hawthorne thereby shows that the harnessing of love by politics not only deforms our personal experience of power—making it seem natural, homely—but also thwarts the very possibility of representing the tactics and strategies of politics, because in rejecting the political operations in question, we would end up rejecting love as well. In *Blithedale* we return to the tragic personal and political effects of love—but here the tragedy of the personal is also, explicitly, a political tragedy. Coverdale's reading of his love plot, evident in his juxtaposition of the "hitherto unwedded bride" with the buried events of American history, is that its failure grows from the failure of American political praxis to appropriate and incorporate his, and others', visionary passion; his retrospective bitterness about the failure of Fourierism on the farm grows from his inability to find an alternative discourse to that of love within which he might even imagine gratification.

From another point of view, however, Coverdale's use of the analogy of the unwedded bride to describe the series of utopian failures whose histories are obliterated by a national amnesia, suggests that in *Blithedale* the bride's plot, the love plot, contains the series of buried "events" that would constitute American history if that history could be written; and while Coverdale is out of control, in love with love and with writing about it, Hawthorne, the figure of the author in the preface, reveals its strategic purport.

The preface to *Blithedale* reiterates the by-now familiar Hawthornean lament about his inability to write pure romances in America: "In the old countries, with which Fiction has long been conversant, a certain conventional privilege seems to be awarded to the romancer. . . . Among ourselves, on the contrary, there is as yet no such Faery Land, so like the real world, that,

in a suitable remoteness, one cannot well tell the difference . . . ."
(III: 2–3). Here Hawthorne discusses the way American authors
are censored in their very mode of representation by America
itself. The national myth, the preconscious pretext inscribed in
the mind of every reader-citizen, is so powerful that certain things
cannot be said in the face of its blinding light; the generic conventions of representation legislated by this nation make every
text, whether the author likes it or not, a symptomatic ideological
construct. The political coercion of the author takes place in
practice by the insistence of the public on reading everything in
terms of mimetic representation: the author, who is not necessarily aware of this coercion, nonetheless feels "pressed very
heavily upon him" (III: 2) the message that he must not write
in the mode of utopian history while always writing in the tragic,
the temporal, the individual. (Coverdale gladly does this; he is
a monster of the individual, and uses the analogy of the bride-
as-world to convince us that even utopian thought is a priori
impossible.)

The author's only hope for relative freedom from writing
only historical novels starring triumphant individuals would be
to find "an available foothold between fiction and reality" (III:
2). In *Blithedale,* the space of straddling is the threshold between
the individual and the collective modes of thinking about history—the place where the unwedded bride meets the buried
truth. But which is the bride—fiction, because embodying the
fantasy of love—or reality, because, as Zenobia so passionately
argues, the bridal condition is woman's fate, her harsh material
experience? The dust of deluded generations occupies the same
contradiction, since its diachronicity gives it the privilege of
romance as well as the claim of the material event. Each is a
fantasy and a materiality, each the occasion for theory.

Thus while Hawthorne blames America for his inability
to write "pure Romance" (this is what Coverdale thinks he does
write, while his narrative refers to some other kinds of stories),
he also has his revenge on America by disallowing the category
of pure genre, and, writing in "this epoch of annihilated space"
(III: 195), locates his "Faery Land" in the places where American narrative discourse is forbidden to go, places buried under
the dust of unused libraries, unread documents, and finally the
dust generated contemporaneously, by progress. And he does
this, in a sense, by overemphasizing the question of genre in
Coverdale's text: calling it *The Blithedale Romance,* and insisting so strongly on the love plot that it breaks down under
the pressure of its application.

All of Hawthorne's American romances display his resistance to theory—about literary genre, about sex, about history.

In *The Scarlet Letter,* it is speculation in the sphere of "theory" that constitutes, in the narrator's view, Hester Prynne's most heinous crime against the state and society. In *Seven Gables,* the theorizing of the Pyncheon and the Maule clans that falsely justifies their claims to power, property, and moral propriety are ridiculed by the narrator, who nonetheless ends up smoothing out the deformities of collective, national history with the privilege of the utopian narrative gaze. And in *Blithedale,* where individual and collective theories of desire are brought into practice, love becomes the only occasion for narrative, and narrative becomes the record of the violations such theorizing brings about. His resistance to the theoretical authority of all traditional, patriarchal law is magnified in the case of Coverdale, whose folly finally shows that the substitution of love for the law does not clarify but blinds the lover/theorist's vision, skewing his representation and obliterating the historical interest of his narrative, by his too intense focus on the *hymen* of history.

Thus for Hawthorne the "hitherto unwedded bride" configures ambivalence about what theoretical speculation might reveal about the relation of national and personal identity. The obsession within these narratives with the woman's sexual purity taps into her time-honored place as the generic repository of knowledge inaccessible to men—she is "knowing." This imputation of special female knowledge, in Hawthorne's work, provokes fantasies of communion and of domination, releasing a desire among men to "know" her, either in or regardless of her own terms. Hawthorne's texts reproduce these fantasies about female sexual difference—but in part to expose and undermine the patriarchal privilege that has marked American national identity. His contradictory representations of woman exhibit the problem of constructing a knowing historical discourse, one that honors individual and collective fantasy while revealing corruption in their local operations. In *The Blithedale Romance* love stands in for the problematic alterity of the tragic and utopian senses of history: the novel bears the scars of its knowledge on the body, its text.

Notes

1. Hawthorne deploys what I would call a "logic of the hymen" when virginity and "wedded" marriage become the opposition around which Coverdale maps out the political, ethical, and textual terrain of Blithedale.

Jacques Derrida has elaborated how this kind of figure works: to demarcate that meaning which exceeds and undermines the claim of metaphysical thinking that intention or presence can determine the proper operation of meaning and identity. He calls this the logic of the "supplement." A theoretical boundary that is also a ring to be passed through, the hymen, represents, to Derrida, the surplus meaning that cannot be contained *within* any system of interpretation as well as "the space between" that demarcates linguistic and sexual difference, paradigm conditions under which the discipline of interpretation is made necessary. See especially "The Double Session."

2.   Critics of *The Blithedale Romance* have traditionally taken up the question of how to read the novel through its utopian and tragic trajectories by championing fiercely the cause of either one or the other. One mode, most forcefully represented by Nina Baym, argues that the story is predominantly about individual characters whose individual dramas have some relation to their local historical context and yet are ultimately about personal freedom and, as she has elsewhere written, the subject's "existential independence" from history and society. Taylor Stoehr's *Hawthorne's Mad Scientists* exemplifies the other school, in which *Blithedale* stages the collective historical experience of American culture. But neither Baym's nor Stoehr's mode of reading accounts for the way that Hawthorne sees the management of these different textual materials as central to the *problem* of adjudicating these different modes of identity. See Baym, "Hawthorne's Women: The Tyranny of Social Myths" 263; "*The Blithedale Romance*: A Radical Reading"; "The Significance of Plot in Hawthorne's Romances" 66. Other recent readers who share Baym's point of view on this text are: Kent Bales; John C. Hirsch; John Harmon McElroy and Edward L. McDonald; John Carlos Rowe, "The Metaphysics of Imagination: Narrative Consciousness in Hawthorne's *The Blithedale Romance*" in *Through the Custom-House* 52–90; Mary Suzanne Schriber.

For interesting examples of the historicist/"reflectionist" mode of reading *Blithedale* (there are many because of its roots in Brook Farm), see Stoehr; David Reynolds; Claudia D. Johnson; Maria Tatar.

3.   For an opposing position, see Edgar Dryden, who reads love in *The Blithedale Romance* as exclusively a redemptive, utopian force.

4.   The possibility that "bachelor" really means "virgin" (in Coverdale's case) is suggested in a number of ways. One of these is that when Coverdale imagines that Zenobia is too "womanly" to be a virgin he utters, " 'Zenobia is a wife! Zenobia has lived, and loved!' " (III: 47). In so doing he substitutes a legal position for a description of her sexual experience: the analogy with "bachelor" is clear. Hawthorne's journal contains another germane entry: "Supposing a man to weigh 140 lbs. when married, and after marriage to increase to 280 lbs.—then, surely, he is half a bachelor; especially if the union be not a spiritual one" (VIII: 314). While allowing for the possibility of spiritual marriage, here Hawthorne emphasizes that marriage and bachelorhood describe sexual experience or practice.

Sexuality is also the issue in Hawthorne's other use of his phrase "hope or fear," in "Alice Doane's Appeal," where the narrator rehearses his failure to seduce publishers and audiences with his texts: paralyzed by bitterness, "I have not much to hope or fear" (XI: 269). Both of these narrators use this locution to mark the state of relinquished desire. Having left the realm of hope or fear (a sexual and political realm as well as a description of their relation to the vocation of writing), these narrators are consigned to lives of vicarious affect; in each instance, this alienation from pleasure, which also signifies the failure of creativity and immersion in nostalgia, is paradoxically crucial to the construction of national and erotic narrative.

5.   Coverdale is said to be important in the history of the Bible not only because he produced the first complete English translation of it; he is also considered a "popularizer," one for whom readability was more important than philological rigor and accuracy in translation. His work was considered valuable for its "literary" quality; some of Coverdale's more beautiful phrasing was retained in later, more accurate translations of the Bible.

I am indebted to Jennifer Krauss's unpublished paper "Hawthorne's *Blithedale* and the American 'Proposal'" for this insight about the Coverdale-Standish relation. Krauss argues that the Miles Standish-John Alden-Priscilla Mullens triangle is also an originary American love plot underlying Hawthorne's novel. Just as crucial to Standish's amorous preview of Coverdale is his military history, especially his centrality in undermining the community of love at Merry Mount, in the Plymouth colony, in 1625. This gloss might motivate the enormous amount of military language used by *Miles* Coverdale (*miles*: Latin, soldier). Moreover, Standish's reputation as fop, braggart, authoritarian, and impotent lover has an uncanny resemblance to Coverdale's.

6.   The passage actually reads "*nudus ara, sere nudus*" (I. 299).

7.   While in John Dryden's 1695 translation the phrase is translated "Plough naked, swain, and naked sow the land," in two major nineteenth-century editions *nudus* is either veiled, simply, "in thin attire" (trans., Davidson 1875) or allegorized entirely, as a message "that the farmer should be industrious, and turn the summer to the best account" (ed. Cooper 1839).

8.   Coverdale turns Zenobia's polemic against the historical oppression of women into a dirty joke. She exclaims, "How can [woman] be happy, after discovering that fate has assigned her but one single event, which she must contrive to make the substance of her whole life? A man has his choice of innumerable events." He replies, "A woman, I suppose ... by constant repetition of her one event, may compensate for the lack of variety" (III: 60).

9.   Eve Kosofsky Sedgwick offers the word "homosocial" to stress how desire "between men" is represented mainly through the social representations and practices of the patriarchal will-to-power. Sedgwick would agree with Coverdale that while relations among men are fractured by the confusion of desire and power, there appears to be a confluence of interests among women. In Coverdale's narrative, such gender distinctions become central to a pathological fantasy of his own powerlessness with respect to women, who are united (against him) in their self-knowledge; Sedgwick, while more self-aware than Coverdale, repeats this fantasy as truth.

10.　Hawthorne is known to have reread Fourier right before writing *Blithedale*. He writes Horatio Bridge that "in the summer of 1851 he was reading Fourier with a view . . . to his next romance" (Stewart 122).

11.　See also Brisbane 1969. Brisbane himself "translated" Fourier's doctrines to American contexts: he writes that Fourier's associations follow the principle of libidinal economy: man's "passion can only be gratified by a prolonged action of the body in the physical world" according to the principles of "love" and "attraction" (211–13; 459).

See also Keith Taylor 121. Taylor notes that the New Amorous World of Fourier extended its earlier theory of state-mandated sexual practice by instituting a Court of Love that would regulate issues as specific as who would sleep with whom—Fourier's ideas were not eugenically oriented in the mode of John Humphrey Noyes (of New York's Oneida Community) but were intended to produce the optimum (for pleasure) distribution of sexual favors within the community. The idea of a Court of Love has its own uncanny and tragic manifestations in *Blithedale*.

12.　Cited in Barbara Taylor. Originally from Fourier 43. Taylor writes that Fourier's emphasis on the liberation of women, a discourse that Coverdale picks up with less self-consciousness than he might, characterized an "entire generation of socialist activists," including the American utopian movement of the early and mid-nineteenth century (x). See also Foster.

13.　Tuveson writes that by 1850 the theory of utopian fruition through natural development heralded by Fourier, Comte, and Condorcet was archaic, and presumably would have been recognized as such; the "book of history" replaced the "book of nature" because "in the actions of nations . . . is to be found the proof of a divine and supremely merciful Mind; for nature shows nothing beyond a kind of engineering perfection, whereas history reveals movement and ends in human history" (85).

14.　Mather writes of Eliot that he (like Hollingsworth) "made it his daily practice 'to enter into that Closet, and shut his Door, and pray to his Father in secret'" (I: 531).

15.　This particular rock or "Pulpit" does not figure centrally in histories of Eliot and his work with the Indians. In addition, Eliot did not usually preach to the Indians at Roxbury (his first church assignment in New England was at Roxbury, but his missionary work was initiated at Concord, and then on his lands at Natick). Only on one occasion did the Indians gather for purposes of worship there (see Eliot 1834). For a more limited, "symbolic" reading of Eliot's Pulpit in *Blithedale*, see Stay.

16.　Francis 298–305. Francis's *John Eliot* provided Hawthorne with much of the source material as well as the tone of the *Grandfather's Chair* section on Eliot.

17.　James Holstun suggests that Exodus 18—where Moses learns to govern by delegating power within the community, creating variously "rulers of thousands, and rulers of hundreds, rulers of fifties, and rulers of tens" (Exodus 18:21)—is a strange text for an enterprise such as Eliot's, since it aims at instituting utopian "procedures which will make [Eliot's] own authority unnecessary." Holstun suggestively situates Eliot's utopianism in the context of other textual utopias, such as More's *Utopia,* in order to describe the way his praying towns raised "the possibility of an unprecedented integration of religious and political life" (122).

18.   Bancroft's reading of Eliot's project is typical: "Foremost among these early missionaries—the morning star of missionary enterprise—was John Eliot. . . . His actions, his thoughts, his desires, all wore the hues of disinterested love. His uncontrollable charity welled out in a perpetual fountain" (Bancroft 94–95).

19.   The first half of the nineteenth century witnessed a strong interest in Eliot. For example, not too long before the writing of *Blithedale,* a monument to Eliot was erected. Hawthorne might have seen Henry Dearborn's widely distributed "A Sketch of the Life of the Apostle Eliot Prefatory to a Subscription for Erecting a Monument to his Memory." Dearborn specifically includes Eliot in a history of important translators of the Bible that includes Miles Coverdale (19). See also Jacobs and Winslow for other typical contemporary enshrinements of Eliot. I isolate Francis's influence on Hawthorne's reading of Eliot because in *Grandfather's Chair,* "Grandfather now observed, that Dr. Francis had written a very beautiful Life of Eliot, which he advised Laurence to peruse" (VI: 49–50).

20.   The Massachusetts Historical Society publication of "Tracts Relating to the Attempts to Convert to Christianity the Indians of New England" contains glowing self-interpretation from Eliot himself, along with supporting letters by the Reverends Shepard, Whitfield, Mayhew, and Winslow. It is important to note that these letters were public documents used mainly to raise funds for the Colony's, and especially Eliot's, missionary work.

21.   Hawthorne would have read of the resistance to Eliot in Mather and Francis (both of whom are unsympathetic to Eliot's critics) and in Hutchinson's *Massachusetts-Bay* (which reports the criticism of Eliot without comment).

22.   Hollingsworth says, "But I offer my edifice as a spectacle to the world that it may take example and build many another like it. Therefore I . . . mean to set it on the open hill-side"; Coverdale's response is to wonder why "Hollingsworth should care about educating the public taste in the department of cottage-architecture, desirable as such improvement certainly was" (III: 80).

Works Cited

Bales, Kent. "The Allegory and the Radical Romance Ethic of *The Blithedale Romance.*" *American Literature* 46 (March 1974): 41–53.

Bancroft, George. *History of the Colonization of the United States.* Vol. 2. Boston, 1837.

Barthes, Roland. *Sade, Fourier, Loyola.* Trans. Richard Miller. New York: Hill and Wang, 1976.

Baym, Nina. "Thwarted Nature: Nathaniel Hawthorne as Feminist." *American Novelists Revisited: Essays in Feminist Criticism.* Ed. Fritz

Fleischmann. Boston: G. K. Hall, 1982. 58–77.

———. *The Shape of Hawthorne's Career.* Ithaca: Cornell UP, 1976.

———. "Hawthorne's Women: The Tyranny of Social Myths." *The Centennial Review* 15 (1971): 250–72.

———. "*The Blithedale Romance*: A Radical Reading." *Journal of English and Germanic Philology* 67 (1968): 545–69.

———. "The Significance of Plot in Hawthorne's Romances." *Ruined Eden of the Present: Hawthorne, Melville, and Poe.* Eds. G. R. Thompson and Virgil L. Lokke. West Lafayette, IN: Purdue UP, 1981. 49–70.

Brisbane, Albert. *Social Destiny of Man or Association and Reorganization of History.* 1840. New York: Augustus M. Kelley, 1969.

Dearborn, Henry A. S. "A Sketch of the Life of the Apostle Eliot Prefatory to a Subscription for Erecting a Monument to his Memory." Roxbury, 1850.

Derrida, Jacques. "The Double Session." *Dissemination.* Trans. Barbara Johnson. Chicago: U of Chicago P, 1981. 173–286.

Dryden, Edgar. *Nathaniel Hawthorne: The Poetics of Enchantment.* Ithaca: Cornell UP, 1977.

Ehrmann, Jacques. "The Tragic/Utopian Meaning of History." *Yale French Studies* 58 (1979): 15–30.

Eliot, John. "The Examination of the Indians at Roxbury, The 13th Day of the 4th Month, 1654." *Collections of the Massachusetts Historical Society.* 3rd ser. 4 (1834): 269–87.

———. *The Christian Commonwealth: Or, The Civil Policy of the Rising Kingdom of Jesus Christ. Written Before the Interruption of the Government. 1659. Collections of the Massachusetts Historical Society.* 3rd ser. 9 (1846): 127–64.

Foster, Lawrence. *Religion and Sexuality: Three American Communal Experiments of the Nineteenth Century.* New York: Oxford UP, 1981.

Fourier, Charles. *Oeuvres Complètes.* Paris, 1841–45.

Francis, Convers. *Life of John Eliot, The Apostle to the Indians. The Library of American Biography* 5. Boston, 1836.

Hawthorne, Nathaniel. *The Centenary Edition of the Works of Nathaniel Hawthorne.* 20 vols. Columbus: Ohio State UP, 1963–.

———. *The Blithedale Romance.* Vol. 3 of *The Centenary Edition of the Works of Nathaniel Hawthorne.*

———. *The Whole History of Grandfather's Chair.* Vol. 6 of *The Centenary Edition of the Works of Nathaniel Hawthorne.*

———. *The American Notebooks.* Vol. 8 of *The Centenary Edition of the Works of Nathaniel Hawthorne.*

———. *The Snow-Image and Uncollected Tales.* Vol. 11 of *The Centenary Edition of the Works of Nathaniel Hawthorne.*

Hirsch, John C. "The Politics of Blithedale: The Dilemma of the Self." *Studies in Romanticism* 11 (1972): 138–46.

Holstun, James. *A Rational Millennium: Puritan Utopias of Seventeenth-Century England and America.* New York: Oxford UP, 1987.

Hutchinson, Thomas. *The History of the Colony of Massachusetts-Bay.* 2nd ed. 2 vols. London, 1760.

Jacobs, Sarah S. *Nonantum and Natick.* Boston: Massachusetts Sabbath School Society, 1853.

Jennings, Francis. *The Invasion of America.* Chapel Hill: U of North Carolina P, 1975.

Johnson, Claudia D. "Hawthorne and Nineteenth-Century Perfectionism." *American Literature* 44 (Jan. 1973): 585–95.

Krauss, Jennifer. "Hawthorne's *Blithedale* and the American 'Proposal.'" Unpublished essay, 1984.

Massachusetts Historical Society, Collection of. 3rd ser., IV (1834): 1–287.

Mather, Cotton. *Magnalia Christi Americana; or, The Ecclesiastical History of New England.* 2 vols. 1852. New York: Russell and Russell, 1967.

McElroy, John Harmon and Edward L. McDonald. "The Coverdale Romance." *Studies in the Novel* 14 (Spring 1982): 1–16.

Murray, Peter B. "Mythopoesis in *The Blithedale Romance.*" *PMLA* 75 (Dec. 1960): 591–96.

Reynolds, David. *Beneath the American Renaissance: The Subversive Imagination in the Age of Emerson and Melville.* New York: Knopf, 1988.

Rowe, John Carlos. *Through the Custom House.* Baltimore: Johns Hopkins UP, 1982.

Salisbury, Neal. "Red Puritans: The 'Praying Indians' of Massachusetts Bay and John Eliot." *William and Mary Quarterly* 3rd ser. 31 (Jan. 1974): 27–54.

Schriber, Mary Suzanne. "Justice to Zenobia." *New England Quarterly* 55 (March 1982): 61–78.

Schroeder, John. "Miles Coverdale as Actaeon, as Faunus, and as October: With Some Consequences." *Papers on Language and Literature* 2 (Spring 1966): 126–39.

Sedgwick, Eve Kosofsky. *Between Men.* New York: Columbia UP, 1985.

Sherbo, Albert. "Albert Brisbane and Hawthorne's Holgrave and Hollingsworth." *New England Quarterly* 27 (1954): 531–34.

Stay, Byron L. "Hawthorne's Fallen Puritans: Eliot's Pulpit in *The Blithedale Romance.*" *Studies in the Novel* 18 (Fall 1986): 283–90.

Stewart, Randall. *Nathaniel Hawthorne.* New Haven: Yale UP, 1948.

Stoehr, Taylor. *Hawthorne's Mad Scientists.* Hamden, CT: Archon Books, 1978.

Tatar, Maria. *Spellbound.* Princeton: Princeton UP, 1978.

Taylor, Barbara. *Eve and the New Jerusalem.* New York: Pantheon Books, 1983.

Taylor, Keith. *The Political Ideas of the Utopian Socialists.* London: Frank Cass and Co., 1982.

Tuveson, Ernest Lee. *Redeemer Nation.* Chicago: U of Chicago P, 1968.

Vaughan, Aldan. *New England Frontier: Puritans and Indians, 1620–1675.* Boston: Little, 1965.

Virgilius Maro, Publius. *Georgics.*

Trans. John Dryden. *The Works of the English Poets.* 100 vols. Ed. Thomas Park. London, 1818.

———. *Opera; or The Works of Virgil.* Ed. J. G. Cooper. New York, 1839.

———. *The Works of Virgil.* Trans. Davidson. Ed. Theodore Alois Buckley. New York, 1875.

Winslow, Ola Elizabeth. *John Eliot: "Apostle to the Indians."* Boston: Houghton Mifflin, 1968.

Veiled Ladies: Toward a History of Antebellum Entertainment

Richard H. Brodhead

When she is not at Blithedale, the Priscilla of Hawthorne's *The Blithedale Romance* has a career. She makes public appearances as the Veiled Lady: clothed in a silvery white veil, which purportedly insulates her from terrestrial reality, she goes onstage as a human conduit to occult knowledge, giving sibylline answers to the questions her audience puts. Hawthorne, we know, felt a final dissatisfaction with this figure of his creation. When *Blithedale* was finished but unnamed he considered "The Veiled Lady" as a possible title for the book but ruled that "I do not wish to give prominence to that feature of the Romance."[1] But would he or no, prominence is just what *Blithedale* gives the Veiled Lady. The book begins with Miles Coverdale "returning to my bachelor-apartments" from "the wonderful exhibition of the Veiled Lady" (5). Its plot machinations—unusually intricate for a Hawthorne novel—all turn on moves to rescue Priscilla from or to re-imprison her in her onstage role. And if any figure in *Blithedale* might be said to be figurally belabored, it is the Veiled Lady, this book's prime site of symbolic overdevelopment. The question I want to put in this essay is what, historically, is on Hawthorne's mind when he writes *Blithedale* in 1851–52, and by extension, what cultural situation a novelist would have had to address at this moment of American literary history. If I begin with the Veiled Lady, it is on the assumption that she embodies answers to questions of this sort.

What cultural history could Hawthorne's Veiled Lady stand for? She is "a phenomenon in the mesmeric line" (5), and she has as her most obvious referent the "magnetized" subjects used by the importers of mesmeric lore—Charles Polen and his many imitators—to demonstrate theories of animal magnetism to American publics after 1836. (In her clairvoyance the Veiled Lady is meant specifically to demonstrate the supermagnetized state that Mesmer's follower the Marquis de Puysegur termed "extraordinary lucity." [2]) More generally the Veiled Lady images, as a salience of contemporary life, the cultural attraction of what *Blithedale* calls "new science[s]" (5), that congeries of systems—Swedenborgianism, phrenology, utopian socialism, and Grahamite dietary lore are other examples—that developed into something between fad philosophies and surrogate religions in the American 1840s. Grouped as she is with Hollingsworth, Zenobia, and the Blithedalers, Priscilla shows such new sciences as literally living together with many other social movements of comparably recent birth: penal reform, the women's rights movement, communitarianism, and so on. In this sense, this exhibit of the "new truths" of mesmerism appears as one manifestation of the variously directed energy of social and intellectual reconstruction that touched almost all aspects of American culture in the 1840s, known by the generic label "reform."

But history teaches us that the hectic innovations of antebellum reform developed alongside the establishment of new forms of social normality in America, in particular the normalization of the nineteenth-century model of middle-class domestic life; and Hawthorne's Veiled Lady is figuratively implicated in this development quite as much as in the history of reform.[3] Priscilla is a woman, but the Veiled Lady is a presentation or representation of a woman; and the representation that the Veiled Lady embodies intricately reflects the representation of "woman" in the domestic ideology of Hawthorne's time. The Veiled Lady is a lady, but in being *veiled* she is made into a lady who does not appear in public. As such she images woman being publicly created into a creature of private space, native of that separate nonpublic, nonproductive zone marked off in nineteenth-century ideology as the home or woman's sphere. Bred in a "little room," her existence has been circumscribed in such a way that extradomestic space has become terrifyingly alien to her: "The sense of vast, undefined space, pressing from the outside against the black panes of our uncurtained windows, was fearful to the poor girl, heretofore accustomed to the narrowness of human limits" (36), Hawthorne writes, in a perfect description of the agoraphobia that Gillian Brown has presented as the psychological equivalent of middle-class women's domestic enclosure.[4]

As it erases her as a public figure, the Veiled Lady's veil specifically puts her body out of sight, or paradoxically makes her appear without a body; and in this sense the Veiled Lady might be called a figure for the disembodiment of women in nineteenth-century domesticity, that is, for the construction of "woman" as something separate from or opposed to bodily life and force. "Wan, almost sickly" of complexion, her brown hair falling "not in curls but with only a slight wave" (27), possessed (in the emphatically undisembodied Zenobia's contemptuous term) of "hardly any physique" (34), Priscilla's carefully noted body type minutely reflects the one that (as Lois Banner has shown) was normalized as a feminine ideal in America in the antebellum decades, that pallid, fragile-appearing, unvoluptuous, unrobust physical type that realized, at the bodily level, a social model of domestic leisure and feminine unproductiveness.[5] In Priscilla's "tremulous nerves"—a sensitivity so overdeveloped as to render her liable to regular collapses of spirits and strength—Hawthorne describes the neurasthenia that is the medical signature of this social type.

When she is veiled, this woman, already strongly repressed at the level of physical life, loses her physicality altogether and becomes what woman most essentially is in the nineteenth-century domestic conception: the embodiment of spiritual forces. Augustine St. Clare's mother in *Uncle Tom's Cabin,* the ideal woman as the cult of domesticity dreams that ideal (Little Eva is her reincarnation), is so fully identified with spirit that St. Clare can say of her: "*She* was *divine*! She was a direct embodiment and personification of the New Testament" (*Uncle Tom's Cabin* 333). Produced as she is, the Veiled Lady too can be said to be "in communion with the spiritual world," indeed to "behold the Absolute!" (201). The "tremulous nerves" that are the sign of her physical devitalization confer on her at least the appearance of spiritual privilege, or in the book's locution, "endow her with Sibylline attributes" (2). So too the veil that bounds her off from public and physical life is (or is at least said to be) what *creates* her as spiritual being: by "insulat[ing] her from the material world," this mark of delimitation "endow[s] her with many of the privileges of a disembodied spirit" (6).

The figure of the Veiled Lady may originate in the history of American cult movements and pseudosciences, I am suggesting, but this figure is not readable wholly in terms of such movements. In the terms of her constitution she precisely reflects another development just as much a part of *Blithedale*'s historical moment as mesmeric exhibits or communitarian experiments: the cultural construction of a certain version of "woman," and of the whole set of social arrangements built upon this figure of domestic life. This, much more than mesmerism or even reform, is the real subject of historical meditation in the Veiled Lady portions of *Blithedale.* Yet what is most interesting about the Veiled Lady is that this personification of woman domestically defined is in no sense domestic.

Produced as a creature of physical invisibility, the Veiled Lady nevertheless leads a life of pure exhibitionism. Rendered an insular or private spirit, her sphere is nevertheless always the public sphere, and her work is not to make a home but to "come before the public" on the most spectacular of terms. In this respect she challenges us to find a rather different historical meaning for her than any we have established thus far.

What the Veiled Lady is most essentially is an image of woman as public performer; and if we insisted on reading this image as historically based, she could help us to the realization that the same period already known to us as the decade of reform and of the establishment of a more privatized and leisured model of middle-class domesticity could also be described as the time of the emergence of some women—specifically women in the entertainment sector—to an exaggeratedly public life.[6] Behind the Veiled Lady we could see arrayed the new female celebrities who, first in the 1840s, then more decisively around 1850, began to appear before audiences newly huge in scale, and to be *known* to publics much greater yet. Mesmerism did not produce a female celebrity of this order. But as a "name" attraction the Veiled Lady could find her likeness in Fanny Elssler, the Viennese dancer who made a triumphal tour of America in 1841. Or she could find her likeness in Jenny Lind, whose American tour exactly at *Blithedale*'s moment—Lind concluded her eighteen months of concerts in May 1852, the month *Blithedale* was completed—consolidated enduring patterns of American mass-cultural stardom: the road tour with entourage, the mobbing of the star's vehicle and the surrounding of her hotel, the conversion of ticket acquisition into a high public drama (tickets to Jenny Lind's concerts were auctioned off at newsworthy prices), the exposure of the well-guarded star in carefully arranged public appearances. (When she came before the public Lind too was dressed in white.)[7]

Or the Veiled Lady could find her likeness in another group of entertainers who emerged into mass visibility at just the same time: the women novelists who attained to a new degree of popularity right at *The Blithedale Romance*'s moment. The scale of the American market for literary goods, we know, expanded abruptly at this time. Where a "decided hit" might have sold five or six thousand copies in America heretofore, around 1850 books like Susan Warner's *The Wide, Wide World* and Maria Cummins's *The Lamplighter* began to sell tens (and in the case of *Uncle Tom's Cabin* hundreds) of thousands of copies. Born together with this new scale of circulation was a new kind of publicity broadcasting such authors' wares *as* popular, indeed proclaiming them the object of insatiable and universal demand: the literary publicity campaign that seized on the mass medium of journalism to announce the staggering sales record of a newly published book was pioneered by the printer of *Uncle Tom's Cabin* in *Blithedale*'s year, and became industry standard almost at once.[8] As the focus of these developments, the new best-selling writers of the early 1850s found audiences and became names on terms quite similar to Jenny Lind's. Ruth Hall, the successful author-hero of Fanny Fern's book of that name (1855), has a steamship named after her, as a suitable tribute to (and advertisement of) her popular fame (176). Fanny Fern herself had a railroad parlor car named in her honor, among other trumpetings of her name. When *Uncle Tom's Cabin* was published in 1852 Stowe became, exactly, a celebrity. Visiting New York after completing the novel, Stowe got into one of Jenny Lind's last concerts—long since sold out—*as* a celebrity, by being recognized as the famous Harriet Beecher Stowe. Her English tour of 1853 recapitulated the Jenny Lind tour with a writer in the singer's place. Stowe drew her own dockside crowds, had her own travel plans publicly announced, packed her own halls, appeared before audience after audience as her celebrated self: found a career, like Lind or like the Veiled Lady, as a famous object of public attention.[9]

Or, to draw the many sides of this figure together, we might say that the Veiled Lady registers the creation of a newly publicized world of popular entertainment taking place simultaneously with the creation of a newly privatized world of woman's domestic life.

Such likenesses suggest that what lies behind *Blithedale* is a development specific to the history of entertainment quite as much as any development in general social life. What the Veiled Lady registers, we might say, is the historical emergence, at midcentury, of a more massively *publicized* order of entertainment in America. She images a remaking of the social organization of entertainment by which artistic performance (broadly understood) came to reach larger and more stabilized mass publics, and by which participation *in* performance came to yield enlarged public visibility, to women above all. Or, to draw the many sides of this figure together, we might say that the Veiled Lady registers the creation of a newly publicized world of popular entertainment taking place simultaneously with the creation of a newly privatized world of woman's domestic life. She embodies the suggestion that the same contemporary cultural processes that worked in one direction to delimit women to de-physicalized and deactivated domestic privacy also helped open up an enlarged publicity women could inhabit, in the entertainment field—a suggestion rich in historical implication.

After all, the steep escalation of literary sales figures around 1850 must be understood to have reflected not only improved production factors like cheaper printing technologies or more active marketing campaigns, but quite as essentially the historical creation of a new social *place* or *need* for literary entertainment to fill. The mass-market novels of the 1850s point to middle-class domesticity as the scene they address because it was above all the institution of this social formation that created literature its new mid-nineteenth-century place. As I have shown elsewhere, the canons of domestic instruction that defined the home as a private, leisured, nonmaterialistic, feminine space in the antebellum decades also and with almost comparable insistence defined reading as a preferred domestic activity ("Sparing" 88–92).[10] In consequence of this linkage, the implementation of this social model in the decades after 1830 had the secondary effect of enlarging demand for reading for the home — and so too of creating public roles for literary producers and public attention for literary works.

The new, popular women novelists whom the Veiled Lady images in part are the figures who most fully seized the public life that domestic privacy helped construct. As Mary Kelley has shown, by using their own feminine domestic competences to address the domestic concerns that identified the new mass audience, these women were able to escape from domestic confinement and capture a new public role: the role of author. (But as Kelley also notes, winning a transdomestic social place did not help such authors escape from domestic self-conceptions. Among other manifestations of this entrapment, they typically attained to public identities without feeling entitled to assert themselves as public creatures: hence their regular use of pseudonyms, the literary equivalent of that highly public erasure of oneself in public embodied in the Veiled Lady's veil. "I have a perfect horror of appearing in print," Catharine Sedgwick wrote before the publication of her first novel, echoing the Veiled Lady's terror of the public or published domain. "We all concur in thinking that a lady should be veiled in her first appearance before the public" (qtd. in Kelley 129–30), Sedgwick's brother wrote at this time, a sentiment Professor Westervelt would share.[11]). The historical situation that writers like Elizabeth Wetherell, Fanny Fern, and Marion Harland — behind the veil, Susan Warner, Sara Willis Eldridge Parton, and Mary Virginia Terhune — capitalized on was, we need to remember, not theirs alone. They were only the most successful exploiters of a cultural restructuring that affected the whole field of literary writing, and adjacent entertainment fields as well. Accordingly, if we find Hawthorne meditating on such public-private figures in the Veiled Lady of *Blithedale,* we need to understand that they embody for him not just new literary competition but the new social conditions of literary production that he too finds himself working under at this time: a situation in which artistic creation has had a potentially massive new public life created for it on the condition that it align itself with a certain structure of private life.

At this point it is important to acknowledge that the historical situation of the literary that *Blithedale* addresses cannot be understood from *Blithedale* alone. Most glaringly, Hawthorne shows no grasp of the enabling side of the publicity that he knows as new at this time. The Veiled Lady is a victim of her display; in celebrity she is only exploited. Her real historical sisters-in-celebrity won wealth, power, prestige, and a measure of independence from their performers' careers. The saucy and independent-minded Fanny Fern—to cite the figure most antithetical to the droopy, dependent Priscilla—entered into a prenuptial contract giving her sole control of the property her royalties had amassed: a Priscilla who struck for such a deal would represent a revision indeed (Kelley 158).[12] The successful author's gloating over the bank stock she now owns at the end of *Ruth Hall* suggests a second possible attainment newly open to the woman-celebrity of this time: not just wealth but the pleasure wealth brings as a mark of achievement and entitlement. (A Priscilla who took pleasure in performance or its rewards would be someone else.) The Veiled Lady displays no talent, her "performance" is a hoax of someone else's devising. But Lind sang, Elssler danced, Southworth and Stowe and Warner wrote, Fanny Fern spoke her piece: the opening that brought them publicity also expanded their field of *expression,* certainly not the least of their gains. Hawthorne is in no position to see this side of the contemporary picture, which we must learn of from other accounts. But partial though it is, *Blithedale* makes its most interesting sense as a reading of the new literary situation of its moment; and *Blithedale* has things to teach about this newly emerging order not easily learned from other sources.

To name a first: *Blithedale* reflects a world in which artistic performers, and preferentially women, have won a new capacity to amass large audiences for themselves. But it also suggests that the development that puts performance in this new relation to popularity installs it in other relations at the same time. The Veiled Lady wins celebrity not by herself but through her bond to Professor Westervelt. This "attraction" is one half of an entertainment partnership the other member of which is her manager. As such this figure brings back to our attention the mid-nineteenth-century female celebrity's typical dependence on a male handler to achieve her public "life." P. T. Barnum was Jenny Lind's Westervelt. Chevalier Wyckoff, who Barnum beat out for the right to manage Jenny Lind, was Fanny Elssler's manager, or in Barnum's phrase the "speculator" who had Elssler "in charge" (Barnum 173).[13] Fanny Fern and Mrs. E.D.E.N. Southworth found the eventual sustainer of their long-lived popular success in Robert Bonner, publicist-publisher of the *New York Ledger.* At the bittersweet close of *Ruth Hall* the popular author Ruth stands at her husband's grave with her daughter and the man in her new public/literary life, her publisher-agent John Walter.

More than a manager, Westervelt is in the full sense of the term the Veiled Lady's *producer.* Having contracted for the rights to Priscilla as an entertainment property, he has made her *into* the Veiled Lady, has created a public identity for her and created public attraction *to* this identity—and he has done so not disinterestedly but as a way to increase the take. In this respect *Blithedale* reminds us that the handlers newly prominent in the popular entertainment of its time are really the sign of such entertainment's entrance into new relations to market forces. The Jenny Lind chapter in P. T. Barnum's autobiography *Struggles and Triumphs*—which spells out the terms of the performer-manager contract that *Blithedale*'s "Fauntleroy" chapter left vague—is fitly called "The Jenny Lind Enterprise."[14] In herself a woman, in Barnum's hands Jenny Lind became a business venture, a singer made *into* Jenny Lind the musical wonder by Barnum's incessant promotional activities, to the end of enriching them both. Similarly the literary-historical meaning of the new mass-market novels of the 1850s is not just that they were more popular than earlier books but that they mark a historical change in the meaning of the word "popular," a term that now comes to denote not just "well-liked" or "widely read" but specifically production *into* a certain market status through commercial management of a book's public life. The new promotional campaigns mounted by the publishers of such works to an altogether new extent *produced* public demand for them, demand which was then republicized as a way of creating further demand. Jewett's early ad for *Uncle Tom's Cabin* "TEN THOUSAND COPIES SOLD IN TWO WEEKS!" or James Cephas Derby's hyping of *Fern Leaves from Fanny's Portfolio* (1853) "FANNY FERN'S BOOK, 6,000 Copies Ordered in Advance of Publication!" promoted these books *as popular,* made their popularity the basis of their market identity (Geary 378, 382). And of course the publicity that made these books known to the public also made them wares marketed to the public: it is not for nothing that we establish the popularity of such works by enumerating their sales.

In *Blithedale* the Veiled Lady's public life is managed toward commercial ends, but it is the particular nature of this management to be hard to see. A curious but persistent feature of narration in this book is that the many dramatically crucial scenes in which Priscilla's deployment as Veiled Lady is arranged or contested all take place off the narrative record. The Veiled Lady's performance thus opens the novel, except that it is finished just before Coverdale begins his tale. The scene in which Old Moodie then intercedes with Hollingsworth to take Priscilla to Blithedale occurs between chapters, so that we never learn what understanding he reached with Hollingsworth or what relation his act had to her career of display—though there is a later hint that her contract with Westervelt has just run out. The subsequent interview in which Westervelt by some means (blackmail?) talks Zenobia into returning Priscilla to his charge occurs before Coverdale's eyes, but out of his earshot. The scene of the Veiled Lady's recapture—the scene in which Zenobia lowers the veil back over Priscilla—is seen and heard but wholly misunderstood: "we thought it a very bright idea of Zenobia's, to bring her legend to so effective a conclusion" (116), Coverdale says of this reveiling, with even greater than usual obtuseness. A presumably contemporaneous scene in which Hollingsworth agrees to the plan of turning Priscilla over to Westervelt ("he bade me come" [171], Priscilla later states—but in consideration of what? of Zenobia's offer of her fortune?) is missing altogether. Later, Coverdale sees Priscilla through his hotel window in the city, but he fails to see how she got there or where she is taken next. In "The Village-Hall" he sees her exhibited again, but she is again produced out of nowhere; when Hollingsworth now intervenes to rescue her from onstage life—for reasons we never see him arrive at—he too takes her we know not where. Finally, when Hollingsworth rejects Zenobia's schemes for Priscilla's and his life, our man on the scene arrives a little late, and so succeeds in missing this decisive exchange.

Did ever a book miss so much of the story it purports to tell? But this insistent narrative *missing,* usually thought merely inept, is itself deeply interesting in the context I am considering. In its narrative organization *Blithedale* constructs a zone in which highly interested arrangements are made and remade around the figure of a female entertainer, and it renders that zone at once controlling of the apparent action and yet imperfectly available to knowledge. In this respect the book might be said to image not just the management of high-visibility performance as commercial attraction but the simultaneous effacement, in such entertainment, of the interests and deals through which its public life is contrived. The new popular entertainment of the mid-nineteenth-century works, in part, through just this cloaking of its business end. Barnum, an apparent exception to this statement, made no secret either of his role in Jenny Lind's tour or of the terms of their commercial engagement. But even this most exhibitionistic or least *veiled* of publicists erased a portion of his act. His publicity for Lind works by creating the fascinating sense that she both is and is not his creation, that she is both the object of his shameless exploitation and at the same time a self-directing agent beyond the reach of his consumeristic wiles. But through its apparent frankness about its own motives such publicity conceals the extent to which Barnum both manufactured the appearance of the "untouched" Jenny and exploited that appearance as a marketing resource. The divineness of "the divine Jenny" was essential to her appeal; but Barnum helped establish her appearance of divineness, for example by arranging for her to sing Handel oratorios. When Jenny Lind gave her concert proceeds to public charities, Barnum publicized her charitableness and so made her yet more commercially valuable; in other words, he arranged a commercial payoff by advertising her separation from commercial ends. Fanny Fern's *Ruth Hall* provides a much more overt instance of a popular entertainment that hides the commercial ground of its generation. *Ruth Hall* tells of a contentedly domestic woman left destitute by her husband's death and threatened with the loss of her child until, in her darkest hour, she finds her way to the work of writing. Against all odds, by dint of unforeseen talent and strength of maternal will, Ruth establishes herself as a best-selling author and literary celebrity (Fern prints sample fan mail), and is at last able to reconstitute her broken family with the proceeds of her literary success. This book tells one story of the relation of women to writing; but that story keeps us from suspecting another story quite different in character—the story of how Fern's own book came to be written. Susan Geary has recently established that the writing of *Ruth Hall* was first proposed not by Fern but a publisher—Mason Brothers—eager to add this profitable author to its fold; that so far from winning its way to popularity by its irresistible strengths, the book was made popular through a highly premeditated and unprecedentedly intricate advertising campaign; and that so far from merely earning, after publication, the reward her book deserved, Fern was moved to write the book by the terms Mason Brothers offered "up front," not least their pledging, in the language of their contract, "to use extraordinary exertions to promote the sale thereof, so as, if possible, to make it exceed the sale of any previous work" (Geary 383–89).

Performance with this backstage: a veiled zone of contrivance in which potential popular entertainments are dreamed up and contracted for with an eye to their commercial profit; a zone in which strategies are contrived to *make* the mass popularity no longer allowed to just happen; a zone that allows itself to be known to exist, indeed that shows its commercialism a little as part of the glamorization of its product; but a zone that shuts the public out from detailed knowledge of its motives or arts of contrivance: *this* is show business as show business begins to exist in America at *Blithedale*'s historical moment. This recognition would help us to the further perception that the entertainment industry that is one of the most decisive identifying marks of the modern cultural order has its inception in America not *in* modernity but in the age of the so-called cult of domesticity, taking the literature produced for domestic consumption as one of its first sites of industrial development. But if it helps bring this little-recognized fact into sharpened focus, *Blithedale*'s most interesting historical suggestion is that the same restructuring of entertainment that produced these arrangements in the sphere of cultural production around 1850 produced corresponding novelties in the sphere of consumption: changes figured, I would suggest, in Miles Coverdale.

Coverdale and Priscilla are incongruous as lovers, but they constitute a couple in several related senses. Coverdale is, the book repeatedly suggests, the "man" who corresponds to Priscilla's version of the term "woman." Imaged as Theodore in Zenobia's tale "The Silvery Veil," his prurient interests in yet insurmountable terror of female sexuality are read as the masculine by-products of the cultural construction that disacknowledges or requires the veiling of woman's erotic embodiedness. But in no less important a sense Coverdale is also the spectator constituted by the Veiled Lady's version of spectacle. Passive in person, Priscilla only acts when she goes onstage, into a separate zone of spectacle marked off from its seated audience. Such a construction of *acting* finds its complement in someone else's passive, nonperforming *watching,* in short in the Coverdalean habit of mind. The language of *Blithedale* urges us to give the word "observer," as a term for Coverdale, the intensified sense of he who exists only in and as a watcher. "As if such were the proper barrier to be interposed between a char-

This recognition would help us to the further perception that the entertainment industry that is one of the most decisive identifying marks of the modern cultural order has its inception in America not in *modernity but in the age of the so-called cult of domesticity, taking the literature produced for domestic consumption as one of its first sites of industrial development.*

acter like hers, and a perceptive faculty like mine" (160), Coverdale huffs when Zenobia lowers the curtain on his peeping, his words baring his assumption that others are full persons and performers, but he a mental faculty only equipped to register their performances. "You are a poet—at least, as poets go, now-a-days—and must be allowed to make an opera-glass of your imagination, when you look at women" (170), Zenobia later mockingly retorts, correctly identifying Coverdale's relation as self or mind to the instrument used by spectators of nineteenth-century mass entertainments to enable them (just) to *see*.[15]

"Men of cold passions have quick eyes" Hawthorne writes in a remarkable notebook entry, by which I take him to mean: people who systematically deaden themselves at the level of primary drives arrange a surrogate life—contrive to be quick, not dead—in their sense of sight (*American Notebooks* 169). What makes Coverdale powerful as a description of the spectator is not just his self-delimitation to a visual self but the book's sense that eye-life has become his way of *having* life. In a moving passage Coverdale speaks of "that quality of the intellect and heart, that impelled me (often against my will, and to the detriment of my comfort) to live in other lives" (160), and these words well explain what makes watching a compulsive or compulsory activity for him. Life as Coverdale understands it is not what he has or does but something presumed to be lodged in someone else. Watching that someone, inhabiting that other through spectatorial self-projection and consuming it through visual appropriation, becomes accordingly a means to "live" *into his* life some part of that vitality that always first appears as "other life."

What the entertainments of the mid-nineteenth century *did* to the mass publics that consumed them, like all questions about the real history of literary reception, is something we cannot know without considerable aid from speculation. But there is good evidence to support *Blithedale*'s surmise that the formation of entertainment new in America at its time sponsored a Coverdalean mode of participation. All of the spectacles we have considered strongly reinforce the habit of motionlessly seeing. When Jenny Lind was touring America, Barnum had another crew scouring Ceylon for elephants and other natural wonders which, reimported and publicly displayed, became his other great enterprise of 1851, Barnum's Great Asiatic Caravan, Museum, and Menagerie—a show that opened a wonderworld to audiences willing to experience wonders in the passive or spectatorial mode (Barnum 213–14). (Barnum arranged for Jenny Lind to review the circus parade in New York City; in other

words, to appear in public as an exemplary watcher.) The crowds
that mobbed Stowe on her arrival in England were, in her words,
"very much determined to look" at her: on this tour Stowe
became at once a figure of fame and an object of visual consumption (qtd. in Wilson 345). And what could the proliferation
of novel reading at this time reflect if not a mass extension of
habits of bodily deactivation and of the reconcentration of self
into sight? The reader of every nineteenth-century novel made
him- or, more likely, herself a Coverdale to the extent that she
conferred the status of "characters" on performatively generated others (Little Eva, Zenobia, Ruth Hall), while consigning
herself to the category of perceptual faculty or *reader,* enterer
into others through an action of the eye. Ellen Montgomery,
the heroine of Susan Warner's *The Wide, Wide World* (1851),
begins the novel Coverdale-fashion, looking out the window:
shut into a world of enclosed domestic idleness, she scans the
space across its boundary for something for her eye to inhabit.
When she enters the ideally constructed domesticity of the
Humphreys household she finds an object for this visual appetite
in reading: in Warner's account, novels offer the residents of
immobilized private space adventure through the eye.

Quite as interestingly, there is abundant evidence that the
form of mass entertainment new in America around 1850 held
its audience in the position *of* audience by seeming to embody
consumable "life." N. P. Willis's further-information-for-the-
curious *Memoranda of the Life of Jenny Lind* (1851)—a book
built on press releases supplied by Barnum, and so aimed to
create the interest it pretended only to address—treats Lind as
a public figure whose celebrity invites inescapable curiosity about
her personal life. "The private life of Jenny Lind is a matter of
universal inquisitiveness" (163), Willis informs the reader in a
chapter on her "Private Habits and Manners" (166); then, instructing us in how such inquisitiveness might be mounted and
targeted, he himself muses on the love life of this great singer:
"One wonders, as one looks upon her soft eyes, and her affectionate profusion of sunny hair, what Jenny's heart can be doing
all this time. Is fame a substitute for the tender passion? She
must have been desperately loved in her varied and bright path"
(159).[16] (The relation to Coverdale's speculations on Zenobia's
sexual history or his urge to peep behind the petals of Priscilla's
erotic bud will be clear at once.) Through such promotion Lind
is made into a public embodiment of a fascinating private life,
and her audience is invited to try to get some fascination into
its own life by consuming the public spectacle of hers: no wonder

interested spectators actually invade this female performer's private dressing room in a Willis incident uncannily like *Blithedale*'s tale of Theodore (Willis 163–65).[17] *Ruth Hall* is as personal a work as the 1850s produced. It tells Fern/Parton's personal history of struggles and triumphs with hot display of her personal loves and resentments (resentments above all against her brother N. P. Willis, the villain of the piece.) But this book's intimacy of record was inseparable from its public or market life. What *Ruth Hall* offered its readers was the chance to "live" a public figure's "hidden" private life by buying and reading a book—and lest the public not be in on the opportunity for vicariousness the book embodied, Mason Brothers publicized its "obscure" personalness, running ads that tantalizingly asked: "IS RUTH HALL AUTOBIOGRAPHICAL?"[18] So it is that a buried, commercial publicity operation, by producing the sense that a rare "life" lies veiled inside the most public of performances, could further its audience's disposition to seek "life" through the consumption of such performances, and so convert private men and women into a huge paying public: in other parlance, a Westervelt creates a Veiled Lady and thereby produces a Coverdale, and by extension a literary mass market as well.

The strategies by which "life" is made to seem available in consumable objects and experiences and the appetite *for* "life" used to draw publics into stabilized bodies of consumer demand are as familiar as daily life itself in modern consumer culture. The products or productions that draw Coverdale by their apparent "surplus of vitality" (96) have their successors (to name no more) in the mass-circulation magazine that sold itself not as pictures to look at but as *Life*; or the soft drink that has offered not to quench our thirst but to help us "Come Alive"; or the car that, at this writing, is inviting us to buy it as a way to discharge our obligation (the ads quote James) to "Live all you can; it's a mistake not to."[19] One historical use of *The Blithedale Romance* is to take us back, if not to the origins, then at least to the early history of a social system held together by the public simulation of "life" as a marketing art and a private imperative to remedy deficiencies of "life" in one's life—a system, *Blithedale* tells us, that has its first large-scale social manifestation in the 1840s and 1850s, and that begins its operations in the entertainment sphere. But if the hunger for a "life" felt as alienated into other lives drives the man or woman of this time into spectatorial dependence on commercial entertainment, we might ask at this point, what gives rise to this driving sense of lack? *Blithedale*'s answer, I take it, is privacy: that this need is a product *in* the self of a social-historical construction of privacy as the self's living "world."

Quite as much as he is an observer, Coverdale is a figure of private life. The spaces he seeks out are always strongly bound off from the public or collective realm: an apartment (the name itself equates dwelling space with separation); a hermitage; the single-family dwelling "just a little withdrawn" (80) that is this communitarian's dream of a utopian social space. At home in the private, Coverdale also carries the private within him as a structure of habitual understanding. The self, this character assumes, is "inviolate" only in the world of its "exclusive possession" (99): to live in the communal, by parallel assumption, is to have one's "individuality" (99) in continual danger of violation. Other characters claim the public—or the public *too*—as their proper theater of action; but when they do so Coverdale's privatizing mind instinctively reads back from their public assertion to the state of private or "individual affections" alleged to "cause" such assertion: "I could measure Zenobia's inward trouble, by the animosity with which she now took up the general quarrel of woman against man" (121), is Coverdale's understanding of Zenobia's feminism. A privatized and privatizing mind, the privacy Coverdale embodies is defined not just through its cult of confinement within the "safe" private sphere but also through its attenuation of the erotic in private life—Coverdale's "apartment" is a "bachelor apartment"—and its exclusion of active, productive labor from the private world: Coverdale is the "idle" or "half-occupied" man (247, 133), his apartment the scene of "bewitching, enervating indolence" (19). This is to say that Coverdale represents a human self constructed upon the same social plan that we have seen imaged in the Veiled Lady: the nineteenth-century middle-class construction that locates the self's home or fulfilled state in the enclosed, physically attenuated, leisured, *private* world of domestic life.

But as the veil imprisons the lady condemned to wear it, so the social construction of the private that Coverdale embodies has the peculiarity of being at once desperately clung to and deeply self-impoverishing. Safe at home, his adventures in communitarianism now long behind him, Coverdale finds the private home a sheer emptiness: "Nothing, nothing, nothing" (245) is the weary tale his private life has been able to generate. And it would be easy to guess that what has established this home as a space of deficiency are the very acts of exclusion that established it in the first place. Having shut out the collective

world, Coverdalean privacy has *made* itself the place of "lone-
liness" (70); having sealed itself in from the public, the overtly
erotic, the productive, and the active, it has made those modes
of life into an "other life" apart from itself and has replaced
them, within itself, with a positive sense of their lack. Life in
certain of its primary and potent forms, *Blithedale* says, is what
the nineteenth-century cult of domesticity insists on not having
in its life *and what it therefore also* hungers to repossess. At
least as *Blithedale* figures it, this is why the contemporary structure of privacy imaged in Coverdale at once closes in on itself
and builds, at the heart of private space, means for a surrogate,
spectatorial relation to the life it has put outside. Coverdale's
hermitage functions at once to protect a self that feels inviolate
only in private and to make that self a watcher, a spectatorial
participant in Zenobia and Westervelt's richer intimacies. The
private bedroom that shields Coverdale at Blithedale becomes,
in its enclosure, an auditorium, a place to listen in on the "awful
privacy" (39) of Hollingsworth's adjacent intimacy. The city
apartment that guards Coverdale's privacy also drives him to
seek entertainment by converting the world of others into a
domestically viewable visual field—and so leads him to become,
at the moment when he is most fully *at home* in the book, first
a reader of novels, then a viewer of the Veiled Lady being
readied for the stage.[20]

The Veiled Lady, I began by saying, images the constructions of a certain version of private life and a certain version
of public spectacle as two sides of a single process. We are now
in a position to say what the logic is that holds these two historical developments together. We could now speculate that a
more publicized and spectatorial entertainment order and a
more leisured, privatized domestic model arose at the same
time in America because it was the nature of that domestic
model to create a *need for* such entertainment: a need for a now
foregone life to be made repossessible in a form compatible
with the deactivations this new order prescribed. By learning
how to aim its products toward this life-hunger a new entertainment industry was able to mobilize domestic privacy as a
mass entertainment market. But that industry could insert itself
in the domestic realm because it met needs produced by that
realm: chief among them the need to acquire extradomestic life
in the spectatorially consumable form of *other* or *represented*
life.[21]

What I have been speculatively reconstructing here—with
Blithedale's aid because this history has not proved fully knowable *without* its aid—is the situation of literature in antebellum

America: a matter that includes the histories of literary production and consumption but that is not wholly external to literature itself. Literary works, it might be worth insisting, do not produce their own occasions. They are always produced within some cultural situation of the literary, within the particular set of relations in which literature's place is at any moment socially determined. Literature's situation in America in the late 1840s and early 1850s was that it was being resituated: placed into the entangled new relations to publicity, to domestic privacy, to the commercial and the promotional, and to vicarious consumption that I have described here. When this change took place, writers could exploit its new structure of literary opportunity in various ways. What they could not do was to ignore the cultural conjunction it produced: could not ignore it because it set the terms for their work's public life.

If we ask the long-postponed question why this set of relations should be so much on Hawthorne's mind in *Blithedale,* then, the most forcible answer would be that they preoccupy him at this time because they define his own new literary situation. Hawthorne himself, after all, found a newly enlarged public for his work around 1850, after more than twenty years of writing in obscurity. Hawthorne too acquired augmented public life at this time at least in part by being taken in charge by his own producer-promoter, the publisher James T. Fields. Hawthorne too began to have his "private life" advertised at this time as part of the creation of his allure: literary mythologizings of Hawthorne's "reclusive" personality and tours-in-print past Hawthorne's private home began in the early 1850s, with full cooperation from Hawthorne's promoters. And Hawthorne too entered into the predicaments of high visibility at this moment: how, in coming before a large, impersonal audience, still to keep "the inmost Me behind its veil" (*SL* 4) becomes this privacy-loving public figure's problem in 1850 just as much as it is Catharine Sedgwick's or The Veiled Lady's.[22]

The Blithedale Romance, accordingly, needs to be understood not just as a depiction of self-evident cultural realities but more specifically as an act of reconnaissance into an emerging cultural form. In writing this book Hawthorne uses his work to *work out* the shape of the field writing has now been placed in, and to measure the meaning of his work's new situation. But the novelists of this time all face the same situation, which they explore in works of their own. *The Wide, Wide World* is in one aspect a fictional history of this same entertainment revolution.

In a central scene Warner memorably contrasts the bee characteristic of an older social order—an entertainment in which the private is not split from the communal, pleasure not split from productive labor, and the performers not other people than the enjoyers—with the passive, leisured, privatized entertainment form (reading) characteristic of modern domesticity, the scene of its own consumption. Melville, who repositioned himself as an antipopular author in face of the same emerging situation that Hawthorne and Warner embraced on other terms, wrote his history of this development in *Pierre* (also 1852), a book that finds its threefold adversary in the cultural organization that encloses sympathy within domestic confinements; a literary market that hypes talent into literary celebrity; and a cultural ordering that sets the literary in opposition to unrepressed bodily life.[23] Fanny Fern, unlike Melville a courter of popularity and unlike Warner an enjoyer of fame, made a different accommodation to the literary situation she too found around her. She takes her more sanguine measure of the same ground in *Ruth Hall,* a book that plots the birth of the popular writer at the junction of a business of literary production and a domesticity in need of its wares. Ruth's fan mail—the proof of her celebrity status—makes clear that a home audience consumes her work to help satisfy cravings domestic life has not allayed.

Not long after this moment, American literature had other situations socially created for it. The Beadle's Dime Novels already in full commercial flower by 1860 embody a quite different world of popular writing, organizing a mass audience on other terms than a domestic one. By that year a nonpopular "serious" literary zone was successfully institutionalized as part of the establishment of a self-consciously high culture in America, a development that laid the ground for a quite different figure of the author to emerge later on. But those structures were not yet in place a decade before. The dominant world of writing in mid-nineteenth-century America was the highly vicarious, highly managed, privacy-addressing, mass-public one that came together around 1850; and the central fact of literary life then was that a writer who hoped to reach a significant public would have to engage a communication system structured on those terms. Small wonder that the author's *work* at this time is to figure out what this situation means: a work performed, among other ways, through the writing of the story of The Veiled Lady.

Notes

I would like to thank the Nathaniel Hawthorne Society and the Department of English at the University of California at Santa Barbara for spirited discussions of an earlier version of this essay. My thanks, too, to my colleague Lynn Wardley for sharing her extensive knowledge of this subject.

1.   Hawthorne to E. P. Whipple, 2 May 1852 (*Letters* 536).

2.   On the American history of mesmerism see Fuller, esp. 16–47. Puysegur and the concept of a clairvoyance-yielding "lucity" are discussed on 10–11.

3.   Among the many works on nineteenth-century domesticity as an ideological construct and social reality see particularly Douglas, Cott, Ryan, and my "Sparing the Rod." The last two works deal extensively with the symbiotic relations between domestic enclosure and public reform movements.

4.   See Brown. For another discussion of the cultural history of privacy and of the highly charged bounding off of public and private space in the antebellum decades, see Haltunnen, esp. 102–12.

5.   Banner discusses the cultural authority of what she calls "the steel-engraving lady" (45–65).

6.   To be fully understood, the quite spectacular emergence of women into public artistic celebrity around 1850 would have to be grasped together with the much more heavily obstructed movement of women into other forms of public life at the same time. Priscilla is partly defined in opposition to Zenobia, who contemplates a countercareer as a feminist political orator. Zenobia's historical correlatives are the women who asserted themselves as speakers in the antislavery and women's rights causes in the late 1830s and 1840s, who found their ways barred by the still strongly enforced social insistence that women not speak in public before mixed male-female audiences. O'Connor's useful volume reminds us that women were enrolled as students at the coeducational Oberlin College, but were not allowed to perform the public-speaking exercises in oratory classes; and that many women publicly prominent in education had male spokesmen read their messages aloud when called on to speak in mixed company (22–40). Calvin Stowe read Harriet Beecher Stowe's responses to the crowds she drew on her English tour (Wilson 349).

7.   Banner discusses Fanny Elssler's tour, 63–64. On Jenny Lind's American concert tour see Barnum, esp. chapters 17–19, and Harris 111–42.

8.   The most comprehensive treatment of 1850s literary promotion and the expansion of the American book market is Geary. See also the discussion of publication and promotion in Kelley's comprehensive history of antebellum best-seller writers (3–27).

9.   Kelley 3, Wilson 291 and 344–86. Stowe was assured of an English "reception as enthusiastic as that of Jenny Lind" (Wilson 334). An important related discussion of "the modelling of a highly visible identity under . . .

new circumstances of conspicuous performance" (164) is Fisher's. But Fisher locates in the 1890s the developments I see beginning in the late 1840s.

10.   All discussions of the joint birth of mass-market fiction and middle-class privacy must acknowledge their debt to Ann Douglas, whose *Feminization of American Culture* first suggested the American version of this linkage, and to the still important chapter "Private Experience and the Novel" in Watt (174–207).

11.   Kelley's discussion of female literary pseudonyms (124–37) is a crucial contribution to the historical meaning of women's veiling in the mid-nineteenth century.

12.   Barnum's Jenny Lind chapters make clear that she profited from her performance career quite as much as he did.

13.   On Bonner, see Kelley 3–6, 21–24, and 161–63. Kelley's evidence suggests how much generosity such a manager might be capable of, and what benefits a woman might gain through her dealings with him, facts that must not be underrated. (In *Ruth Hall* Ruth thinks of her manager as a real brother, unlike her miserable actual brother Hyacinth.) But it is a tendency of Kelley's argument to slip over the market relation that a bond *to* a publicist-promoter necessarily involved: Kelley thus treats this relation as background or introductory information, instead of as a relation that helps *constitute* the female literary "success."

14.   In the same vein Barnum calls Lind's tour "an enterprise never before or since equalled in managerial annals" and gloats: "I had marked the 'divine Jenny' as a sure card," and so on (170–72).

15.   On actor and spectator in nineteenth-century European culture see for instance Richard Sennett's discussion of Pagliaccian virtuosity and the new etiquette of audience silence (195–218).

16.   Willis's reverie continues, in a locution truly astonishing: "To see such a heaven as her heart untenanted, one longs to write its advertisement of 'To Let'" (160). Readers of the Willis *Memoranda* will be struck by the close analogies to Priscilla in Lind's "white garb of purity" (132), her pallid and "insensuous" appearance (140–41), her upbringing as a "poor and plain little girl" locked "in a little room" (5), and so on.

17.   "Your uninvited presence here is an intrusion," Lind tells the invaders of what *Blithedale* would call her "private withdrawing room" (110–11); but the celebrity privacy that brands public entrance intrusion in fact invites just such intrusion, as Willis virtually says.

18.   See Geary, 388–89. As Geary notes, the really fascinating question this publicity raises—whether Fern wrote up her life in the knowledge that it would be marketed in this way—is impossible now to answer.

19.   Rolls Royce ran this advertisement in the April 1988 issue of *Gourmet*.

20.   Does my phrasing sufficiently suggest that I see *Blithedale* as prophetically describing the "living room" of the modern private home, focused

on the sound system, television, and VCR? That the average American watches television seven or more hours a day *in* such enclosures is the social fact *Blithedale* helps foresee. On the American tradition of opposition to privacy as a spatial and social construct see Hayden.

21. My understanding that mass-cultural instruments can build social groups into markets because they also meet those groups' socially created needs has been influenced by Ohmann. Like Fisher, Ohmann focuses these developments in the 1890s.

22. Further evidence that the issue of Hawthorne's writing around 1850 is the issue of enlarged publicity would be found in the 1851 preface to *Twice-Told Tales* and in his other novels of 1850–52, which both open with a crisis of public exposure: Hester's exposure on the Puritan scaffold in *The Scarlet Letter* and the "going visible" that accompanies Hepzibah's opening of her shop in *The House of the Seven Gables.* On the promotion or public creation of Hawthorne in the 1850s and after, see my *School of Hawthorne,* 48–66.

23. For Melville's struggle to describe "life" and its alienation in contemporary writing see for instance this remarkable passage:

> Pierre is young; heaven gave him the divinest, freshest form of a man; put light into his eye, and fire into his blood, and brawn into his arm, and a joyous, jubilant, overflowing, upbubbling, universal life in him everywhere. Now look around in that most miserable room, and at that most miserable pursuit of man, and say if here be the place, and this be the trade, that God intended for him. A rickety chair, two hollow barrels, a plank, paper, pens, and infernally black ink, four leprously dingy white walls, no carpet, a cup of water, and a dry biscuit or two. Oh, I hear the leap of the Texan Camanche, as at this moment he goes crashing like a wild deer through the green underbrush; I hear his glorious whoop of savage and untamable health; and then I look in at Pierre. If physical, practical unreason make the savage, which is he? (*Pierre* 302)

Works Cited

Banner, Lois W. *American Beauty.* New York: Knopf, 1982.

Barnum, P. T. *Struggles and Triumphs.* New York: Penguin American Library, 1981.

Brodhead, Richard H. *School of Hawthorne.* New York: Oxford UP, 1986.

———. "Sparing the Rod: Discipline and Fiction in Antebellum America." *Representations* 21 (1988): 67–96.

Brown, Gillian. "The Empire of Agoraphobia." *Representations* 20 (1987): 134–57.

Cott, Nancy. *The Bonds of Womanhood: "Woman's Sphere" in New England, 1780–1835.* New Haven: Yale UP, 1977.

Douglas, Ann. *The Feminization of American Culture.* New York: Knopf, 1977.

Fern, Fanny. *Ruth Hall and Other Writings by Fanny Fern.* Ed. Joyce

W. Warren. New Brunswick: Rutgers UP, 1986.

Fisher, Philip. "Appearing and Disappearing in Public: Social Space in Late-Nineteenth-Century Literature and Culture." *Reconstructing American Literary History.* Ed. Sacvan Bercovitch. Cambridge: Harvard UP, 1986.

Fuller, Robert C. *Mesmerism and the American Cure of Souls.* Philadelphia: U of Pennsylvania P, 1982.

Geary, Susan. "The Domestic Novel as a Commercial Commodity: Making a Best Seller in the 1850s." *Papers of the Bibliographical Society of America* 70 (1976): 365–93.

Haltunnen, Karen. *Confidence Men and Painted Women: A Study of Middle-Class Culture in America, 1830–1870.* New Haven: Yale UP, 1982.

Harris, Neil. *Humbug: The Art of P. T. Barnum.* Chicago: U of Chicago P, 1973.

Hawthorne, Nathaniel. *The American Notebooks.* Vol. 8 of *Centenary Edition of the Works of Nathaniel Hawthorne.* Columbus: Ohio State UP, 1962–.

———. *The Blithedale Romance.* Vol. 3 of *Centenary Edition of the Works of Nathaniel Hawthorne.*

———. *The Letters, 1843–1853.* Vol. 14 of *Centenary Edition of the Works of Nathaniel Hawthorne.*

———. *The Scarlet Letter.* Vol. 1 of *Centenary Edition of the Works of Nathaniel Hawthorne.*

Hayden, Dolores. *The Grand Domestic Revolution: A History of Feminist Designs of American Homes, Neighborhoods, and Cities.* Cambridge: MIT P, 1981.

Kelley, Mary. *Private Woman, Public Stage: Literary Domesticity in Nineteenth-Century America.* New York: Oxford UP, 1984.

Melville, Herman. *Pierre; or, the Ambiguities.* Evanston: Northwestern UP and the Newberry Library, 1971.

O'Connor, Lillian. *Pioneer Women Orators.* New York: Columbia UP, 1954.

Ohmann, Richard. "Where Did Mass Culture Come From? The Case of Magazines." *Politics of Letters.* Middletown: Wesleyan UP, 1987. 135–51.

Ryan, Mary. *Cradle of the Middle Class: The Family in Oneida County, New York 1790–1865.* Cambridge, Eng.: Cambridge UP, 1981.

Sennett, Richard. *The Fall of Public Man.* New York: Knopf, 1977.

Stowe, Harriet Beecher. *Uncle Tom's Cabin.* New York: New American Library, 1981.

Watt, Ian. *The Rise of the Novel.* London: Chatto and Windus, 1957.

Willis, N[athaniel] Parker. *Memoranda of the Life of Jenny Lind.* Philadelphia: Robert E. Peterson, 1851.

Wilson, Forest. *Crusader in Crinoline: The Life of Harriet Beecher Stowe.* Philadelphia: Lippincott, 1941.

Pictographs as Autobiography: Plains Indian Sketchbooks of the Late Nineteenth and Early Twentieth Centuries

Hertha D. Wong

1

When scholars talk about Native American autobiography the assumption is that they mean the ethnographer-collected life histories of the late nineteenth and early twentieth centuries. Because autobiography has been considered a distinctly Western impulse emphasizing individuality and has been defined as the story of one's life written by oneself, precontact personal narratives spoken, performed, and painted by more communally oriented indigenous peoples have generally been overlooked. Thoughtful critics like Arnold Krupat insist that "Indian autobiography has no prior model in the collective practice of tribal cultures" (31). But long before Anglo ethnographers came along, Native Americans were telling, performing, and painting their personal histories. One potential preliterate model of autobiography, at least among Plains Indian males, is the pictographic personal narrative. The symbolic language of pictographs allowed preliterate Plains Indians to "read" about each other from painted robes, tipis, and shields. According to Helen H. Blish, pictographic hides were a "widely practiced" form of artistic personal history. Such "personal records" were "quite common . . . among the Plains Indians," and, says Blish, "these are the most frequently found pictographic records" (21).[1]

By the late nineteenth century such Plains Indian traditions of personal history began to intersect with Euro-American autobiography. When Native Americans began to communicate to others outside of their cultures, such individual self-expression encountered new challenges. Often their personal narratives were solicited by an ethnologist, historian, or other "friend of the Indian." Always they had to negotiate the difficult terrain of translation—from a native language to English, from an oral or pictographic to a written form, from a Native American culture to a Euro-American culture.

The resulting "bicultural composite composition," noted by some critics to be "the principle constituting the Indian autobiography as a genre" (Krupat 31) or as its "most distinctive characteristic" (Sands 57) holds true for nineteenth-century pictographic personal narratives as well as for as-told-to life histories. These "bi-cultural documents" (Brumble 2–3) reveal the artistic and literary traditions of two distinct cultures. Even though the final shape and content of the life histories were determined by white editors, Indian narrators seem to have told their life stories in their native narrative forms—forms which were shaped originally by the cultural patterns of the tribe, but which then were modified according to the needs of a new audience, purpose, and setting.

When examining this bicultural transformation, we must consider not only the narrator and his or her editor, but also the constraints of language on the process of self-expression. Literary theory that suggests how language is on the border between self and other enables us to see how language is engaged in a power struggle between these two opposing forces (Bakhtin 293–94). If the power struggle between self and other is evident within the language use of one individual, it is intensified fourfold when individuals seek to express themselves with the assistance of other persons. When two individuals come from different cultures and speak different languages, the situation is compounded again. There is an interaction not merely of two individuals with their respective senses of self and other, but there is also an interplay of two linguistic communities with their differing assumptions, preconceptions, denotations, and connotations. How, then, does a Native American express a genuine sense of self when that self is mediated not only by one's own language, but by the language of another? How does one define a self in a hostile world? Is the act of expressing one's self in the language and forms of the "enemy" an attempt at communication, an indication of negotiation, or an act of capitulation?

Precontact forms of personal narrative often focused on a self constructed through communal identity. Late nineteenth- and early twentieth-century solicited autobiographies, however, are not only concerned with a cohesive tribal identity, but with that identity in conflict with Euro-American culture. With this in mind, the anthropological theory of acculturation offers an apt model by which to consider these transitional texts. Rather

How, then, does a Native American express a genuine sense of self when that self is mediated not only by one's own language, but by the language of another? . . . Is the act of expressing one's self in the language and forms of the "enemy" an attempt at communication, an indication of negotiation, or an act of capitulation?

than a one-way process—a minority group adapting to the white mainstream society—acculturation is a dual process with both groups interacting with and learning from each other. Certainly acculturation involves two distinct cultures, but the point of contact between the two results in a third culture, what Robert F. Murphy calls "a boundary culture" (262). We can think of late nineteenth- and early twentieth-century Native American autobiography as a type of literary "boundary culture" where two cultures influence one another simultaneously.[2] Although this paper is about how this border encounter changes Native American forms of pictographic personal narrative, it is vital to remember that Euro-American notions of narrative were also challenged in their turn.

These Native American collaborative autobiographies can be thought of as cultural border skirmishes and as miniatures of those treaty conferences which, according to A. M. Drummond and Richard Moody, were "our first American drama" (15). The resulting collaborative "bi-cultural document" might be seen as a personal treaty—an attempt to negotiate between one's individual or tribal identity and a new dominant culture. Native American autobiographies are interesting, then, not merely because of what they tell us of the cultural, religious, and historical aspects of an individual and the tribe, but for the dramatic way in which they record the human encounter with change, with new and threatening circumstances. If we accept the assumption that we can shape and recreate ourselves through language, we can examine the development of some patterns of Native American autobiography in which we see individuals who attempted to recreate themselves in language and who tried to refashion themselves in a foreign language for an alien audience.

2

Precontact Plains Indian males did not simply *tell* the stories of their personal exploits in hunts and battles, they *portrayed* them in various artistic forms.[3] Pictographs were often painted on tipis, shields, cloth, or hides. As Helen H. Blish notes, nineteenth-century ethnographer Garrick Mallery called such personal records "bragging biographies" and "partisan histories" since they are individual records of one person's exploits (21). Such "picture-writing" was meant to record and to communicate rather than to please aesthetically. Before 1830 these pictographic narratives were a type of shorthand. In fact, according to art historian Karen Daniels Petersen, the "characteristic features of this art style" included "little interest in anatomical details," "relative scale," or "perspective" (*Howling Wolf* 7–8). One well-known example is the pictographic robe of Mah-to-toh-pa (The Four Bears), a Mandan chief. In 1832 George Catlin visited the Mandans and reported that Mah-to-toh-pa wore a robe with "the history of all his battles on it, which would fill a book . . . if they were properly enlarged and translated." This robe with "all the battles of [Mah-to-toh-pa's] life emblazoned on it by his own hand" was "the chart of his military life" (I: 145, 147–48).[4] Mah-to-toh-pa's pictographic robe, then, tells the story of his heroic exploits. Following the traditional pattern of coup tales (tales of a warrior's brave deeds), he identifies the hero (often by portraying a characteristic symbol of himself such as his lance adorned with eagle feathers), the strategic position (the warrior's relation to his enemy), the weapons used by both the warrior and the enemy, and the number of opponents (often represented by their tracks, arrows, or bullets rather than their bodies). The result is a visual narrative of Mah-to-toh-pa's accomplishments, much like John Sturrock's description of the product of "the new model autobiographer" who, in the process of creating associative autobiography, presents a spatial "diagram of the autobiographer" rather than a linear narrative description (61). This pictographic narrative came to life as speech and performance when Mah-to-toh-pa, sitting upon his robe and pointing to his paintings, would brandish his knife and reenact the battles. Such a dramatic rendering of the episodes is more impressive than merely looking at the pictures which serve as a mnemonic device for the teller, as a personal and historical record for the individual and the tribe, and as a monument to individual bravery and achievement. Although a few Indians learned of Euro-American artistic techniques earlier, according to Petersen, it was not until "the decade of the 1830s that a few Indians began to draw and paint in the white man's medium of pencil and watercolors on paper for whites" (*Howling Wolf* 9). Learning from the Swiss artist Karl Bodmer about "realistic portraiture," Mah-to-toh-pa drew in pencil and then painted with watercolor a more realistic, detailed version of one of his triumphs in battle (9).

As well as painting pictographic hides, the "prominent tribal leaders" of the Kiowa and Kiowa-Apache painted their tipis (Ewers 8). From 1891 to 1904, James Mooney, the ethnologist for the Smithsonian Institution, collected "small-scale models of painted tipis" described by the oldest Kiowa and Kiowa-Apaches who remembered and owned these tipis and painted by Kiowa artists—Paul Zotom, Charley Ohettoint, and Silverhorn (Ewers 10). Before 1870 such ornamented tipis were used to signify the elevated status of an individual within the tribe. These "earliest mural artists in North America" obtained designs and colors for their art work through personal visions, brave war deeds, inheritance, or marriage (Ewers 8). Designs were often handed down from one generation to the next so that a tipi design was closely associated with the individual owner and his family, in much the same way as a European family crest symbolizes a collective heritage. Some owners even "came to be known by the names of their tipis" (Ewers 8). Both the design and the colors are personal expressions rendered in a set of conventional symbols, what James Mooney referred to as "Kiowa heraldry" (Ewers 10). Although the tipi usually had an individual owner, several men generally worked together to create this artistic autobiographical narrative, an intratribal collaboration soon to be supplemented with bicultural collaboration.

3

By 1870 Euro-Americans had virtually exterminated the buffalo and, along with these sacred animals, the physical and spiritual sustenance of the indigenous peoples of the Plains. Hostilities between Plains Indians and Anglos, as we know, often flared into warfare. According to Indian art historian Dorothy Dunn, "painting and drawing now became an urgent personal record of dying days" rather than the earlier heraldic expressions of self. Plains Indian men continued to paint pictographic personal narratives, but now the materials, the occasion, and the audience had been altered abruptly. It is not surprising that "much of the new art emerged in army prisons—Fort Robinson, Fort Omaha, Fort Sill, Fort Marion, and others in which the Indians had been confined" for protecting their own homelands (7), including "847 extant pieces of art done by twenty-six Plains Indian warriors" who had been imprisoned in Fort Marion (Petersen, *Plains Indian Art* ix).

Two such examples are found in the *1877 Sketch Books* of Zo-Tom, a Kiowa, and Howling Wolf, a Cheyenne, who were held prisoners in Fort Marion in St. Augustine, Florida. Like many Indian prisoners, Zo-Tom and Howling Wolf sketched and painted on whatever material was available to them. After seeing their drawings, Eva S. Fenyes (then Eva Scott), an artist herself, ordered art pads for them and asked them "to fill the

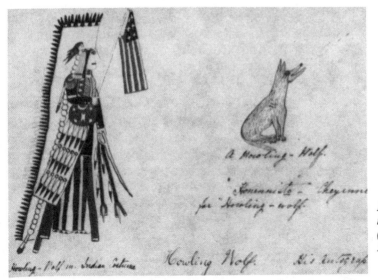

Figure 1. "Howling Wolf in Indian Costume." (Courtesy of Southwest Museum, Los Angeles.)

two sketchbooks with colored drawings" (Dunn 11). It was not until 1969 that Fenyes's daughter, Leonora Scott Muse Curtin, published reproductions of these drawings because they "provide a rare and fascinating opportunity of seeing the Indians as they saw themselves in bygone times" (Dunn 12).

Of the two artists, Howling Wolf is the less explicitly autobiographical. Although he begins his sketchbook with depictions of his personal activities, he shifts his focus to portrayals of tribal life.[5] Plate 1 (Figure 1) is a drawing of Howling Wolf in full Cheyenne warrior regalia.[6] He wears a long warbonnet, breechcloth, breastplate, silver hair-plates, and a bird war charm tied in his hair. He carries his personal shield, sword, coup sticks, and ironically (to a contemporary eye), a pendant US flag. In addition to these innovative details of costume, he reverses the traditional flow of action. Instead of the narrative action moving right to left, as it does in the conventions of earlier hide paintings, we read this picture from left to right. Rather than the conventional Plains Indian autograph—in this instance, a shorthand sketch of a howling wolf above or below Howling Wolf with a line connecting the pictographic autograph to the person—Howling Wolf includes a somewhat realistic drawing of *honennisto,* or a howling wolf, without the connecting line. Petersen notes that at least "within Fort Marion, the name-symbol device became obsolescent"; it was used in less than 20 out of 460 drawings (*Plains Indian Art* 53). Howling Wolf uses it, but with innovations. In Plate 2 he presents a picture of himself as a small boy with his father and mother—all dressed in traditional Cheyenne clothing. After this brief

Figure 2. "Zo-Tom Coming to Capt. Pratt with flag of truce in '71." (Courtesy of Southwest Museum, Los Angeles.)

presentation of his parents, Howling Wolf's personal account turns into an artistic tribal documentary as he depicts people in ceremonial garb—chiefs, warriors, medicine men, and brides and grooms; and tribal activities—hunting, fishing, singing, dancing, drumming, riding, fighting, and counseling. It is important to remember, however, that in precontact times one's individual identity was linked so intimately to one's tribal identity that personal and tribal history were often one and the same.

Zo-Tom's drawings, on the other hand, are more consistently autobiographical since he focuses more persistently on his personal narrative. Read from start to finish his pictographs reveal some of the changes he underwent in this transitional period. Although the drawings are not strictly chronological, they do tell a story of change over time. On one narrative level, the drawings depict his journey from the freedom of the plains to his imprisonment at Fort Marion in Florida. On another level, they reveal his journey from the old Kiowa ways of life (represented by scenes of hunting, fighting, moving, trading, gambling, and celebrating) to his new Euro-American way of life (in this case, represented by a drawing of Zo-Tom studying English).

Zo-Tom's first drawing depicts a Kiowa camp with nine men and women pursuing assorted activities amongst the painted tipis. Plate 2, entitled by the editor, "Chief Receiving a Stranger of Importance," shows the respectful Kiowa reception of a white military officer. After this initial intercultural encounter, there is no more mention of Indian-white interaction until Plate 18 in which the Kiowa prepare to surrender to Captain Pratt. Plates 3 to 17, like Howling Wolf's, deal with Plains Indian daily activities—dancing, chasing Navajo, gambling, trading, sleeping, celebrating, cooking, eating, marrying, burying, moving, hunting, and fighting other tribes. After Plate 18, "Surrender at Mt. Scott," Zo-Tom depicts the journey to Fort Sill in Oklahoma and from Fort Sill to Fort Marion in Florida, with a few flashbacks depicting the old days. In Plate 23 (Figure 2) Zo-Tom presents himself as the warrior carrying the flag of truce to Captain Pratt in 1871. Like Howling Wolf, Zo-Tom ignores the traditional right to left movement of hide paintings. Captain Pratt and Zo-Tom meet face to face in the center of the page. Both extend their right arms in a peaceful greeting. In his left hand, Pratt grips a sword, while Zo-Tom holds a rifle and carries a quiver of arrows. Traditionally, a mid-nineteenth-century pictographic painter would depict details of the enemy's costume, enough at least to identify tribal affiliation and rank. Accordingly, Zo-Tom provides numerous details of Captain Pratt's military uniform, including buttons, stripes, boots, and spurs. In addition, he provides comparable details of his own outfit—what looks like an army jacket adorned with Kiowa designs, leggings, moccasins, breastplate, and shield. This extended treatment of his own costume may result from using Euro-American art materials (paper and pens rather than hide and bone) that allowed for more detailed treatment of subjects. As a result, notes Petersen, the "name-symbol device" was replaced by "a costume-symbol" (*Plains Indian Art* 54). The horses, too, are rendered in detail. Pratt's horse is large and brown with horseshoes, while Zo-Tom's is small, black, and unshod. Also, Zo-Tom's horse has been adorned with feathers (signifying brave escapades) and has had his tail tied (perhaps indicating recent participation in battle). One final innovation to the conventions of pictographic painting is even more remarkable. To be certain the viewer knows that *he* is the one dealing with Pratt, Zo-Tom adds one thing. He (or perhaps the editor) writes his name in English above the picture.

In Figure 3, "A Great Battle" (Plate 26), Zo-Tom provides a detailed pictographic narrative of Kiowa warriors and the US Army engaged in battle. This pictograph "in basic respects, in scheme of composition and style of life figures, corresponds to mid-nineteenth century hide paintings" (Dunn 17). He uses the main conventions of hide and tipi painting—front view of torso with the rest of the body seen from the side; detailed orna-

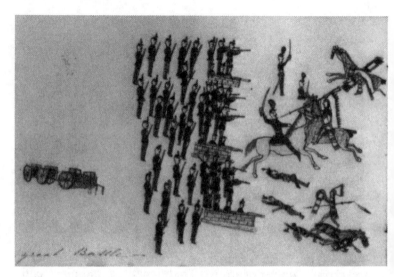

Figure 3. "A Great Battle." (Courtesy of Southwest Museum, Los Angeles: 2 Parts.)

mentation of the enemy; wounds depicted as dark spots with blood streaming from them; and movement depicted from right to left. He also uses some of the basic formats of the coup narrative: he indicates the affiliation and status of warriors and soldiers by providing details of costume and horses, and he presents the strategic positions of both sides. Note how the US soldiers are barricaded together on the left, while the Indian warriors are attacking from the right. Zo-Tom, however, does not rely entirely on such conventions; he also "extends precedents developed in hide painting" (Dunn 19–20). His new additions include his treatment of the military barricades and wagons and the fact that the drawing is "more representational" than the older hide paintings (Dunn 17).

From this battle, Zo-Tom proceeds to draw the dreary exterior and interior of Fort Marion in St. Augustine, Florida, in the penultimate two plates. His final drawing, "A Class of Indians in Fort Marion, with Their Teacher (Mrs. Gibbs)" (Figure 4), completes his account of his personal journey and serves as the climax to his cultural conversion narrative. Instead of the long-haired, brilliantly attired and ornamented Kiowa warriors of his earlier drawings, he draws seven clean-cut Indian students in blue pants and snug black coats who sit, lining a long school bench, at a long desk. Mrs. Gibbs, the teacher, stands, prim and pleasant, to the left. Dutifully, the Indian students read names from flashcards. Zo-Tom has written his name above one student and Making Medicine's above another.

Each name, written in English, is connected by a line to its owner (in a modification of a traditional Plains Indian autograph). Zo-Tom's name appears again, more discreetly, on the flashcard held by the student next to him. Thus Zo-Tom has become a new person and a new subject—literally. In this new life, he is a subject of study both for Fenyes and for himself.

To a certain degree Zo-Tom and Howling Wolf use mid-nineteenth-century Plains Indian artistic principles and conventions in their personal narratives, yet they also introduce

Figure 4. "A Class of Indians in Fort Marion, with their teacher (Mrs. Gibbs)." (Courtesy of Southwest Museum, Los Angeles.)

Figure 5. Fenyes's title page for Zo-Tom. (Courtesy of Southwest Museum, Los Angeles.)

new elements such as an occasional written word to aid in explanation, more realistic depictions of animals and people, and frequent drawings of landscape. The original purpose—to describe one's personal heroics—is still accomplished, but in forms modified to be comprehensible to a white audience. Furthermore, a new purpose—to translate one's culture—has been added. The collaborative nature of these drawings continues from preliterate Native American collaborations in painting tipis and hides, but now there is only one collaborator—a white sponsor. Fenyes did not sit with Zo-Tom and Howling Wolf advising them about how to draw, nor did she edit their final pictures. She did, however, add two major contributions.

Fenyes added the descriptive titles for each drawing and the general titles for each sketchbook. Her selection of titles for these sketchbooks is revealing: "The Life of the Red-Man, Illustrated by a Kiowa Brave" (Figure 5) and "Scenes from Indian Life, Drawn by Howling Wolf" (Figure 6). Such titles disclose her interest in depicting a generalized presentation of Indians, rather than the personal artistic interpretations of individuals. This approach was shared by many ethnographers who were interested in presenting a picture of "some representative . . . individual," rather than in describing the personality of a "definite personage" (Radin 2). Along with inventing the titles, Fenyes did the calligraphy and design for the title pages, leaving a space in the center of each for a picture of the Indian artist.

By providing the sketchbooks, Fenyes helped to shape the pictures produced. It is no accident that Zo-Tom and Howling Wolf each have twenty-nine pages of drawings (although Zo-Tom uses the back of one page to make a two-page drawing of

Figure 6. Fenyes's title page for Howling Wolf. (Courtesy of Southwest Museum, Los Angeles.)

"A Great Battle," and Howling Wolf occasionally draws two related pictures on one page, thus modifying the available space). The very size, shape, and texture of the medium influence how the artist will proceed. Thus the European artistic sensibilities of their sponsor determined, in part, the artists' output. Such a seemingly casual collaboration is far less intrusive than the more active involvement of many ethnographer-editors who often rearranged their Indian informants' recorded oral narratives, imposing a strict chronology and excising "tedious" repetitions. Without such direct interference, the traditional Plains Indian pictographic modes of personal narrative continued with only a few modifications made in order to enhance their accessibility to a white audience in this "evolving bi-cultural expression" (Dunn 25).[7] Petersen points out that Indian adaptation of European materials did not begin in prison. In fact, "blank or partly used ledgers, army rosters, daybooks, memorandum books, and sheaves of paper often found their way into Indian hands through gift, trade or capture" (*Plains Indian Art* 25). Even before the buffalo were exterminated, many "warriors adopted the white man's materials for recording the pictographic history of their brave deeds" (25).

4

A more conspicuously modified pictographic personal narrative was composed over fifty years later by White Bull (*Pte San Hunka*), a Teton Dakota chief who, like Zo-Tom and

Howling Wolf, fought whites in the 1870s and claimed to have killed General George Armstrong Custer at the Battle of the Little Big Horn. White Bull's 1931 written and pictographic personal narrative is clearly influenced by the request and expectations of his solicitor-editor. Chief White Bull's narrative was commissioned by Usher L. Burdick of North Dakota who paid him fifty dollars for a "Sioux History Book." White Bull wrote part of his account in Dakota and drew part of it in traditional pictographs in a business ledger, using "a combination of ink, lead pencil, and colored crayon" (Howard vii). Editor James H. Howard begins White Bull's personal narrative with a letter (from White Bull to Burdick) which reiterates the arrangements made with Burdick, at the same time encouraging a more generous payment. White Bull writes: "Friend, you have asked me to send [return] something and I have done as you wished. What you say is so, but I would like to say this. My war record, as I have written it, is accurate and I have written it for you. You said you would give me fifty dollars for it and that is all right, but I would like to earn more, and as you see I have written much more" (Howard 1–2). This letter makes it clear that White Bull is not writing for his own edification, but for a monetary compensation. His "personal narrative," then, was not merely solicited; it was purchased. Such considerations may help explain, in part, what White Bull includes in his narrative.

After the letter of explanation, White Bull begins his personal narrative with a brief account of several buffalo hunting expeditions. After the traditional hunting stories, White Bull presents his genealogy. Following this brief personal reckoning (1–3), White Bull devotes pages 4 through 8 to his winter count (which he purchased from Hairy-Hand)—a pictographic Dakota history covering the years 1764/65 to 1816/17 and 1835/36 to 1930/31.[8] White Bull, however, recorded events in writing, not in pictographs, even transferring Hairy-Hand's pictographic versions of events painted on hide to his own written versions on paper.

From tribal history, he returns to his personal history, which focuses upon hunting and warring. After another set of hunting stories, this time for buffalo and bear, and a political genealogy, White Bull's personal narrative indeed becomes a "war record." He devotes pages 11 through 46 to his war honors, arranging them by type—counting coup in battle (11–32) (Figure 7), rescuing fallen comrades (33–38) (Figure 8), and stealing enemy horses (39–46) (Figure 9). For these he includes traditional Dakota pictographs, but adds to them copious labels and expla-

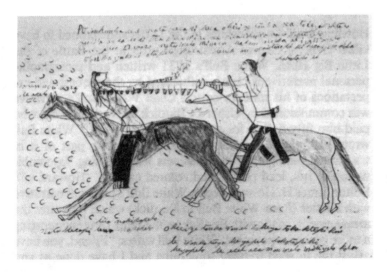

Figure 7. "White Bull Counts Coup on a Flathead." (Courtesy of Chester Fritz Library, University of North Dakota and University of Nebraska Press.)

nations written in Dakota. In Figure 7 (Plate 8) White Bull, on the right, chases down and counts coup on a Flathead who fires a gun at him (note the curlicue lines coming from the gun indicating gunsmoke). Traditional nineteenth-century hide-painting conventions include flow of movement from right to left, hoofprints to indicate number and direction of warriors, small heads and elongated bodies of horses, and wound marks (note the two dark spots dripping blood on the enemy's horse's side). White Bull's "feathered banner," notes Howard, was "commonly associated with the Strong-heart and Crow-owners warrior societies" (42). According to Howard, the text above the Flathead's horse's head may be translated as "They were charging me from this direction" (42). This is obvious to a reader of picture-writing because of the hoof marks leading in that direction. The Dakota text at the bottom right reiterates the basic information: "There was a big fight and this was the first man killed. Because of it I was highly praised by the Lakotas. It was a glorious fight, my friend" (42).

In Figure 8 (Plate 27) White Bull, wearing a full warbonnet, rescues a wounded Cheyenne. (That the wounded man is Cheyenne is indicated by the salamander war charm tied in his hair. Note also the wound in his side.) This is an especially brave deed since you can see the hoofprints, gunsmoke, and flying bullets (indicated by short lines). In a kind of pictographic synecdoche, one gun, on the left, represents a full collection of warriors. The Dakota writing above identifies White Bull and his Cheyenne friend, Sunrise, and describes the action, the en-

Figure 8. "White Bull Rescues a Wounded Cheyenne." (Courtesy of Chester Fritz Library, University of North Dakota and University of Nebraska Press.)

emy, the witnesses, and the battle location (66–67). In Figure 9 (Plate 29) White Bull is shown stealing nine horses from a Crow camp. The camp, on the right, is depicted as a circle of thirteen tipis. In the middle of the circle is the Dakota label Howard translates as: "This is the Crow camp" (69). Hoofprints within and around camp indicate the original position of the horses. The squiggly line above camp denotes a stream. The writing above provides basic information about the exploit, while the brief labels near each horse describe their worth. "Four of the adult horses are labeled '*le waste*' ('this was a good one'),'' explains Howard, "and the two colts are labeled '*cincala*,' meaning 'young ones'" (69). Just as Zo-Tom's pictographic narrative is clarified by the addition of an occasional word, White Bull's drawn personal history is enlivened, at least for a white audience, by the additional detail provided in his written narrative.

In contrast to his numerous drawn and written depictions of his early life, White Bull includes only two written accounts (conspicuously lacking pictographs) of his later life at the agency. In these accounts he catalogs his titles and achievements obtained in his new life. He served as an Indian policeman, a tribal judge, a chairman of the tribal council, a catechist, and so forth. Finally, White Bull ends his personal narrative with three of his updated pictographs (pictographs which include written commentary) in which rather than focusing upon the present, he returns to his depictions of the past.

White Bull's narrative movement, which fluctuates between personal and tribal foci, may highlight his traditional

Figure 9. "White Bull Steals Crow Horses." (Courtesy of Chester Fritz Library, University of North Dakota and University of Nebraska Press.)

sense of tribal identity. On the other hand, his inclusion of tribal history (especially the winter count) may arise from Burdick's desire for a "Sioux History Book" or White Bull's own desire for a longer account which might mean a more financially profitable endeavor. If White Bull's narrative moves liberally between personal and tribal history, it also roams freely between past and present, dwelling heavily upon the past. Clearly, the expectations of his Euro-American editor shape White Bull's personal account. Even though White Bull's narrative is organized, in traditional Plains Indian fashion, according to his brave deeds and war honors, it follows a general chronological progression. With such a pattern one might expect his personal narrative to end with his later life at the agency, but White Bull defies such a Euro-American expectation in three ways.

First, he devotes only two pages to this part of his life. Even though he had held many honorable positions and had achieved a respected status in both the Dakota and white communities, and even though he had lived this "later life" for more than fifty years, he does not elaborate upon his experiences. Such a contracted treatment of so many years filled with so much activity suggests a distinct selection principle on White Bull's part. White Bull's minimal description of this part of his life reflects the reluctance of a great many Indian people to talk about their reservation experiences. Zo-Tom and Howling Wolf, remember, devote most of their attention to their prereservation days of freedom. The Crow chief, Plenty-coups, will say only this: "when the buffalo went away the hearts of my people fell to the ground, and they could not be lifted up again. After this nothing happened. There was little singing anywhere" (311).[9]

Second, unlike his depictions of the honors obtained in his earlier life, White Bull draws no pictographs for his later life. Instead, he catalogs his achievements in writing. Perhaps a traditional Plains Indian pictographic mode simply was not suitable to depict his nontraditional actions as a policeman or a tribal chairman or a church catechist. Although his ceremonial dancing or his Custer battle reenactments or his apprehension of "antagonistic" Utes for the US government seem to lend themselves to pictographic expression, he does not give them such artistic treatment. Perhaps the detail he bestowed upon the pictographs of his hunting and war deeds of the distant past and the sparse catalog he wrote of his recent past indicate the relative importance he placed upon these two sets of events. It is as if his real life ended fifty years before, at the age of thirty-one, when, as he says, he "followed the ways of the whites, as the President instructed" (Howard 76).

If White Bull were to end his personal narrative with his brief written list of achievements since living "the ways of the whites," we might conclude that he diminished his treatment of his later life because he gloried in his adventurous past or that he yearned for his lost youth or that he simply ran out of time because of a deadline and so brought it to a hurried conclusion (also explaining the lack of pictographs for this stage of his life). White Bull, however, does not end his personal narrative with his reservation life. He includes three final pages, each with a pictograph accompanied by a written explanation. What is striking here is that these pages focus once again upon the distant past, a third way White Bull confounds a sense of chronology. In Plate 37 White Bull draws a picture of his tipi. On the next page (in Plate 38), he draws "The Ceremonial Camp of the Circle of the Miniconjou," labeling several items and explaining about life "a long time ago" (Howard 80).

The final Plate (39) (Figure 10) shows White Bull in "the full ceremonial costume of a Teton chief" (Howard 81). This is not, however, a depiction of White Bull as a young warrior. Rather, it is a picture of the contemporary White Bull (the eighty-one year-old autobiographer) in the costume he wore "on festive occasions," "at the gatherings of the Lakotas," or "riding in parades" (Howard 81). Thus, the two penultimate pages of White Bull's personal narrative return to "a long time ago" when he lived in a tipi and the Miniconjous came together for ceremonials. His final pictograph, however, unites (for the first time in his account) the distant past with the present. The

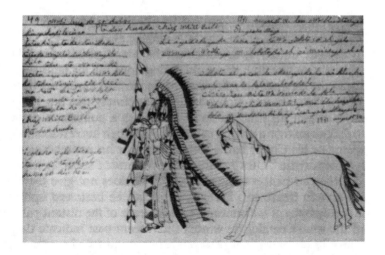

Figure 10. "White Bull in Full Dress." (Courtesy of Chester Fritz Library, University of North Dakota and University of Nebraska Press.)

present-day White Bull is shown in his "long ago" ceremonial clothing in which he reenacted and/or recalled historical deeds for a contemporary audience.

White Bull's narrative is a fascinating example of transitional Plains Indian autobiography in that his personal narrative was solicited and purchased by a white history buff. It was both drawn and written, thus combining Native American and Euro-American autobiographical forms. White Bull's written explanations and labels themselves suggest a white audience (a Plains Indian audience would need no explanation) and thus reveal an attempt at a type of translation from one cultural code to another. White Bull's personal narrative was also translated, edited, and published by James H. Howard, a Euro-American scholar. Chief White Bull's narrative, then, has been triply mediated by Euro-American society: Burdick's request and expectations, White Bull's modification of traditional pictographic forms, and Howard's translation. Yet a sense of White Bull—courageous, proud, and deeply attached to his tribal past—emerges from his hybrid autobiography which mixes past and present, Miniconjou and white, and pictograph and writing, all of which are representative of the boundary culture in which he lived.[10]

5

Zo-Tom's and Howling Wolf's pictographic sketchbooks from the late nineteenth century and White Bull's pictographic and written Dakota ledger book from the early twentieth century provide insights into one of the precontact Plains Indian male traditions of personal narrative and its subsequent adaptation for a white audience. Relying on earlier artistic conventions of Plains Indian hide and tipi painting, these three artist-autobiographers use new materials and modify pictographic conventions for a white audience. These men were not sellouts. Each of them fought against the encroaching Euro-Americans. Zo-Tom was "in the last group of Kiowa warriors to surrender, February 18, 1875" (Petersen, *Plains Indian Art* 173), and two months later, Howling Wolf was arrested at the Cheyenne Agency for being a "ringleader" (*Plains Indian Art* 221). A year or so later, White Bull fought at the Battle of Little Big Horn (1876). Only when they had no alternative did they agree to translate their personal exploits and tribal experiences into pictographic narratives modified for a white audience. Certainly all were motivated by economic factors. The work of Zo-Tom and Howling Wolf was in great demand by wealthy, curious, or sympathetic whites. The going price for a Fort Marion Indian sketchbook was $2.00 (*Plains Indian Art* 64) and White Bull, remember, earned $50.00 for his "Sioux History Book." Each of them was willing, under pressure, to examine the white way of life. Years after converting to Christianity, however, all three men returned to tribal ways. After serving as a deacon of the Episcopal Church, Zo-Tom became a Baptist and finally a member of the Native American Church which blends Christian and tribal beliefs and ceremonies with the use of peyote. Howling Wolf and White Bull also gave up "the Jesus road" and, by the end of their lives, joined the Native American Church. Under the harshest conditions, these pictographic autobiographers attempted to communicate in modified Plains Indian forms to their white audience. They provided ethnographic details of tribal costume and custom and personal details of individual accomplishments. These pictographic sketchbooks, then, provide an insight into a distinctly traditional Plains Indian form of autobiography as it was being adapted to colonialism.[11]

Traditional Plains Indian pictographic personal history continued to be evident in the transitional autobiographies of the late nineteenth and early twentieth centuries. Often these forms were modified to make them comprehensible to a white audience. Such Plains Indian personal narratives were supplemented by commentary from ethnographers and editors who were often responsible for the final shape of the autobiography as well as its original solicitation. Thus, as Native Americans and Euro-Americans clashed and negotiated historically, representatives of these two distinct cultures interacted textually within the pages of transitional autobiography. As Anglo editors attempted to translate Native American languages, cultures, and personalities into their own language and cultural framework, one result was a blend of traditional Native American pictographic forms of personal history and Euro-American written modes of autobiography. Such a life story, "a self-contained fiction" (Titon 276), is an attempt to refashion one's self. If autobiography is an act of self-creation, Native American transitional autobiography is an act of self re-creation in which a Native American conceives of himself or herself anew as a result of this boundary culture encounter.

Acknowledging Plains Indian pictographic paintings as one distinctly native form of autobiographical activity is not only important in piecing together a uniquely Native American tradition of autobiography. Such pictographic narratives have consequences for literary discourse in general, and for autobiography theory in particular. Pictographic narratives challenge the Eurocentrism of our American literary canon, they dispute the ethnocentric definition of self assumed by many theorists of autobiography, and they defy the primacy of the written word. American literature does not begin with Captain John Smith's 1620 account of New England; it does not even begin with explorer narratives. It begins in pre-Columbian oral and artistic traditions of indigenous peoples. Similarly, Native American autobiography does not begin with Western imposition of European forms on native peoples. Rather, what we can at least call autobiographical activity emerges on its own terms from preliterate native peoples. By the late nineteenth century, oral and pictographic forms of personal narrative intersect with Western autobiographical forms, continuing a long tradition of adaptation and development.

Notes

1. See also Lynne Woods O'Brien and H. David Brumble III's latest book.

2. In *For Those Who Come After*, Arnold Krupat refers to such transitional autobiographies as "the textual equivalent of the frontier" (33).

3. As well as the hide and tipi paintings mentioned below, Plains Indian males narrated their stories in their personal adornment. In *Indian Art in*

America, Frederick J. Dockstader notes how Plains Indian face painting, hair designs, and clothing expressed a "concept of self" (46).

4.   This robe was not the only part of Mah-to-toh-pa's outfit that was decorated with pictographs of his achievements. For Catlin's description of Mah-to-toh-pa's mountain-sheep shirt, leggings, etc., see 146–47.

5.   The Howling Wolf and Zo-Tom sketchbooks I describe were recently donated to the Southwest Museum in Los Angeles by Curtin's daughter. Another Howling Wolf sketchbook is owned by A. H. (Anna Bourke) Richardson's family and is housed in the Joslyn Art Museum in Omaha, Nebraska. According to Petersen, the Field Museum, the Massachusetts Historical Society, and Yale University have other Howling Wolf drawings, while Hampton Institute, the Museum of the American Indian, Yale University, and Boles and Jolly have Zo-Tom drawings.

6.   Throughout this paper, Plate will refer to the original sketchbook and Figure will refer to the illustration accompanying this text.

7.   A similar artistic autobiography is that painted in watercolor by Running-Antelope, a chief of the Hunkpapa Dakotas, for Dr. W. J. Hoffman in 1873. This "continuous record of events" includes "the most important events in the life of Running-Antelope as a warrior" between 1853 and 1863. Each of the eleven watercolors is a detailed coup account with Running-Antelope's name depicted pictographically in each. Along with the drawings, Running-Antelope provided an oral interpretation. See Mallery, II: 571–75.

8.   These page numbers refer to White Bull's original ledger book housed in the Special Collections Department of the Chester Fritz Library, University of North Dakota, Grand Forks, not to Howard's edition.

9.   In addition, Brumble notes that "the reluctance of early Indian 'informants' to open up 'their souls in the inwardness of true autobiography' is widely remarked upon" (3).

10.   It is interesting to note that another artistic form of personal expression, blanket weaving, went through a similar change, but with different results. Anthony Berland and Mary Hunt Kahlenberg trace the design changes of Navajo blankets from prehistoric times to the twentieth century (3). In the late nineteenth century most of these changes were due to the demands and desires of the market (the wealthy Euro-American purchasers from the East coast) which insisted upon borders, subtle colors, "suitably 'barbaric' designs," and wool rugs rather than cotton blankets (142–45). Some Navajo women, "weaving for trade rather than for the tribe" (141), gave up one means of traditional self-expression in return for economic improvement.

11.   According to Petersen, the Fort Marion sketchbooks "may prove to be the Rosetta Stone of Plains Indian pictorial representation" (*Plains Indian Art* x).

Works Cited

Bakhtin, M. M. *The Dialogic Imagination.* Trans. Caryl Emerson and Michael Holquist. Ed. Michael Holquist. Austin: U of Texas P, 1981.

Berland, Anthony, and Mary Hunt Kahlenberg. *Walk in Beauty: The Navajo and Their Blankets.* Boston: New York Graphic Society, 1977.

Blish, Helen H. *A Pictographic History of the Oglala Sioux.* Lincoln: U of Nebraska P, 1967.

Brumble, H. David, III. *American Indian Autobiography.* Berkeley: U of California P, 1988.

———. Introduction. *An Annotated Bibliography of American Indian and Eskimo Autobiographies.* Lincoln: U of Nebraska P, 1981.

Catlin, George. *Letters and Notes on the Manners, Customs, and Conditions of the North American Indians.* Vol. 2. 1844. New York: Dover Pubs., Inc., 1973. 2 vols.

Dockstader, Frederick J. *Indian Art in America.* Greenwich, CT: New York Graphic Society, n.d.

Drummond, A. M., and Richard Moody. "Indian Treaties: The First American Dramas." *The Quarterly Journal of Speech* 39F (1953): 15–24.

Dunn, Dorothy, ed. Introduction. *1877: Plains Indian Sketch Books of Zo-Tom and Howling Wolf.* Flagstaff, AZ: Northland P, 1969.

Ewers, John. *Murals in the Round: Painted Tipis of the Kiowa and Kiowa-Apache Indians.* Washington, DC: Smithsonian Institution P, 1978.

Howard, James H., ed. *The Warrior Who Killed Custer: The Personal Narrative of Chief Joseph White Bull.* Lincoln: U of Nebraska P, 1968.

Krupat, Arnold. *For Those Who Come After: A Study of Native American Autobiography.* Berkeley: U of California P, 1985.

Mallery, Garrick. "Picture-Writing of the American Indians." Tenth *Annual Report* of the Bureau of Ethnology to the Secretary of the Smithsonian Institution. 1888–89. II. Ed. John Powell. 1892. New York: Dover, 1972. 571–75.

Murphy, Robert F. "Social Change and Acculturation." *Transactions of the New York Academy of Sciences.* 2nd Ser., 26.7 (1964): 845–54.

O'Brien, Lynne Woods. *Plains Indian Autobiographies.* Boise: Boise State College, 1973.

Petersen, Karen Daniels. *Howling Wolf: A Cheyenne Warrior's Graphic Interpretation of His People.* Palo Alto: American West Pub. Co., 1968.

———. *Plains Indian Art from Fort Marion.* Norman: U of Oklahoma P, 1971.

Plenty-coups. *Plenty-coups: Chief of the Crows.* Ed. Frank Bird Linderman. 1930. Lincoln: U of Nebraska P, 1962.

Radin, Paul. Introduction. *The Autobiography of a Winnebago Indian.* 1920. New York: Dover, 1963.

Sands, Kathleen Mullen. "American Indian Autobiography." *Studies in American Literature: Critical Essays and Course Designs.* Ed. Paula Gunn Allen. New York: MLA, 1983. 55–65.

Sturrock, John. "The New Model Autobiographer." *New Literary History* 9 (1977): 51–63.

Titon, Jeff Todd. "The Life Story." *Journal of American Folklore* 93 (1980): 276–292.

Early Histories of American Literature: A Chapter in the Institution of New England

Nina Baym

When, in the second decade of the twentieth century, academics defined a field of study called "American literature," they did so by appropriating and sophisticating a narrative already constructed in the plethora of American literary history textbooks that had been published between 1882 and 1912. Putnam; Houghton Mifflin; Ginn; American Book Company; Silver, Burdett; Macmillan; Henry Holt; A. C. McClurg; Scribner's; Harper; D. C. Heath; D. Appleton—these and other publishers commissioned American literary histories for high school and college use, and had them frequently revised and updated.[1] By situating select works and authors—above all authors—in a narrative, these textbooks attempted to configure American literature to serve the aims of American public education: forming character and ensuring patriotism.[2] As one of them put it, American literature "is valuable to the young student and future citizen of the Republic just in proportion as it seems to mirror our American ideals and as it shall have a tendency to build up the reader into a worthy citizenship" (Burton v). The histories were written for the most part by professors of New England origin employed at elite colleges; they cribbed from each other routinely and meshed with an array of handbooks, anthologies, memoirs, and biographies (many put together by the same professors) to create the tendentious narrative that launched the academic field and continues to influence it.

Constructing history in a shape to further the purpose of schooling, the textbook writers made literary works and authors display the virtues and achievements of an Anglo-Saxon United States founded by New England Puritans. The histories were expressly derived from national history as it had been iterated throughout the nineteenth century in a variety of forms, chiefly in connection with the Whig political project.[3] The story that they told, simply put, is this: in the face of numerous obstacles, a bona fide literary culture had developed in America before the Civil War. Before about 1830 there was no such culture in America; after 1830 there was. "Literary" here meant belletristic, having to do with literature written for its own sake rather than for some other end. No sermons or political documents qualified. "Culture" here meant a documentable social scene wherein the production of belles lettres was encouraged, its producers esteemed, and the cultural products themselves disseminated. The story showed how this country, at first hostile or indifferent to belles lettres and lacking entirely in literary culture, came to develop both.

This literary culture, according to the story, emerged in New England among groups of Cambridge and Concord authors linked socially through the amenities of Boston, where a powerful publishing and critical apparatus supported them and circulated their writings around the nation. The main authors— Emerson, Hawthorne, Lowell, Longfellow, Holmes, and Whittier—were descendants of Puritans whose work expressed Puritan values in nineteenth-century terms. The histories encouraged respect, veneration, and gratitude toward these men who had achieved American literature on behalf of the rest of us, and implied that affiliation with them would assimilate the reader to the national culture they represented and displayed.

The Whig project of installing New England as the original site of the American nation had been designed to unify the unformed and scattered American people under the aegis of New England by creating a national history anchored in that region. Conservative New England leaders knew all too well that the nation was an artifice and that no single national character undergirded it. And they insisted passionately that peace and progress called for a commonalty that, if it did not exist, had at once to be invented. By originating American history in New England and proclaiming the carefully edited New England Puritan as the national type, they hoped to create such a commonalty, instilling in all citizens those traits that they thought necessary for the future: self-reliance, self-control, and acceptance of hierarchy.

It did not take long for intellectual leaders to see that the public, or common, schools might be an important agent in this process. Common schools, one must remember, were designed for children whose parents could not afford private instruction, a group increasingly composed of newly arrived, non-English immigrants. By no accident, both Connecticut and Massachusetts established Boards of Education in 1837, during the decade when substantial numbers of Irish began to settle in

New England, and more specifically in the Panic year of disproportionate suffering among the working poor (see Williams; McGrane). New England educational reformers, led by Horace Mann of Massachusetts and Henry Barnard of Connecticut, theorized the school as a socially conservative force. The greatly expanded and rigorously standardized apparatus they hoped to put in place was meant to keep young people in school for a long time and turn them out as literate, rational, reliable citizens.[4]

Indirectly, their program called for many more teachers and many more textbooks, facts that the publishers—the largest segment of whose business had always been textbooks—grasped quickly. It was not apparent at first, however, that belles lettres could play a role in this brave new world of schooling. Mann thought that literacy necessarily undergirded any republic, but he distrusted imaginative literature because he distrusted the imagination; for his part, Henry Barnard thought the King James Bible sufficient for all classroom reading needs (Mann 33–34, 36–37; Curti 143).[5] Insofar as American belles lettres—or belles lettres of any sort—entered the schools in the antebellum era, it did so only through extracts in compilations like McGuffey's. Pared to their obviously declarative content, these extracts enunciated patriotic, moral, and Christian sentiments, and in true Whig fashion attributed the enlightened, prosperous, independent, intelligent, Christian, honest, hardworking, sober, and moral American character—along with the republican institutions that such a character had created—to New England Puritan origins.[6]

In the last two decades of the nineteenth century, the supposed menace to which the first generation of school reformers had responded seemed, to many, to have reappeared in far more frightening form. The outcome of the Civil War had barely reimposed union when industrialization and immigration brought back the specters of cultural chaos and social violence once again. Industrialization created enormous new wealth and distributed it unequally, producing a group of newly wealthy people who knew nothing of the New England way and an equally ignorant, far more dangerous class composed largely of immigrants, a wretchedly poor class packed into restless and rootless urban slums. Public school teachers could hardly expect to be invited to reform the newly wealthy; in the new poor they found their opportunity. Educators proposed to reach the working class through its children, by greatly expanding the time in school required of such children. There emerged, now, a need for more subjects to fill up this time. The question was how to invent and tailor subjects for the goal of Americanization, the timely term which described the project.

What could be better suited for the Americanizing of the young immigrant, some argued, than a literature authored by native-born Americans—preferably of several generations' descent—composed in English, expressing American values and representing American themes and events? What more likely to deflect the (usually foreign-born) poor from their desire to have a substantial piece of the country's settled wealth than exposure to an idealism from whose lofty perspective the materialist struggle would seem unworthy? The old textbook compilations could not provide the necessary tools for this new enterprise; one needed instruction in literature itself, immersion in works of truth and beauty within a nationalist framework supplied by historical and biographical guides.[7]

The publishing company most prepared to help establish such an approach to teaching literature in the schools was Houghton Mifflin, which held the copyright to all the Cambridge-Concord authors.[8] We can see the company at work in an 1888 address to teachers on the place of literature in the schools, delivered by Horace Scudder, director of Houghton Mifflin's Education Department. Scudder praised the common schools system as the safeguard of the American way, and observed that the system was now responding in two appropriate ways to "the danger which threatens the nation" (10)—a danger he described as "the relations of labor to well-being" and as "the cry of Labor in Poverty."[9] Poor children were to receive both an industrial (i.e., vocational) education and a literary education—vocational education to earn a decent living, literary education to reconcile them to that standard of living by inculcating spiritual values. Since religious diversity had made the Protestant Bible obsolete for public education, literature was the best substitute: "in literature, above all, is this spirit enshrined" (33).[10]

American literature had particular value for American students because it provided an easier access to American history than history itself, which tended to be cluttered with names and dates; and because its well-born authors, in the face of the powerful material temptations of American life, had chosen the spiritual way. In making this choice, the classic writers of the mid-nineteenth century reincarnated the self-denying moral values of the Puritan founders. "The lives and songs of Bryant, Emerson, Longfellow, Whittier, Holmes, and Lowell have an imperishable value regarded as exponents of national life"; along with Hawthorne, Irving, and Cooper, who "associate with them in spiritual power," they "have been the consummate flower of American life," and "it is through their works that spiritual light most surely and immediately may penetrate our common schools" (25–26).

Houghton Mifflin offered its Riverside Literature Series pamphlets as the material base for implementing this spiritual program in the elementary schools.[11] Although Scudder seemed certain that sheer repetition by itself would suffice to flood the child's mind with irresistible spiritual light, Houghton Mifflin as early as 1883 published a historically organized primer of American literature (written by Charles Richardson) to guide the students' apprehension of the important works. And, as more and more people needed to know about this literature in order to teach it, textbooks for higher levels of schooling developed apace. Invariably, these textbooks were literary histories. Though Houghton Mifflin benefited most from the sale of textbooks of primary works, all publishers stood to benefit from the market for literary history that they aimed to shape and expand as much as possible.

In view of the Americanizing aims of the American literary history textbooks, the histories rather emphasized than played down the English origins of the American nation, thereby instructing classrooms of children of non-English ancestry to defer to the Anglo-Saxonism of their new country's heritage.

In view of the Americanizing aims of the American literary history textbooks, the histories rather emphasized than played down the English origins of the American nation, thereby instructing classrooms of children of non-English ancestry to defer to the Anglo-Saxonism of their new country's heritage. This most important point was often left implicit, but it appears to have been well understood. Certainly it came through strongly when a historian asserted that American literature could never be anything other than "the literature of a part of the English people, under new geographical and political conditions" (Richardson I:1). Paradoxically, non-Anglo-Saxons could become American only to the extent of their agreement that only those of Anglo-Saxon lineage were really Americans.[12]

Emphasis on English precedence served the historical plot, for it allowed historians freely to concede that literature in the United States was belated and inferior to English literature and then to use this backwardness as the starting point of their story. That literature had been produced at all in the United States— this was the whole happy point, the triumphant occasion for the celebration of American literature in school. The celebrated literary works did not need to be masterpieces; it was enough that they were certifiably belletristic and that there were enough of them to show that a literary culture existed around them.

Although it was their status as aesthetic objects that justified the history being written, they were not made the objects of aesthetic analysis. And works of solitary genius—like the novels of Charles Brockden Brown—merited notice as instances of the *failure* of a literary culture to develop, and therefore emphasized by contrast the different situation in New England.

Warming to their trials-and-triumph plot, the opening pages of these texts gleefully specified the many difficulties that a would-be literary culture faced, including: the absence of a unique national language as well as a primitive period of national history; the geographical separation of the nation from European cultural centers and its tardy exposure to intellectual currents; or, alternatively, the advanced state of transportation permitting too-easy access to the superior literatures of England and Europe; and of course the all-absorbing material hardships of American life, among which subduing nature and exterminating the Indians posed particular challenges.[13] Yet, ultimately, such obstacles were seen as minor compared to the impediment posed by the unliterary character of early Anglo-Americans themselves in their two incarnations as hedonistic Virginia Cavalier and dour New England Puritan.

It was hardly surprising, then, that—as all the histories agreed—no literary culture developed in America before the nineteenth century.[14] On the contrary, the surprise was rather that it had developed at all. To make its belatedness all the more salient, historians routinely denigrated the literary quality of whatever early American writings they chose to acknowledge. "The literature of the Colonial age in Virginia is so scanty and uninteresting as to deserve little attention" (Pattee 14); the "literature of Virginia during these early years is comparatively meager and poor" (Bronson 11); "if pure literature be the test, there is very little, after all, to detain us" in New England (Burton 3–4); Puritan literature is "hopeless" from the "point of view of intrinsic aesthetic value" (Trent 2); "The Day of Doom," like the *Bay Psalm Book* and Anne Bradstreet's poems, is not literature—"the student notes it only as a curiosity, and as a pitiful indication of the literary poverty of the days and the land in which it was popular" (Richardson II:6–7).

Since all agreed that American literary culture finally established itself in New England, the plot moved American writing toward belles lettres and toward New England simultaneously. Moses Coit Tyler's two scholarly volumes on Colonial literature, published in 1878, provided the source for most of what was written by other historians on the early period.[15] Ignoring his own announced plan to trace "the rise of American literature at the several isolated colonial centres" until 1765 when "the scattered voices of the thirteen colonies were for the first time brought together and blended in one great resolute utterance" (I:v), Tyler, following Palfrey, quickly reduced the Colonies to two: "during the first epoch in the history of American literature, there were but two localities which produced in the English language anything that can be called literature: Virginia and New England" (I:80). Everybody followed Tyler's lead—not because Tyler was original but, on the contrary, because his approach was familiar and because he had applied traditional history to the literary-historical field.[16] "All our northern colonies developed from those planted in Massachusetts, and all our southern from that planted in Virginia" (Wendell and Greenough 25); "Such literary activity as existed was divided at first between Virginia and New England" (Burton 2). Virginia and Massachusetts are "the fountain heads of all that is strongest in our national and our literary history" (Pattee 10).

Next Tyler narrowed the field further by announcing that no more literature was written in Virginia after the first twenty years of settlement (I:80). He gave New England about two-thirds of the space in each of his volumes and spent much of the non-New England space speculating on why literature written elsewhere was scanty and poor.[17] His explanations, derived again from standard political history, proved useful to other literary historians. "Conditions of life in the Colonial South were distinctly unfavorable to any great achievement in literature" (Pancoast 20). "Colonial Virginia lacked the mental stimulus of life in towns and cities, where mind kindles mind by contact; if books were written, it was difficult to get them printed; and if they were printed, there were few people to read them. In such conditions the production of a large body of literature is not to be expected" (Bronson 14). "With no metropolis to furnish the needed contact of mind with mind, with material needs making large drains upon their energy, with the chase and other rural sports satisfying their rudimentary instincts for pleasure, and, above all, with no deep-seated artistic impulses and few inherited literary traditions and aspirations," Virginians naturally "produced little literature and developed little culture of importance" (Trent 6). "The Virginia gentleman preferred field sports and indoor social diversions to letters" (Burton 3).

As if to make the point more emphatically, the historians

unanimously chose John Smith (with whom Tyler had begun his history) as the greatest Virginia writer. In shorter histories he was the *only* Virginia writer. The very brevity of his residence on the North American continent proved that Virginians were not serious about founding a nation. One literary historian observed that John Smith "never ceased to be an Englishman" and that he was probably included in American literary history only because of the "paucity of readable colonial books and writers" (Trent 3–4).

According to Tyler, New England was literary because it was intellectual, by which he meant idealistic, interested in ideas that are ideals. Virginians "came here chiefly for some material benefit," New Englanders "chiefly for an ideal benefit. In its inception New England was not an agricultural community, nor a manufacturing community, nor a trading community: it was a thinking community" (Tyler I:98). Again other historians fell in line. "Concentration of population" in New England "stimulated intellectual activity and made easier the establishment of common schools"; the level of intelligence "was very high, and there was from the first a literary class, composed chiefly of clergymen and magistrates, who had the capacity, learning, and industry to write many books" (Bronson 16–17). Contrasting "the high average of intelligence and character among the New England colonists" with "the idle, profligate, and disorderly elements which entered into the making of Virginia" a textbook called Massachusetts "the most intellectual of all the Colonies"; it was there that popular education, "the only foundation on which a republic such as ours can safely rest, was begun" (Pancoast 24–25).

New England, in fact, "produced so large a proportion of American books during the seventeenth century that we hardly need consider the rest of the colonies" (Wendell and Greenough 33–34). But even though New England alone produced literature, it was by no means unrepresentative. Far from it. For those who did not write also did not stay, did not establish our American institutions, and did not multiply across the continent. "The settlers of Massachusetts differed from the early Virginians in almost every respect. They did not seek America for worldly gain; they were not adventurers cast up by the tide of chance, nor were they carried across the sea by a wave of popular enthusiasm. They were earnest and prayerful, prone to act only after mature deliberation, and they had come to America *to stay*" (Pattee 19).

The high seriousness of the New England colonialists was

interpreted (with a little help from Matthew Arnold and other racial theorists of the day) as a defining quality of the Anglo-Saxon mind. This mind believes that there is a "necessary connection between art *and* ethics" so that "between two books of equal literary merit, but unequal purpose, it gives greater and more lasting favor to the more useful book" (Richardson I: 339–40). The English inheritance of moral seriousness in the New England Puritan that first made the American nation possible later gave American literature its distinct character. Without William Bradford and John Winthrop "we could not have had Emerson and Hawthorne" (Richardson I:12).

If American literature, when it developed, could not be anything other than didactic and moralistic, the historical problem, however, was that at the start New Englanders were so moralistic and didactic that they could produce no literature—no belles lettres—at all. Richardson, the first historian who took the story up to the present day, asserted that "Puritan theology in New England could no more produce poetry than it could paint a Sistine Madonna. Its theological force was intense, but it was neither gracious nor serene . . . of the poetic art it had not an idea" (II:1), and that New England "was virtually blind to the infinite vision which makes life worth living, and inspires religion, philosophy, literature, and arts, and science to struggle toward a more perfect expression" (II:284). More mildly, another wrote that "while the tone of New England was conspicuously intellectual, and while conditions favorable to the encouragement of the intellect were by no means lacking, the whole mental life was cramped by an almost complete devotion to questions of theology and point of doctrine" (Pancoast 28). So if it was true that we could not have had Hawthorne and Emerson without Bradford and Winthrop, it was still a question how we could have had them *with* Bradford and Winthrop. Nothing less than a transformation of the New England character was required, one in which morality and didacticism were freed from theology and dogma on the one hand and merged with beauty and artistic craft on the other. In a word, it was necessary to produce secular Puritans before New England could produce literature.

In the historical narrative offered by our first literary historians, disconsolate belles lettres wandered from region to region, finding no resting place except briefly in New York, until at last New England, prepared by the Unitarians, welcomed and transformed it, through its own intense spirituality and moral earnestness, into something truly national. In this union of (feminine?) literature with (masculine?) New England, belles lettres was uplifted and New England was softened and beautified. "The mission of all the great New England writers of this age was to make individuals freer, more cultivated, more self-reliant, more kindly, more spiritual. Puritan energy and spirituality spoke through them all" (Halleck 268).

Skipping rapidly past Jefferson and Washington, as well as Franklin and Brockden Brown, the historians agreed that the first true national literary culture was established in New York. "The 'rosy fingers' of this long-expected dawn were first to brighten the skies above the Hudson" (Richardson II:23–24). Irving, the first American author whom we enjoy reading, is "the father of our American prose" who stands "at the threshold of the greater period of our literature" (Pancoast 116). Irving, of course, did not stand at the threshold alone; a gregarious man, he was a member of the Knickerbocker School. The emergence of a school, rather than of a singular, gifted writer, signified the belated formation of a true, if frivolous, literary culture. Secular, commercial New York was the right place to hatch an American literature because it was open to the liberal currents streaming across the Atlantic; but it could not nurture such a literature into maturity. For in that city, "then as now," an "excess of the commercial spirit over the intellectual and artistic" hindered true literary achievement (Bronson 112–13), and literature was produced from the first as "an article of trade" (Woodberry 65). Knickerbocker writing was "urbane and elegant rather than profound or forcible" (Higginson and Boynton 83). Except for Bryant, the one New Englander among them, the Knickerbockers "placed the chief emphasis on the power to entertain" (Halleck 109); they were "a band of young New Yorkers attempting, with the exception of Bryant, nothing very earnest nor very wise, but working on human materials in the artistic spirit for the artistic end of pure delight" (Bates 106). Bryant alone charged his work with "that depth of moral power that was his heritage from Puritanism, and marked in the next generation the literature of New England, setting it off from the literature of New York" (Woodberry 59).

Since New Yorkers "never dealt with deeply significant matters," only New England could produce "the serious literature of America" (Wendell and Greenough 184–85). But New England in the Knickerbocker age "lagged behind" New York because of a "narrowness and lack of general cultivation which resulted from the strictness of its religion" (Pancoast 159). The region could not play "that leading part in the purely literary development of the country which it afterward assumed. It had no names to match against those of Irving and Cooper" (Beers 115). Something had to intervene before there could be a "transfer of the leadership from New York to New England" (Pattee 196). What intervened was the particularly New England response to the European liberalism that had created Knickerbockers in New York—not a Knickerbocker school but a theological movement that, "though not immediately contributory to the finer kinds of literature, prepared the way, by its clarifying and stimulating influences, for the eminent writers of the next generation. This was the Unitarian revolt against Puritan orthodoxy. . . . That we do now possess a national literature, is in great part due to the influence of Channing and his associates" (Beers 115, 118). The Unitarian movement emancipated "the New England mind from these narrow ideas" and led to "the rise of the greatest group of writers the country has yet produced" (Pancoast 159).

The underlying New England character endured through this "mental revolution which changed the whole character of New England and turned into new channels the current of its thought and literature" (Pattee 196). Thus, the literature it eventually produced was "a characteristic outbreak of the mighty moral passion of New England. A Knickerbocker literature, essentially artistic and entertaining, was not for her. When her great hour of utterance came, it was the old Puritan flood of idealism broken loose again. The liberalization of theology through Channing and Parker, the European influences brought to bear upon American thought and taste by Allston and Dana, Everett and Ticknor, Longfellow and Lowell, resulted in that New England renascence whose supreme achievements were the Transcendental essays and poems of Emerson, and the mysterious romances of Nathaniel Hawthorne" (Bates 117–18). The Unitarians had rejected Puritanism while preserving the Puritans' "deep reserves of poetry, and capacity for independent thought" (Pancoast 161). Then, "released from the weight of formalism and asceticism, and at the same time quickened and uplifted by influences of a most congenial and stimulating character, the New England mind ceased to expend itself wholly on theology, and asserted through a group of great writers those literary powers which had been so long suppressed. In its great literary epoch, the reserve power, the stored-up energy and repressed sympathies of New England, first found an adequate outlet in literature" (Pancoast 164).

The central New England writer, corresponding to Irving

in New York, was the man deemed most responsible for moving beyond Unitarianism into a literary utterance separated from any particular doctrinal program, and hence transforming Puritanism itself into literature. Emerson was this writer. His centralization is not, as many present-day Americanists believe, a twentieth-century construction: it coexists with the institution of New England in American literary history, which is to say with the institution of American literature itself. One text called him "the foremost representative of the powerful influence which New England has exerted on American life and on American literature" (Brander Matthews 93). Another put him "in the center of the remarkable little group of New England writers who stood for God and country, who were idealists, yet thoroughly of the soil, into whose words the very genius of their land seems to have passed" (Burton 135). A third said that Emerson, though not necessarily "a greater writer than any of the men who surrounded him," was "most representative of the whole movement" and "the most influential in shaping its form and character" (Pancoast 165). A fourth called Emerson "the most eminent figure among the Transcendentalists, if not indeed in all the literary history of America" (Wendell and Greenough 254). And still another said he was the "foremost figure of the age. . . . Puritanism, the old search for God in New England, ended in him; and he became its medium at its culminating moment of vision and freedom" (Woodberry 83, 92).

But, again, Emerson was not merely the ideal center of a national literature; he was the actual, historical center of a group of many like-minded men and a few women (Margaret Fuller and Harriet Beecher Stowe), all actively and deliberately engaged in building American literature and all exemplary, in different ways, of the New England mind. Six in particular— Longfellow, Emerson, Hawthorne, Whittier, Lowell, and Holmes—"constitute a large part of the strength and beauty of American literature." Historians stressed that these were not only New Englanders, but were also Massachusetts residents, all but one born in Massachusetts, and that most of them lived in or near Boston or Cambridge. They did so to remind students that:

> New England had from colonial days been the intellectual and literary leader of the country; Massachusetts was the head of New England, and Boston was the eye of Massachusetts. By heredity, tradition, and acquired momentum

the Bay State still kept the lead in mental activity; Unitarianism and the Transcendental movement added an intellectual freedom and freshness not elsewhere attained so early in like degree; and Harvard College, its roots now deep in the past, bore in larger measure with every succeeding year the beautiful fruit of a ripe culture. (Bronson 177)

"As they grew up and began to write, these authors became friends; and their friendship lasted with their lives" (Brander Matthews 124). Concord was one of two "spiritual suburbs of Boston"; the other was Cambridge, where the university scholar could live "withdrawn in an academic retirement" yet "within easy reach of a great city, with its literary and social clubs, its theaters, lecture courses, public meetings, dinner parties" (Beers 161). Pattee, Wendell, and other historians specified elements of the network besides Harvard: the Saturday Club, the *North American Review,* the Lowell Institute, the *Atlantic Monthly,* Ticknor and Fields. No solitary could have been the center of a literary history whose purpose was to show the emergence of a literary culture, no matter what his literary gifts. It was, indeed, Emerson's gifts for society, his demonstrable place in both Concord and Boston circles, that fitted him for the central role that he was made to play in American literary history.

The six major writers, in fact, were each central to the project in a different way, and the histories frequently represented them as quasi-allegorical personifications of some aspect of what, even in these pre-Millerian days, was called the New England mind. The basic scheme installed Whittier as the Reformer, Longfellow as the Poet, Holmes as the Wit, Lowell as Man of Letters, Emerson as Teacher or Philosopher (a designation that may explain his especial popularity with educators), and Hawthorne as Artist. The histories acknowledged other writers than the key figures, and disposed them in different ways on the peripheries of their narrative. Occasionally, historians signaled toward a large anonymous group of texts by mentioning the need to elevate youthful taste above them. The didactic, sensational, and sentimental work that almost certainly comprised most of what was read in nineteenth-century America besides journalism and religious writing had no place in these narratives. In fact, the obliteration of such writings, along with the literary centers that supported them—New York and Philadelphia—was evidently an aim of this historical project.[18]

Historians did, however, name two other types of writers,

which I will distinguish as minor and marginal. Minor writers were the lesser adherents of the schools that produced the major writers. Fitz-Greene Halleck and Rodman Drake as Knicker-bockers; Margaret Fuller, Bronson Alcott, and Henry David Thoreau as Transcendentalists—these are among the names that most often recur as minor figures. Their shortcomings high-lighted the major writers' excellences, while their presence in the narrative once again emphasized the cultural aspect of literary production.

Not so with two disruptive American figures, Poe and Whitman, who could not be left out of the narrative because English and European critics esteemed them highly. It became a challenge to plot a story that acknowledged them in order to exclude them. They were cast as pretenders—writers who were not "really" American—and thus as foils to the central authors. Emerson could oppose Poe or Whitman; Hawthorne was particularly useful to counter Poe, and Longfellow to counter Whitman.

Typical commentary on Poe runs like this: Poe has been "admired, imitated, and translated as hardly another of the native writers," which is an "interesting and curious" fact, because Poe "is not representatively American at all." His work "has no local color, and it does not reflect our native ideas or ideals; it tells little or nothing of the soil whence it springs, of the civilization behind it" (Burton 66). Poe seems "out of place in American literature, like an importation from the Old World," teaching no lesson and writing only "to chill the blood by mere revolting physical horror" (Pattee 172, 181). His "place in our literature is one of peculiar isolation," as he "wanders in his unsettled and struggling career from city to city"—a cosmo-politan, a wandering Jew, who "stands essentially alone" (Pancoast 263–64).

But insofar as Poe was judged a real artist by sophisticated European critics, denying him a role in American literature might make the historians seem parochial. Since "in place of moral feeling he had the artistic conscience" (Beers 213), they looked for a New England writer who had moral feeling *and* artistic conscience. They found that figure in Hawthorne, whom they always described as the "artist" in the New England group. To be sure, the Hawthorne who is made to play this role is not an isolated figure; his love of solitude is offset by his deep roots in New England literary culture both as a descendant of the Puritans whose deeds he records and whose temperament he shares, and as an active participant in the New England Renaissance, friend of Longfellow, resident of Concord, member of the Saturday Club, an author published by Ticknor and Fields and the *Atlantic.*

We read, then, that Poe "cannot affect our whole lives as does a Hawthorne in prose, nor can his eye sweep from zenith to nadir in the poetic vision of Emerson" (Richardson II:136). "The tragedy in Hawthorne is a spiritual one, while Poe calls in the aid of material forces"; if Poe's poetry "had the sweet home feeling of Longfellow or the moral fervor of Whittier, he might have been a greater poet than either" (Beers 218–19). Both Poe and Hawthorne were "dwellers in the dusk, but the shadow that haunted Poe crept from the charnel-house, while Hawthorne's, sprung from the sinful heart of man, showed still a glint of heaven" (Bates 299). "Poe lavished on things comparatively superficial those great intellectual resources which Hawthorne reverently husbanded and used. That there is something behind even genius to make or mar it, this is the lesson of the two lives" (Higginson and Boynton 209). "From whatever cause, Poe's life and character, when placed beside that of Longfellow or of Lowell, stand out in sharp and tragic contrast." His work shows how "the worship of beauty entirely for itself, dissociated from any sense of design or regard for essential and ethical value, inevitably degrades the worshiper" (Fisher 255). As Hawthorne's shadow, Poe entered largely into the way in which literary histories represented Hawthorne as a blend of Poe-like qualities tempered by New Englandism.

Whitman challenged the internal coherence of the historical account even more than Poe because as a self-styled democratic poet he laid claim to a quality that some had identified with the United States since Tocqueville. Actually the word "democracy" seldom appeared in American literary histories before 1900, given their Whig orientation. But throughout the life of this genre, the histories countered Whitman's claim to be a people's poet by pointing out that the people themselves ignored or rejected him. And they chose the beloved patrician, Longfellow, to withstand him.

"A poet in whom a whole nation declines to find its likeness cannot be regarded as representative" (Woodberry 243). "Of all our poets, he is really the least simple, the most meretricious; and this is the reason why the honest consciousness of the classes which he most celebrates—the drover, the teamster, the soldier—has never been reached by his songs" (Higginson and Boynton 233). His work is "as utterly removed from the people as he himself was close to them in his daily life. The scholars

Longfellow and Lowell are the poets of thousands of humble homes; Whitman is as yet the admiration of a little clique among the most cultured upper class. Called the founder of a national American literature, by a singular irony he is better known to the intellectual aristocracy of England than among the people of his own land" (Pancoast 301–02). When the "barbaric yawp" of Walt Whitman was heard in the land, "the American public, so far as it heeded him at all, was affronted, and with right good reason" (Bates 199). Longfellow, the "most widely read and loved of American poets" contrasts sharply with "such a 'cosmic' singer as Whitman, who is still practically unknown to the 'fierce democracy' to which he has addressed himself"; "Whittier and Longfellow, the poets of conscience and feeling, are the darlings of the American people. The admiration, and even the knowledge of Whitman, are mostly esoteric, confined to the literary class" (Beers 162, 165, 236). The representation of Longfellow as the genial, beloved, and immensely popular poet had much to do with his function as a defense against Whitman, just as Hawthorne's representation was in part a creation of the specter of Poe.

Poe and Whitman failed as writers, the historians urged, because internally they lacked national traits and externally they lacked a sustaining literary culture. These two lacks were not unrelated. If they had been more "American," they would have been more successful. In this way, the idea of success entered the narrative obliquely; the truly American writer will be recognized by his culture and find an honored place in it. Some historians identified Poe as a Southerner, others as a New Yorker, but all agreed that he was in essence a rootless wanderer. (Pattee compared him to the Wandering Jew.) It could not be denied that Whitman was a New York City man; despite his native ancestry, historians described him as though he were an unassimilated immigrant, one who voiced values that the institution of American literature in the schools was designed to obliterate. "One begins to see why Whitman has been so much more eagerly welcomed abroad than at home. His conception of equality, utterly ignoring values, is not that of American democracy, but rather that of European. His democracy, in short, is the least native which has ever found voice in our country" (Wendell and Greenough 375).

Toward the end of the thirty-year period encompassed by these history books, attitudes toward Poe and Whitman began to soften. Woodberry, who had written a biography of Poe, ranked him with Bryant, Irving, Cooper, Emerson, Hawthorne,

Longfellow, and Lowell in the "first class" of authors "whom the nation as a whole regards as its greatest writers in pure literature" (203). Trent observed that Poe's "fame has been so steadily rising in America that it is becoming possible for critics of standing to hold that Hawthorne's superiority to him is not a settled point" (376). Halleck recorded that Poe had an "almost world-wide reputation for the part which he played in developing the modern short story" (299) and, comparing Hawthorne, who "saw everything in the light of moral consequence," to Poe, who "cared nothing for moral issues," even suggested that it was a Puritan literary criticism that faulted Poe (306). And as his reputation rose, Poe's unworldly purity became more a matter for critical notice.

Whitman called for reassessment as the usefulness of the term democracy for the American system became more manifest. In light of the origins of the new immigrants, Whitman— who had been careful to remind readers in "Song of Myself" that he was "born here of parents born here from parents the same, and their parents the same"—was reinterpreted as a visionary ahead of his time, whose lack of reception among the populace showed that democracy had not yet arrived. In a move that prefigured Matthiessen, some now saw him as an idealist, a lesser Emerson. Thus, though the winds of change rippled over the surface, the New England anchorage held firm.

The brief celebration with which literary histories in the 1880s ended their didactic narrative became, over the thirty years in which the genre flourished, an ever longer and more conflicted coda. Appearing first when the great New England generation was finishing its work, the literary histories had attempted to institutionalize the work of that generation as the achievement of a long-prefigured literary project. Thirty years later the achievement could only be seen as ephemeral; no second generation of New Englanders was carrying on the tradition, which meant in effect that no tradition had been established after all. Not through the works of the New England writers themselves, but in the stories that literary histories told about them in the classroom, a New England literary culture was installed in this country.

Perceiving that New England had "lost its long monopoly" (Beers 260), most historians saw the contemporary scene as a time of diffuseness in which literary activity, dispersed across the continent as well as among a very large number of independent, entrepreneurial writers, had lost definition as well as excellence. There was nothing in the present moment like the "sharply defined group of which Emerson, Hawthorne, Longfellow, Whittier, Holmes, and Lowell were the leaders"; amidst a "host of book-makers" no one now attained "the stature of Longfellow and Hawthorne, and the other leaders of the early school. It is a period of minor poets and novelists" (Pattee 345). "Although there have never been so many authors as there are to-day, and although the average of literary skill is probably higher than ever before, there is now no towering figure and no dominating personality. And those who are at the head of American literature at the end of the nineteenth century are not men of the same general type as the greatly-gifted New Englanders whom they succeeded; and their aims and their ideals are not the same" (Brander Matthews 229). At present there is a "halt of our literary genius"; the "field is open, and calls loudly for new champions" (Woodberry 252, 253).

In their conclusions, historians pointed regularly to: a striking increase in the production of long and short fiction along with a decrease in poetry; the dominance of the school of realism in fiction, with Henry James and William Dean Howells as its chief practitioners and advocates; the development of a distinct type of humorous literature; and—decentralization and diffusion notwithstanding—the rise (or return) of New York City as the chief American literary center. The association of Boston with the spiritual, New York with the material, had explained why the Knickerbockers failed to produce major literature. Now, as literature slipped out of Boston's control, these associations led to the doleful suggestion that the motive force of history itself had changed, and was becoming material. (Henry Adams was soon to be canonized as a literary artist precisely to score this point.) American men of letters, "sucked in ever greater numbers into the vortex of New York . . . are spun about, like mere bankers and brokers, in the whirl"; today's literature "is abundant, varied, clever, but if genius is among us, it walks unrecognized" (Bates 130). Now that New York was the country's literary center, novels and poems have "become mere commercial commodities . . . manufactured in cold blood at specified times, at specified rates, and while fierce competition has greatly raised the standard of mere literary art, it has not breathed into the product that indefinable *something,* the presence of which makes work immortal" (Pattee 350).

As we have seen, it was chiefly fear of the materialization of American values—or, more precisely, fear of the spread of

It was chiefly fear of the materialization of American values—or, more precisely, fear of the spread of materialist goals to people who could not hope to satisfy their ambitions without thorough renovation of the social system—"the relation of labor to well-being" as Scudder had phrased it—that shaped these literary history textbooks in the first place.

materialist goals to people who could not hope to satisfy their ambitions without thorough renovation of the social system— "the relation of labor to well-being" as Scudder had phrased it—that shaped these literary history textbooks in the first place. Canvassing the contemporary scene for hopeful signs that the tradition would continue, historians inevitably translated the question: will American literature remain, or again become, true to the American spirit?—into the question: who are the heirs to the New England Renaissance (Wendell's phrase) and where can we find them? Isolated New England local colorists conveyed at best a diminished and unacculturated version of the earlier period. Realists and naturalists were often skillful but their implication in the worst tendencies of American life made them thoroughly ineligible. Their very skill became the reason for an attack on intellectualism as un-American; this attack meshed with the long-standing distrust of pure aestheticism to produce an ideal of American literature as a body of writing neither overly intelligent nor overly accomplished: a moral literature for a moral people.

The historians found what they were looking for, at least provisionally, in a nebulous rural West populated mainly by Saxons along with some Germans who, as Teutons, shared the requisite racial heritage. Here might be the locus of a future American literature. They saw a new dawn first, tentatively, in Bret Harte, and then more certainly in Mark Twain and Abraham Lincoln. Wendell's American literary history of 1901 had concluded with an elegy on "The Decline of New England" and an attack on Whitman; the coauthored textbook version he produced in 1907 ended by celebrating Mark Twain. Another textbook closed with Lincoln, "a conservative, not a radical force, one proceeding from the democratic West, not from old aristocratic Boston" and "a fitting and auspicious name with which to close an account of the development of American literature" (Trent 578–79).

The Cambridge History of American Literature, which both contributed to and reflected the ongoing construction of American literature as an academic profession, was structured to reflect the expertise of individual professors, and it parceled out the field into separate scholarly properties rather than telling a historical story.[19] It is no wonder then that its chapters "mainly read like isolated essays in a collection printed without benefit of transitions and continuity"; and yet, even so, an implicit if unexamined narrative remained "obvious" in its conventional periodization and choice of major authors (Vanderbilt 156). In a move that seems to have been meant to free them from the traditional narrative's constraints, the scholars of the *Cambridge History* expanded the definition of American literature beyond the belletristic to consider it as an expression of the national intellectual life. But in so doing, they were led to a much higher estimation of the historical importance of the New England Colonial and Revolutionary periods in our literature, so that the basis of the origins narrative was actually strengthened. Parrington's *Main Currents in American Thought* depended on the narrative of prefiguration and fulfillment that had been instituted as the historical basis of American literary study, and indeed restated it at the very moment that it declined to confine American literature to belles lettres. Nor had this narrative frame been escaped in the attacks launched on the professors by men like John Macy or Van Wyck Brooks. For they did not deny that the professors accurately recorded the history of what American literature had been—they argued rather that it was time to escape from American literary history, to start American literature anew. What Macy and Brooks clearly grasped, however, was the essentially conservative motive involved in a program to constrain literature within a historical account.

If, however, belles lettres was no longer the point of the story, and different authors had become central figures in American literature, and some of the New Englanders were written out of the narrative, and emphasis shifted from the achievements of a literary culture to those of solitary individuals, how could it be that a new historical narrative did not replace the old? With the Puritan and Revolutionary periods valued more highly than they had been in the old literary histories, and installed even more tenaciously as the origins of American literature, there was really no other story to tell. And, therefore, canonical change was much less far-reaching than it appeared to those advocating it. Their newly canonical authors were still white and Anglo-Saxon; many of them were also New Englanders. They admired Thoreau and a New Englandized Whitman and an Anglo-Saxon Mark Twain. Removing the Cambridge group from the center, they left the Concord group at the pinnacle. Non-New Englanders were added to the canon only if they could be assimilated to this still New England center, still preferably as a matter of racial inheritance, but at least as a matter of shared ideology.[19] The equivalence of the New England and national characters remained the guiding principle of American literary studies, with or without the protective sheathing of a narrative specifically about belles lettres and literary culture as a social formation.

Perry Miller studied literature as intellectual history rather than belles lettres; his work appears in many respects to be a sophisticated rewriting of Tyler. And practitioners in the field of early American literature continue to argue for the importance of their field on the ground that the texts they study are the basis of later American literature. As for Matthiessen, his *American Renaissance* appropriated and revised Wendell's catchy phrase with something that looked much broader; but his American Renaissance, though more democratic than Wendell's, was no less New Englandish in tone. He eliminated Cambridge but kept Concord. Emerson was detached from Longfellow but buttressed by Thoreau and a Whitman who was not a sensual urban working-class poet but a Transcendental idealist. Melville moved to the literary center not as a New Yorker but as friend and soul mate to Hawthorne. And Emerson and Hawthorne repeated their traditional roles as New England philosopher and New England artist, respectively. Matthiessen's oft-noted omission of Poe indicates—notwithstanding the elaborate aesthetic apparatus of *American Renaissance*—that American literature is the place to look for national ideals, not for fancy writing.[21] Not until Edward H. Davidson represented Poe as a moral writer, the double, not the opposite, of Hawthorne, did that writer win his firm place in the canon.

The myth critics with their frontier vision attempted more deliberately than Matthiessen to escape the New England narrative. But, as we have seen, the western solution had already emerged in the 1890s (so did Turner's frontier thesis of American history) as a way to reject aspects of American life that the New Englanders had also been used to reject—the city, industry, commerce, mass culture, immigrants, along with their attendant literary movements. The frontier in 1950s myth criticism served similar purposes. Though again devaluing the genteel social networks of antebellum Boston, such criticism apotheosized lonely and intransigent New England types, like Thoreau or—what would otherwise seem an extraordinary anomaly—Emily Dickinson. The mythic frontiersman existed on a mythic frontier that could be anywhere. As the frontier became a metaphor, New England was released from its geographic specificity and identified with the state of mind represented by the frontier myth, an allegory of the American.[22] Likewise, scholars who proposed to study the literature of the South argued that since New England had become as crass and commercial and full of the foreign born as New York, only the South was left to represent what an earlier New England had stood for.[23] Even recent feminists have affiliated with New England by tracing a canon of American women writers back to the foremother Anne Bradstreet, and then moving it forward to the present through Emily Dickinson.[24]

Between the continuing supposition that American authors necessarily articulate a New England vision, and the still-functioning preference that they actually *be* of New England descent, the originary narrative of American literary history remains in place even among many who earnestly wish to escape it. There are many reasons for this tenacity, including such inevitable human matters as inertia and vested interest. But since this origins narrative, whether or not it is a true account of the origins of American literature, certainly represents the origins of "American literature," the field of study, it would be necessary to dismantle the field itself to achieve this goal. And since we are teachers as well as scholars, and the didactic and rhetorical aims that shaped "American literature" as a school subject as well as a scholarly subject continue in force, we may have no option but to replace the rejected story with another narrative very much like it. If we practice American literature in the classroom for the ultimate aims of forming students' characters and making them better citizens, we find ourselves— to our surprise—carrying on Whig goals, no matter how radical our claims; we walk in the paths laid down by the first American literary historians.

Notes

1. Several of these textbooks were listed in Jones 78–118; some are mentioned in passing by Brodhead 60–63. In his valuable study, Vanderbilt describes many of these individual literary histories with particular attention to the works of Tyler, Richardson, and Wendell (81–153). None of these scholars, however, dwells on the historical narrative presented in these textbooks.

2. Students of historiography agree that modern history writing is an aspect of the formation of nation-states in the modern era. See, e.g., Levin *History,* Callcott, Gellner, and Hobsbawm and Rangers. The inescapable narrative (hence fictional) form of history writing has been much theorized: see, e.g., Danto, Mink, White *Metahistory* and *Content of the Form,* Ricoeur, Wallace Martin 71–75. In Colacurcio, the identity of history with story is implied rhetorically: "Could we not then tell some really vital and self-sufficient story? The ideal of unity, coherence, and development seems, always, almost

within our grasp" (111); similarly, the historical pluralist Kolodny longs for the day when we can tell "a coherent, integrated story about our literary past" (297). Two essays by Carafiol—"The New Orthodoxy" and "The Constraints of History"—argue that American literary study is captive to an archaic essentialism, and call for abandoning the "faith in an 'American' literature" along with the accompanying "quest for a 'coherent story' about American writing" because such faith and quest are inconsistent with a posttheological age ("Constraints" 617). The question, however, may be seen less as theological than national. We do not live in a postnational age.

3.   For the American Whig worldview and its need for history, see Hart, Welter, Jean V. Matthews "Whig History" and *Rufus Choate,* Howe, Hall, McWilliams, and Buell.

For the foundation of Whig thought in the Federalism that preceded it, see Buell, Hall, Hart, and also Charvat *Origins of American Critical Thought,* Greenslet, Simpson *Federalist* and *Man of Letters,* Fischer, Goodman, Tyack *George Ticknor,* Story.

Even more than Bancroft's volumes, the formal, full-scale histories crucial to American literary history were Richard Hildreth's six-volume *History of the United States,* published between 1849 and 1852 and designed to oppose Bancroft's celebratory democratic politics, and John Gorham Palfrey's five-volume *History of New England,* three volumes of which appeared between 1858 and 1864, volume IV in 1875, and the last, completed by his son, posthumously published in 1889. Palfrey had disseminated his views over the years in the *North American Review.* Buell and McWilliams see Bancroft's New England filiopietism as more or less identical to that of the Whigs, but (in my view) Bancroft differs because he allots considerable space to all of the thirteen colonies, esteems the contribution of Virginia highly, and refuses to identify the American character solely with the New England founders. His text, too, is coded with the words "freedom" and "democratic" where the Whig historians use "liberty" and "republican."

4.   See Mann, Curti, Tyack *One Best System,* Katz, Lazerson, Messerli, Schultz. The goal of character formation was not directed exclusively to primary and secondary mass education; see Stevenson for Yale and Hall for Harvard. The difference is that the elite schools attempted to form the character of leaders, the public schools those of followers—or, more precisely, of those who would choose and then defer to leaders.

5.   See Messerli 340 ff. for Mann's rejection of Elizabeth Peabody's suggestion that Nathaniel Hawthorne should write for the school district library series, and also his advice to Richard Henry Dana about how to revise *Two Years Before the Mast*: "Many of the scenes and events, which the work describes would also admit the introduction of moral sentiments, suited to the class of readers for which it is intended" (345). On surveillance in nineteenth-century culture, the prime theoretical work has of course been done by Michel Foucault; closer to home is Rothman—which, however, does not discuss schools. On Barnard, see Curti 143.

6.   For a content analysis of nineteenth-century school textbooks, see Elson. On 167–69, Elson discusses the typical representation of the Puritans as the

nation's founders. She observes also that most of these early readers (McGuffey's is an exception) were compiled or written by New Englanders.

7.   Textbooks for very young children put more emphasis on individual life history than national history. The history textbook answered to a presumed greater sophistication in the student, offering a more complicated structure within which to situate the exemplary authorial lives already learned about. As the subtitles of several of these books indicated, they were designed for "schools and colleges" interchangeably—that is, the high schools whose population was growing and where much of the nation's teacher training took place; and the colleges where increasingly in the 1880s a course or two on American literature was made available in English departments—perhaps also with the preparation of schoolteachers in mind. Few literary histories composed for any level of schooling contained much in the way of literary extract or literary analysis, and several prefaces pleaded with teachers to use the history text together with some sort of anthology—thus suggesting that in many cases literary history could have been taught without any reliance on primary works at all.

8.   The roles of Houghton Mifflin and its predecessor, Ticknor and Fields, in promoting New England authors, are well known. See Ballou, especially 328–49 and 492–516; and Jones: "The standardization of American authors—the creation of the canon of Great Names in our literature—is the product of this New England empire, more specifically of Ticknor and Fields and their publishing successors" (86). Charvat has written at length about Ticknor and Fields's structuring of the American literary canon: see *Literary Publishing in America* and *The Profession of Authorship in America*; Tryon certainly overstates the personal influence of Fields but provides much invaluable information, as does the joint project of Tryon and Charvat, *The Cost Books of Ticknor and Fields*.

9.   Brodhead identifies Scudder as a key figure in the canonization of Hawthorne (59–64 passim). Brodhead is interested in the way in which New England authors were made part of the cultural apparatus to which an emergent middle class aspired: my focus is on the deployment of literature in a somewhat different, more evidently political, project. Scudder's expressed ideas about education meshed with those of such prominent educators of his day as Edwin P. Seaver, Secretary of the Massachusetts Board of Education from 1880 to 1904, whom he must have known (see Lazerson). My parenthetic references to Scudder cite the Riverside Literature Series pamphlet of October 1888, containing three addresses: "Literature in School," "Nursery Classics in School," and "American Classics in School."

10.   In 1884 the Synod of Catholic Bishops instructed every parish to build a parochial school for educating Catholic children. Had this plan succeeded, it would have removed much of the target population from the public schools. The King James Bible had to be sacrificed to keep Catholic children in public schools.

11.   A Houghton Mifflin circular of 1890 lists 42 titles in the Riverside series, including 13 by Longfellow, 10 by Hawthorne, along with a few by Whittier, Lowell, Holmes, and John Burroughs, as well as one each by

Thoreau, Bayard Taylor, Charles Dudley Warner, and Emerson. Benjamin Franklin has three pamphlets, George Washington one, Abraham Lincoln one.

12.   Many New England intellectuals at the turn of the century were certain that Anglo-Saxon behavior could be practiced only by those of Anglo-Saxon descent. On New England racialism in the last two decades of the nineteenth century see Solomon "Intellectual Background" and *Ancestors and Immigrants,* Gossett, Persons, Hedrick. Jones discusses racialism in English departments and identifies the vogue for teaching Anglo-Saxon as an outgrowth of it (79–115).

Palfrey's 1876 introduction to Volume V of his history, expressing the ideology with chilling clarity, is worth quoting at length: "It has not yet appeared that the Celtic or the African constitution, or that of the aboriginal red man or of strays from one or another despotism of continental Europe or of the heathen East, is competent to struggles and exploits, or to an acute, far-seeing, courageous, and persistent policy, like those by which the later greatness of New England was founded and fashioned by the God-fearing builders of that community. The structure and temper of the society into which these foreign elements are received, may be expected to do much towards moulding them into a congenial shape. But how far may such assimilation of thought and character be expected to go? Can these alien races be educated to carry on the work which minds of antecedents so different laid out; may they become capable of improving upon its principles and methods, or are they likely to have their own aptitudes and tastes so modified as to enter with intelligent zeal into the plans of the intelligently zealous men who preceded them here? And how much time will such a process take? And meanwhile is there more or less danger of a lowering of the native style of thinking and character by compromises with the ignorance and incapacity and wrong-headedness which are to be instructed and reformed and cultivated, and by submission to their hurtful dictation for the sake of a temporary advantage from their favor?" (V:ix). For a sense of how immigrants introjected and struggled against the contradictions in their exposure to American literature and history, see Sollors, and Dearborn.

13.   For example: "American literature had no infancy. That engaging *naiveté* and that heroic rudeness which give a charm to the early popular tales and songs of Europe find, of course, no counterpart on our soil. Instead of emerging from the twilight of the past, the first American writings were produced under the garish noon of a modern and learned age" (Beers 9; reissued in later years under different titles); American literature in the first two centuries "is not that of a people slowly emerging from barbarism and creating their own civilization through the long toil of ages. On the contrary, it is the literature of a people already highly civilized, but transplanted to another continent, where they set up in the wilderness" (Bronson 7); in America we could never produce "the rude chant, or primitive epic, because when our English forefathers first settled here they had passed far beyond the stage of national development which makes such creations possible" (Pancoast 4).

14.   For example: "Pure literature, or what, for want of a better term we call *belles lettres,* was not born in America until the nineteenth century was

well under way" (Beers 51); Americans of the nineteenth century alone produced "literature of any importance" (Wendell and Greenough 6—a revised version of Wendell's 1900 *Literary History of America*); not until the nineteenth century had fairly begun did "the dawn of American literature begin to brighten" (Pattee 67); "Nearly all of our most lasting and important contributions to literature" were written between 1809 and 1897 (Pancoast 11); "The writers who have made us famous and taken a fixed place in our galaxy fall after the opening of the nineteenth century" (Burton 10).

15.   Tyler had planned to write the whole history of American literature but never finished his project; he published two more volumes, on the literature of the American Revolution, in 1897, nearly twenty years after the Colonial volumes.

16.   In a recent bibliographical essay, Philip Gura decries the mode of Puritan studies instituted by Perry Miller, in which, among other things, "The literature of the colonial period most often has been viewed as a prologue to the literature of the United States in the nineteenth century rather than having been considered in its own rights and terms," and "New England has served as a proxy for the British North American colonies generally, with the result that the literature of the distinct regions within the British American empire has not been properly assessed." In a brief rejoinder, David Levin calls attention to the active practice of other early Colonialists like Morison and Murdock ("Survivor's Tale"). My point is that the origins of this origins story go further back still. What Gura finds objectionable is what American literary history was written *for*.

17.   Tyler gives Franklin only two pages in the Colonial volumes, reserving fuller treatment for the planned Revolutionary volumes. Franklin is still studied on Tyler's terms.

18.   Obliteration of writing by women was not evidently part of the program; but the focus on formal social networks of a masculine cast—Harvard, the Saturday Club—led inexorably to that result.

19.   The standard book on the formation of professions in academia is Bledstein.

20.   So, for example, Parrington writes that "remembering the mingled strains of Melville's ancestry, the critic is tempted to discover in his New England blood the source of his transcendental visions" (II:251).

21.   As Frederick Crews points out, F. O. Matthiessen has recently become the center of attack by what he terms the "New Americanists," who want to revise the canon for political reasons. Crews singles out essays by Donald Pease and Jonathan Arac (Michaels and Pease, eds.). Nonetheless, Arac and Pease hew to the Matthiessen canon when writing more generally about American literature.

22.   Reising connects the myth critics and the textual critics. An earlier study of this connection can be found in the selections and introductions in Kartiganer and Griffith.

23. Here, too, an early American literary history anticipated the movement; one historian proposed the South as a likely locus for future American literature because, on the one hand, men in the South were now "running mills as well as driving the plow," replacing plantations with small farms, instituting free public schools, demanding compulsory education for all, establishing excellent institutions of higher learning, and encouraging "writers and a reading public, both with progressive ideals"; and, on the other, the region "retains much of her innate love of aristocracy, loyalty to tradition, disinclination to be guided by merely practical aims, and aversion to rapid change," because "the original conservative English stock, which is still dominant, has been more persistent there and less modified by foreign immigration" (Halleck 291). For a recent critique of the historical representation of southern literature, see Kreyling.

24. See, for example, Watts, Walker, Wendy Martin.

Works Cited

Ballou, Ellen B. *The Building of the House: Houghton Mifflin's Formative Years.* Boston: Houghton, 1970.

Bates, Katherine Lee. *American Literature.* New York: Macmillan, 1897.

Beers, Henry A. *Outline Sketch of American Literature.* New York: Chautauqua, 1887.

Bledstein, Burton J. *The Culture of Professionalism: The Middle Class and the Development of Higher Education in America.* New York: Norton, 1976.

Brodhead, Richard. *The School of Hawthorne.* New York: Oxford UP, 1986.

Bronson, Walter C. *A Short History of American Literature, Designed Primarily for Use in Schools and Colleges.* Boston: Heath, 1903.

Buell, Lawrence. *New England Literary Culture: From Revolution to Renaissance.* New York: Cambridge UP, 1986.

Burton, Richard. *Literary Leaders of America.* New York: Chautauqua, 1903.

Callcott, George H. *History in the United States, 1800–1860: Its Practice and Purpose.* Baltimore: Johns Hopkins UP, 1970.

Carafiol, Peter. "The Constraints of History: Revision and Revolution in American Literary Studies." *College English* 50 (1988): 605–22.

———."The New Orthodoxy: Ideology and the Institution of American Literary Scholarship." *American Literature* 59 (1987): 626–38.

Charvat, William. *Literary Publishing in America, 1790–1850.* Philadelphia: U of Pennsylvania P, 1959.

———. *The Origins of American Critical Thought, 1810–1835.* Philadelphia: U of Pennsylvania P, 1936.

———. *The Profession of Authorship in America.* Columbus: Ohio State UP, 1968.

Charvat, William, and W. S. Tryon. *The Cost Books of Ticknor and Fields and Their Predecessors, 1832–1858.* New York: Bibliographical Society of America, 1949.

Colacurcio, Michael J. "Does American Literature Have a History?" *EAL* 13 (1978): 110–32.

Crews, Frederick. "Whose American Renaissance?" *New York Review of Books* 27 Oct. 1988: 68–81.

Curti, Merle. *The Social Ideas of American Educators.* New York: Scribner's, 1935.

Danto, Arthur. *Analytical Philosophy of History.* Cambridge, Eng.: Cambridge UP, 1965.

Davidson, Edward H. *Poe: A Critical Study.* Columbus: Ohio State UP, 1957.

Dearborn, Mary V. *Pocahontas's Daughters: Gender and Ethnicity in American Culture.* New York: Oxford UP, 1986.

Elson, Ruth Miller. *Guardians of Tradition: American Schoolbooks in the Nineteenth Century.* Lincoln: U of Nebraska P, 1964.

Fischer, David Hackett. *The Revolution of American Conservatism: The Federalist Party in the Era of Jeffersonian Democracy.* New York: Harper, 1965.

Fisher, Mary. *A General Survey of American Literature.* Chicago: A. C. McClurg and Company, 1901.

Gellner, Ernest. *Nations and Nationalism.* Ithaca: Cornell UP, 1983.

Goodman, Paul. "Ethics and Enterprise: The Values of the Boston Elite, 1800–1860." *American Quarterly* 18 (1966): 437–51.

Gossett, Thomas F. *Race: The History of an Idea in America.* Dallas: Southern Methodist UP, 1963.

Greenslet, Ferris. *The Lowells and Their Seven Worlds.* Boston: Houghton, 1946.

Gura, Philip F. "The Study of Colonial American Literature, 1966–1987: A Vade Mecum." *William and Mary Quarterly* 45 (1988): 305–41.

Hall, Peter Dobkin. *The Organization of American Culture, 1700–1900: Private Institutions, Elites and the Origins of American Nationality.* New York: New York UP, 1982.

Halleck, Reuben Post. *History of American Literature.* New York: American Book Company, 1911.

Hart, Thomas R., Jr. "George Ticknor's *History of Spanish Literature*: The New England Background." *PMLA* 69 (1954): 76–88.

Hedrick, Joan D. "Harvard Indifference." *New England Quarterly* 49 (1976): 356–72.

Higginson, Thomas Wentworth, and Henry Walcott Boynton. *A Reader's History of American Literature.* Boston: Houghton, 1903.

Hobsbawm, Eric, and Terence Rangers, eds. *The Invention of Tradition.* Cambridge, Eng.: Cambridge UP, 1983.

Howe, Daniel Walker. *The Political Culture of the American Whigs.* Chicago: U of Chicago P, 1979.

Jones, Howard Mumford. *The Theory of American Literature.* Ithaca: Cornell UP, 1948.

Kartiganer, Donald M., and Malcolm A. Griffith, eds. *Theories of American Literature.* New York: Macmillan, 1972.

Katz, Michael B. *The Irony of Early School Reform: Educational Innovation in Mid-Nineteenth Century Massachusetts.* Cambridge: Harvard UP, 1968.

Kolodny, Annette. "The Integrity of Memory: Creating a New Literary History of the United States." *American Literature* 57 (1985): 290–307.

Kreyling, Michael. "Southern Literature: Consensus and Dissensus." *American Literature* 60 (1988): 83–95.

Lazerson, Marvin. *Origins of the Urban School: Public Education in Massachusetts, 1870–1915.* Cambridge: Harvard UP, 1971.

Levin, David. *History as Romantic Art: Bancroft, Prescott, Motley, and Parkman.* New York: AMS Press, 1967.

———. "A Survivor's Tale." *William and Mary Quarterly* 45 (1988): 345–47.

Mann, Horace. *Lectures on Education.* Boston: Ida & Dutton, 1855.

Martin, Wallace. *Recent Theories of Narrative.* Ithaca: Cornell UP, 1986.

Martin, Wendy. *An American Triptych: Anne Bradstreet, Emily Dickinson, Adrienne Rich.* Chapel Hill: U of North Carolina P, 1984.

Matthews, Brander. *Introduction to American Literature.* New York: American Book Company, 1897.

Matthews, Jean V. *Rufus Choate: The Law and Civic Virtue.* Philadelphia: Temple UP, 1980.

———. "'Whig History': New England Whigs and a Usable Past." *New England Quarterly* 51 (1978): 193–208.

McGrane, Reginald Charles. *The Panic of 1837: Some Financial Problems of the Jacksonian Era.* Chicago: U of Chicago P, 1924; New York: Russell & Russell, 1965.

McWilliams, John P., Jr. *Hawthorne, Melville, and the American Character: A Looking-Glass Business.* New York: Cambridge UP, 1984.

Messerli, Jonathan. *Horace Mann: A Biography.* New York: Knopf, 1972.

Michaels, Walter Benn, and Donald E. Pease, eds. *The American Renaissance Revisited: Selected Papers from the English Institute, 1982–83.* Baltimore: Johns Hopkins UP, 1985.

Mink, Louis. "Narrative Form as a Cognitive Instrument." *The Writing of History: Literary Form and Historical Understanding.* Eds. Robert Canary and Henry Kozinki. Madison: U of Wisconsin P, 1978. 129–58.

Palfrey, John Gorham. *History of New England.* 5 vols. Boston: Houghton, 1858–89.

Pancoast, Henry S. *An Introduction to American Literature.* New York: Henry Holt, 1898.

Parrington, Vernon L. *Main Currents in American Thought.* 1927. New York: Harcourt, 1954.

Pattee, Fred Lewis. *A History of American Literature, with a View to the Fundamental Principles under-*

lying Its Development: A Textbook for Schools and Colleges. New York: Silver, Burdett & Company, 1896.

Persons, Stow. The Decline of American Gentility. New York: Oxford UP, 1973.

Reising, Russell. The Unusable Past: Theory and the Study of American Literature. London: Methuen, 1986.

Richardson, Charles F. American Literature, 1607–1885. 2 vols. New York: Putnam's, n.d.

Ricoeur, Paul. Time and Narrative. 3 vols. Chicago: U of Chicago P, 1984–88.

Rothman, David J. The Discovery of the Asylum: Social Order and Disorder in the New Republic. Boston: Little, 1971.

Schultz, Stanley K. The Culture Factory: Boston Public Schools, 1789–1860. New York: Oxford UP, 1973.

Scudder, Horace. Literature in School. Boston: Houghton, 1888.

Simpson, Lewis P., ed. The Federalist Literary Mind. Baton Rouge: Louisiana State UP, 1962.

———. The Man of Letters in New England and the South. Baton Rouge: Louisiana State UP, 1973.

Sollors, Werner. Beyond Ethnicity: Consent and Descent in American Culture. New York: Oxford UP, 1986.

Solomon, Barbara Miller. Ancestors and Immigrants: A Changing New England Tradition. Cambridge: Harvard UP, 1956.

———. "The Intellectual Background of the Immigration Restriction Movement in New England."

New England Quarterly 25 (1952): 47–59.

Stevenson, Louise L. Scholarly Means to Evangelical Ends: The New Haven Scholars and the Transformation of Higher Learning in America. Baltimore: Johns Hopkins UP, 1986.

Story, Ronald. The Forging of an Aristocracy: Harvard and the Boston Upper Class, 1800–1870. Middletown: Wesleyan UP, 1980.

Trent, William P. A History of American Literature, 1607–1865. New York: D. Appleton, 1903.

Tryon, W. S. Parnassus Corner: A Life of James T. Fields. Boston: Houghton, 1963.

Tyack, David B. George Ticknor and the Boston Brahmins. Cambridge: Harvard UP, 1967.

———. The One Best System: A History of American Urban Education. Cambridge: Harvard UP, 1967.

Tyler, Moses Coit. A History of American Literature. I: 1607–1676; II: 1676–1765. New York: Putnam's, 1878.

Vanderbilt, Kermit. American Literature and the Academy. Philadelphia: U of Pennsylvania P, 1986.

Walker, Cheryl. The Nightingale's Burden: Women Poets and American Culture before 1900. Bloomington: Indiana UP, 1982.

Watts, Emily Stipes. The Poetry of American Women from 1632 to 1945. Austin: U of Texas P, 1977.

Welter, Rush. The Mind of America, 1820–1860. New York: Columbia UP, 1975.

Wendell, Barrett, and Chester Noyes Greenough. *A History of Literature in America.* New York: Scribner's, 1907.

White, Hayden. *The Content of the Form: Narrative Discourse and Historical Representation.* Baltimore: Johns Hopkins UP, 1987.

———. *Metahistory: The Historical Imagination in Nineteenth-Century Europe.* Baltimore: Johns Hopkins UP, 1973.

Williams, E. I. F. *Horace Mann, Educational Statesman.* New York: Macmillan, 1937.

Woodberry, George E. *America in Literature.* New York: Harper & Brothers, 1903.

Bio-Political Resistance in Domestic Ideology and *Uncle Tom's Cabin*

Lora Romero

Throughout the decade before she wrote *Uncle Tom's Cabin* (1852), Harriet Beecher Stowe suffered from hysterical episodes that left her bedridden for weeks at a time. These attacks were so severe that from May 1846 to March 1847 she left her husband and their three young children in Cincinnati for Dr. Wesselhoeft's Hydropathic Institute, a fashionable water-cure establishment in Brattleboro, Vermont, recommended to her by her sister Catharine Beecher.[1]

The illness from which Stowe suffered in the 1840s may have, in part, dictated her choice of the subject matter for *Uncle Tom's Cabin* (1852). When read together, *Uncle Tom's Cabin* and Stowe's letters on her illness suggest that the novelist identified the white hysterical housewife with the black Southern slave, seeing both as victims of a patriarchal power that violates the integrity of the self.[2] Because the discourse on hysteria addresses the issue of subjectivity at the same time that it expresses concern for the health of the body, Stowe's figuration of the hysteric as the archetypal victim of patriarchal government in *Uncle Tom's Cabin* encodes, as we shall see, a feminist-abolitionist critique within hygienist norms. Not only does Stowe's medicalizing of feminist critique derive from her sister Catharine Beecher's hygienist concept of bodily economy in her writings on housekeeping, but Beecher's domestic ideology also provides a medical feminism to which Stowe added an abolitionist component when writing *Uncle Tom's Cabin*.[3]

The biographical factors informing Stowe's political consciousness take shape within, and themselves evince, a larger restructuring of political power in relation to medical knowledge in antebellum America. Foucault suggests that "bio-power" or "bio-politics"—the integration of the medical and political—increasingly characterizes the exercise of governmental power in Western countries beginning in the eighteenth century.[4] Since that time "political technologies that [invest] the body, health, modes of subsistence and lodging" have proliferated—technologies directed toward "*policing*" but of a sort not to be "understood in the limiting, repressive sense we give the term today, but according to a much broader meaning that encompasse[s] all the methods for developing the quality of the population and the strength" of nations (Donzelot 6). Reading the relation between Stowe's hysteria and political critique in *Uncle Tom's Cabin* articulates the history of the bio-political both as discourse and as "the materiality of power operating on the very bodies of individuals" ("Body/Power" 5), in this case the body of the hysterical Stowe.

Feminist scholarship has long recognized the status of both domestic ideology and *Uncle Tom's Cabin* as political critique, but my claim that feminist-abolitionist resistance itself forms an important part of the history of the exercise of governmental power might, at first, seem to imperil such a reading of Stowe's and Beecher's work. Jane Tompkins, for example, asserts that the domesticity of Stowe's novel delineates a feminist "*alternative . . .* world, one which calls into question the whole structure of American society" (144). In Tompkins's remark feminist-abolitionist critique stands in a relationship of alterity to political power and social institutions. Political resistance originates *outside* of established political relations, in the home. In the critical tradition represented by Tompkins, only from such a privileged point can cultural critique transcend "the whole structure of . . . society."[5]

Although my reading of abolitionism and feminism as integral to the rise of bio-power in the United States undermines an oppositional analysis of the two movements, it does *not* illustrate the recuperation of resistance by that which it opposes. Bio-power renders irrelevant the power/resistance binarism upon which Tompkins's analysis depends. In *The History of Sexuality* Foucault displaces the binary with the multiple, asserting that society is "not a structure," but a network of "nonegalitarian and mobile" power relations (93). All of these relations have their limits. While he allows for "hegemonic effect" when some superstructural force "traverses the local oppositions" within otherwise competing power relations and "links them together" (94), Foucault de-essentializes hegemony. A "whole" society to whose monolithic sameness resistance could oppose an equally monolithic difference does not exist; for Foucault, resistance to power *cannot* be grounded in radical alterity. Without a "binary and all-encompassing opposition between rulers and ruled at the root of power relations," there can be "no single locus of great Refusal, no soul of revolt, source of rebellions, or pure law of the revolutionary" (95–96). "Bio-political resistance" is *not* oxymoronic. Thus resistance may be retheorized as historical rather than radical alterity. My reading of the bio-politics of antebellum feminist and abolitionist critique analyzes political resistance as *defined* rather than *contained* by its entanglement in power relations.

1. Feminist Hygiene and Stowe's Hysteria

A conflict between two perceptual modes, absorption and abstraction, structures Stowe's private letters on housekeeping from the late 1830s and the 1840s, a conflict which expresses the impact of the hygienist component of domestic ideology upon Stowe's interpretation of her own hysteria. These letters suggest that Stowe believed that she had a tendency to become absorbed in the physical details of domestic work and that, in order to recover from her illness, she needed to develop a household system, a domestic economy, to abstract herself from "minutiae."

In an 1845 letter to her husband, Stowe describes the drudgery of housework as a perilous visual activity. She describes herself not just (like all other nineteenth-century housewives) "working hard," but also "looking into closets, and seeing a great deal of that dark side of domestic life which a housekeeper may who will investigate too curiously into minutiae . . ." (qtd. in Charles Stowe 111). If this letter presents the dark side of domestic labor as the somatic activity of focusing on particular household details, the specific symptomatology of Stowe's hysteria represents a retreat from such absorptive domestic vision. The author found herself paying for periods of intense domestic labor with ensuing episodes of hysterical blindness and a related "neuralgic complaint that settled in [her] eyes," which, as she put it, rendered her unable "to fix them with attention on anything" (101). Stowe was not so much blinded by her hysteria as incapable of discerning discrete objects. Confined to a darkened room during these attacks, she symbolically eluded absorptive vision at the same time that she actually eluded domestic labor.

Stowe's letters suggest that the author imagined that her failure to impose a larger intellectual system or economy upon household specifics had resulted in her absorption in domestic details and her consequent illness. Stowe opposes absorption in domestic minutiae to what she calls "systematic" housekeeping. She writes to a friend in 1838 that "all [her] days [are] made up" of domestic "details" (92), and in a later letter to her husband admits that she is "constitutionally careless and too impetuous and impulsive easily to maintain that consistency and order which is necesssary in a family . . ." (qtd. in Wagenknecht 54). The topic of "system and order in a family" inspires Stowe to effuse in one letter she wrote while at Brattleboro, "I know that nothing can be done without it; it is the keystone, the *sine qua non* . . ." (qtd. in Charles Stowe 115). Systematic household organization, symbolizing the housewife's control over otherwise unorganized physical details, represents Stowe's attempt to imagine household labor as something more than manual labor. Expressing a rejection of absorptive domestic vision, Stowe's hysterical blindness answers her fear of being reduced to "a mere drudge with few ideas" (92).

Like Stowe, Beecher understood hysteria to result from absorption in details. In *Letters to the People on Health and Happiness* (1855), Beecher translates external multiplicity, the myriad of household details, into internal fragmentation, hysteria. She rapturously hails systematization as remedying the increasing "nervousness" of American women (111). Systematization, the domestic skill that allowed women to displace the patriarch from the home, conjoins faculties dissevered by patriarchal government and in doing so repairs the self-division that, for Beecher, defines hysteria.

The competing terms (discrete details versus overarching systems) shaping Stowe's interpretation of the origin of her illness also structure Beecher's domestic ideology. A single hygienist dictum informs virtually all of Beecher's writing on housekeeping: no faculty should be developed at the expense of any other. Disproportion must be avoided at all costs. Hysteria is the mark of patriarchal oppression. Beecher uses the concept of bodily economy to articulate a feminist critique of patriarchal government of the home.[6] Beecher, like others committed to educational reform in the late eighteenth and early nineteenth centuries, believed that patriarchal interests had dictated the content of traditional, middle-class female education.[7] In instructing girls exclusively in the ornamental graces requisite for obtaining an advantageous familial alliance through the marriage contract, that education had privileged the development of certain pleasing and marketable skills in women, such as dancing and piano playing. Educational reformers lamented the rarefied and partial product of such an upbringing. They responded with an educational method that they believed would cultivate the whole woman instead of only a few marketable accomplishments—hence Beecher's obsessive dismissal of partiality from female experience.

Beecher banishes disproportion by banishing precisely those absorbing household details that her sister found so problematic. "There is no one thing, more necessary to a housekeeper, in performing her varied duties," proclaims Beecher, who dedicates an entire chapter of her *Treatise on Domestic Economy* (1841) to the subject, "than *a habit of system and order,"* for "the affairs of a housekeeper [are] made up . . . of ten thousand desultory and minute items" (18). In regard to the organization of the troublesome "minutiae of domestic arrangements" (149), Beecher recommends that the housewife devote specific days to specific tasks. In a systematic household Monday might be devoted to mending, Tuesday to washing, Wednesday to ironing, and so forth. For Beecher, the real issue is hygienic rather than merely practical, for a "wise economy is nowhere more conspicuous, than in the right *apportionment of time* to the different pursuits" (144–45). Systematization "modif[ies] any mistaken proportions" in a woman's development (147). It allows her to cultivate various faculties instead of only a few.

Beecher links disproportion to the opening of a gap between mind and body. She designs her postpatriarchal pedagogy to close this gap through the harmonious development of all the faculties (an economy of the body). Referring in her *Letters* to the use of domestic help in wealthy families, Beecher laments that even in America, where there is no genuine aristocracy, one "portion of the women have all the exercise of the *nerves of motion,* and another have all the *brain-work."* She explains the great virtue of properly systematic housework: "it would exercise every muscle in the body, and at the same time interest and exercise the mind" (111). Disproportional development leads to self-division, hence the alarming incidence of "nervousness" and hysteria among Americans, for, when "equalization of the nervous fluid" is "withheld, the sensibility of the other portions of the brain is liable to become excessive, unnatural, and less under the control of the will" (103). Beecher thinks of labor in the systematic household as active rather than reactive, its stimulus being internal not external, determined by the housekeeper rather than by factors out of her control. Systematic housekeepers, writes Beecher, "control circumstances" rather than allowing "circumstances [to] control them" (*Treatise* 148). For Beecher, domestic economy maintains bodily economy by encouraging women to exercise their will over physical details. In narrowing the gap between mind and body, domestic economy enhances subjectivity and thus combats hysteria.

Stowe's representation of absorptive labor in an essay she wrote on nervousness helps explain the logic of Beecher's belief that the housewife's enslavement to circumstances creates hysterical women. In "Irritability" the novelist speaks of overwork as an "overdraft on the nervous energy, which helps us to use up in one hour the strength of whole days" (76) and compares it to alcohol, tobacco, and coffee, indulgences Beecher repeatedly denounces. According to Stowe, such stimulants permit one to shine "for a few hours of extra brightness," but with an artificial glow. Artificial brightness, produced under the stimulus of excessive labor or narcotic indulgence, destabilizes subjectivity. To be artificially stimulated is to surrender self-determination and willpower and to make the body work independently of the mind. Beecher believes that systematization enhances female subjectivity by coordinating handwork and brainwork, relocating the stimulus for activity within the housewife by creating an economy of the self in which all the faculties surrender control to the will.

Beecher's call for the educational conjunction of physical and intellectual culture partakes in a larger grounding of female subjectivity in resistance to patriarchal control over the home. Other domestic ideologues (both British and American) called for the creation of an integrated female self. These educators also wanted to institute the home, rather than the marriage market, as the focus of female education. If women were to spend the greater part of their adult lives in the home, then their education should prepare them for that life, not prepare them for a lifetime in the ballroom, the theater, or the drawing room. Hannah More, the British author who influenced Beecher, asks, "Do not we educate [our daughters] for a crowd, forgetting they are to live at home? for the world, and not for themselves? for show, and not for use?" (40). According to More, patriarchal education engenders a craving for excitement that domestic life could never gratify and hence produces fragmented female selves, torn between desire and domestic duty. Domestic education of the sort envisaged first by More and later Beecher represents the attempt to imagine a form of household government that would enhance, not undermine, subjectivity.

Because the sphere of female activity defined by Beecher and other female educators is circumscribed by the boundaries of the home, one could argue that domestic ideology extends rather than subverts patriarchal power. Carroll Smith-Rosenberg presents the hysterical woman as a rebel against the coercive ethos of "will, control, and hard work" personified in the ideal domestic woman, whom Smith-Rosenberg sees as the discursive product of patriarchal power. As Jacques Donzelot points out, however, analyses such as these essentialize patriarchal hegemony. "For feminists," writes Donzelot, the rise of the domestic woman "seems of slight importance when weighed against a patriarchal domination seen as essentially unchanged across the centuries." The power/resistance binarism supporting Smith-Rosenberg's argument may "nurture . . . combat," but it also "conceals" historical changes in the family (xxii). Women's colleges, the growth of teaching and nursing as careers for women, the entrance of women into public life through their alliance with social professions, were "the springboard" women "needed for the recognition of [their] political rights" (xxiii). Even if such developments enforced behavioral norms and values that, to use Smith-Rosenberg's words, prepare women "to undertake the arduous and necessary duties of wife and mother" (205), they also legitimated certain versions of female financial and social autonomy, without which female political enfranchisement was unthinkable. Although antebellum domestic feminism may at points intersect and even collaborate with patriarchal power, that does not make the former reducible to the latter.

2. Social and Bodily Economy

Nancy Armstrong has argued that British domestic ideology signals a "cultural change from an earlier form of power based on sumptuary display to a modern form that works through the production of subjectivity" (80). Armstrong's comment applies also to American domesticity, which produces a female subject in the act of resisting patriarchal power.

Beecher's domestic ideology also bears resemblance to a late eighteenth-century European educational analysis of the body's relationship to the state that, according to Donzelot, expressed itself through a political discourse on the health and welfare of the working classes and through a domestic discourse on the preservation of women and children. French educators, physicians, and politicians expressed a concern for the waste of labor resources through state oppression of the working classes at the same time that they exposed the "wasteful" and "artificial" education of the children of the wealthy. Valuable human resources were being squandered both at the bottom and the top of the social scale. The "impoverishment of the nation and the etiolation of its elite" would result, warned these authorities (9). Donzelot describes the bio-politics as a two-part agenda, one, a call for bodily economy to preserve the bodies of upper-class women and children, and the other, a call for social economy to preserve the bodies of the working classes (12–13). Bio-political resistance unites the working classes with upper-class women and children against the patriarch. It demands that these two groups wrest control over their bodies away from him, stabilize their unstable subjectivities, and practice self-government.

Donzelot's account of bio-politics helps explain Stowe's apparent translation of the terms by which she understood her hysteria into a fictional representation of Southern slavery. In *Uncle Tom's Cabin* bodily economy and social economy merge in a feminist-abolitionist critique of patriarchal power. The very same hygienist logic behind Stowe's understanding of her hysteria governs her analysis of slavery, a coincidence suggested by the parallels her novel articulates between "nervous" white women and overworked black slaves.

In *Uncle Tom's Cabin* the lack of an economy of the body among white women raised in unsystematic aristocratic households recapitulates in its structure the dissociation of mind and body produced by a society in which "a lower class" is "given up to physical toil and confined to an animal nature" so that "a higher one thereby acquires leisure and wealth for a more expanded intelligence and improvement and becomes the directing soul of the lower" (II: 21). This system, as pro-slavery apologist Henry Hughes put it, makes blacks "manualizers" and whites "mentalizers" (86).

The Southern white woman's lack of *wholeness* reflects and is predicated upon the division of labor into mentalizers and manualizers. Significantly, the hysterical and sickly Marie St. Clare is not, as Stowe puts it, a "whole woman." Rather, as Stowe twice repeats, she is "a fine figure, a pair of bright dark eyes, and a hundred thousand dollars" (I: 222, 224). The partial product of patriarchal education, the daughter raised for what Armstrong calls "sumptuary display," becomes an "unsystematic" housekeeper (I: 295). As in Beecher's narrative of the etiology of nervous disease, ill-health in *Uncle Tom's Cabin* originates in the division between mind and body, a gap to whose presence Marie St. Clare's "enervated" nervous system (II: 144), her lapses into "hysterical spasms" (II: 118), and her failure to be a "whole woman" attest.

Even more vividly than Marie's hysterical outbursts, however, Little Eva's fatal illness suggests the bio-political dimension of Stowe's feminism. In representing Eva's slow decline, Stowe wages a bio-political critique of patriarchal power. The novelist describes how the child's body is being used up too quickly. In her illness Eva, who is about eight years old, seems suddenly to undergo puberty. The consumptive flush, as has often been remarked of nineteenth-century representations of the disease, resembles the flush of awakening sexuality—a similarity that suggests that Stowe thinks of Eva, as much as the slave, as a victim of preindustrial southern discipline. Eva's father Augustine St. Clare notes something unnatural and precocious about his daughter. He is struck by "the daily increasing maturity of the child's mind and feelings," and all notice a new "womanly thoughtfulness" gracing Eva's behavior as her disease progresses (II: 67).

Contemporaneous discussions of consumption further illuminate how Eva's illness symbolizes the dissociation of mind and body produced by patriarchal government. Dr. William Alcott advises that the "common custom of pushing forward the intellect at the expense of the body" lies behind many cases of consumption (273). Alcott sees in consumption a failure to maintain an economy of the body, a dangerous and disproportionate development of one faculty (the imagination) at the expense of development of another faculty (the body).

Moreover, in the dissociation of mind and body depicted in Eva's illness, the novelist creates a version of her own hysteria. At one point St. Clare wonders if Eva isn't growing "nervous"—a suggestion that Eva dismisses, while Stowe notes "a nervous twitching about the corners of her mouth" (II: 28). As Dr. James Clark, a mid-century authority on consumption, writes, there "is more nervous sensibility than is natural to the [consumptive] patient" (31), and Alcott concurs (269). According to Stowe, the nervous are "soon used up" ("Irritability" 71), consumed. Little Eva's precociousness, the rapid consumption of her flesh, her apparent nervous susceptibility, all express Stowe's feminist critique of a patriarchal power that discourages proportional development in women and deprives them of self-government.[8]

In *Uncle Tom's Cabin*, the South uses up black slaves even more conspicuously than it consumes white women. Stowe deems slave labor in the southernmost states as less hygienic than those of more northern regions, for the "general prevalence of agricultural pursuits of a quiet and gradual nature, not requiring those periodic seasons of hurry and pressure that are called for in the business of more southern districts, makes the task of the negro [in states like Kentucky] a more healthful and reasonable one" (I: 23). Because preindustrial Southern labor is task- rather than time-oriented, Stowe can transform the intense physical activity of slaves engaged in absorptive labor into a kind of consumptive fever. As Simon Legree summarizes his treatment of slaves, "Use up, and buy more, 's my way . . ." (II: 173). During the "heat and hurry of the [cotton-picking] season" (II: 183), the overseer's whip temporarily "stimulate[s]" slaves "to an unnatural strength" (II: 191), and hence, in the logic of mid-century hygiene, the bodies of blacks are used up all the more quickly. The term "used up" adumbrates the hygienist maxim upon which Stowe dilates "Irritability": it is better "to labor for years steadily, diligently . . . avoiding those cheating stimulants that overtax Nature" than it is "to pass life in exaltations and depressions, resulting from overstrained labors, supported by unnatural stimulus" (82). The patriarchal stimulus to labor is unnatural in that it comes from outside rather than from within and thus leaves the slave exhausted.

There is nothing remarkable about the fact that Stowe's representation of slavery should refer to the horrific intensity of labor in the fields or that part of Stowe's appeal comes from depicting the toll that slavery takes upon the body. Obviously, attention to the physical effects of slavery on the body furthers both Stowe's realism and her polemic intent; that Stowe embeds her critique of coercive power in the specific logic of bodily economy *does* warrant remark.

Hygienist notions of absorptive labor, and their implicit political critique, even determine Stowe's representation of slave labor of a less intensive variety than field work.

Hygienist notions of absorptive labor, and their implicit political critique, even determine Stowe's representation of slave labor of a less intensive variety than field work. The St. Clare's cook Dinah reproduces the southern disciplinary system in her method of managing the St. Clare kitchen. Stowe notes that, even though the kitchen is generally characterized by the most extreme disorder, Dinah "had, at irregular periods, paroxysms of reformation and arrangement, which she called 'clarin' up times' " (I: 302). Labor manifests itself like a spasm or a fever in these "irregular periods." Stowe's language suggests an analogy between Dinah's "clarin' up times" and those "periodic seasons of heat and hurry" characteristic of field work when she refers to the cook's occasional attempts to put the kitchen in order as "periodic seasons" of household reform (I: 303).

Dinah's spasmodic relation to labor symbolizes her spasmodic relation to discipline, the gap that patriarchal government generates between power and subject, the same gap that Stowe also suggests in her representation of Marie St. Clare's lack of "wholeness" and of Little Eva's illness. Stowe's hygienist critique of patriarchal government stresses the inadequacy of power that disrupts the economy of the self. My point is not that Stowe's abolitionist-feminism addresses issues of the body but rather that a nineteenth-century concept of physical health structures the entire logic of Stowe's critique of patriarchal power. Stowe's critique, in other words, is bio-political.

3. The Subject of Resistance

Although Beecher's feminism can be aligned with Stowe's feminist-abolitionism on the basis of the bio-politics they share, bio-politics does not stipulate a conservative or progressive political position. While Stowe translated her belief in the need for an economy of the body into an abolitionist best-seller, Beecher's hygienist fear of the partial and of the detail led her to oppose abolitionism. In her *Essay on Slavery and Abolitionism* (1837), Beecher represents the antislavery movement as a variety of mania by which "the minds of men are thrown into a ferment" (94). Abolitionist leaders, writes Beecher, are probably otherwise moral and reasonable individuals, but because of political measures that require disproportionate fixation on a single idea, a significant portion of the movement's leadership is composed of "men accustomed to a contracted field of observation, and more qualified to judge of immediate results than of general tendencies" (21). Bio-power determines the discursive materials through which various political positions articulate themselves but does not completely determine individual interpretations of those materials into specific political affiliations.

Because the materials of bio-power are subject to multiple, although not infinite, interpretations and uses, Foucault asks that we reconceive power as "power relations" and resistance as "resistances" (*HS* 96); however, in the particular versions of bio-politics represented in Beecher's and Stowe's work, the integration of the political and medical discourages us from thinking of the relationship between power and resistance as anything other than a "binary and all-encompassing opposition." Perhaps we should think of bio-politics not as a particular political interest or stance so much as a way of conceiving the political. Beecher's hygienist analysis of abolitionism is really less concerned with that particular movement than it is a critique of politics in general. Any engagement in politics, for Beecher, threatens the self (throws "the mind of men . . . into a ferment"), because all political beliefs are partial and involve devotion to details at the expense of larger systems. Any relation to power, whether as its victim (in the case of the hysterical housewife) or as its agent (in the case of the hysterical abolitionist), leads to self-division.

To imagine power as something that creates self-division is to imagine power as simultaneously absolute and negative. In discussing the "separation in the subject between *psyche* and *soma*" figured in hysteria, D. A. Miller suggests that, paradoxically, the hysteric, whom I have been representing as like the slave, may be the figure of the liberal subject par excellence. Hysteria, Miller writes, allows us to imagine the radical autonomy of the individual from the society around her, for "what the body suffers, the mind needn't think" (148). The body of the hysteric, like the body of the slave, is coerced by power, but the mind of both hysteric and slave remains absent and aloof. In Stowe's and Beecher's bio-political imaginations, the nervous woman and the slave are archetypal *objects of power,* but the hygienist body/mind binarism built into the representation of hysteric and slave does not permit them to become the *subjects of power.* Subjectivity, selfhood, individualism are invested in one half of the binarism whereas political relations, power, and society pertain only to the other half. This negative inscription of power enables the oppositionalist understanding of resistance. The hysteric and the slave, as discursive entities, serve simultaneously as figures of utter disempowerment and transcendental resistance, of a resistance whose purity is guaranteed by its radical alterity from what Tompkins calls "the whole structure of society."

That the mind and body could become utterly dissevered, no matter how oppressive the circumstances, is, at best, a dubious proposition. If people could be made into just bodies, slavery would seem less appalling than it is, but Henry Hughes's division of society into manualizers and mentalizers rests on a proposition not just offensive but absurd, that some people are things. Stowe's original subtitle for her novel—*The Man That Was a Thing*—conveys the absurdity of the legal fiction that makes subjects into objects. It expresses the pathos of the situation of human beings treated as though they were simply bodies, and yet, paradoxically, Stowe's concept of resistance to enslavement requires that sometimes people be things.

Even when Stowe represents the resistance to patriarchal government that her novel would appear to legitimate, the hygienist mind/body binarism allows her to imagine the self in a relation of complete exteriority to the political power exercised in the act of rebellion. When George Harris can no longer tolerate his master's abuse and determines to escape slavery or die trying, Stowe represents this as George's loss of control over his body. He "had [formerly] been able to repress every disrespectful word; but the flashing eye, the gloomy and troubled brow, were part of a natural language that could not be repressed—indubitable signs, which showed too plainly that the man could not become a thing" (I: 29). Curiously, in the very moment that George becomes determined to be more than a body, more than a thing, Stowe reduces him to his body.

When George's wife Eliza learns her master has sold their son to a slave trader, she too loses the capacity for self-government. Although she believes she is "wicked" to run away, she explains to her friends that she "can't help it" (I: 63, 64). They express approbation of her actions by asserting that she did "what no kind o' mother could help a doin'! " (I: 139). Eliza's loss of control over her body manifests itself in "[p]ale, shivering . . . rigid features and compressed lips" that make her look like "an entirely altered being from the soft and timid creature she had been hitherto" (I: 60). Not until she has reached Indiana with her son does the "supernatural tension of [her] nervous system [lessen]" and the apparently hysterical Eliza falls into a sort of nervous exhaustion (I: 82).

Stowe's insistence on the mind/body binarism in her representation of first George's and later Eliza's acts of resistance allows the body to suffer "what the mind needn't feel." These two episodes record Stowe's inability to conceive of the subject in any relation to the political. Rebellion in *Uncle Tom's Cabin* is not a political act but rather the radical separation of the individual from all political activity. In Stowe's mind, power and resistance are so polarized that she cannot imagine resistance as the assertion of a legitimate political position against an illegitimate one. Instead, the novelist represents resistance as what Foucault calls the "great soul of revolt," a radically independent self, rebelling against political power in general, rather than some particular and malignant manifestation of power.

Stowe's inability to think of the subject in relation to the political is perhaps even clearer in her characterization of the abolitionist Ophelia's demeanor. St. Clare's cousin from Vermont is as "inevitable as a clock, and as inexorable as a railroad engine." The mechanical metaphors express her disdain for "all modes of procedure which [have] not a direct and inevitable relation to accomplishment of some purpose they definitely had in mind" (I: 229). Stowe represents Ophelia (in what has to be a significant metaphor in an abolitionist novel) as the "absolute bond-slave" of her personal moral code (I: 230), including her

In Stowe's mind, power and resistance are so polarized that she cannot imagine resistance as the assertion of a legitimate political position against an illegitimate one.

abolitionism. Despite Ophelia's obedience to a personal political code rather than external coercion, Stowe suggests Ophelia's mechanical deportment is a self-division comparable to that of the slave laboring under the whip. Although St. Clare's cousin comes from an abolitionist family and expresses strong political views on the issue of slavery, Stowe undermines the legitimating grounds of the abolitionism as a political position when she shows Ophelia recoiling in horror at the sight of whites touching black slaves. Ophelia's automatism suggests that the gap between the subject and the political cannot be bridged.

Even though Simon Legree represents a political position antithetically opposed to Ophelia's, Stowe also understands his pro-slavery ideology too as fundamentally exterior to the self. The novel's final chapters, which show Legree descending into alcoholism and insanity, suggest that Stowe's villain had all along been maddeningly ambivalent about the morality of slavery and that only a Herculean act of self-government, analogous to Ophelia's enslavement to her politics, has enabled him to hold slaves in the first place. His "bullet head" and aggressively mechanical behavior testify to the effort of repressing a prepolitical consciousness of the moral sin involved in slaveholding.

Significantly, when Legree's self-government begins to unravel, Stowe symbolizes it with an image of the body uncannily coming to life. On her deathbed Eva gives a lock of her hair to Tom, who later comes into Legree's possession. This lock of hair "like a living thing, twine[s] itself round Legree's fingers" and his memories when he confiscates it from his new possession (II: 216). Eva's memento animates Legree's long-dead memory of the lock of hair that his own saintly mother sent him on her deathbed, hair which also "twined about his fingers" (II: 218). Legree wonders "if hair could rise from the dead!" (II: 220). The uncanniness of this scene consists in the body's (the hair's) refusal to act like a *thing*. Stowe identifies Legree's repressed feelings about slavery with Mrs. Legree's lock of hair, and she configures Legree's eroding ability to repress those emotions as the body uncannily taking on a life of its own.

Integrating the medical and political permits Stowe to imagine in the split between body and mind a transcendent liberal subject radically independent of political power and society in general. One episode especially conveys how absorptive vision returns as the novel's abolitionist desideratum. Augustine St. Clare compares the danger of looking too minutely into the details of the slave system to the danger of looking too minutely into his cook Dinah's slovenly habits of kitchen management.

"If we are to be prying and spying into all the dismals of life," he informs his northern cousin Miss Ophelia, who asks him how he can live with his knowledge of the abuse suffered by slaves, "we should have no heart to anything. 'T is like looking too close into the details of Dinah's kitchen. . ." (II: 8). St. Clare later quotes the axiom by which his father conveniently disposed of the matter of the maltreatment of slaves: "General rules will bear hard on particular cases" (II: 17).

In her letters on hysteria Stowe represents herself as a "housekeeper" who "investigate[s] too curiously into minutiae." Stowe was committed to eliciting on behalf of her political cause the absorptive vision and commitment to the particular that St. Clare disavows. According to *A Key to Uncle Tom's Cabin* (1853), general rules, like those promoted by Bird and St. Clare, have impeded emancipation: "The atrocious and sacrilegious *system,*" Stowe claims, referring to the institution of slavery, "fails to produce the impression on the mind that it ought to produce because it is lost in generalities." She concludes that she herself "cannot give any idea of the horribly cruel and demoralizing effect of [slavery], except by presenting *facts in detail*" (349; my emphasis). Facts in detail, investigation into minutiae, absorptive vision—these can topple political belief and abstract theories. Whereas Stowe's earlier letters on hysteria express a Beecherian feminist critique of the detail in favor of the system, in *Uncle Tom's Cabin* the hysterical violation of economy and wholeness entailed by privileging the detail functions simultaneously as the product of patriarchal power and the grounds of resistance to it.

4. The Cultural Subject

The difficulty of divesting our political imaginations of the prophylactic binarism, the difficulty of imagining a *subject* of power, is suggested by the tendency of even Foucauldian literary criticism to depend upon a body/mind dyad in describing how power works. Foucauldian critics speak of power in the nineteenth century as "internalized . . . institutional control" (Miller 122) and the "inward" relocation of "external discipline's traditional corrective tools" (Brodhead 78). To understand biopower as internalized physical discipline, as the introjection of the prison cell or the slave master's whip, is to apply the mind/body binarism to consciousness itself. In these tropes power stands in a belated relation to subjectivity. Foucault interrogates this strictly negative concept of power when he questions the "repressive hypothesis" in *The History of Sexuality*. In figuring power as introjected social control these critics fail to challenge "a human subject on the lines of the model provided by classical philosophy, endowed with a consciousness which power is then thought to seize on" ("Body/Power" 58). In *Discipline and Punish* Foucault insists that we "must cease once and for all to describe the effects of power in negative terms." Power "produces," he writes, and precisely what it produces is a subject (194).

Foucauldian criticism on nineteenth-century literature has relied on the oppositional concept of resistance as radical alterity, no doubt because of the difficulty of imagining a productive relationship between the self and power. Inspired by *The History of Sexuality*'s assertion that where "there is power, there is resistance, and yet, or rather consequently, this resistance is never in a position of exteriority in relation to power," followers of Foucault have deconstructed the central binarism of oppositional criticism by demonstrating how political critique fails to occupy such a position of exteriority and hence is recuperated by power.[9] Only within the logic of the oppositionalist binarism, however, are the failure to stand outside of power and the fact of containment synonymous. Resistance may not transcend power relations altogether, but that does not mean that it merely reproduces the same power relations or that all power relations must reproduce the status quo.

Similarly, thinking of bio-power as having a productive relation to the self does not render it the mere pawn of social control. Foucault writes that "the subject constitutes himself in an active fashion, by the practices of self, these practices are nevertheless not something that the individual invents by himself. They are patterns that he finds in his culture and which are proposed, suggested and imposed on him by his culture, his society and his social group" ("Care of the Self" 11).

In a somewhat different context, the feminist philosopher Judith Butler suggests an alternative model of subjectivity in relation to power which does not depend upon the existence of the liberal subject radically free of "the whole structure of society." Butler describes a "cultural self" created as a "process of interpretation within a network of deeply entrenched cultural norms" (128). This "cultural self" is grounded but not contained, and power invests it in both positive and nondeterminist ways. Butler's concept of the cultural subject suggests a way of thinking ourselves out of the power/resistance binarism informing *Uncle Tom's Cabin* and domestic ideology and still operating in feminist oppositional criticism and, far more subtly, in Foucauldian criticism itself.

Notes

I want to thank Cathy Davidson, Catherine Gallagher, Walter Michaels, Jeff Nunokawa, Michael Rogin, Margit Stange, Eric Sundquist, and Lynn Wardley for their important suggestions and helpful insights.

1.   Forrest Wilson provides the most detailed account available of Stowe's illness. On Dr. Wesselhoeft's Hydropathic Institute, see Kemble and Weiss, 209–18, and on Beecher's relationship to the water cure, see Sklar, 204–09.

2.   A discussion of the political problematics of Stowe's identification of white women and slaves is beyond the scope of this study. They are very ably detailed by Sanchez-Eppler.

3.   Ammons in "Stowe's Dream of a Mother-Savior," Brown, Tompkins, Brodhead, Fisher, Matthews, and Crumpacker all discuss Stowe's relation to her sister's domestic ideology.

4.   Foucault writes that bio-power takes on issues such as "the problems of birthrate, longevity, public health, housing, and migration" and that "its aim is to strengthen the social forces—to increase production, to develop the economy, spread education, raise the level of public morality; to increase and multiply" (*History of Sexuality* 140; *Discipline and Punish* 208).

5.   For other examples of feminist oppositional readings of Stowe and domesticity, see Ammons's "Heroines in *Uncle Tom's Cabin*" 153 and Baym 189.

6.   Cf. Barker-Benfield's discussion of what he sees as the inherently misogynist concept of bodily economy, and Leach's statement that the concept of bodily economy served the interests of "an emerging hierarchical corporate capitalist system dominated by men" (350–51).

7.   On the reform of female education in this period, see Cott 115–16; Kerber 203–21; Sklar 75–76; Donzelot 39; and Armstrong 59–95.

8.   I realize that my interpretation of Little Eva's illness and death goes against critical consensus, which has represented Eva's consumption in positive terms, as part and parcel of the larger transcendence of "the physical" necessitated by evangelical belief that "it is the spirit alone that is finally real" (see Tompkins 133). But Stowe's Christianity was of a more muscular variety than critics have generally assumed. In an article appearing in her "The Chimney-Corner" series, Stowe actually attacked revivals of religion because they so "often end in periods of bodily ill-health." Stowe states in this article that the body *need not* be transcended by the true believer. In fact, "[t]he body, if allowed the slightest degree of fair play, so far from being a contumacious infidel and opposer, becomes a very fair Christian

helper, and, instead of throttling the soul, gives it wings to rise to celestial regions" ("Bodily Religion" 90).

9.   A particularly relevant example of the tendency of Foucauldian criticism to reproduce a pre-Foucauldian conception of power is Brodhead's "Sparing the Rod." There Brodhead asserts that Stowe wants to abolish slavery—but only to replace it with a disciplinary maternal love that is not at all liberating but rather a "new [order] of coercive power" (87). When he suggests that because bourgeois antebellum child-rearing practices enforced behavioral norms they were a form of "coercive power" analogous to slavery, Brodhead effectively collapses the difference Foucault posits between punishment and discipline. While Brodhead is right that neither black slave nor white child is "free" in an absolute sense, Foucault's point is precisely that there exists a whole spectrum of power relations occupying the space between enslavement and absolute freedom.

Works Cited

Alcott, William A. *Lectures on Life and Health.* Boston: Phillips, Sampson, 1853.

Ammons, Elizabeth. "Heroines in *Uncle Tom's Cabin.*" *Critical Essays on Harriet Beecher Stowe.* Ed. Elizabeth Ammons. Boston: Hall, 1980. 152–65.

———. "Stowe's Dream of the Mother-Savior: *Uncle Tom's Cabin* and American Women Writers Before the 1920s." *New Essays on Uncle Tom's Cabin.* Ed. Eric J. Sundquist. New York: Cambridge UP, 1986. 155–95.

Armstrong, Nancy. *Desire and Domestic Fiction: A Political History of the Novel.* New York: Oxford UP, 1987.

Barker-Benfield, G. J. *The Horrors of the Half-Known Life: Male Attitudes Toward Women and Sexuality in Nineteenth-Century America.* New York: Harper, 1976.

Baym, Nina. *Novels, Readers, and Reviewers: Responses to Fiction in Antebellum America.* Ithaca: Cornell UP, 1984.

Beecher, Catharine E. *An Essay on Slavery and Abolitionism.* 1837. Freeport, New York: Books For Libraries, 1970.

———. *Letters to the People on Health and Happiness.* New York: Harper, 1855.

———. *Treatise on Domestic Economy.* 1841. New York: Schocken, 1977.

Brodhead, Richard H. "Sparing the Rod: Discipline and Fiction in Antebellum America." *Representations* 21 (Winter 1988): 67–96.

Brown, Gillian. "Getting in the Kitchen with Dinah: Domestic Politics in *Uncle Tom's Cabin.*" *American Quarterly* 36 (Fall 1984): 503–23.

Butler, Judith. "Variations on Sex and Gender: Beauvoir, Wittig and Foucault." *Feminism as Critique: On the Politics of Gender.* Ed. Seyla Benhabib and Drucilla Cornell. Minneapolis: U of Minnesota P, 1987. 128–42.

Clark, James. *The Sanative Influence of Climate.* Philadelphia: A. Waldie, 1841.

Cott, Nancy F. *The Bonds of Womanhood: "Woman's Sphere" in New England, 1780–1835.* New Haven: Yale UP, 1977.

Crumpacker, Laurie. "Four Novels of Harriet Beecher Stowe: A Study in Nineteenth-Century Androgyny." *American Novelists Revisited: Essays in Feminist Criticism.* Ed. Fritz Fleischmann. Boston: Hall, 1982. 78–106.

Donzelot, Jacques. *The Policing of Families.* Trans. Robert Hurley. New York: Pantheon, 1979.

Fisher, Philip. *Hard Facts: Setting and Form in the American Novel.* New York: Oxford UP, 1985.

Foucault, Michel. "Body/Power." Trans. Colin Gordon, et al. *Power/Knowledge: Selected Interviews and Other Writings, 1972–1977.* Ed. Colin Gordon. New York: Pantheon, 1980. 55–62.

———. *Discipline and Punish: The Birth of the Prison.* Trans. Alan Sheridan. New York: Vintage, 1979.

———. "The Ethic of Care for the Self as a Practice of Freedom: An Interview." Trans. J. D. Gauthier. *The Final Foucault.* Ed. James Bernauer and David Rasmussen. Cambridge: MIT P, 1988. 1–20.

———. *The History of Sexuality: An Introduction.* Trans. Robert Hurley. New York: Vintage, 1980.

Hughes, Henry. *Treatise on Sociology.* Philadelphia: Lippincott, 1854.

Kemble, Howard R., and Harry B. Weiss. *The Great American Watercure Craze: A History of Hydropathy in the United States.* Trenton: Past Times, 1967.

Kerber, Linda K. *Women of the Republic: Intellect and Ideology in Revolutionary America.* Chapel Hill: U of North Carolina P, 1980.

Leach, William. *True Love and Perfect Union: The Feminist Reform of Sex and Society.* New York: Basic, 1980.

Matthews, Glenna. *"Just a Housewife": The Rise and Fall of Domesticity in America.* New York: Oxford UP, 1987.

Miller, D. A. "*Cage aux folles*: Sensation and Gender in Wilkie Collins's *The Woman in White*." *The Novel and the Police.* Berkeley: U of California P, 1988. 146–191.

More, Hannah. *Strictures on the Modern System of Female Education.* 3rd American ed. Boston: J. Bumstead, 1802.

Rugoff, Milton. *The Beechers: An American Family in the Nineteenth Century.* New York: Harper, 1981.

Sanchez-Eppler, Karen. "Bodily Bonds: The Intersecting Rhetorics of Feminism and Abolitionism." *Representations* 24 (Fall 1988): 28–59.

Sklar, Kathryn Kish. *Catharine Beecher: A Study in American Domesticity.* New York: Norton, 1976.

Smith-Rosenberg, Carroll. "The Hysterical Woman: Sex Roles and Role Conflict in Nineteenth-Century America." *Disorderly Conduct: Visions of Gender in Victorian America.* New York: Knopf, 1985. 197–216.

Stowe, Charles. *Life and Letters of Harriet Beecher Stowe.* Boston: Houghton, 1889.

Stowe, Harriet Beecher. "Bodily Religion: A Sermon on Good Health." *Atlantic Monthly* Jan. 1866: 85–93. 93.

———. *A Key to Uncle Tom's Cabin.* New York: AMS, 1967. Vol. 2 of *The Writings of Harriet Beecher Stowe.* 16 vols. London: Thomas Bosworth, 1853.

———. "Irritability." *Little Foxes.* Boston: Ticknor and Fields, 1868. 53–90.

———. *Uncle Tom's Cabin; or, Life Among the Lowly.* 2 vols. Boston: J. P. Jewett, 1852.

Sweetser, William. *A Treatise on Consumption.* Boston: T. H. Carter, 1836.

Tompkins, Jane. *Sensational Designs: The Cultural Work of American Fiction, 1790–1860.* New York: Oxford UP, 1985.

Wagenknecht, Edward. *Harriet Beecher Stowe: The Known and the Unknown.* New York: Oxford UP, 1965.

Wilson, Forrest. *Crusader in Crinoline: The Life of Harriet Beecher Stowe.* Philadelphia: Lippincott, 1941.

Beyond Transcendence or Beyond Ideology: The New Problematics of Cultural Criticism in America

Giles Gunn

If one were looking for a way to describe contemporary American literary and cultural studies, one could scarcely do better than associate it not, as in Daniel Bell's phrase, with the "end of ideology," but rather with its rebirth. By this I mean that almost everywhere in humanistic scholarship these days, one finds people exploring cultural mind-sets that are presumed to define the conceptual and emotional frames within which readers like writers, historical actors like historical interpreters, determine what constitutes meaning. Nor is this analysis of ideology the preoccupation of any particular school of inter- pretation or specialty alone. Concern with ideology is no more exclusively the preserve of neo-Marxists than of Derrideans, of Renaissance scholars or of gender critics. Instead it serves to focus the work of most contemporary thinkers who seek to relate the products of individual consciousness to more collec- tive forms of mentality and to the systems of power that de- termine their significance.

Contemporary interest in ideology has not, however, de- veloped without certain problems of its own. One of them, though comparatively minor, is related to slippage in the term itself. In current American scholarship, for example, ideology refers to everything from ideas in the service of power to com- plex semiotic systems that, as Clifford Geertz has proposed, map the political world, simultaneously demarcating its bound- aries and furnishing directions about how to move around with- in it. About the only things these definitions share are that ideology is often disguised in the operations of cultural life, that its concealment results from the fact that ideological form is inevitably synecdochical, and that by substituting parts for wholes, ideologies seek to legitimate (or delegitimate) various kinds of social privilege.

A more serious problem derives from the difficulties that this "ideologization" of so much American scholarship creates for the possibilities of cultural criticism itself. If culture amounts to nothing more than a set of ideological formations permeating the semiological worlds that constitute it, as many of its modern students imply, then in what sense is it possible to achieve sufficient perspective on such formations to bring those worlds under critical scrutiny, much less to propose ways of revising them? In the writings of many of the most interesting contemporary American scholars — Philip Fisher, Myra Jehlen, Sacvan Bercovitch, Jonathan Arac, Walter Benn Michaels — this question is essentially rhetorical. Ideology not only conditions meaning in culture; it constitutes the whole of it. And it virtually does so by furnishing all of the terms by which culture might otherwise be challenged and surmounted from within. Walter Benn Michaels puts it this way: "Although transcending your origins in order to evaluate them has been the opening move in cultural criticism at least since Jeremiah, it is surely a mistake to take this move at face value: not so much because you can't really transcend your culture but because, if you could, you wouldn't have any terms of evaluation left — except, perhaps, theological ones" (18).[1] Therefore, as Myra Jehlen argues, critics must move toward a position that is "beyond transcendence" by moving back in the direction of those cultural — which is to say ideological — prejudices of gender, class, and race that make us the socially specific creatures that we, like our subjects, are (*Ideology* 1).

Jehlen's immediate reference is to those realms of unmediated spirit or eternal verity that were purportedly sought, or predictably defended, by the classic — and predominantly male — writers of the American Renaissance. But her phrase actually extends to any critical attempt to seek methodological refuge in some theoretical standpoint transcendent to experience itself. Such recursive gestures in the direction of a position putatively, as Lionel Trilling phrased it, "beyond culture" are now held, like their chief intellectual supports — the correspondence view of truth, the copy theory of knowledge, and the mimetic conception of art — to be mere creations of culture, and creations that have no other purpose than to subordinate one form of mentality to another. By privileging such semisacred abstractions as Reason, God, Liberty, Nature, the Over-Soul, Individualism, Democracy, the West, History, the People, or, latterly, the Orient, the Feminine, Blackness, Material Conditions, or the Third World, all forms of transcendentalism, so ideological critics contend, simply serve as disguised expressions of the will to power.

1

This diagnosis has by now become one of the familiar features of poststructuralist criticism in general. Suspicious of all conceptual attempts to hypostatize cultural alterity, the new ideological criticism seeks to redirect attention to those racial, economic, and sexual factors that are more material to aesthetic as well as social and political production. But as Edward Said has pointed out, this "Manichaean theologizing of the 'Other'" is by no means restricted to criticism that is prestructuralist. Rhetorical recourse to "transhuman authority," together with an often telltale reliance on varieties of indeterminacy, paradox, undecidability, the unthinkable, silence, the abyss of meaning, and nothingness is no less a feature of the contemporary criticism that foregrounds logocentricity and the disciplinary state than it is of that which privileges the single, separate, or what is otherwise known in America, thanks to Quentin Anderson, as "the imperial self."

According to Said, this critical deference to the metaphysics of cultural otherness reflects a residual religious nostalgia that inflects even the most militant modernist and postmodernist methodologies, and has converted many of them, no matter what their professed allegiances, into another variant of what can still nonetheless be described as "religious criticism" (291). By "religious criticism" Said means a good deal more than criticism that operates within the intellectual shelter of some traditional orthodoxy; he means all reflection that, he thinks, shares with most other religious discourses an interest in premature closure, in metanarrative, and in pious subservience to what William James called "the transempirical."

Said sets over against this a criticism that is worldly, iconoclastic, and "secular." Antithetical to all "organized dogma," this criticism would not only resist all forms of totalization, but would also be suspicious of all institutionalizations of "professionalism," in short, a criticism that is concerned to advance what Said calls "noncoercive knowledge produced in the interests of human freedom" by remaining disbelieving, cosmopolitan, and, above all, "oppositional" (29). Oppositional or secular criticism, as he envisions it, seeks to challenge and, where possible, to deconstruct all the forms in which literary study, whether intentionally or not, has collaborated in the maintenance of cultural, which in the modern West is to say, religiohumanistic piety; and along with others, like Jonathan Culler, Said associates the possibility for such oppositional thinking with a criticism that is not only intransigently adversarial but emphatically comparative.[2] Indeed, Said and Culler both come very close to identifying secular or oppositional criticism with the field or specialization of comparative literature itself, and they define comparative literary study, by which they really mean comparative cultural criticism, as essentially a critique of religion, or, rather, a critique of the potential forms of collusion, perhaps even conspiracy, between organized religion and the critical defense of the Western literary tradition that, so they hold, is implied by the titles of such widely known books as *The Genesis of Secrecy, The Great Code, Deconstruction and Theology,* and *Violence and the Sacred.*

Whether oppositional alterity is anything we can in fact think and thus practice—or even conceive and thus enact by thinking its opposite (since, as Derrida would say, "thinking . . . the opposite . . . is still in complicity with the classical alternatives" [95])—ideological critics like Jehlen would most likely put it differently. While sharing Said's suspicion that all forms of "religious criticism" are ethically retrograde and intellectually bankrupt, they would dispute his hope to establish a new basis for criticism in relation to "its difference," as he says, "from other cultural activities and from systems of thought and method" (29). The argument is based on the grounds that the process by which any cultural form produces and reproduces meaning—through developing mental sets that privilege certain semiotic systems for recognizing meaning and ignoring, suppressing, or effacing others—is largely hidden even from itself. Thus all texts, the more radical ideological critics would argue, even secular critical texts, are at best representations, at worst symptoms, of the process by which all cultures, like all languages, mask the effects of the ideas they promote.

2

This view of ideology is currently associated most closely in American humanistic scholarship with the "new historicism," and can be differentiated from the "old" by its construing the text as the site of a particular kind of production rather than a specific kind of reflection or refraction. The "old historicism" was, and is, defined most simply, and not inaccurately, in the well-known words from the preface to Edmund Wilson's *Axel's Castle,* as the attempt to provide "a history of man's ideas and imaginings in the setting of the conditions which shaped them" (x). Most old historicists, Erich Auerbach no less than Perry Miller, M. H. Abrams and Walter Jackson Bate no less than F. O. Matthiessen and Roy Harvey Pearce, have also understood this kind of history to be, in its way, broadly moral: they have assessed the value of what Wilson called "man's ideas and imaginings" in direct proportion to the amount of resistance they offer to their shaping conditions. Where these historicists have differed among themselves is over the question of what sorts of resistances the intellect and the imagination encounter in any given period, and what sorts of strategies, gestures, achievements constitute an overcoming of them.

The new historicism is based on the premise that to understand any representative human actions and aspirations historically is to come to terms with the way they are sedimented with, in Wittgenstein's sense, all the past "forms of life" that went into any given formulation of the principles informing them. To historicize them, then, is to see them configured both as products of meaning and also as processes for its creation. The new historicism aspires to subvert continually our tendency to foreground and possibly reify specific facts or objects of study (say, a literary text) by displacing "the immediately given fact," as Alan Trachtenberg has written, "with the profoundly mediated [cultural] process" by which it comes to us (36). The object is to resituate the text in the sociopolitical and economic sites of its production and thus to unmask the ideological factors that have concealed its true purpose.

How does one reconstruct after the fact the process by which the literary text rewrites or restructures the historical or ideological subtext, thus in part disguising its own productive operations?

The new historicism therefore always entails an interpretive rewriting of the literary text itself. But this rewriting assumes that the text itself is a rewriting of an ideological or historical subtext, "it being always understood that that 'subtext' is not immediately present as such, not some common-sense external reality, nor even the conventional narratives of history manuals, but rather must itself always be (re)constructed after the fact" (Jameson 81).

But how does one do this? How does one reconstruct after the fact the process by which the literary text rewrites or restructures the historical or ideological subtext, thus in part disguising its own productive operations? According to Jameson, the answer involves a fundamental reconception of historiographic method. To reconceive the text as exemplifying the production of meaning and not merely its reflection, one cannot conceive of the text as emerging from a prior moment in some developmental process. Nor can one define the text in relation to some external ground or context that is assumed to lie beyond it. To reconceive the text as an instantiation of meaning production, one must interrogate its materials for their formal and conceptual conditions of possibility. "Such analysis," Jameson writes, "thus involves the hypothetical *reconstruction* of the materials—content, narrative paradigms, stylistic and linguistic practices—which had to have been given in advance in order for that partial text to be produced in its unique historical specificity" (57–58).

From this perspective, the ideological is not something added onto or inserted into the aesthetic. It should be conceived rather as something inscribed within the aesthetic in a way that makes aesthetic creation, and therefore literary production as a whole, an ideological act in and of itself. Unless I am mistaken, however, to reconceive their relationship in this way also transforms the historical recovery of ideology into a fundamentally aesthetic act, since the historical reconstruction of the ideological is essentially an act of the imagination. And this reconstruction of the material conditions of possibility for the emergence of any text with this unique historical specificity produces what Jameson concedes to be a "hypothetical" structure.

Hence the point for the new historicist is not to establish a theoretical or critical perspective beyond the ideological but to resituate critical and theoretical reflection wholly within it. Yet this only raises the question as to whether the critic can ever escape the ideological contamination of his or her own processes of reflection. If he or she can, then the practices of ideological criticism confute its own premises. If not, then the moral aim of cultural criticism (to the degree that moral discrimination remains a meaningful critical activity to begin with) is reduced to little more than unmasking the mendacious.

3

In American literary and cultural studies, one of the most sophisticated and persuasive as well as influential advocates of ideological criticism in the new historicist mode (whether or not he is to be accurately described as a new historicist himself) is Sacvan Bercovitch. Yet his work is to be differentiated from other new historicist proponents of the study of the ideological by virtue of the lengths to which he has been increasingly prepared to carry it. For not only does he associate ideology with hegemony and history with self-fashioning; he also maintains in "The Problem of Ideology in American Literary History" that the interlinked system of ideas, symbols, and beliefs comprising ideology and controlling processes of historicization constitutes the chief means "by which a culture—any culture—seeks to justify and perpetuate itself" (635). So conceived, ideology is not only conservative but also coercive. What distinguishes it from other symbolic or semiotic systems with which it might be compared (art, religion, science, everyday gossip) is how it absorbs all the elements of cultural conflict within itself, converting the "rituals of diversity," as Bercovitch says, into "a rite of cultural assent" (635).

Bercovitch's most powerful expression of this view is still to be found in his well-known *The American Jeremiad.* A brilliant revisionist study of the rhetorical form that Perry Miller first isolated, a sermonic form that Puritan clergy employed on Election Days and other civic occasions to remind a backsliding people of their covenantal obligations to build a Holy Commonwealth in the New World, Bercovitch argues that Miller misinterpreted the function of the jeremiad. Far from defining the moral and spiritual costs of running this theological "errand into the wilderness," as Miller believed, and thus acquainting the faithful of New England with the exorbitant religious price of cultural accommodation, the jeremiadic declarations of seventeenth-century transgression, through their ritual repetitions of remonstrance, kept alive a sense of the sacredness of the original errand thus being betrayed; and by surviving a succession of historical transformations, these litanies of iniquity were, by the nineteenth century, to become the chief literary vehicle for the expression of the central American faith, or what Bercovitch, in the essay mentioned previously, calls simply "the American ideology" (635).

As the earliest form of cultural criticism in America, Bercovitch argues that the jeremiad became the principal instrument of socialization, the most potent discursive formula for developing national consensus. And even where the myth that lay at the heart of this consensus generated its detractors, as during the period known as the "American Renaissance," the ritualized rhetoric of the jeremiad still provided American authors like Melville, Hawthorne, or Stowe, who were inclined to rebel against aspects of that myth, not merely the terms but also the form to try to transcend it from within.

It therefore very nearly goes without saying that the efforts of writers like Emerson, Thoreau, Melville, and Whitman to transcend ideology by defining a position resistant, if not immune, to it were essentially futile. As Bercovitch remarks with perfect consistency but questionable reasoning, when the American Jeremiahs of the nineteenth and twentieth centuries thunder against their culture, they thunder in vain. The whole of their intellectual and literary revolt simply amounts to a rejection of America as it is—commercial for Emerson, materialist for Thoreau, racist and spiritually hypocritical for Melville, historically divided and emotionally stunted for Hawthorne, physically alienated and socially rigidified for Whitman—for the sake of creating in their art a vision of America as it ought to be—the commonplace converted into the sublime for Emerson, a middle landscape for Thoreau, the boundless realm of spiritual quest for Melville, a new era of sexual and spiritual frankness between human beings for Hawthorne, the insouciance and adventure of the Open Road for Whitman—but either way, they remain coiled within the very "American ideology" they would escape.

More recently, Bercovitch has found the monolithic sound of this last phrase both misleading and inaccurate, conceding that "the American ideology" is more like a rhetorical battleground of competing and often antagonistic outlooks than a symbolic synthesis. But he still insists that it retains sufficient coherence to reflect the interests and conceptual forms of the American middle class as it has evolved during three centuries of historical contradiction and discontinuity, and that it has thereby achieved "a hegemony unequaled elsewhere in the modern world" ("Problem" 636). Thus for all of his admirable circumspection about its univocality, Bercovitch is still prepared at times to accord "the American ideology" the power to convert all overt forms of cultural dissent into covert forms of cultural consensus and to reduce all expressions of political radicalism to the gestures of a reactionary politics:

> It undertakes above all, as a condition of its nurture, to absorb the spirit of protest for social ends; and according to a number of recent critics, it has accomplished this most effectively through its rhetoric of dissent. In this view, our classic texts re-present the strategies of a triumphant middle-class hegemony. Far from subverting the status quo, their diagnostic and prophetic modes attest to the capacities of the dominant culture to co-opt alternative forms to the

point of making basic change seem virtually unthinkable, except as apocalypse. This is not at all to minimize their protest. The point is not that our classic writers had no quarrel with America, but that they seem to have had nothing but that to quarrel about. Having adopted the culture's controlling metaphor—"America" as synonym for human possibility—and having made this tenet of consensus the ground of radical dissent, they redefined radicalism itself as an affirmation of cultural values. (645)

Despite Bercovitch's intentions to open up interpretation rather than close it off by "recognizing," as he puts it, "the limitations of ideology," there is, on his own account, nowhere beyond ideology from which to do so.[3] His own critique is no more capable of surviving the demolition of his argument than, by his own account, is Melville's or Emerson's. Like them, he too is imprisoned within the ideology of America, but only because he has supposed, or rather postulated, that its nineteenth-century critics invested the word "America" with precisely the same sense of human possibility as did the purported targets of their revisionism. To state this differently, by inscribing the ideological within the aesthetic, Bercovitch aestheticizes ideology by reducing the issue of its hegemony to a question of rhetoric that merely yields, in Jameson's terms, another "hypothetical" structure.

There are other difficulties in Bercovitch's position. For one thing, he, like other ideological critics, conflates the notion of ideology, or political templates for changing reality, with the concept of worldview, or metaphysical templates for describing reality. Therefore, he is left without any way of explaining how, as Leo Marx has demonstrated, a worldview like progressivism, which envisions American history as a record of continuous progress, could produce such different modern ideologies as, on the one hand, contemporary neoconservatism, which is committed to some variant of market capitalism, and, on the other, contemporary democratic socialism, which is committed to some form of collective solidarity (40–41).

For another, by everywhere assuming, though nowhere demonstrating, that the central fact of American history from colony to nation has been the steady growth of the middle class, and by insisting that this class has consolidated its power in the US chiefly through its rhetorical ability to define itself ideologically in terms of the sacred symbol of "America" itself, he nearly winds up re-treading an argument for American exceptionalism. This is accomplished by confusing the claim that all rhetorics of "redemptive" (meaning soteriological) American themes strengthen the hegemony of the middle class with the claim that, in the same way and to the same degree, the hegemony of the middle class is strengthened by any rhetorics redemptive of the thematics of America as such.

Last but not least, Bercovitch overlooks or discounts the counterideological, or at least potentially culturally subversive, impulses of this "redemptive rhetoric" in America by situating its origins in the seventeenth century, with the paradoxical effects of the Puritan jeremiad, rather than a century or more earlier, with the Renaissance development of what deserves to be called, after Walt Whitman, "New World metaphysics."[4] By locating the origins of America's culturally redemptive rhetoric in the self-contradictory oppositions of jeremiadic declension, Bercovitch glosses the fact that from its earliest European expressions—in everything from Christopher Columbus's "Letter to Lord Sanchez . . . on his First Voyage," Amerigo Vespucci's *Mundus Novus,* and Peter Martyr's *Decades of the New World* to Thomas Hariot's *Briefe and True Report of the New-found Land of Virginia,* Sir Walter Raleigh's *The Discovery of Guiana,* Shakespeare's *The Tempest,* and Francis Bacon's *The New Atlantis*—the term "America" has always served the political interests both of cultural consensus and of cultural dissensus.

In this sense, as Bercovitch would agree, "America" was invented before it was discovered, or discovered, as Edmundo O'Gorman has shown, in large part as a result of its "invention," and its symbolic invention was determined in no small measure by the Renaissance need to define a set of spiritual possibilities that were genuinely alternative to those that had become exhausted in Europe principally for Western men. The rhetorical history of America thus begins not with the betrayal of its symbolic definition in the colonial and postcolonial eras but rather with America's symbolic creation in the precolonial era. Furthermore, that history turns out to be a complex and contradictory record not only of how Europeans (and European ideologies) first imagined America and, conversely, how America (or the symbolic versions of it) eventually altered the imaginations and the ideologies of Europeans, but also of how the symbol's "sacred" meanings have never wholly lost their culturally adversarial tenor even when they have lent themselves to co-option by the vehicles of cultural or ideological dominance, indeed, even when they were produced at the expense of effacing the existence of "America's" native inhabitants. How else explain the almost palpable sense of moral, not just conceptual dissonance to which Bercovitch's own rhetoric can appeal, especially when it reveals discrepancies between professions of belief—with which the sacred symbol of America was, and still is, associated—and the social, political, and ethical practices it has tacitly as well as expressly promoted?

But these various objections ultimately boil down to one which derives from the philosophical prejudice built into a position like Bercovitch's and other ideological critics: that cultural texts are unable to engage in processes of reflection on the values that generate them without at the same time being subsumed by those values. Walter Benn Michaels expresses a typical example of this view when, in *The Gold Standard and the Logic of Naturalism,* he notes the futility of attempting to determine what it meant for Theodore Dreiser to approve or disapprove of consumer culture by observing that "it seems wrong to think of the culture you live in as the object of your affections: you don't like it or dislike it, you exist in it, and the things you like and dislike exist in it too" (18).

In addition to presupposing that culture is monolithic and essentially seamless, that it encompasses the whole of experience and is at every point consistent within itself, this view tends to conflate culture with ideology without furnishing any precise reasons as to how or when they are the same. Thus Michaels can first argue that "Even Bartleby-like refusals of the world remain inextricably linked to it—what could count as a more powerful exercise of the right to freedom of contract than Bartleby's successful refusal to enter into any contracts? Preferring not to, he embodies . . . the purest of commitments to laissez-faire, the freedom in contract to do as one likes" (18–19)—and then turn around and admit that such reasoning may be completely fallacious if, as Brook Thomas suggests, "Bartleby's persistent 'I would prefer not to' undermines the contractual ideology that dominated nineteenth century law" (qtd. in Michaels 19).

One question that is left hanging here—as it does over much ideological criticism—is how to decide between such alternatives. By what principle of interpretation, or in view of what material or textual evidence, does one determine that ideology does, or does not, encompass a given case? A second concerns the precise relationship between cultural form and ideological function. Not a little ideological criticism presumes that the effects of certain practices are inevitably predefined, at which

What gets lost in this blanket application of ideological categories to social practices is any sense either that ideologies function in different ways in different circumstances or that they are sometimes divided within and against themselves.

point, as Gerald Graff notes in an unpublished paper entitled "Criticism among the Crocodiles: Ideology, Literary History, and the Students," ideology becomes reduced to "a preestablished calculus of subversive and repressive traits," whereupon "any textual leaning toward individualism, naturalization, totalization, unified subjectivity, universalism, Cartesian dualism, narrative closure, the specular gaze, and determinate textual meaning can be designated as repressive, panoptic, and normalizing." Or to switch to the American cultural register, any reference to Nature, self-reliance, spiritual antinomianism, the innocent eye, the tragic vision, the frontier, pragmatic thinking, the machine in the garden, worlds elsewhere, experience, liberalism, or otherness itself, invokes what Bercovitch is otherwise fond of calling, in *The Puritan Origins of the American Self*, "the myth of America" (136–86).

What gets lost in this blanket application of ideological categories to social practices is any sense either that ideologies function in different ways in different circumstances or that they are sometimes divided within and against themselves. Kenneth Burke reminded us as long ago as 1931 that whatever else it is, an ideology is simply "an aggregate of beliefs sufficiently at odds with one another to justify opposite kinds of conduct" (163). There is also a blurring not only of the relationship between ideology and hegemony—the more or less articulate and formal meanings, values, and convictions by which a dominant group defines and extends its authority or power over others is not identical with the whole repertoire of practices and predispositions by which such meanings become experienced as whole, lived realities—but also of the difference between resemblances, parallels, analogies, and other structures of typification, on the one side, and homologies, or correspondences in origin and development as opposed to appearance and function, on the other (Williams 101–14).

Clearly, for example, the rhetoric of market capitalism in the antebellum period and its association with the concept of political freedom meant one thing to the American slave, Frederick Douglass, and quite another to white slaveholders. To Douglass, the ideological linkage between capitalism and liberty quickened his resolve to escape by enabling him for the first time to envisage what it might mean to lay claim to the rights of his own labor. To his Southern owners, on the other hand, the same rhetorical association further legitimated their practices by enabling them to view the "peculiar institution" as extending their rights as free people to hold property. Or, to

take another example of the different ways that ideology functions in different circumstances, even within the circumstances
of different rhetorics: if Herman Melville and the Young Americans of the 1830s and 1840s were both responsive to the antebellum challenge to create a culture commensurate with
America's democratic possibilities, they responded to that challenge in significantly different ways. What the Young Americans
wanted was simply a literature that would capture the spirit of
Jacksonian nationalism. What Melville produced in *Moby-Dick*
was a text that in drawing out the tragic dimensions of his
democratic and capitalist materials, while inverting the theological myth of historical entitlement to which they provided
ideological support, sought to reassociate the idea of "America"
or the "New World" with a realm of experience that (as he
dramatizes in "The Pacific") transcends all his culture's historically and culturally available God terms, including itself.

These examples obviously would not satisfy Bercovitch.
While conceding that free market values energized Douglass's
desire to escape the slave system, Bercovitch maintains that on
a deeper level those same values inevitably manipulated and
constrained Douglass, virtually reenslaved him, by restricting
his definition of freedom to the terms of "self-possessive individualism" provided by the ideology of antebellum Northern
culture ("Problem" 648). And Bercovitch would no doubt argue
that, so long as Melville's desire to overcome the God terms
provided by his culture still derived from the critique he made
of those same God terms, his quest never succeeded in escaping
the ideological system in relation to which it defined itself. But
by this point ideological criticism risks becoming wholly circular, even tautological. What is worse, this ideological self-
reflexivity is almost inevitably achieved, as Milan Kundera attempted to demonstrate in *The Unbearable Lightness of Being,*
at the price of rendering everything that it would encompass
but cannot quite subsume simultaneously trivial and meaningless, weightless and banal.

Even where, as new historicists and others have shown so
convincingly, ideology is omnipresent, it need not be construed
as necessarily omnipotent. But to perceive its dominance as
limited, or at least as potentially limited and even selective,
requires reconceiving critical inquiry itself and the place of ideological analysis within it. What is needed is a form of critical
inquiry that, like the new historicism, sees the ideological as
inscribed within the aesthetic but does not go on to interpret
this to mean that the aesthetic is merely another hostage of the

ideological. To reconceive critical inquiry in this fashion is to resituate it midway between the kind of so-called religious criticism, to invoke Said's term again, that merely deforms otherness through Manichaean idealizations of it, and the "secular criticism," as Culler defines it, that constitutes itself solely through the making absolute of intellectual contrariety or opposition. Rather than effacing difference, like the first, or fetishizing it, like the second, critical inquiry should be devoted to comprehending difference by repositioning its interpretation and discussion in the sociopolitical and psychosexual spaces of its actual or imagined implications for practice.

4

Among American intellectuals, if not modern intellectuals, one of the very first to understand this fact within the terms of this present discussion was, so far as I know, William James. That is, James was the first American thinker to argue that while ideology, or something very much like it, colors the whole of our conceptual life as human beings, it does not, or at least need not, determine all the ways we can reflect on this process.

There is no little irony in the fact that some of James's richest reflections on this process occur in an essay entitled "Humanism and Truth." On James's reading, humanism should have taught us that experience comes to us initially in the form of questions that are then digested or assimilated through reference to fundamental categories wrought so long ago into the structure of human consciousness that at least within specific cultural traditions they seem practically irreversible. This apparent irreversibility in turn allows the categories themselves not only to dictate "the general frame within which answers must fall" but also "gives the detail of the answers in the shapes most congruous with all our present needs" (168). We thus encounter experience culturally, James argued, as "now so enveloped in predicates historically worked out that we can think of it as little more than an *Other,* of a *That* . . . to [which] we respond by ways of thinking which we call 'true' in proportion as they facilitate our mental or physical activities and bring us outer power and inner peace" (169).

To the humanist this meant, or should mean, James deduced, that reality is, as a Pierre Macherey or even a Louis Althusser might as easily say, "an accumulation of our own intellectual inventions" (or interpretations) and truth therefore a function of the relation between our notions and our needs (169). But James differentiated his own position from that of many contemporary ideological critics who take their cues from an Althusser or a Macherey—Bercovitch among them— by insisting that our needs do not thereby inevitably imprison us within our notions. For James reasoned that even if we cannot determine whether these inventions or interpretations of ours, these ideological "Others" or "Thats," possess any absolute or real structure—or if they have any, whether that "structure resembles any of our predicated *whats*"—we can, James concluded, assisted by the critical imagination, determine the difference it makes to think so, or the alterations in experience that would be necessary if we thought otherwise (169).

This is the task that James assigned to the much maligned theory of critical inquiry he termed pragmatism. Better described a generation later by Dewey as "the discipline of severe thought" (35), pragmatism was devised as a procedure for liberating, in Foucault's words, "the power of truth" from "the truth of power." James and Dewey both believed, in other words, that if truth, as we would now say in this ideological age, is always related to some system of power, humanists can still emancipate it "from the forms of hegemony, social, economic, and cultural, within which it operates at the present time" (Foucault 133). The challenge is to develop critical strategies for determining what our encounters with experience as an ideological predicate do to us and what our re-predicating of experience as a form of conceptual alterity does to it.

Dewey described this for himself as a process of "intellectual disrobing" in which we seek to examine the forms of cultural sense-making we call values to see what the wearing of them does to us and what happens to them when we put them on. Dewey by no means supposed that anyone can shed entirely the garments of culture and recover in experience the condition of actually living without them, but he did hold with much recent hermeneutic theory that, by imaginative reconstruction and intelligent analysis of the situations from which values arise and the results in which they issue, one can repossess what he described as a kind of "secondary naivete," or cultivated innocence of the sort that is sometimes available to us in, say, aesthetic experience. Beyond this, Dewey insisted more emphatically than James that the crucial intellectual meaning of the "discipline of severe thought" known as pragmatism lay not in its importance as an end in itself but as our chief instrument for furthering culture as a whole. Only by emancipating and expanding the meanings of which experience is capable, Dewey wrote, can culture advance; and only by critically assessing the valuations of which cultural experience is composed can the meanings potential to it, but not yet effectively realized within it, be successfully liberated. Such liberation was to Dewey as well as to other pragmatists but another name for social reform.[5]

It could therefore be said that pragmatism affords the possibility of doing cultural criticism from a perspective that is not only "beyond transcendence," as Jehlen conceives it, but also "beyond ideology," as Bercovitch describes it. Such a perspective is located beyond ideology and transcendence alike not because it can escape their superventions but only because it can resist their simplifications. As James noted as early as 1876 in an article on "The Teaching of Philosophy in Our Colleges," pragmatism may be no more than "the habit of always seeing an alternative, of not taking the usual for granted, of making conventionalities fluid again, of imagining foreign states of mind" (178); but it is a habit capable of cultivation precisely because the dominance of all social systems, the hegemony of all ideologies is, as Raymond Williams maintained, inevitably selective. Since no social system can exhaust what Said calls "the essential unmasterable presence that constitutes a large part of historical and social situations" (241), there is always potential space left over—James termed it the increment of "the More"—for what Williams described as "alternative acts and alternative intentions which are not yet articulated as a social institution or even [a] project" (252).

This is the space that pragmatic criticism, to be sure in various ways, likes to explore—Said's no less than James's, Poirier's, Goodman's, or Bernstein's, Rorty's no less than Dewey's, or Cavell's, or Lentricchia's—by reconceiving texts not only as, in deconstructionist terms, undecidable objects, nor as, in variants of Marxist criticism, ideological templates, but also as sites of effective action, as scenes of forceful statement— "with consequences," as Said writes, "that criticism should make it its business to reveal" (225). From this it should be clear that while pragmatic criticism advocates no particular policies, it does possess a specifiable politics. It is a politics distinguished by the democratic preference to render differences conversable so that the conflicts they produce, instead of being destructive of human community, can become potentially creative of it.

This is a politics that can still be called humanistic, then, not because it is based on some unitary conception of humanity, much less because it assumes that any conception of the human must be grounded in a structure of things impervious to the contingencies of experience itself. It is humanistic for two other reasons: first, because it views all attempts to make cultural discourse monologistic or univocal as forms of totalism, even possibly of totalitarianism; and, second, because in the realm of critical and theoretical practice it measures all forms of totalism, and especially of totalitarianism, against the distinctly dialogical and moral gauge that Hayden White finds in Fredric Jameson: "any theory must be measured by its capacity, not to demolish its opponents, but to expropriate what is valid and insightful in its strongest critics" (144).

Notes

1.   This is, as we shall see, an odd way to put it, especially for a new historicist like Michaels. In addition to supposing that theology is something other than a cultural form, it implies that there is some kind of reflective practice or theoretical discourse that could or does exist above history.

2.   Said's position is most fully adumbrated in the two chapters from *The World, the Text, and the Critic*; Culler's in "Comparative Literature and the Pieties" (esp. 30–32). Of the two, Said's seems the more moderate. At times he speaks as though "secularity" involves little more than a skeptical, self-consciously situated criticism "reflectively open to its own failings" and by no means value free. At other times, however, he speaks of "secular" or "oppositional criticism" as one which is not only suspicious of all totalizing, reifying, dominating habits of mind, but also as one wholly defined by its "difference from other cultural activities and from systems of thought or of method." The more the identity of this kind of criticism is based upon self-consciously maintained differences from every other mental activity or form, the more it succumbs, because of its wholly oppositional nature, to a totalization of its own.

3.   One of the many attractive features of Bercovitch's writing is his willingness to declare the "principles" of his own "ideological dependence": "I hold these truths to be self-evident: that there is no escape from ideology; that so long as human beings remain political animals they will always be bounded in some degree by consensus; and that so long as they are symbol-making animals they will always seek in some way to persuade themselves (and others) that *their* symbology is the last, best hope of mankind" ("Problem" 636). From these sensible principles concerning the ubiquity of ideology it does not follow, however, that the coerciveness of ideology is absolute.

4.   See Edmundo O'Gorman's *The Invention of America* and my *New World Metaphysics*, esp. xix–xxii, 3–37.

5.   For a fuller discussion of these points, see my "John Dewey and the Culture of Criticism."

Works Cited

Anderson, Quentin. *The Imperial Self.* New York: Knopf, 1971.

Bercovitch, Sacvan. *The American Jeremiad.* Madison: U of Wisconsin P, 1978.

———. "The Problem of Ideology in American Literary History." *Critical Inquiry* 12 (1986): 631–53.

———. *The Puritan Origins of the American Self.* New Haven: Yale UP, 1975.

Bercovitch, Sacvan, and Jehlen, Myra, eds. *Ideology and Classic American Literature.* Cambridge: Cambridge UP, 1986.

Burke, Kenneth. *Counter-statement.* Berkeley: U of California P, 1968.

Culler, Jonathan. "Comparative Literature and the Pieties." *Profession 86.* 30–32.

Derrida, Jacques. *Writing and Difference.* Trans. Alan Bass. Chicago: U of Chicago P, 1978.

Foucault, Michel. *Power/Knowledge: Selected Interviews and Other Writings, 1972–1977.* New York: Pantheon, 1980.

Geertz, Clifford. *The Interpretation of Cultures.* New York: Basic, 1973.

Gunn, Giles. *New World Metaphysics.* New York: Oxford UP, 1981.

———. "John Dewey and the Culture of Criticism." *Works and Days* 5 (1987): 7–26.

James, William. *Pragmatism and Other Essays.* New York: Washington Square P, 1972.

———. "The Teaching of Philosophy in Our Colleges." *Nation* 23 (1876): 178.

Jameson, Fredric. *The Political Unconscious.* Ithaca: Cornell UP, 1981.

Marx, Leo. "Pastoralism in America." Bercovitch and Jehlen 36–39.

Michaels, Walter Benn. *The Gold Standard and the Logic of Naturalism.* Berkeley: U of California P, 1987.

O'Gorman, Edmundo. *The Invention of America.* Bloomington: Indiana UP, 1961.

Said, Edward W. *The World, the Text, and the Critic.* Cambridge: Harvard UP, 1983.

Trachtenberg, Alan. "Comments on Evan Watkins' 'Cultural Criticism and the Literary Intellectual,' " *Works and Days* 3 (1985): 35–39.

White, Hayden. *The Content of the Form.* Baltimore: Johns Hopkins UP, 1987.

Williams, Raymond. *Politics and Letters: Interviews with* New Left Review. London: New Left Books, 1979.

Wilson, Edmund. *Axel's Castle.* New York: Scribner's, 1931.

The Ties that Bind: Race and Sex in *Pudd'nhead Wilson*

Myra Jehlen

Literary fictions can no more transcend history than real persons. Though certainly not universally acknowledged, in the current criticism this truth has replaced the former truth that literature was a thing apart. Once banned from the interpretation of books for violating the integrity of the imagination, considerations of race and sex (and of class) have entered into even the most formalist readings.[1] Race and sex are now found organic to problems of organic form. As a result, those problems have become vastly more complicated than when a literary work was thought to invent its own sufficient language. For then the task of the critic, though complex, was also simple; it was to show how all parts worked together, in the conviction that coherence would be revealed. A poem or story was a puzzle for which critics could be sure they had all the pieces and that these dovetailed.

Now neither assurance is available; one cannot be certain a work seen as engaged in history is internally coherent, or that the issues it treats finally hang together. This development is not altogether congenial to literary critics who mean to analyze works, not to dismantle them. But if we take literature's link to history seriously, we will have to admit that it renders literature contingent, like history itself. My case in point is *Pudd'nhead Wilson* whose writing posed problems that the history of racial and sexual thinking in America made impossible to resolve. The ideologies of race and sex Mark Twain contended with in this novel were finally not controllable through literary form. They tripped the characters and tangled the plot. *Pudd'nhead Wilson* exemplifies the tragedy of the imagination, a literary kind that, ironically, only a historical criticism can fully appreciate.

Pudd'nhead Wilson builds its plot upon a plot. The subversive schemer is a young slave mother named Roxana (Roxy) who is thrown into panic one day by her master's casual threat to sell some of his slaves downriver, deeper into the more hellish South. Reasoning that if the master can sell these, he can as readily sell her baby, Roxy first determines to kill herself and the child rather than lose it to the slave market. Then she finds another way. Not only a mother but the mammy of her master's child, she simply switches the infants, who look so much alike that no one suspects the exchange. In contrast to their perfect resemblance as babies, the two boys grow up totally unlike. The black child taking the white's name of Tom (for Thomas à Becket Driscoll), becomes a treacherous, cowardly thief, while the white child, assuming the black name, Valet de Chambre, shortened to Chambers, is gentle, loyal, honest, and brave. Tom's path of petty crime leads eventually to murder, and his victim is his putative uncle and guardian, the much loved benevolent Judge Driscoll. A pair of visiting foreign twins are wrongly accused of the crime and are about to be convicted when Pudd'nhead Wilson, a local sage in the tradition of shrewd Ben Franklin, uncovers the real murderer who is, coincidentally, the real black. The amiable foreigners are vindicated, the real white man is freed from his erroneous bondage and restored to his estate, and the murderer is punished. Since he is not really a gentleman but a slave, he has to be punished as a slave and is sold downriver.

Twain starts off simply enough with a farce whose characters' opportunistic prevarications expose established lies. The lie Roxy exposes when she successfully replaces her master's child with her own is that racial difference is inherent. As the basis for slavery, this racism is unambiguously false, its inversion of human truth dramatized in Roxy's dilemma: she can jump in the river with her baby or live in daily peril of its being sold. Given those alternatives, her stratagem appears righteous and even fair, despite its concomitant enslavement of the white baby. Without condoning this but simply by focusing on Roxy and her child, the story enlists the reader wholly on their side, since the failure of the scheme can mean only the separate sale of mother and child, or their common death.

But then things take an odd turn which will culminate in an about-face, the reversal ultimately going so far as to transform the exposure of Roxy and her son into a happy ending that rights wrongs, rewards the good, punishes the bad, and restores order all around. When, at the eleventh hour, Pudd'nhead Wilson unmasks Tom and justice is done, the reader is actually relieved and gratified. If by this intervention the story does not exactly celebrate the return of the escaped slave to bondage or his sale to the demons of tidewater plantations, neither does it lament these events. Roxy's broken spirit and the double defeat of her maternal hopes are pitiable sights, but there is a consolation prize. In *Pudd'nhead Wilson*'s finally rectified moral economy, Roxy's punishment is quite moderate. Not only are the legal authorities of the town of Dawson's Landing forbearing, but "The young fellow upon whom she had inflicted twenty-three years of slavery continued [the pension she had been receiving from Tom]" (114). Exemplary generosity, to be sure, and a startling turnaround: for Roxy, who once was so helplessly enslaved that her only recourse was suicide, is now being represented as herself an enslaver. Adding insult to injury, the pension her victim bestows upon her makes her appear still more culpable. Roxy and her baby exit as the villains of a story they entered as the innocently wronged.

Twain recognized that this about-face required explanation. One reason Tom turned out so badly and Chambers so well, the narrator suggests, is because they were brought up in opposite ways. "Tom got all the petting, Chambers got none. . . ." The result was that "Tom was 'fractious,' as Roxy called it, and overbearing, Chambers was meek and docile" (18–19). Slavery is made to counter racism here in much the way it does in *Uncle Tom's Cabin* and not to any better effect. Here the black man made Christlike by his sufferings is really white, so that, in the absence of real blacks similarly affected, the case is not fully made. All that these distortions of character argue is the evil of human bondage, not the equality of master and slave. For Stowe countering racism was incidental; indeed, she had only a limited interest in battling it, needing only to establish the humanity of the slaves in order to prosecute her central case, which was against slavery. But this was not Twain's situation when he published *Pudd'nhead Wilson* in 1894, thirty-two years after Emancipation. This novel, and its story of the baby exchange, has little to do with slavery: the plot does not follow Chambers the white slave to depict the horrors of his condition; instead, it settles on Tom, the black master, and the crimes he has all his freedom to perpetrate. In appropriate contrast to Stowe's novel, *Pudd'nhead Wilson* is only peripherally concerned with the atrocities of the slave system. Although Chambers is sadly disadvantaged by his years of servitude, his debility has too little force to motivate the novel and nothing much comes from it or is expected to. On the contrary, everything comes from Tom's ascension to power—all of it bad.

Nothing in the original premise of the story predicts this

sad development, so the obvious question is *Why does Tom, the former slave, turn out so villainous and dangerous a master?* The most congenial explanation—that Tom has been fatally corrupted by his translation into the class of oppressors—omits too much of the story to serve. Twain offers it only halfheartedly, presenting the real white planters as a decent lot, absurd in their chivalric poses, inadequate to their ruling tasks, but men of integrity, faithful to their "only religion," which is to be gentlemen "without stain or blemish." Even their slave owning seems less evil than careless. The description of Pembroke Howard as "a fine, brave, majestic creature, a gentleman according to the nicest requirements of the Virginian rule" mingles affection with mockery, and while his dash is balderdash, there are worse things, like Tom. His sale of Roxy treacherously and symbolically downriver is presented as transcendently evil, an act so wicked as to brand him an unnatural son and a denatured man. To underline the exceptional quality of this betrayal, Twain shows him prepared to sell his mother twice over, for when she escapes and seeks his help against pursuing slave hunters, only her threat to repay him in kind prevents him from turning her over.

It is more than a little perverse that the two characters actually seen trafficking in slavery are both black. Percy Driscoll's threat to sell his misbehaving slaves is the novel's original sin that leads to Roxy's desperate deed. Having the sale itself take place offstage and specifying that, unlike Tom, the Judge only sells to his relatively humane neighbors and not to the Simon Legrees of the Deep South, serves to attenuate our sense of the planter's guilt. Yet the story pointedly reports Tom's plan to sell his boyhood companion Chambers, a plan foiled by Judge Driscoll who buys Chambers to safeguard the family honor; "for public sentiment did not approve of that way of treating family servants for light cause or for no cause" (22); Tom's corrupting environment, therefore, does not explain why the disguised black is both more deeply and differently corrupted than his fellow slave owners, a development that is the more startling because it reverses the initial expectations of virtue inspired by his first appearance as a hapless babe.[2]

But if no explanation emerges directly from the novel, consider its historical context. 1894—the year of its publication—was the eve of McKinley's election and a period of accelerating racism marked by the bloody spread of Jim Crow. The formative experience of *Pudd'nhead Wilson*'s era was the defeat of Reconstruction, not the end of slavery. In that context the story of the replacement of a white baby by a black one has a local urgency we may miss at this distance. The progress from a good thing to a bad as the black boy grows up to murder the town patriarch who is his uncle, and to rob, cheat, and generally despoil the whole village, as well as plunging his mother into a worse state than before, makes as much sense in history as it fails to make in the story.

For in the story Tom's villainy appears only arbitrary. As much as Twain justifies Roxy's revolution by appealing to the transcendent motive of maternal love, making her insurrection finally inevitable and in no way a sign even of inherent rebelliousness, he damns Tom from the start as "a bad baby, from the very beginning of his usurpation" (17). So the good black is a woman; the bad, a man. The good woman, complicated enough within herself to act for the bad, while remaining good, is black; the black, lacking interiority and simply expressing a given identification which is barely an identity, is a bad man. With this formula, *Pudd'nhead Wilson* emerges as a remarkable exploration of the anxieties aroused by a racist social structure, as a literary locus classicus of one modern (in its integrating of individualist concepts of identity) paradigm of race, and perhaps most strikingly, as the exposition of the relation between the paradigm of race and a modern one of gender. The conjunction of race and sex is more often pictured as an *intersection* but here it is an *interaction*. Moreover, this interaction does not simply join but combines them so that in certain pairings they are more stringently limiting than when taken separately.

When Twain associates the black race with the female sex, he represents racism in the uncontroversially repugnant form of slavery. Roxy's force and shrewdness work to disprove stereotypes of servility. Her sovereignty over the children extends naturally to the story of which she is a sort of author. She achieves the highest status available to a fictional character when she and the narrator are the only ones who know what is going on and can truly identify the participants. The white baby's mother is dead and his own father fails to recognize him. Roxy alone knows who and what he is. Furthermore, the way she knows this bears its own antiracist implications; since both babies have flaxen curls and blue eyes, her discrimination can have nothing to do with physical characteristics. Thus as she identifies them, *who* Tom and Chambers are is entirely independent of *what* they are: they embody the American ideal of individualism, the belief that a man is what he makes of himself, potentially anything he determines.

The progress from a good thing to a bad as the black boy grows up to murder the town patriarch who is his uncle, and to rob, cheat, and generally despoil the whole village, as well as plunging his mother into a worse state than before, makes as much sense in history as it fails to make in the story.

Consonant with this liberal view, *Pudd'nhead Wilson* initially defines black character in universal traits as benign as Roxy herself. If Roxy at times succumbs to the lure of unattended objects, "Was she bad?" Twain muses. "Was she worse than the general run of her race?" "No. They had an unfair show in the battle of life, and they held it no sin to take military advantage of the enemy—in a small way." Twain insists, "in a small way, but not in a large one" (11). Even as he writes this, Roxy takes the very large military advantage of exchanging the infants. But the petty thievery, in this case not even her own, that has called down the wrath of her master and thus precipitated this ultimate transgression *was* a very small crime. If Roxy's pilfering turns to pillage, the novel suggests that this is not her fault, hardly even her doing, but that of a criminal society that monstrously deforms both marginally guilty relations and purely innocent ones.

The night of the exchange, Percy Driscoll, whose threat to punish any theft by selling the thief has raised for Roxy the specter of her child's own commodity status, sleeps the sleep of the just. By contrasting the white master's smug oblivion to the black slave's anguished wakefulness, the one scene in which she becomes the story's consciousness, Twain condones and even endorses her crime. The novel continues to side with her when it is not Roxy but Percy Driscoll who enforces the children's inequality by permitting the ostensibly white boy to abuse the child whom the father fails to recognize as his son. In this representation of the political economy of slavery in terms of the family, the author's voice speaks against the regnant patriarchy, espouses the oppressed, applauds subversion. Fathers in Mark Twain are not a nice lot, and boys are frequently abused. A black woman enslaved by white men is the natural ally of white boys. Would that all boys had mothers like Roxy!

Tom's becoming a man, however, rearranges this scheme radically. His passage into manhood, marked by his return from Yale, seems to start the story over. At Yale he has been a desultory student but has acquired a number of grown-up ways that pose unprecedented grown-up problems. His indifferent intellect has prevented any deeper penetration, but Tom has acquired the superficies of elite culture, its dainty dress and its mannered ways. The local youths naturally scorn such refinements, but when they set a deformed black bell-ringer dressed in parodic elegance to follow Tom about, the young popinjay is debunked more profoundly than anyone in the story suspects. It is unclear just what is being satirized: is it simply Tom's pretensions or some special absurdity of black foppery? Since the characters are unaware that their parody of Tom possesses this additional dimension, it becomes a joke shared by the narrator and the reader, a joke with a new target.

Twain had already mocked black dress when he described a despairing Roxy adorning herself for her suicide. Her ribbons and feathers, her wondrously gaudy dress, are certainly meant to reflect on her race, but the butt of the joke is not race per se. Being black is not given as ridiculous, though blacks may behave ridiculously. In the later episode being black is itself absurd: the private joke we share with the narrator is the very fact of Tom's negritude, that while pretending to be a highfalutin gentleman, he is really a "Negro." The novel begins here its turnaround from the initial view implicit in the identical babies, that human beings are potentially the same, to the final dramatization in the Judge's murder, of black duplicity and violence as inherent racial traits.

Tom's grown-up inferiorities make his spoiled childhood irrelevant. He cannot have acquired his fear of dueling, for instance, from being raised a southern gentleman. While his overexcited peers in Dawson's Landing fall to arms at the least imagined slight, Tom turns tail at the first sign of a fight. This is only one of a constellation of traits defining Tom as a different sort of beau ideal, the very type of the upstart Negro of post-Reconstruction plantation fiction: cowardly, absurdly pretentious, lazy and irresponsible, a petty thief but potentially a murderer. Born the generic, universal baby, Tom has grown into a very particular sort of man, unlike both his white and his black fellows, because on the white side, he is not capable of being a master, and on the black, he has been dangerously loosed from the bonds that keep other black men in check.

I want to stress the next point because it is central to the racial/sexual paradigm developed in *Pudd'nhead Wilson*. The white man who has taken Tom's place might have been expected, in the context of the novel's increasingly essentialist view of race, also to manifest an essential nature. He does not. "Meek and docile" in adaptation to his powerless state, Chambers yet does not become a white man fatally misplaced among blacks, as Tom is a black man fatally misplaced among whites. This asymmetry embodies a typing that applies only to the inferior race. The superior race, when defining itself in the terms of modern individualism, claims not a better type, but the general norm—universality, or the ability to be any type and all of them.

Unhappily for Chambers, however, universality imparts only potential, a capacity to become rather than an already defined (therefore limited) being. That is, what characterizes the norm embodied in the superior race, instead of a particular set of traits, is universal potential. Such potential realizes itself in relation to environment: ironically, the white "Chambers" is far more vulnerable to the shaping force of the exchange, for had Tom remained a slave he would have unfolded into essentially the same man, though a crucially less powerful one and for that reason a less harmful one. So Chambers, unlike Tom, adapts to his sad situation and is shaped by it. In one important respect his adaptation represents one of the novel's most basic, though unacknowledged issues. I suggested earlier that while in Roxy, Twain endorses a black woman's subversion of the white patriarchy, in Tom he rejects a black man's takeover. The fate of Chambers begins to explain why Twain distinguished so sharply between mother and son by revealing the stake in his relation to the latter.

That stake is manhood. Through Tom's usurpation, the white community of Dawson's Landing risks losing its manhood. A black woman exercising the authority of motherhood in a white society may call in question the domestic ideology of white womanhood. In *Pudd'nhead Wilson* this domestic ideology means the genteel sentimentalism of aunts and widows. Had it been only a question of Roxy's passing off her child as the child of a white lady, the baby switch would have been a disturbing but limited affair. But the far more encompassing event of a black man occupying the place of a white man, wielding the same power, usurping (Twain's repeated term) the authority of white fatherhood, connotes a global reversal: instead of being emancipated, the iconoclastic boy who typically articulates Twain's abhorrence of genteel culture is emasculated. The subversion in Tom's usurpation of white identity turns Chambers into a woman, for feminization is the lasting result of that unfortunate man's slave upbringing. Once a black slave, he can never take his place among his real peers: "The poor fellow could not endure the terrors of the white man's parlor, and felt at home and at peace nowhere but in the kitchen" (114). Note that Chambers's loss of manhood is clearly regrettable only because he is white. A black man may be improved by the attenuations of femininity, as Twain's motherly Jim is elsewhere. One stereotype of the black man threatens violence and uncontrollable sex. The other has him contemptibly effeminate. Black men are seen simultaneously as excessively male and insufficiently masculine. Entangled in these ideological contradictions, Tom is incoherently both. While his final act is a stabbing, at an earlier point in the story he robs houses disguised as a woman. The witnesses who fail to recognize in a dress the man they know as a white gentleman are actually seeing the real Tom, who thus shows himself not to be a real man.

By the logic of the different *kind* of identity that real men develop, a black mother can be the ally of rebellious boys, but a black father would rob them of their very identities as heirs to the mantle of universal (white) manhood. We stand with Roxy when she defies the social order to save her son. But when this child grows up, he embodies a revolution which has displaced the erstwhile ruling children, usurping their manhood. Once this implication has been realized by the story's unfolding, even the benignity of Roxy's crime seems retrospectively less certain. On the last page of the novel, the story finally represents the exchange not as freeing the black child but as enslaving the white.

That was all along implicit in a situation whereby the only way to free Tom is to enslave Chambers. This unhappy reciprocity, however, is not manifest in the story as long as it focuses on mothers and children. The maternal economy in this novel is a welfare state. Its central concern is not production but distribution, and even when it is unfair, it has primarily to do with giving: allocating privileges and goods among the more or less undifferentiated members of a group who seek more not from each other but from the mother/state. Production, not distribution, is the chief care of the market/capitalist economy of the US in the late nineteenth century; and in that context, distribution is a matter of competitive acquisition.

Much has been written about the relation of these two economies which in some respects confront and in others complement each other.[3] The peculiar slant of *Pudd'nhead Wilson* comes from presenting them not, as usual, synchronically, as simultaneous dimensions of one society, but diachronically, the market economy following the maternal. Thus sequentially related, with each one in its time defining the fictional universe, their contradictions emerge more sharply, along with the way that the hierarchy of family and state, private and public, gives the market the last word. It certainly has the last word in *Pudd'nhead Wilson*. While a mother may take something from one child and give it to another who needs it more but not deprive the former, in an economy in which personally recuperable profit is the bottom line, taking away and giving has ultimately

The maternal economy in this novel is a welfare state. Its central concern is not production but distribution, and even when it is unfair, it has primarily to do with giving: allocating privileges and goods among the more or less undifferentiated members of a group who seek more not from each other but from the mother/state.

to show up on the ledger. And when self-sufficient individuals—which means men and fathers—possess unequal amounts of power or wealth, reallocation, however equitable, means deprivation: one gets only by taking away from the other. At the point at which the story of Tom and Chambers leaves the nursery and enters the marketplace, Tom, once the innocent and even rightful recipient of the freedom he unjustly lacked, becomes a usurper, while Chambers is seen to have been robbed.

The maternal and market economies which in their turn dominate the plot of *Pudd'nhead Wilson* coexist to a degree. Though the story starts out in Roxy's control, the market wields overwhelming force from the first since the power of whites to sell blacks to other whites inspires the exchange of the babies. But at this point, even though slavery functions as a harsh necessity in Roxy's world that will ultimately deprive her of all power, the market as such is not yet the primary setting. Indeed, when this necessity first manifests itself, she resists successfully, temporarily returning her world to its prior order and keeping both babies. All through their infancy and childhood she administers her welfare system, taking care of both of them as fairly as she can under the circumstances, despite the fact that her own child is in the master position and would be favored if she were to implement fully the unfairness of the slave system. When Tom is no longer a mother's child but his own man, however, he takes over the fictive universe and administers it his way. His administration participates directly in the patriarchal economy, and in this new context the baby exchange realizes its meaning in the trade of Chambers's white manhood for Tom's black impotence, and vice versa.

Because the asymmetries of race and of sex are parallel, Roxy's innate character as a mother is congruent with being a black woman. Paradoxically, even ironically, this very limit permits Twain to endow her with a considerable potential for transcendence, the way that Flaubert, say, endows Emma with much of his own sense of self without ever questioning the nontranscendence of female selfhood.[4] So Roxy, a black woman, actually approaches individualist selfhood, while her son is denied it altogether and is depicted as capable of achieving self-creative powers only by the outright usurpation of whiteness. On the other side, Chambers's failure to achieve manhood, in dramatizing the transcendence of white identity which defines itself by going beyond nature, also points up a terrible vulnerability that springs from the very quality that makes white men superior. For to be capable of making oneself and one's world is a very fine thing, but it has its price. The price of white men's power of self-creation is the risk of failing not only to achieve but to be, while women (though not always as fictional characters) and blacks are essentially, and thus invulnerably, what they are born. This inequality of vulnerability counterbalances racial inequality, coming first, in the ideological and psychological world of *Pudd'nhead Wilson,* to equate the plights of blacks and whites, then finally to make blacks appear stronger or at least more threatening.

An essentialist identity requires, for the good of the community, more social control. An essentialist identity is too little vulnerable to be allowed as much freedom as selves that are constrained by their own vulnerability. It is generally recognized that the ratio of self-making to being determines the status of modern individuals, so that the more a man is his own author, the higher he ranks and the more authority he wields. The converse is less often articulated; an essentialist identity not only brands the socially inferior but necessitates their submission. In one scene of *Pudd'nhead Wilson* this logic very nearly justifies slavery.

When Chambers reveals to Roxy that her errant son is a dissolute gambler, who at the moment owes the huge sum of two hundred dollars, Roxy is stunned: "Two—hund'd—dollahs! . . . Sakes alive, it's mos' enough to buy a tollable good second-hand nigger wid." Now the irony here is that the two hundred dollars Tom has gambled away are two hundred dollars *he* would fetch, being himself "a tollable good second-hand nigger." Thus the possibility of buying and selling human beings, which up until now has implied such intolerable violations of natural law as the separation of mothers and children, has become, astonishingly, a way to measure and *preserve* genuine value: Tom's worthlessness as a white man is measured by his gambling away his worth as a slave. Lest we not grasp this point fully, Twain spells it out in the ensuing dialogue. Chambers's report that Tom has been disinherited for his scandalous conduct infuriates Roxy who accuses her supposed son of lying, calling him a "misable imitation nigger." Chambers retorts, "If I's imitation, what is you? Bofe of us is imitation white— dat's what we is—en pow'full good imitation, too . . . we don't 'mount to noth'n as imitation niggers" (35). But Chambers *is* an "imitation nigger," since he is really white. He is also really honest and good, as he shows by openly declaring his purported blackness, unlike the true blacks in the story who lie about race. Once again the reader of *Pudd'nhead Wilson* understands a scene by knowing better than the characters and that better knowledge is the reality, the truth, of racial difference.

This scene plays directly to the concealed switch of Tom and Chambers and exactly negates its original thrust that whites and blacks can be exchanged because in *fact* blacks can be essentially white—read: universally human. However exchangeable the mistakable physical characteristics of blacks and whites, they represent how apparent likeness can mask real and profoundly different beings. Initially, clothing and social status are seen as hiding real human resemblance. These same superficial differences have come to mask real difference, and the bodily likeness of Tom and Chambers that first expressed their common humanity now renders their total opposition invisible. People may *appear* equal, it says, but they are really not.

What matters in this scene is the real difference between Tom and Chambers, while what had mattered about them at the start was their real likeness. Coincidentally in the same episode, Roxy herself sadly dwindles as the narrator ascribes her anger at Chambers (for reporting Tom's disinheritance) to her fear of losing "an occasional dollar from Tom's pocket" (35). This is a disaster she will not contemplate, the narrator laughs. But earlier Roxy defined herself in relation to a larger disaster, not the loss of a dollar but the sale of her baby. And when two pages later Tom actually does refuse his mother a dollar, the novel's shift of perspective is complete: where the injustice of racial inequality was first measured by the violation of Roxy's natural motherhood, now inequality will be justified by the spectacle of the emancipated and empowered Tom's unnatural sonhood. Roxy's subsequent threat to expose him is directed at his falseness; for the "truth" about Tom is that he is false, not really who he is or should be. Henceforth the story of *Pudd'nhead Wilson* is not about interchangeable babies irrationally and unjustly rendered master and slave, but about a black man who has taken a white man's place. Roxy herself, who first identified Tom as a universal baby—who revealed him as "white" as any baby—now calls him a "nigger."

The first name she had bestowed on her child was the name of a servant, Valet de Chambre. The fine sound of it appealed to her, Twain explained, though she had no notion what it meant. But we do, and when we first laugh at it we do so out of affectionate condescension. When later Roxy exchanges this name for that of a lord, Thomas à Becket, we begin to see that both names have their serious implications: they project spurious identities that yet determine what each man becomes. In the end, however, we find that we have been wrong twice, first when we took the names lightly, but second when we took them as seriously damaging misnomers. Valet de Chambre was all along the correct identification of a man born a servant and for a time dangerously misnamed a master.

Roxy's final renaming of Tom does not merely exchange one name for another but redefines the very nature of his identity. When she called her son Tom and thereby made him the equal of whites, it was on the grounds that he was indistinguishable from whites. Scrutinizing his golden babyhood dressed in white finery, she marveled: "Now who would b'lieve clo'es could do de like o'dat? Dog my cats if it ain't all I kin do to tell t'other fum which, let alone his pappy" (14). When babies are fledgling individuals, one as good as another in anticipation of each one's self-making, fathers cannot tell one from another—paternity is irrelevant. But when race enters into identity, paternity becomes all-important.

Roxy announces Tom's blackness to him by saying "You ain't no more kin to old Marse Driscoll den I is!" With this she claims him—"you's my *son*" (41)—but the grounds for this claim is a renunciation. Even as she demands that he recognize her maternal authority—"You can't call me *Roxy,* same as if you was my equal. Chillen don't speak to dey mammies like dat. You'll call me Ma or mammy, dat's what you'll call me" (42)—she abdicates the transcendent authority that earlier enabled her to name *him* into an identity she had more than borne: created. Henceforth he may call her "Ma or mammy" and accede to her orders, but for both this will ratify subjection, even servitude. Yet the reclamation of this maternal authority is limited, bounded by the surrounding patriarchy. "You'll call me Ma or mammy," Roxy storms, "leastways when dey ain't nobody aroun." For him to recognize her as his mother in public would reveal his real identity as a slave, whereupon Roxy would lose him to the authority of his father, and to the paternal authority of the slave system. Roxy had been able to make Tom free, when she was in charge and nature and race were in abeyance, but making him a slave requires her to invoke white patriarchal authority. For Tom may be black through his mother, but he is a slave through his father.

By a consummate irony, the revelation of his real white father seals Tom's status as a black son: a chastened Tom surrenders to his new status by asking timidly, "Ma, would you mind telling me who was my father?" The final link connecting Tom to his mother—identifying him as a slave—is her knowledge, her ability to call on the name of a white man. And through the medium of Roxy's pride as she tells him that his father was "de highest quality in dis whole town—Ole Virginny stock, Fust Famblies," the authority of Cunnel Cecil Burleigh Essex parodically but surely reaches forward from that past all-generating moment when he could command Roxy to bear his son, to declare that son now a black slave. "Dey ain't another nigger in dis town dat's as high-bawn as you is," she ends, proffering an identity that is the fatal opposite of the one she had conferred on him at the start of the story. "Jes' you hold yo' head up as high as you want to—you has de right, en dat I kin swah" (43).

One sign of Roxy's demotion to the status of just another fond mother is that she is wrong about this: Tom has neither the right nor the capacity to hold up his head. Despite his excellent white descent, he is simply not of cavalier mettle. On the occasion when he runs away from a challenge to duel, Roxy herself sadly draws the inevitable conclusion—not even his superior white sire can redeem his fatal flaw: "It's de nigger in you, dat's what it is. Thirty-one parts o' you is white, en on'y one part nigger, en dat po' little one part is yo' soul. 'Tain't wuth savin'; 'tain't wuth totin' out on a shovel en tho'in in de gutter. You has disgraced yo' birth. What would yo' pa think o' you? It's enough to make him turn in his grave" (70).

Roxy's racism is comically undercut certainly, but in the service of what alternative view? We are the more at a loss for a proper liberal riposte in that Roxy's parting shot travels directly to the end of the novel and its definitive return of Tom to the now unproblematical status of "nigger." "Ain't nigger enough in him to show in his finger-nails," she mutters, "en dat takes mightly little—yit dey's enough to paint his soul" (70). It was because of his white, thus raceless or race-transcendent fingernails that she could raise him to the status of master. Now it turns out that his fingernails did not accurately represent the case. Rather, as all discover, his identity lies in his fingerprints, and no one transcends his or her fingerprints.

Pudd'nhead Wilson's resort to fingerprints to establish Tom's true identity solves more than the Judge's murder. It provides a more encompassing resolution of the novel as a whole, for his astounding revelation restores both racial and sexual order. Indeed, in that any satisfactory ending would require that the truth be revealed and, since only Roxy could reveal it, it is not easy to imagine how else Twain could have ended his story. For Roxy to solve the mystery would not constitute an ending, not so much because her confession would be dramatically unlikely but because by identifying Tom and Chambers accurately, she would reassert precisely the power to identify that has so badly compromised Dawson's Landing. For Roxy to name her son and his white counterpart a second time would confirm her authority, thus perpetuating the racial dilemma of *Pudd'nhead Wilson.* Reconstruction would continue.

In Pudd'nhead Wilson, however, Twain finds an alternative truth teller. Male to a fault in his entire self-sufficiency, Wilson counters, then surpasses Roxy's authority: to the babies' identical fingernails which enabled Roxy to declare them identical, Wilson opposes fingerprints representing the apotheosis of difference, uniqueness. Fingerprints are individually distributed, not racially, so they cannot testify to Tom's race, only to his personal character. Nevertheless, in the courtroom scene, Wilson invokes the telltale fingerprints categorically, to identify the individual miscreant as himself the representative of a category.

Wilson, who represents the category of authoritative white men commanding both law and language, begins by announcing this authority to the community: "I will tell you." This is what he tells them: "For a purpose unknown to us, but probably a selfish one, somebody changed those children in the cradle." So far is the story from casting doubt on any aspect of this emerging elucidation, its miraculous verity is reinforced when the narration turns briefly to Roxy, who thinks, pathetically, that "Pudd'nhead Wilson could do wonderful things, no doubt, but he couldn't do impossible ones," and that therefore her secret is safe. But what is impossible to her is as nothing to Wilson. Having named the exact time of the exchange (thus returning to the crime's origin to master it whole) and having identified the perpetrator, he continues in the irrefutable idiom of scientific formulas: "A was put into B's cradle in the nursery; B was transferred to the kitchen, and became a negro and a slave . . . but within a quarter of an hour he will stand before you white and free!" He controls time and place. "From seven months onward until now, A has still been a usurper, and in my finger-records he bears B's name." And now the coup de grace: "The murderer of your friend and mine—York Driscoll, of the generous hand and kindly spirit—sits among you. Valet de Chambre, negro and slave." Roxy's response is poignantly telling. Before the miracle of white masculine omniscience, she can only pray: "De Lord have mercy on me, po' miserable sinner dat I is" (112–13).

Wilson's godlike authority has appropriated the story, raveling the order of the white community as he unravels the case. In the process, the story redraws its characters and issues in stark blacks and whites and is also rewritten with a new beginning, one that brushes Roxy's motive aside with the casual conclusion that whatever her reason, it was just selfish (in context, a stunningly ironic term that the text leaves uninflected).

And what about Pudd'nhead himself, the instrument of resolution? What is his relation to the order he restores? In the first place, while he embodies the authority of the white patriarchy, he is not himself a father but a bachelor, a lone, even an outcast figure whose own authority the village has only this moment recognized and then only because of his trick with the fingerprints. While he rescues the established order, he is acutely, at times bitterly, aware that those who administer it are not often worthy of their power. The joke that earns him the nickname "Pudd'nhead" has turned out more serious than it seemed. On his first day in town, Wilson became a fool in the eyes of his neighbors when he declared that he wished he owned half of a loudly barking dog so that he might kill his half. Now he has saved half a dog, while the other half dies. There is nothing joyous in restoring the status quo of Dawson's Landing. Twain may have been reluctant to see black men acquire the power of whites and may have viewed their bid for a share of power as outright usurpation. He did not vindicate white society. This is a familiar dilemma in his works, which frequently end, as does *Pudd'nhead Wilson,* in a stalemate between radical criticism and an implicit conservatism expressed in the refusal, or the inability, to imagine significant change. The stalemate here seems particularly frustrating: change must be defeated yet nothing of the established way of life appears worth preserving.

Pudd'nhead Wilson's concluding depression also sounds the depth of the most profoundly embedded images in the American mind, those of race and sex. Separate yet interacting, these images sometimes activate the imagination, and sometimes disable it, trapping it as Mark Twain's seems to have been by the impossible adjuncts of racial equality and white authority, of maternal justice and patriarchal right. When in the end Twain reestablishes by the fiat of law the rule of the white fathers, he does not do it gladly. Pudd'nhead Wilson, an outcast and a failure, playing out his charades alone in his study, represents the writer as outcast and failure. If he also represents the writer as lawgiver who defends the system he hates even from its victims trying to overcome their oppression, this is not a productive paradox but a paralyzing contradiction. As an expression of his author's anguish, Pudd'nhead Wilson would really have liked to kill his half of the dog, but was afraid finally of leaving the house unguarded.

Notes

1. I use the term "sex" instead of "gender" not to reject the argument that sexual identity is a social construction but to sidestep it in order to evoke the material condition itself, the way sex is interpreted into gender being precisely the subject of the essay. I am aware that one view holds that there exists no material condition as such, or none we can apprehend, so that the language of gender (gender as a language) is all we know of sex and all we need to know. To this my response is implicit in what follows, that gender, like any ideological construction, describes the interactions of several realities at least one of which is not the creature of language but material—the world out there. Gender is all we know of sex but not all we need to know. The essay also depicts the inadequacy of ideological knowledge.

2. The first description of the two children distinguished only by the "soft muslin and . . . coral necklace" of one and the "coarse tow-linen shirt" of the other recalls the similarly contrasting costumes of the Prince and the Pauper. In that story, however, the little pauper fulfills all sentimental expectations and, far from usurping the throne, returns it more secure to its rightful owner. Are there implications in the virtue of this poor boy, versus the vice of the black boy, for different authorial attitudes toward class and race?

3. Here I would mention specifically that portion of the literature which has reevaluated the sentimental tradition as a female, sometimes feminist critique of the male ideology of the market. See especially Tompkins and Ammons.

4. I have discussed this phenomenon more fully in "Archimedes and the Paradox of Feminist Criticism."

Works Cited

Ammons, Elizabeth. "Stowe's Dream of the Mother-Savior: *Uncle Tom's Cabin* and American Women Writers before the 1920s." *New Essays on* Uncle Tom's Cabin. Ed. Eric J. Sundquist. Cambridge: Cambridge UP, 1986. 155–195.

Jehlen, Myra. "Archimedes and the Paradox of Feminist Criticism." *Signs* 6 (1981): 575–600.

Tompkins, Jane. *Sensational Designs: The Cultural Work of American Fiction, 1790–1860.* New York: Oxford UP, 1985. 122–146.

Twain, Mark. *Pudd'nhead Wilson.* Ed. Sidney E. Berger. New York: Norton, 1980.

The Vanishing American

Walter Benn Michaels

When Tom Outland discovers that his friend Roddy Blake
has sold their collection of Indian "relics," he makes him an
outraged speech that Roddy ruefully describes as a "Fourth of
July talk" (245). The burden of the speech is that Roddy has
failed to understand "the kind of value" the relics have to Tom;
the Fourth of July part involves the accusation that Roddy,
"like Dreyfus," has sold his "country's secrets" to a German.
"They belonged to this country, to the State, and to all the
people," Tom says, and "You've gone and sold them to a
country that's got plenty of relics of its own" (245). Although
Roddy thinks his mistake has been to sell Tom's "private property," insofar as the relics are a public "trust," he is more a
traitor than a thief. And insofar as the relics belong to the
"State" only because they belonged to the Indians whom Tom
describes as his and Roddy's "ancestors," Roddy's lack of patriotism is really a lack of (what Tom calls) "filial piety" (251).
Roddy has thought of their "find" as "no different than anything
else a fellow might run on to: a gold mine or a pocket of
turquoise," but Tom has come to think of it as a collection of
family heirlooms, the "pots and pans that belonged to my poor
grandmothers a thousand years ago" (243). In selling the relics,
then, Roddy has betrayed his country by betraying his family,
all the boys, "like you and me," Tom says, "that have no other
ancestors to inherit from" (242). And Tom himself spends the
rest of that summer on the mesa in an orgy of "filial piety"
(251), reading the *Aeneid* and "tidying up" the ancestral "ruins,"
imagining himself as the pious Aeneas rather than as the un-
patriotic Dreyfus.

This experience is not available to Roddy Blake, who can't
read Latin and who persists in thinking that Dreyfus was framed;
indeed, Tom's whole speech is, Roddy says, "away out of" his
"depth." And Roddy is surely right to call attention at least to
its peculiarity. The equation of "relics" with state "secrets" is
odd, as is the more general preoccupation with ancestors. But
the contrast to Dreyfus and the fact that *The Professor's House*
was written mainly in 1924, the year in which postwar nativism
climaxed in the passage of the Johnson Immigration Act, may

help to dispel at least some of the oddity. The Johnson Act did not only limit the number of immigrants to 150,000 a year (as opposed to the approximately one million a year of the period immediately preceding the War): it did so (through the Reed Amendment) by linking the "annual quota of each nationality" to the "number of inhabitants of the United States having that national origin" (qtd. in Hutchinson 192), thus requiring a "racial analysis" of the current American population and making everyone's ancestry an essential element in the future determination of eligibility for American citizenship. Giving a *real* "Fourth of July talk" to the National Education Association in 1924, Calvin Coolidge cited the Johnson Act as one of his administration's chief accomplishments in the effort, as he put it, to help "America . . . remain American" (28); from this perspective, the fact that Tom's patriotism takes the form of an interest in his ancestors recapitulates the newly official interest in everybody's ancestors.

But Tom's preoccupation with his ancestors is, in any event, less surprising than his claim that the ancestors in question are *his*. This is surprising not only because Tom is "a kind of stray" who has "no family" (185) and not only because whatever family he once had obviously wasn't Indian, but also because the Indians themselves belong to a "race" that Cather insists has "died off" (119). Her cliff dwellers embody absolutely the myth of the Indians as a "vanishing race" and Tom's claimed descent from them is not only false but on her and his own terms impossible; since the cliff dwellers were "utterly exterminated" (221), *no one* is descended from them. But just as the Johnson Immigration Act helps make sense of Tom's preoccupation with ancestors by insisting on a new connection between one's racial descent and one's qualifications for American citizenship, so another text of 1924, the Indian Citizenship Act, helps make sense of his desire to claim descent from Indians.

Throughout the nineteenth and early twentieth centuries, Indians had been anomalies with respect to American citizenship, regarded first as citizens of their tribes and then, with the passage of the Dawes Act of 1887, as potential citizens of the US. Indian potential for citizenship was identified with the ability to adopt "the habits of civilized life" (Prucha, *Documents* 174) and Indian policy was increasingly directed at "the absorption of the Indians into our national life, not as Indians, but as American citizens" (Morgan 177). Thus a series of government initiatives, from the Lacey Act of 1907 (authorizing the Secretary of the Interior to grant individual Indians individual control of their "pro rata share" [Prucha, *Documents*

210] of tribal funds), through the Sells "Declaration" of 1917 (authorizing a series of measures designed to "speedily achieve" the "ultimate absorption of the Indian race into the body politic of the Nation" [214–15]), to the Citizenship for World War I Veterans Act of 1919 (authorizing citizenship for every veteran who "desires" it [215]) encouraged the normalization of the Indians' status as citizens. And the Citizenship Act of 1924, declaring "all non-citizen Indians born within the territorial limits of the United States . . . to be citizens of the United States" (218) represented the triumphant end of this process. Where the Johnson Act identified the racial groups which were to be prevented, if possible, from becoming American, the Citizenship Act celebrated that racial group which had succeeded. Better, in Cather's terms, to be the imaginary Indian Tom Outland than the real Jew Louie Marsellus, better (in Scott McGregor's words) "Outland" than "outlandish" (43).[1]

In fact, however, the Citizenship Act of 1924 did not mark anything like the successful culmination of the policy of assimilation; in fact, the policy of assimilation failed: as the Indian hero of Zane Grey's *The Rainbow Trail* (1915) puts it, "the white man's ways and his life and his God are not the Indian's. They never can be" (41).[2] Instead of being absorbed into the body politic, Indians were increasingly relegated to "a peripheral role in society" (Hoxie 236). And from this perspective, the Citizenship Act could seem at best a futile gesture, at worst a cynical acknowledgment of the ultimate irrelevance of citizenship to the Indians' predicament.

But the discrepancy between the status envisioned for them by the Citizenship Act and the actual social status of the Indians should not be understood to exhaust its meaning. The perceived impossibility of assimilating large numbers of Eastern European immigrants had led to the erection in the Johnson Act of barriers to citizenship; the actual failure to assimilate the Indians led through the Citizenship Act to citizenship. Undoubtedly, as Robert F. Berkhofer points out, the Congress was more afraid of "millions of Southern and Eastern Europeans" than of "a few hundred thousand pacified Indians" (177). In any event, however, the sense in which these two Acts were opposed—one designed to exclude, the other to include—is less striking than the sense in which they were complementary: they were both designed to keep people from *becoming* citizens. The Johnson Act guaranteed that aliens not become citizens by putting a halt to mass immigration; the Citizenship Act guaranteed that Indians not become citizens by declaring that they already were citizens. Both Acts, that is, participated in a recasting of American citizenship, transforming it from a condition that could be achieved through one's own actions (immigrating, becoming "civilized," getting "naturalized") to an identity that could better be understood as inherited.[3] "America," as Charles W. Gould had described it in a racist tract of 1922, was "A Family Matter" and the only way to keep the family strong was to "utterly reject . . . foreigners" (4). American traditions, Gould wrote, "cannot be taught, they must come to us with the mother's milk . . . and grow with our nerves and thews and sinews until they become part and parcel of our very being" (163). "Repeal our naturalization laws," Gould urged his readers, "secure our children and our children's children in their legitimate birthright" (165).

At least part of what it means, then, for Tom to claim descent from Indians is to claim exemption from the perils of assimilation and naturalization, perils that Cather insists upon by contrasting him with the man who would be his "brother" when he should be his "rival" (166), Louie Marsellus. For *The Professor's House* is also, as the title of Book One ("The Family") suggests, a family matter and one of its central concerns is with exactly who can and who can't belong to the Professor's family. Tom can: even before his engagement to the Professor's daughter, Rosie, he was "like an older brother" (132); marrying him would have been marrying someone who was already "almost a member of the family" (173). Louie can't: the Professor is amazed by and somewhat contemptuous of his wife's (atavistic, as if she were still committed to the melting pot) willingness "to adopt anyone so foreign into the family circle" (78). And the Professor's other daughter, Kitty, to whom Rosie has been "a kind of ideal" (86), is "done with her sister . . . all at once" (89) upon the announcement of her engagement to Louie. Married to a "stranger," Rosie is lost from the family; the family's regret is that, if it hadn't been for Marsellus, "we might have kept Rosie . . . in the family, for ourselves" (87).

The idea of keeping the family intact by saving sisters from marriage to—or, at least, intercourse with—strangers is a central concern of the American novel in the '20s, one that finds figurative expression in texts like *The Great Gatsby* (1925) and *The Sun Also Rises* (1926) and literal expression in *The Sound and the Fury* (1929). In Hemingway and Fitzgerald, the families from which Robert Cohn and Jimmy Gatz are to be excluded require a blood supplement to count as real families—"aficion" in Hemingway, a more subtle mixture of class and race in Fitzgerald.[4] But in Faulkner the St. Peters are evenly matched by the Compsons. Of course, Kitty St. Peter has no sexual interest in Rosie but then Quentin Compson doesn't have much sexual interest in Caddy either. What he wants is to "isolate her out of the loud world" (220); by saying that he has committed incest to make it so that "it would have been so and then the others wouldn't be so and then the world would roar away." Incest is, from this standpoint, nothing but one of *The Sound and the Fury*'s strategies (along with suicide, castration, and contraception) for avoiding assimilation. Quentin's attempt to keep Caddy from Dalton Ames, like Jason's attempt to keep Quentin from the man in the red tie, are efforts to save the family from strangers; "blood is blood," Jason says, "and you can't get around it" (303). The man with the red tie is one of the show people who have "brought nothing to the town" (243), who, like the Jews, Jason says, "produce nothing" (237–38). Jason has known "some jews that were fine citizens" and he has "nothing against jews as an individual"; "It's just the race" (237). Jews, even New York Jews, are "foreigners" (citizens of somewhere else); Jason is "an American."

But if *The Sound and the Fury,* like *The Professor's House,* is hostile to assimilation, it is, unlike *The Professor's House* or *The Great Gatsby* or *The Sun Also Rises,* skeptical about the stranger's desire to be assimilated. All four of these novels commit themselves to the construction of citizenship as identity (as a function of what you are rather than what you do) but the three earlier ones do so in the context of the foreigner's presumed eagerness to alter his. Neither Dalton Ames nor the man in the red tie (not even, despite his telling Quentin, "I belong to the family now" [136], Herbert Head) manifests the desire expressed in different ways by Jimmy Gatz, Robert Cohn, and Louie Marsellus to belong to the families that Nick Carraway and Daisy Buchanan, Jake Barnes and Brett Ashley, Tom Outland and Rosamond St. Peter can be imagined as belonging to. By the late '20s, the invention of cultural pluralism (an invention that is taking place in these texts of the early '20s) made the mark of the alien his indifference—even hostility—to assimilation. Quentin calls the Italian girl he picks up "sister" but he is Dalton Ames to her real brother Julio, "You steela my seester," Julio says, "I killa heem" (174); in *The Sound and the Fury,* Italians can be Compsons too. But in Hemingway, Fitzgerald, and Cather, the only thing strangers want is to join the family. What is to be feared most is the foreigner's desire to become American.

This itself, of course, represented a significant change from the prewar commitment to "Americanization," which encouraged both immigration and the immigrants' desire to join what

Teddy Roosevelt called "the American race." But it represents at the same time a continuation of the exclusionism that characteristically accompanied the welcoming discourse of the melting pot: Italians, Jews, Poles, and Irish were regarded by Progressive Era America as eligible for citizenship; Asians and blacks were not. Indeed, the very possibility of American citizenship was a function of the event that, according to Progressive racists, had created the American state by creating the conditions of white racial purity, the Civil War. The "Nation" that could not "exist half slave and half free," says Abraham Lincoln in Thomas Dixon's *The Clansman,* "cannot now exist half white and half black" (47). The significance of the Civil War, according to Dixon, was that it replaced class and sectional differences between whites with racial differences between whites and blacks. Hence, while encouraging the immigration of whites (he was an advocate of the melting pot), Dixon advocated also the "colonisation" (repatriation) of blacks, characterizing them (in terms that anticipated those of the '20s) as an "alien" "race," "whose assimilation is neither possible nor desirable." The Civil War had made what Dixon called the "ideal Union" possible by eliminating the racial obstacle to political identity; because (under Jim Crow) no black person could become an American citizen, any white person could. For whites, joining the American race required nothing more or less than learning to identify oneself as an American, rather than as a Southerner or Northerner, an Italian or a Jew.

Citizenship is imagined here as something that can be (except for blacks) and must be (even for whites) achieved, a matter of ideology rather than birthplace. Cather's early short story, "The Namesake" (1907), makes this point by imagining its hero, a sculptor distinguished above all by his relation to America ("He seemed, almost more than any other one living man, to mean all of it—from ocean to ocean" [167].) as both an immigrant and an expatriate. Born in Italy, living in France, his only American experience is a two-year visit to his aunt's house in the suburbs of Pittsburgh, and even here, he "never" feels "at home" (175); the one thing American that inspires in him a "sense of kinship" is a portrait of the namesake, his uncle, "killed in one of the big battles of Sixty-four" (171). And it is this attraction to the uncle that results in his Americanization.

From interrogating the local veterans about the circumstances of his uncle's death, he progresses to reading books about the Civil War and searching the house for the dead hero's memorabilia. The culmination of all this is an exceptionally intense

Indeed, the very possibility of American citizenship was a function of the event that, according to Progressive racists, had created the American state by creating the conditions of white racial purity, the Civil War. The "Nation" that could not "exist half slave and half free," says Abraham Lincoln in Thomas Dixon's The Clansman, *"cannot now exist half white and half black."*

Memorial Day on which, sent by his aunt to fetch the flag from the attic, he discovers an old trunk containing, among other things, a copy of the *Aeneid* with his "own name" written on the front flyleaf and written again, along with a drawing and inscription, on the back flyleaf. The drawing is of "the Federal flag" (178) and the inscription—"Oh, say, can you see by the dawn's early light / What so proudly we hailed at the twilight's last gleaming"—is from "The Star Spangled Banner," which would not officially become, until nine years after Cather's writing (by executive order of Dixon's graduate school classmate, President Wilson), the national anthem, but which here, unofficially, makes the immigrant-expatriate feel, "for the first time . . . the pull of race and blood and kindred" (179). After which he goes back to Paris and starts producing the "monuments" to "the heroes of the Civil War" and the sculptures on American topics ("his *Scout,* his *Pioneer,* his *Gold Seekers*" [170]) that make his artistic career.

In Dixon, the Civil War makes American national identity possible; in Cather, Civil War literature performs the same function. "The Namesake" is essentially a story about assimilation, about a "citizenship" which, although it is linked to "race and blood and kindred," is more a matter of "experience" than of heredity.[5] Where Dixon's heroes become Americans (instead of Northerners or Southerners) by fighting in the War, Cather's hero becomes American (instead of French or Italian) by reading about his uncle fighting in it. The fact that his "citizenship" is, as he himself puts it, "somewhat belated" (170), marks the sense in which he can be said to have acquired rather than inherited it, or rather it marks the transformation of an inheritance into an achievement. This is precisely what, according to Dixon, the Civil War was all about, the transformation of the founding fathers' legacy into their grandchildren's political creation; that's why *The Birth of a Nation* (made, of course, from Dixon's *The Clansman*) was called *The Birth of a Nation.*[6] Cather, by invoking "The Star Spangled Banner" on behalf of the Civil War dead, helps to transform the almost Revolutionary song of 1812 into the national anthem of 1916.

For Dixon, racism was crucial to the reinvention of the American state; only by freeing themselves from slavery, destroying their familial bonds to blacks and intermarrying with their racial kinsmen from across the Mason-Dixon line, could whites become Americans. But antiblack racism plays no role in "The Namesake"; my point in comparing Cather to Dixon is only to suggest that her concern in "The Namesake" with the question of American identity involves the characteristic

Progressive understanding of that identity as essentially political, reenabled by the Civil War as the refounding of the American nation. By the mid-'20s however, by the time, that is, of *The Great Gatsby, The Sun Also Rises,* and *The Professor's House,* although the question of American identity remained an urgent one, it had come to seem less obviously political. In the July Fourth address to the NEA in which he cited the Johnson Act as his administration's major contribution toward enabling "America" to "remain American," Coolidge went on to remark that "acts of legislation" were in themselves of little importance. Real progress toward "increased National freedom" (22) depended not on the "interposition of the government" but on "the genius of the people themselves" (13), and it was this genius that a liberal education, he told his audience of liberal educators, was designed to cultivate. One element in this education would, of course, be what he had called in another speech to teachers, "critical inquiry" into the nature of our "institutions" with an eye toward "a better understanding of the American form of government" (33). But this course of study, a staple of Progressive assimilationism and of the effort toward Americanization that we have seen embodied in "The Namesake," could not be adequate to a conception of identity that went beyond "legislation" to the "genius" of the people. What was required, he told yet another educational audience, was more "intense" study of "the heritage of civilization" (68); "We do not need more government," he said, "we need more culture" (74).

Thus, although it was Coolidge who said that what was good for business was good for America, in his frequent speeches on education, he took a somewhat different line, distinguishing between the "material advantage" and the "cultural advantage of learning" (15) and reminding his listeners that "vocational and trade schools" could be at best a supplement to a "liberal education" (63). Like Cather's Professor, who resists in his university the "new commercialism" and who defends "purely cultural studies" (140), Coolidge compared the "commercial" unfavorably to the "ideal" (69); "It is not the skill of a Fagin that is sought," he wrote, "but, rather, the wisdom of a Madame Curie" (60–61). The "teachings of history" (37), for example, he thought essential to an understanding of why different nations "cling to their customs" and of why reforms that "might produce good results in one country [say, in the wake of the 'Red scare' of 1919–20, Soviet Russia] would be found to be not workable in another" (37–38); it was thus "especially . . . desirable" to obtain "more accurate knowledge of the causes and events which brought about the settlement of our own land and which went into the formation of its institutions" (38). Where the racist writers of the Progressive Era had appealed to the founding authority of the Civil War, racist writers of the '20s— like Lothrop Stoddard in *The Rising Tide of Color against White World-Supremacy* (1920) and in *Re-forging America* (1927)— looked, like Coolidge, beyond the Civil War and beyond even the Revolution to what Stoddard called "the racial and cultural foundations of the early colonial period." Fitzgerald makes fun of Stoddard in *The Great Gatsby*: "*The Rise of the Colored Empires* by this man Goddard" (13) is one of the "deep books with long words in them" that Tom cites as "scientific" evidence that "Civilization's going to pieces." But the famous last scene of *The Great Gatsby*—with its transformation of Nick's eyes into the "Dutch sailors' eyes" seeing once again the "vanished trees" of the "fresh, green breast of the new world" (182)—is as true to Coolidge's exhortation to "search out and think the thoughts of those who established our institutions" as even Stoddard could have wished. And Professor St. Peter's *Spanish Adventurers in North America* is an exercise in "purely cultural studies" designed precisely to provide the "more accurate knowledge of the causes and events which brought about the settlement of our own land and which went into the formation of its institutions" that Coolidge and Stoddard hoped would help America "remain American."

But in *The Professor's House,* not even the Spanish explorers count as the originators of American culture; the episode in the "history" of his "country" (222) that concerns Tom Outland goes back to "before Columbus landed" (119). In this respect, Cather participates in a more general discussion of what was perceived to be a crisis in contemporary American culture, a discussion that, as it began to raise questions about the nature of culture itself, tended increasingly to focus on the American Indian. Indians were the exemplary instance of a society that could be understood as having a culture: thus Edward Sapir, writing on "Culture, Genuine and Spurious" in the *American Journal of Sociology* (1924), characterized Indian salmon-spearing as a "culturally higher type of activity" (316) than the labor of a "telephone girl" or "mill hand" because it worked in "naturally with all the rest of the Indian's activities instead of standing out as a desert patch of merely economic effort in the whole of life." For Sapir, the life of "the average participant in the civilization of a typical American Indian tribe" provided a model of "genuine culture," the experience of society as a "significant whole" (318), and of an individuality that avoids modern fragmentation because it both grows "organically" out of culture and contributes constructively to it: "A healthy national culture is never a passively accepted heritage from the past, but implies the creative participation of the members of the community," Sapir wrote, echoing Coolidge's insistence that, although "We did not acquire our position through our own individual efforts. We were born into it," "it is only by intense application that the individual comes into the . . . possession of the heritage of civilization" (68). "It was possession," Tom says, when he begins "for the first time" to study "methodically" and "intelligently" (251) that summer on the mesa, and when he starts to see things that summer, also for "the first time," "as a whole" (250).

And the Indian is also understood as the exemplary instance of what it means no longer to have a culture. The "fragmentary existence" of the modern Indian—the "integrity of his tribe" destroyed and the "old cultural values" dead—leaves him, Sapir wrote, "with an uneasy sense of the loss of some vague and great good, some state of mind that he would be hard put to define but which gave him courage and joy . . ." (318). The "happiness unalloyed" that Tom experiences on the Blue Mesa is thus the recovery of Indian culture, which is to say, of the very idea of culture. Feeling toward the cliff dwellers the "filial piety" he is reading about in Virgil, he experiences "for the first time" what Sapir called "genuine" culture, the culture the Indians had had but lost, the culture that modern Americans were looking for, the culture that, according to Coolidge, would take the place of "government."

The transformation of the *Aeneid* from a poem about political identity—inscribed, in "The Namesake," with a "drawing" of the "federal flag"—into a poem about cultural identity—inscribed, in Tom's imagination, with the "picture" of the cliff-dwellers' tower, "rising strong, with calmness and courage" (253)—marks in Cather the emergence of culture not only as an aspect of American identity but as one of its determinants. That, after all, was what the classics were for. "Modern civilization dates from Greece and Rome" (47), Coolidge said in an address before the annual meeting of the American Classical League at the University of Pennsylvania in 1921. As Greece and Rome had been "the inheritors of a civilization which had gone before" (47), we were now their "inheritors." Hence, in the effort to form a cultural in addition to a political identity, it was study of the classics rather than the Constitution that would promote (as had the Johnson Act) the modern American's desire "to be supremely American" (56). The answer to the question, "What are the fundamental things that young Americans should be taught?" was "Greek and Latin literature" (44–45).

Coolidge's word for cultural identity was "character" and his interest in education was a consequence of his view that the "first great duty" of education was "the formation of character, which is the result of heredity and training" (51–52). What the Johnson Act (keeping out, among others, the descendants of the Greeks and Romans) would contribute to the heredity side of American character formation, a classical education (studying the literature of the ancestors whose descendants the Johnson Act was excluding) would contribute to the training side. Indeed, insofar as Greek and Latin civilization was itself our inheritance (the civilization ours was descended from), our training could be understood not only to supplement but to double our heredity. More striking still, since we had no biological relation to Greece or Rome (and since the point of the Johnson Act was to make sure that we would continue to have no biological relation to them) our training could be understood not only as doubling but as constituting our heredity; it is only our education in our origins that guarantees that those origins will indeed be ours. "Culture is the product of a continuing effort," Coolidge told the classicists, "The education of the race is never accomplished" (49). The education of the race can never be accomplished because it is only education that makes the race. Our descent from the Greeks and Romans in Coolidge parallels Tom Outland's descent from the Indians in Cather, and the classical education Tom gets among the cliff dwellers exemplifies the "instruction in the classics" that Coolidge hoped would one day "be the portion of every American" (57). In Coolidge and Cather both, identity is a function of inheritance, but what gets inherited is not just a biology—it's a culture.

Sapir called this "social inheritance" and he was careful to distinguish it from the Stoddard-like assumption that "the so-called 'genius' of a people is ultimately reducible to certain hereditary traits of a biological and psychological nature" (311). Insisting that "what is assumed to be an innate racial characteristic" usually turns out to be "the resultant of purely historical causes," Sapir deploys the idea of a culture against the idea of a race. But the advantage of culture here is not purely destructive, that is, Sapir is not concerned to deny the existence of those "distinctive modes of thinking or types of reaction" from which the idea of "a national genius" is abstracted and which writers like Gould and Stoddard identified as racial characteristics. On the contrary, he is concerned to relocate the national genius, replacing biologically inherited traits with "established and all but instinctive forms" (312). Culture does for the anthropologist what biology did for the racist.[7]

In fact, it does more. Replacing biology with culture, as Sapir understands it, involves something more than attributing the transmission of national identity to "more or less consciously imitative processes" instead of "purely hereditary qualities" (309). For if culture were nothing but imitative processes, then it would be nothing more than social environment, whatever beliefs and practices the individual happened to be raised in. And if culture were nothing more than social environment, then the Indian, for example, could never have the experience, so powerfully described by Sapir, of having "slipped out of the warm embrace of a culture into the cold air of a fragmentary existence" (318). Social environment in this respect is too much like genetic inheritance: everyone always has one. But a culture is something that (unlike the genes you happen to have and the things you happen to do) can be lost. Which is why, although it must be inherited, it can never just be inherited: it is "never a passively accepted heritage from the past, but implies the creative participation of the members of the community." If, then, as an inheritance, culture is unlike the citizenship of the melting pot because it cannot simply be achieved, it is also unlike race and environment in that it cannot simply be inherited. The distinctive mark of culture is that it must be both achieved and inherited.

This is why the American Indian—conceived at the same time as biologically unrelated to and as an ancestor of boys like Tom Outland (who is a "stray" and has "no family" but whose cliff-dweller "grandmothers" owned the "pots and pans" that Roddy sells to the Germans)—plays so crucial a role in the developing idea of cultural identity. The "utterly exterminated" tribe of *The Professor's House* and the tribe "without culture" that exterminated them represent, because the one biologically disappeared and the other culturally never existed, the possibility of an identity that insofar as it is neither simply biological nor simply environmental, can be properly cultural. Neither by blood as such nor through education as such can Tom come into "possession" of himself, but only through a process of what is essentially acculturation, a process imaginable only as a kind of education which is simultaneously a kind of blood affiliation. If Tom had really been related to Indians or if he'd grown up speaking Latin around the house, this process would have been impossible. So although Coolidge had protested that Latin and Greek weren't really "dead languages," in fact, it was only because they *were* dead that they could assume the status of cultural standards. If the Italian immigrants disembarking at Ellis Island had spoken Latin, Coolidge wouldn't have urged the schools to teach it any more than Cather would have had Tom read it: a truly "living" language could not be an object of "purely cultural study." And if the Indians had not been perceived as vanishing, they could not have become the exemplary instance of what it meant to have a culture. "The sun of the Indian's day is setting" (137), an old chief tells Nophaie, the hero of Zane Grey's *The Vanishing American*. It is because the Indian's sun was perceived as setting that he could become, I want to argue, a kind of paradigm for increasingly powerful American notions of ethnic identity, for the idea of an ethnicity that could be threatened or defended, repudiated or reclaimed.[8]

It is because the Indian's sun was perceived as setting that he could become, I want to argue, a kind of paradigm for increasingly powerful American notions of ethnic identity, for the idea of an ethnicity that could be threatened or defended, repudiated or reclaimed.

Grey's Nophaie is a Navajo, raised among whites and now returned to his tribe; with "an Indian body and white man's mind" (94), he represents a synergetic combination of the means by which the vanishing Indian was supposed to vanish: cultural assimilation and biological obliteration. Raised among whites, he loves a white woman and because he cannot marry her and will not (loving a member of an "alien" "race" [14]) marry a woman of his own race, he sees that he is "the last of his family and he would never have a child" (114). In the version published by Harper & Brothers in 1925, this turns out to be literally true: offended by the prospect of an Indian man marrying a white woman (the reverse was more acceptable), Harper & Brothers had required Grey to make changes in the original serial (published in the *Ladies' Home Journal* in 1922) that resulted in Nophaie dying unwed under what Grey's son Loren calls "quite mysterious and really illogical circumstances" (vii). But even in the uncensored version, where Nophaie ends up marrying white Marian after all, the spirit of his prediction, his representation of himself as "the last of his family," comes true. For, in marrying Marian, he tells her, "I shall be absorbed by you—by your love—by your children. . . ." Imagining their children as her children (and himself as her), Nophaie treats assimilation exactly as if it were a form of instead of an alternative to biological extinction, and approves it—"It is well" (342). Whether responding to racist demands or rejecting them, Grey made sure that the Indian vanished.

But Grey's title is not (the title of Curtis's famous photograph) "The Vanishing Race" or "The Vanishing Indian"; it is *The Vanishing American*. And if, from the standpoint of assimilationism, this makes a certain sense—since it was in ceasing to be an Indian that the Indian would become an American—

it makes even more sense from the standpoint of the hostility to assimilation that we have seen at work in Cather and that finds an important expression also in Grey. For *The Vanishing American*'s villains are the missionaries who preach to the Indians that by adopting "the white man's way, his clothes, his work, his talk, his life, and his God" they will become "white in heart" (183). In Indians like Nophaie, whose "soul" has "as much right to its inheritance of ideals and faith as any white man's" (103–04), these teachings produce a "spiritual catastrophe." But the War, which dealt in fact a major blow to the project of assimilating the immigrant—"The war virtually swept from the American consciousness the old belief in unrestricted immigration" (Higham 301)—deals a major blow in *The Vanishing American* to the project of assimilating the Indian. That is, like the Indian Citizenship Act, it renders the project of assimilation impossible because unnecessary. For the War reveals the missionaries as themselves *less American* than the Indians. Grey's missionaries are "all German" (213); "their forefathers," as an old Navajo chief puts it, "belonged to that wicked people who practice war. They are not American. They are not friends of the Indian" (227–28). And the Indian, by contrast and "by every right and law and heritage," is "the first and best blood of America." Offered the opportunity to enlist, Nophaie immediately volunteers, "I will go," he says, "I am an American" (224).[9]

The neat trick here of representing the Germans as the ancestral enemies of the Indians (and it is a German who buys the Indian relics that by rights, Tom Outland thinks, should be in the Smithsonian—it is not just, as Indiana Jones puts it, that "they belong in a museum," they belong in an American museum) pales by comparison to the truly astonishing rearrangement of ancestry that the War makes possible. Attempting to persuade his fellow tribesmen to enlist, Nophaie gives what Grey calls "a trenchant statement of his own stand": "Nophaie will go to war. He will fight for the English, who are forefathers of Americans. Nophaie and all the Nopahs are the first of Americans. He will fight for them" (229). If the Indians are the first Americans and the Americans are descended from the English, then the English become the "forefathers" of the Indians and the Indians going off to fight for them are fighting as Americans for their ancestors and against the ancestors of the un-American missionaries. Or to put this from the standpoint not of the Indians *about* whom Grey was writing but of the white Americans *for* whom he was writing, if the Indians are the "first Americans," then the Americans now going off to war are descended from them; the Indians, whose forefathers are the English, are themselves the forefathers of the Americans. Volunteering to fight and so proving themselves as American as the white man, they make it possible for the white man to become their descendant and so to become as American as the Indian.

The readers of *The Vanishing American* are thus understood to bear the same relation to the Indians that Tom Outland does. And when Nophaie vanishes at *The Vanishing American's* end, he is only following in the footsteps of the cliff dwellers whose disappearance as a people made possible their arrival as a culture. In *The Professor's House,* one's ancestors cannot be the members of one's family; this is why the defense of the family against "strangers" like Louie Marsellus is bound to fail—the essence of the family is its inability to maintain the integrity to which the theorists of racial purity were committed. Rosamond is the chief site of this failure; the "peculiar kind of hurt" a man "can get from his daughter" (155) is the destruction of his family: "When a man had lovely children in his house . . . why couldn't he keep them?" the Professor wonders, "Was there no way but Medea's?" (126). Marrying them to their brother (Tom) might have been a way; imagining a family without women altogether might be another: the "happy family" (198) on the Blue Mesa (Tom, Roddy, and Henry) is one such model of America as "a family matter," as is Louie's vision of the Professor's books as his "sons," his "splendid Spanish adventurer sons" (165).[10] But Tom calls such "substitutions" "sad" and they are, in any case, ineffective: he is himself betrayed by Roddy (as the Professor is by Rosie) and Louie gets himself "related to" the books just as he got himself related to Tom, "by marriage."

Thus the only way to save the family is indeed to destroy it, Medea's way, by killing your children or, the Professor's way, by imagining you never had any. For while his family is in Europe (and while his daughter is participating in the production of "a young Marsellus" [273]), the Professor is becoming "the Kansas boy" he once was, who "had never married, never been a father" (265). And "this Kansas boy" is not only much younger than the Professor but much older, he is "a primitive" "nearing the end of his life." Going back to what he calls a "beginning" that is simultaneously an ending, the Professor embodies an "extinction" that guarantees the purity Tom experiences on the Blue Mesa. In Washington, looking for help with what he's found, Tom is sent first to the Indian Commissioner and then, after being informed that the Commission's business is "with living Indians, not dead ones" (226), to the

Smithsonian, where they also—albeit for different reasons—
turn out not to "care much about dead and gone Indians" (235).
Tom, however, has no interest in living Indians; he mentions
them only once to compare the men's "contemptible" habit of
helping to shop for their wives' clothes to the practice of the
pathetic bureaucrat Bixby; and the paradigm of a man who
shops with women is, of course, Louie, who chooses all his
wife's clothes; when the Professor receives the "cruellest" hurt
"that flesh is heir to" (155) from his daughter, it is on a "shop-
ping expedition" (281) with her to Chicago, an expedition that
marks not only the fact that he has lost Rosamond to Louie
but also that, in losing her to Louie, he has, like Rosamond
herself, "become Louie" (86). So in *The Professor's House,* the
only good Indians are the dead ones; and it is to avoid becoming
a living Indian (or a Washington bureaucrat, or a Jew) that the
Professor imagines himself not only dead but (like the cliff
dwellers) extinct.

Cultural purity thus emerges as an ideal of miraculous
preservation, like the Cliff City; a high-tech racial purity that
can survive the cruel hurts that flesh is heir to and even transform those hurts into the technology of survival: becoming
extinct, the Indians become the "first Americans," the "forefathers" of Tom Outland. Or to put the point more precisely,
culture becomes a way of insisting that citizenship is a function
of identity without reducing identity to nothing but biology.
The assimilationism of the early years of the twentieth century,
racist though it was, had understood citizenship as the consequence of certain transforming actions; excluding blacks, it conferred eligibility on all whites and appealed to the political
authority of the Civil War as the founding moment of the
American state. The racism of the '20s (one might, with a nod
to Paul de Man, call it vulgar racism) replaced the political state
with the biological family, the overwhelming difference between
blacks and whites with intrawhite distinctions like those among
Nordics, Alpines, and Mediterraneans, and the Civil War with
the arrival on American shores of the first Nordics. Its antiassimilationism consisted not only in its attempt to limit the
numbers of those who could actually become citizens but also
in its understanding of citizenship as "a family matter"; "blood
is blood," as Faulkner says, and a fellow citizen is someone of
the same blood. *The Professor's House* clearly participates in
this form of antiassimilationism, repulsing at every opportunity
the stranger's attempt to join the family. But *The Professor's
House* also stages a critique of Gould's and Grant's and Stoddard's vulgar racism: the technology by which the family per-

petuates itself is represented as destroying its purity and so the ideal of citizenship becomes participation in a family that, already dead, exists instead as a culture: the Greeks, the Romans, the cliff dwellers.

"Modern American books," complained D. H. Lawrence, are "empty of any feeling," especially by contrast to "the old American books" in which Lawrence found a feeling that seemed to him, writing in 1923, still "new." *Studies in Classic American Literature* claims the status of "classic" for Melville, Hawthorne, and the rest by attempting to add them to a canon that should be understood as already including, Coolidge-style, not only the Greeks and Romans (Lawrence in fact begins with Lucretius and Apuleius), but also the Indians who, as is well known, play a crucial symbolic role in his account of American literature. He identifies Indians with "blood-knowledge" instead of "mind-knowledge," preferring, in what is perhaps the book's most famous formulation, "red-skins" to "pale-faces." But Lawrence's involvement with Indians was more than symbolic: Mabel Dodge had invited him to Taos in the hope of getting him to write a book that would help save the Indians, and for the first two months of his stay Lawrence lived next door to John Collier, the single most important figure in what his biographer has called the "assault" on the Indian Bureau's policy of assimilation. The possibility of the American classic thus emerges out of the antiassimilationism that was excluding aliens and rescuing Indians. The Americanization of Lawrentian ideas about race took place in the context of a nativism that was culminating in the discovery of the Native American.[11]

But where Collier thought of saving what he called "the Indian culture system" (Kelly 326) as a matter of saving the Indians, Lawrence embodied even more clearly than Cather the desire to keep Indian culture alive by killing the Indians off. What Lawrence calls the "Spirit of Place," the "living homeland" that, in words almost identical to Sapir's descriptions of the vanished Indian culture, is available only to the members of a "living, organic, *believing* community" (6), will be available to white Americans, he argues, only when the Indians have disappeared. The "Spirit of Place" can't exert its "full influence upon a new-comer until the old inhabitant is dead or absorbed" (35). So it is only after "the last nuclei of Red life break up in America" that white men will encounter "the demon of the continent." Only the extermination of the Indian will make possible the emergence of Indian culture as "classic" American culture.

Sapir had emblematized in the living Indian the "sense"

of "loss" (318); Tom, reading Virgil among the dead Indians, wakes up "every morning," feeling "that I had found everything, instead of having lost everything" (251). As I have argued and as Lawrence makes clear, what Tom has found is what the Indians have lost, their culture; he has come into "possession" of his identity as an American. But in imagining a culture that can be lost and found, Cather was participating in the construction of a technology that went beyond creating Americans. Indeed, from the perspective of such a culture, Tom and Cather's Indians are only stalking horses for the emerging ethnics of the '20s. They are defined in opposition to Louie Marsellus, but the Indians will be his ancestors too, "outlandish" will take its place alongside "Outland." Hoxie makes a version of this point in his final chapter, "The Irony of Assimilation," when he says that "The assimilation effort, a campaign to draw Native Americans into a homogeneous society, helped create its antithesis—a plural society" (243) and goes on to remark that "Other groups traveled this path to cultural survival"; blacks, Jews, and Catholics "forged a potent political interest group amid the nativist hysteria of the 1920's. Rejection and exclusion ... bred self-consciousness, resourcefulness, and aggressive pride" (246). But Hoxie writes here as if cultural pluralism were simply a reaction against nativism; I have been arguing that the commitment to cultural identity is a form of nativism—it shares with nativism the claim that all politics are identity politics. The cliff dwellers provide for Cather a paradigm of the American but they provide, more generally, a paradigm of cultural identity itself; the rejection, on their behalf, of Louie's efforts to assimilate will become, in time, Louie's assertion of his own Jewishness.

Such assertions have themselves often emerged in the form of vulgar racism, and Werner Sollors, in his extremely important *Beyond Ethnicity: Consent and Descent in American Culture,* has made devastating fun of the willingness of "consent–conscious Americans" to "perceive ethnic distinctions—differentiations which they seemingly base exclusively on descent, no matter how far removed and how artificially selected and constructed—as powerful and as crucial" (13). It would be a mistake, however, to see the commitment to descent (to, in Cather's terms, the family) as undone by the revelation of its artificial (i.e., cultural) component. On the contrary, the very idea of cultural identity requires both the extension and the critique of descent-based, biological identity.

For if political citizenship is essentially a matter of what you do, and familial citizenship is essentially a matter of what you are, the elegance of cultural citizenship consists in its refusal to choose between these options. Thus it must be simultaneously racist and compatible with a certain critique of racism. It is racist in that, refusing to identify "our" culture (whoever "we" are) with whatever it is we do and believe, it imagines instead that our culture is the culture of our ancestors, so that we can be understood, for example, to participate more fully in our culture when we find out about and imitate the social or religious practices of our great-grandparents. Their genetic makeup is (at least partially) ours through biology; their culture is ours only through the biologization of that culture. But culture involves also the critique of biology, for if culture were simply biological, we could never fail fully to participate in it; if our "heritage" were genetically encoded, we would always be in full possession of it.

Hence the extraordinary power of culture as a concept: it is manufactured out of an insistence upon the discrepancy between social and biological criteria of identity but it is at the same time hostile to any attempt to require a choice between the two sets of criteria. On the contrary, the essence of culture is that it cannot be reduced to either the social or the biological; culture's project—the project embedded in the very idea of culture—is to reconcile them.[12] And such a project is as available to Jews about whom there is "nothing Semitic" (43) but their noses as it is to Tom Outland who doesn't exactly look Indian. If, then, *The Professor's House* provides a model of cultural Americanism, it does so only by providing a model of culture that can by no means be limited to native Americans. And it may be this model of culture that has turned out to be—for better or for worse—the great cultural contribution of the classic American literature of the '20s.

Notes

I want to thank Lady Falls Brown and Patrick Shaw for encouraging me to think about Cather by inviting me to the Santa Fe Cather Conference (August 1989) where a version of this essay was first delivered as a talk, and I want to thank Michael Fried for suggesting to me, after reading "The Souls of White Folk," that *The Professor's House* would be a text I would find interesting.

1. Critics of *The Professor's House* tend either to ignore or play down the question of anti-Semitism, attaching it (when they bring it up at all) to Cather's ambivalence about Isabelle McClung's Jewish husband (Edel 212–15) or to her general hostility to the American "preoccupation with material wealth" (Stouck 100–09). This seems to me a mistake but not exactly one

I mean to correct here, since my own interest is less in anti-Semitism as such than in the role played by anti-Semitism (as by love of the classics and admiration for dead Indians) in the reconstruction of American citizenship.

2. In *The Rainbow Trail,* the Indian is called Nas Ta Bega and he is based on a Paiute named Nasja Begay who, with John Wetherill, guided Grey to the giant natural arch, *Nonnezoshe* and through Monument Valley in 1913. It was Wetherill's brothers, Richard and Al, who in December 1888 had discovered the Anasazi ruin that they called Cliff Palace and that became Cather's Cliff City.

3. For an important discussion of the differences between "consensual membership" and "birthright citizenship" (4), see Schuck and Smith 9–41.

4. For a discussion of family, race, and culture in Hemingway and Fitzgerald, see Michaels 193–206.

5. Sharon O'Brien convincingly describes "The Namesake" as an "autobiographical" account of Cather's developing commitment to an "art" with its "source in American soil, American history, and American lives" (329). The question, however, is what is meant by "American."

6. Indeed for Griffith, as Michael Rogin points out in a brilliant essay on race, nationality, and aesthetics both in *The Birth of a Nation* and in Progressivism more generally, the movie itself could be understood to succeed the Klan and Wilsonian Progressivism in a series of "linked attributions of national paternity" (192).

7. Thus in "Franz Boas and the Culture Concept," George W. Stocking writes that Boas's "problem as a critic of racial thought was in a sense to define 'the genius of a people' in other terms than racial heredity. His answer, ultimately, was the anthropological idea of culture" (214). Stocking thinks of racial identity and cultural identity as fundamentally opposed; in my own view, as the following pages will make clear, the idea of cultural identity proved for many to be a way of renovating rather than repudiating racial identity.

8. Actually the number of Indians had increased from 237,196 in 1900 to 244,437 in 1920, and would rise to 357,499 by 1950 (Prucha, *Documents* 57).

9. As a way of guaranteeing their un-American status, Grey makes the missionaries "Bolshevists" (157) as well as Germans, proleptically (from the standpoint of the time when the story takes place) retrofitting (from the standpoint of the time when the story was written) the wartime enemy as the postwar enemy alien.

10. Eve Kosofsky Sedgwick's acute description of the relation between Roddy and Tom as a "gorgeous homosocial romance" (68) becomes all the more convincing in the light of the benefit to racial purity of a nonreproductive sexuality. The happy homosexual family appears here as the eugenically utopian alternative to the unhappy heterosexual one, a machine (even if, as it turns out, a rather fragile one) for turning race to culture.

11.   Which is not to say that American Indian policy proceeded smoothly along antiassimilationist lines. For one thing, Collier's tenure as Commissioner of Indian Affairs was followed by a period of "termination," devoted in part to rolling back Collier's reforms. And, for another, the reforms themselves (particularly with respect to the reorganization of tribal government) were sometimes viewed by the Indians as "crass instances of continuing government paternalism" (Prucha, *Documents* 66).

12.   From this perspective, one might also describe "The Namesake" as at least pointing the way beyond a national to a cultural identity since, even though it insists on the primacy of "experience" in becoming American, the experience insisted upon turns out to be that of discovering that one already is American.

Works Cited

Berkhofer, Robert F. *The White Man's Indian.* New York: Knopf, 1978.

Cather, Willa. "The Namesake." *24 Stories.* Ed. Sharon O'Brien. New York: Meridian, 1987.

———. *The Professor's House.* 1925. New York: Vintage, 1973.

Coolidge, Calvin. *America's Need For Education.* Boston: Houghton, 1925.

Dixon, Thomas, Jr. *The Clansman: An Historical Romance of the Ku Klux Klan.* Lexington: U of Kentucky P, 1970.

Edel, Leon. "A Cave of One's Own." *Critical Essays on Willa Cather.* Ed. John J. Murphy. Boston: G. K. Hall, 1984. 200–17.

Faulkner, William. *The Sound and the Fury.* 1929. New York: Vintage, 1954.

Fitzgerald, F. Scott. *The Great Gatsby.* New York: Scribner's, 1925.

Gould, Charles W. *America, A Family Matter.* New York: Scribner's, 1922.

Grey, Zane. *The Rainbow Trail.* 1915. New York: Pocket, 1961.

———. *The Vanishing American.* 1922. New York: Pocket, 1982.

Higham, John. *Strangers in the Land: Patterns of American Nativism, 1860–1925.* 1955. New Brunswick: Rutgers UP, 1988.

Hutchinson, E. P. *Legislative History of American Immigration Policy, 1798–1965.* Philadelphia: U of Pennsylvania P, 1981.

Hoxie, Frederick E. *A Final Promise: The Campaign to Assimilate the Indians, 1880–1920.* 1984. Cambridge: Cambridge UP, 1989.

Kelly, Lawrence C. *The Assault on Assimilation: John Collier and the Origins of Indian Policy Reform.* Albuquerque: U of New Mexico P, 1983.

Lawrence, D. H. *Studies in Classic American Literature.* 1923. New York: Viking, 1964.

Michaels, Walter Benn. "The Souls of White Folk." *Literature and the Body.* Ed. Elaine Scarry. Baltimore: Johns Hopkins UP, 1988. 185–209.

Morgan, Thomas J. "Annual Report of the Commissioner of Indian Affairs, October, 1889." Prucha, *Documents.*

O'Brien, Sharon. *Willa Cather: The Emerging Voice.* New York: Oxford UP, 1987.

Prucha, Francis P., ed. *Documents of United States Indian Policy.* Lincoln: U of Nebraska P, 1975.

———. *The Indians in American Society.* Berkeley: U of California P, 1985.

Rogin, Michael. *Ronald Reagan, the Movie and Other Episodes in Political Demonology.* Berkeley: U of California P, 1987.

Sapir, Edward. "Culture, Genuine and Spurious." *Selected Writings in Language, Culture, and Personality.* Ed. David G. Mandelbaum. 1949. Berkeley: U of California P, 1985. 308–31.

Schuck, Peter H., and Rogers M. Smith. *Citizenship Without Consent: Illegal Aliens in the American Polity.* New Haven: Yale UP, 1985.

Sedgwick, Eve Kosofsky. "Across Gender, Across Sexuality: Willa Cather and Others." *South Atlantic Quarterly* 88 (1989): 53–72.

Sollors, Werner. *Beyond Ethnicity: Consent and Descent in American Culture.* New York: Oxford UP, 1986.

Stouck, David. *Willa Cather's Imagination.* Lincoln: U of Nebraska P, 1975.

Stocking, George W., Jr. *Race, Culture, and Evolution: Essays in the History of Anthropology.* Chicago: U of Chicago P, 1982.

Stoddard, Lothrop. *Re-Forging America.* New York: Scribner's, 1927.

———. *The Rising Tide of Color Against White World-Supremacy.* New York: Scribner's, 1920.

The Limits of Cultural Studies

José David Saldívar

1

Cultural studies analyses of Chicano literature appeared on the scene just four years ago when Michael M. J. Fischer published his ambitious essay, "Ethnicity and the Post-Modern Arts of Memory," in James Clifford and George E. Marcus's influential anthology, *Writing Culture: The Poetics and Politics of Ethnography* (1986). Since then, the cultural studies movement has enlisted other well-known critics who, in a growing body of work, have begun to examine Chicano cultural practices. In addition to Fischer's study of ethnic American autobiographies and Chicano literature, George Lipsitz, in an essay about the Chicano band Los Lobos, "Cruising Around the Historical Bloc—Postmodernism and Popular Music in East Los Angeles" (1986), and Renato Rosaldo, in his revisionist essay on Chicano studies, "Politics, Patriarchy, and Laughter" (1987), have presented readers with broadly postmodernist and anthropological views of Chicano texts. Cultural studies, as it is practiced in the US, already seems to have taken its place as one of the established contemporary approaches to Chicano literature.

As of yet, there has been no investigation of the kind of cultural criticism Fischer practices and its consequences for Chicano studies. Because of the quantity and the diversity of the interpretations that the cultural studies movement has generated in books such as Clifford and Marcus's and in journals such as *Cultural Critique* and *Cultural Anthropology,* I will limit the beginning of this essay to Fischer's representative analysis of Chicano literature. In the second part, I will focus on Rolando Hinojosa's Chicano testimonial chronicle, *Claros Varones de Belken* [*Fair Gentlemen of Belken County*] (1986), to see if there are ways of characterizing Chicano writing and culture other than the ones the (postmodernist) cultural studies critics typically provide, since "culture," in Hinojosa's text, is not only "constructed," but is also intimately connected with social relations and global power. Finally, I will look briefly at the interdisciplinary work by Guillermo Gómez-Peña, Renato Rosaldo, and Gloria Anzaldúa, whose various artistic, social, and gender analyses concentrate on *fronteras* ("borders")—the invented lines along which different groups work and live with divergent understanding. The general postmodern art-culture system represented in Fischer's essay thus is contested throughout the last two sections of this study, where alternative "border" cultures, histories, and contexts are suggested. Cultures, for Gómez-Peña, Rosaldo, and Anzaldúa, as we will see, are by their very nature heterogeneous and necessarily involve borders.

We might survey briefly the history of the cultural studies movement with an eye toward establishing its beginnings and elucidating its current debates: what do these critics mean by the term, "cultural studies"? According to Stuart Hall, one of its founders, cultural studies "was conceived as an intellectual intervention. It aimed to define and to occupy a space" (16). Hall suggests that "the field in which this intervention was made had been initially charted in the 1950s. This earlier founding moment is but specified in terms of the originating texts, the 'original curriculum,' of the field—Hoggart's *The Uses of Literacy,* Raymond Williams's *Culture and Society* and *The Long Revolution,* E. P. Thompson's critique of the latter and the example of related questions, worked in a more theoretical mode, in *The Making of the English Working Class*" (16). For Hall, there are at least two ways of defining and understanding culture: 1) "an anthropological definition of culture—as cultural *practices*"; and 2) "a more historical definition of cultural practices: questioning anthropological meaning and interrogating it universally by means of the concepts of social formation, cultural power, domination and regulation, resistance and struggle" (27). As Richard Johnson emphasizes, "culture is neither autonomous nor an eternally determined field, but a site of social differences and struggles" (39).

Cultural studies, thus defined, draws upon an analytic sense of "culture," and it includes the study of subordinate and dominated cultures like public schoolchildren in Great Britain or low riders and *cholos* in East Los Angeles, and of popular mass media forms like a TV series. Foremost among its lessons for literary studies is that cultural practices are never politically neutral. On the contrary, cultural studies is committed to transforming any social order which exploits people on the grounds of race, class, and gender. At the level of canon theory and emergent practice, cultural studies argues that the process of selecting and regulating texts that makes up a national canon always results from a socially constructed set of practices and relations.

At its most accomplished, cultural studies does not restrict our aesthetic and political sympathies. As in the work of ethnohistorian-anthropologist Rosaldo or historian Clifford, cultural studies develops a diverse range of rich and subtle perceptions which can be exercised over a wide series of visual, aural, and literary artifacts, thus encouraging us to read and experience these texts in new ways. At its worst, however, cultural studies can (unwittingly) become another normalizing form of what Clifford calls in his book, *The Predicament of Culture* (1988), "culture collecting" and "culture fetishizing"; objects, exotic cultures, diverse experiences, and facts are contextualized and given enduring value in the Western art-culture system (230).

In Fischer's study of ethnic American autobiographies, for example, the anthropologist from Rice University gathers and classifies Armenian-American, Asian-American, Chicano, and African-American autobiographies "in order to ask whether they can revitalize our ways of thinking about how culture operates and refashion our practice of ethnography as a mode of cultural criticism" (195). Fischer is at his most instructive when he theorizes about the invention of ethnicity, which he calls "a process of inter-reference between two or more cultural traditions . . ." (201). Moreover, "ethnicity," Fischer suggests, "is not something that is simply passed on from generation to generation, taught and learned; it is something that is dynamic, often unsuccessfully repressed or avoided" (195). Ethnicity is like a dream for Fischer, full of Freudian displacements, representations, condensations, and secondary revisions. What is even more daring about Fischer's view of ethnicity is that the "ethnic I," like the Western I, the seat of consciousness, is not the integral center of thought, but a dynamic and often decentered and contradictory category constituted by discourse itself. Fischer's essay thus inquires "into what is hidden in language, what is deferred by signs, what is pointed to, what is repressed, implicit, or mediated" (198) in ethnic American autobiographies.

What is disturbing about Fischer's essay, however, is that his work takes on the traditional and normalizing anthropological form of culture-collecting; he presents the reader with an overwhelming catalogue of ethnic textual "data" with far too little discussion of local knowledge and local history. Diverse "ethnic" American experiences of Maxine Hong Kingston,

Charlie Mingus, Michael Arlen, José Antonio Villarreal, Ernesto Galarza, Sandra Cisneros, Rolando Hinojosa, N. Scott Momaday, Leslie Marmon Silko, and Gerald Vizenor (to name only some of the writers Fischer analyzes in his study) are selected, gathered, and detached from their local cultural and temporal occasions. In this act of removal, local meanings are reified in the name of some enduring "redemptive" value in a new postmodernist arrangement. Because Fischer is comparing a number of diverse ethnic experiences, he is forced to make wild claims that only a comparatist (without scholarly training in the respective ethnic American literatures) would make. For example: "Perhaps the most striking feature of Mexican-American writing, present in other ethnic writing, too, but brought to its most explicit and dramatic level here, is interlinguistic play: interference, alternation, inter-reference" (218). Fischer then argues that "*pochismo* or caló, the Chicano slang, takes on a privileged role" (218). Fischer then quotes the Chicana poet, Bernice Zamora (who does not write in caló): "I like to think of caló as the language of Chicano literature" (218). Unfortunately, wishing, for Zamora and for Fischer, does not make it so.

Are "interlinguistic play" and Chicano slang, *pochismo* and caló, really what makes Chicano literature distinctive, or are they something that the professional culture collector imposes? A more rigorous and scholarly study of Chicano literature would make the anthropologist more sensitive to the heterogeneity of Chicano and Chicana voices. Lorna Dee Cervantes, one of the more engaging contemporary Chicana poets and author of *Emplumada* (1981), in contradistinction to Zamora and Fischer, claims, for instance, that "there is a real distinct Chicano as well as Chicana voice. . . . I think men do more code switching and word play mixed with humor as seen in the works by Ricardo Sánchez or Alurista" (105). Cervantes, who is absent from Fischer's study, thus contends that her poetry is less interested in "linguistic trips": "I am more concerned with images, specifically domestic images" (105). Here Fischer is confronted with all the questions about gender and linguistic differences that his postmodernist cultural analysis evades.

As postmodern culture collector, Fischer gathers and classifies Chicano poetic practices that are themselves antithetical to what contemporary Chicano and Chicana writers are now producing. His practice of cultural studies thus treats diverse ethnic American discourses not as heterogeneous voices and utterances, but as prized monological acquisitions from a marvelous ethnic US where everything is readily available for the collector. Fischer thus appropriates "exotic" discourses, facts, and meanings, and makes them stand for abstract wholes—a Chicano text, for example, becomes an ethnographic metonym for redemptive culture.

Fischer's focusing on outmoded Chicano literary practices from the 1960s and 1970s, our "tribal past," blinds him to our emergent present. Confronted with more and more ethnic American experiences, Armenian-American, Native-American, Chicano, and African-American texts, and encountering them with less and less local cultural rigor, specificity, and knowledge, Fischer struggles to maintain a unified perspective about American ethnicity. Indeed, he looks for order in our fragmented world characterized "by the erosion of public enactments of tradition, by the loss of ritual and historical rootedness" (197). Seen in this light, Fischer's practice of cultural studies, the totalizing of diverse historical phenomena in terms of postmodern homogenization, needs to be resisted. As Clifford makes the point, "we need to resist deep-seated habits of mind and of systems. We need to be suspicious of an almost-automatic tendency" in scholars "to relegate non-Western peoples . . . to an increasingly homogeneous humanity" (*Predicament* 246).

2

How then do we tell other stories? How do we tell other histories which are placed in local frames of awareness on the one hand and situated globally, geopolitically on the other hand? One example, Hinojosa's *Claros Varones de Belken* from the US-Mexican border, may suggest different strategies for those interested in the positive practices associated with cultural studies.

Although *Claros Varones de Belken,* the fourth volume of the ten narratives comprising Hinojosa's *gran cronicón* about his imaginary Belken County, Texas, was accepted for publication by Justa Press in Berkeley, California, in the late 1970s, it was not published until 1986, when Bilingual Press produced a Spanish and English version (translated by Julia Cruz).[1] As the author explains, "The contracts were signed, but Justa Publications suffered some reversals . . . y allí se quedó. Nothing was done with it" (*Reader* 182).

As in his previous decentered narratives about this imaginary south Texas county, Hinojosa uses strategies of ellipses, concealment, and partial disclosures—a discourse that experimental anthropologists and cultural studies critics like Clifford, Marcus, and Fischer would recognize as their own—to characterize his vast chronicle of border history and culture. Although written in a fragmented and decentered postmodernist narrative, *Claros Varones de Belken* is, in fact, a chronicle, written within certain formal generic constraints. As Hayden White suggests, the chronicle as form is superior to the annals form of historiography in "its greater comprehensiveness, its organization of materials 'by topics and reigns' and its greater narrative coherence" (16). For White, "the chronicle also has a central subject—the life of an individual, town, or region, some great undertaking, such as war or crusade; or some institution, such as a monarchy, episcopacy, or monastery" (16). Finally, White contends that unlike the historical narrative proper, the chronicle "does not so much conclude as simply terminate; typically, it lacks closure, that summing up of the 'meaning' of the chain of events with which it deals that we normally expect from the well-made story" (16).

What thus appears to be fragmented and postmodern in Hinojosa's *Claros Varones de Belken* is really formal and generic: *Claros Varones de Belken* begins in medias res, and though it promises closure, it does not provide it. Like most chronicles, *Claros Varones de Belken* has a central subject: the conflicts and local wars of Esteban Echevarría, the race wars and the Texas Rangers wars in south Texas, and the more global wars of Jehú Malacara and his cousin, Rafa Buenrostro, who leave south Texas to fight in Korea. Moreover, *Claros Varones de Belken* also has a proper geographical center (south Texas, Belken County, *La Fronteriza,* the border) and a proper social center (Chicano ranching communities versus Anglo-American farming towns); finally, Hinojosa as chronicler provides us with a proper beginning in time (from 1749 to the late 1950s).

Hinojosa consciously situates his work in a tradition of chronicle writing as biographical sketches in *Claros Varones de Belken* by alluding in his own title to Fernando del Pulgar's medieval Spanish chronicle, *Claros Varones de Castilla.* Hinojosa's is thus a highly self-conscious and fashioned discourse. Pulgar, who was a chronicler and author of numerous letters, some of which later became independent essays, was one of the first Spaniards to begin writing chronicles deliberately as a form of biography. Pulgar dedicates his work to the most eminent figures of the noble class and of the clergy in Juan II's and Enrique IV's courts. As various Hinojosa scholars such as Rosaura Sánchez, Yolanda Julia Broyles, and Héctor Calderón have suggested, Hinojosa, with fine irony, subverts the lofty tradition of the Spanish chronicle by focusing not on the powerholders in south Texas, but on the powerless, not on the colonizers, but on the colonized men of Belken County. Like Plutarch and Pulgar before him, Hinojosa is interested in rendering the so-called cardinal virtues of prudence, temperance, fortitude, and justice, so it is not coincidental that many of Hinojosa's male characters are named for such values—Prudencio ("prudence"), Buenaventura ("good fortune"), Malacara ("bad face"), Buenrostro ("good face"), and el Chorreao ("dirty and unkempt").

Claros Varones de Belken is comprised of eight fragmentary sections. As the author tells us early on, "En este cronicón se contaran, entre cosa varia, casos en las vidas de Rafa Buenrostro, Esteban Echevarría, Jehú Malacara, y P. Galindo" ("In the lengthy chronicle, among sundry things, events in the lives of Rafa Buenrostro, Esteban Echevarría, Jehú Malacara, and P. Galindo will be related") (15). Although we learn much about Rafa Buenrostro and Jehú Malacara (for instance, we learn that Rafa is made a widower at eighteen when his wife drowns at a *resaca*; and we see how Jehú Malacara spends his spare time reading the Bible while in the Army, or attending the College of William and Mary part-time), the real focus of *Claros Varones de Belken* are the border characters, P. Galindo and Esteban Echevarría. In fact, the several retellings by Galindo, Rafa, and Jehú of Echevarría's peaceful death under a mesquite tree give the narrative its coherence.

As in *Estampas del Valle y Otras Obras* (1973) and *Klail City y sus alrededores* (1976), here in *Claros Varones de Belken* P. Galindo is absorbed in writing. Like an indigenous ethnographer (an insider talking back), Galindo fleshes out interpretations, records important events, and fills in the gaps left open in the earlier chronicles. As an observer-participant of events in south Texas border culture, Galindo's sketches and short stories are experimental, and, as "un hombre recto," his texts are always properly ethical. Perhaps an alter ego of Hinojosa himself, P. Galindo avoids a smoothed-over, monological form and presents his writings as pieced together, full of lacunae in their own right—what we might call, "history with holes."

As an insider of Klail City, Texas, then, P. Galindo offers us new ways of seeing and understanding Chicano border culture. Very much a traditional observer-participant often confined in his writings to visual description, P. Galindo also explores the consequences of positing cultural facts as things heard: Esteban Echevarría's oral tales at the local cantinas (the chronotope in the narrative where the plot is tied and untied) and the various *corridos,* tangos, and boleros in south Texas which record the Rio Grande Valley's emergent cultural resistance.

What is most significant for the readers of *Claros Varones de Belken* is that Hinojosa, through P. Galindo, uses techniques of digression and incompleteness—Echevarría's oral narratives—to impart oppositional historical knowledge to younger Chicano kinsmen such as Rafa Buenrostro and Jehú Malacara. An episode recalled by Rafa Buenrostro is particularly illuminating:

> Esteban Echevarría told me that when he was still young, the Seditionists rode down Klail's main street; they rode in after dark and camped out at the park that divides Anglo town from Mexican town. . . .
>
> They passed through, according to Esteban, without fanfarrón, as if on a Sunday ride. . . . That same day, later on, Ned Barker arrived in Klail with sixty deputies or so: policemen, marshalls, constables, county officers, rangers, and the usual hangers on. When Barker asked Esteban what he knew, Echevarría said, "They went through here. . . ."
> (34)

This short section of Hinojosa's chronicle presents the reader with a highly compressed view of one of the most dramatic events in the history of the Southwest, the armed insurrection of south Texas Chicanos in 1915 and their defeat by the Texas Rangers.[2] While many of Hinojosa's readers may miss the author's historical allusion, Rafa Buenrostro, a history and literature major at the University of Texas–Austin, knows the complete story: the seditionists, drawn heavily from the Chicano communities along the border, had joined together in order to regain land lost by their parents and grandparents to Anglo-Americans. In Echevarría's reconstruction of American history, the Texas Rangers do not merely suppress the seditionists, but also pave the way for Anglo-American domination in south Texas. Thus Hinojosa stresses the value of local knowledge and local history; that is, a recognition that class actors such as Esteban Echevarría shape local cultures. Nor is the larger global context forgotten in the chronicle, for the outside world of commodities segregating Klail City into Anglo-American and Chicano zones of core and periphery is always there in the text, affecting local matters. As historian David Montejano sees it, the seditionists' acts of revolt, "simply stated, were a response on the part of Texas Mexicans to the new farm developments" (125).

When the first Anglo-American farm seekers arrived in south Texas in 1900, the world they found had a rich Mexican character. "Cattle ranching," Montejano writes, "still dominated the regional economy, as it had since the Mexican settlements had been established in the mid-eighteenth century" (110). What Hinojosa thematizes in his chronicle are the oppositions Echevarría expresses in his childhood memory of the seditionists' ride through Klail City: Mexicans versus Anglo-Americans, seditionists versus Texas Rangers, and newcomers versus old-timers. At the center of these oppositions are the opposed views of economic development. *Claros Varones de Belken,* like the entire *Klail City Death Trip* series, articulates a cultural poetics that is not only prefigured visually but is also an interplay of oppositional histories, economies, voices, songs, and inflected utterances.

What we see and hear before us as readers, then, is a "plural poesis" of south Texas border culture. Formally, *Claros Varones de Belken* dramatizes the author's passion for chronicles and for freedom in the most radical of literary genres—the novel. Eschewing protostructuralist notions of the novel, Hinojosa, through Galindo, Rafa, and Jehú, is not after a unified system. Instead, Hinojosa pursues aggregates of forces, suggestive tropes and metaphors, the possibility of an artistic social act doing something not systematic and predictable (in the Bakhtinian sense), but something new, novel, unexpected.

Claros Varones de Belken is a fluid narrative that exemplifies Hinojosa's larger designs, for the chronicle formally represents an impulse that the author has been stressing since at least 1973. In "The Sense of Place" (1985), Hinojosa puts it this way: "As the census rolls filled up in the works, so did some distinguishing features, characteristics, viewpoints, values, decisions, and thus I used the Valley and the Border, and the history and the people. The freedom to do this also led me to use folklore and the anthropology of the Valley and to use whatever literary form I desired and saw fit to tell my stories: dialogs, monologs, imaginary newspaper clippings, and whatever else I felt would be of use" (23).

To be sure, Hinojosa sees his project as participating in the cultural conversations of the Southwest, where border culture is a serious contest of codes and representations. More specifically, *Claros Varones de Belken* is part of a Chicano artistic and intellectual response to the white supremacist scholars of the 1930s and 1940s like Walter Prescott Webb and his followers, who represented a popular, romanticized history: Native Americans and Chicanos are subdued, ranches are fenced, railroads built, until the Southwest was won. Hinojosa's chronicle negates Webb's triumphalist's literature by representing history from the local and oppositional Chicano perspective. *Claros Varones de Belken* strips away the mythical aspects of the southwestern periphery by dramatizing this history in economic and sociological terms. The fullest description of Hinojosa's counter-discourse can be found in a perhaps nostalgic section of the chronicle entitled "Con El Pie en el Estribo" ["*Going West*"], where Esteban Echevarría tells Rafa Buenrostro about social change, economic development, and ethnic relations in Belken County, how Valley people used to till the land, "but lost it little by little": "Before there was such a thing as Belken County or a Klail City and the rest of it, there were people, Rafa, people. Fields and small towns and that Rio Grande, which was for drinking, not for keeping those on one side away from the others on the other side. No, that came later: with the Anglos and their civil engineers and all those papers in English" (206). This conversation between Hinojosa's eighty-year old native informant, Echevarría, and Rafa, summarizes what some historians call the transformation of a precapitalist, agrarian society into a modern commercial order. Hinojosa thus directs the reader's attention to familiar actors and events in the loosening of the Chicanos' hold on the land. In *Claros Varones de Belken* we see how an organic class society—where a certain social order and class relations made sense to a people—shatters and explodes under the pressures of market developments and the politics of new class groups.

Hinojosa's chronicle functions simultaneously as historical record, as genealogy, and as a cultural critique of traditional southwestern American history. Moreover, his focus on text-making and rhetoric-making (in his use of P. Galindo, Rafa Buenrostro, Jehú Malacara, and Esteban Echevarría) highlights the constructed nature of cultural accounts. Hinojosa thus undermines overly transparent modes of authority (unlike Fischer) and draws attention to what James Clifford calls the historical predicament of ethnography—the fact that it is always caught up in the invention of cultures.

3

In turning to the interdisciplinary work of Gómez-Peña, Rosaldo, and Anzaldúa, we shift from a totalizing interpretation toward analysis informed by Mexican and US border literature and liminality. Unlike Michael Fischer's representation of Chicano writers, these authors do not see themselves as "minority," "subcultural," or "postmodern." Instead, they see themselves in a border field of meaning as "LimIts." According to Houston Baker, Jr., "LimIts" signifies "the prefixal resonances of liminal and the suffixal capitalization and reclamation of the third-person singular category of 'Its' resistance and interability." For Baker, "the colonizer is always coded as 'he' and 'she' of personhood. The colonized, by contrast, is always 'it' " (2). What Baker and, by extension, what Goméz-Peña, Rosaldo, and Anzaldúa demand is a transformation of "limits" into "LimIts" as agency.

Gómez-Peña's essay, "Border Culture: A Process of Negotiation Toward Utopia" (1986), has an experimental sense about it because he indicates that his cultural group of performance artists from the metropolitan Tijuana-San Diego area, Taller de Arte Fronteriza ("Border Art Workshop") forced him to write a different sort of account about border identities, border cultures, and border topography. For Gómez-Peña, *"existen muchas fronteras. Demasiadas"* ("there are many borders, too many"). His essay engages the infinite number of cultural contrasts and shocks he sees on the Tijuana-San Diego border: "mariachis and surfers, cholos and punks, second-hand buses and helicopters, tropical whorehouses and video discotheques, Catholic saints and monsters from outer space, shanty houses and steel skyscrapers, bullfights and American football, popular anarchism and cybernetic behaviorism, Anglo-Saxon puritanism and Latin hedonism. Will they exist in peaceful coexistence or open warfare?" Essentially, what Gómez-Peña calls for in his essay is a new kind of cultural studies "capable of articulating our incredible circumstances."

Gómez-Peña's essay does not contain a standard account of the US-Mexico geopolitical border, for, as he suggests, "the border is not an abyss that will save us from threatening otherness, but a place where . . . otherness yields, becomes us, and therefore comprehensible." In contradistinction to conceptions of the border as the *limits* of two countries, Gómez-Peña and his Taller de Arte Fronteriza group argue for a more unified border "as a cardinal intersection of many realities" (1). In short, Gómez-Peña focuses the reader's attention on the common ground literally shared by North and Latin America: "Latin America lives and breathes in the United States and vice versa" (2). The real innovation in Gómez-Peña's new definition of the border is the author's attempt to situate the shifting borders of the Americas within a range of "demographic, economic, and cultural" facts (2). Any account of border culture should convey for Gómez-Peña a sense of the "borderization" of the American hemisphere: "Whether we want it or not, the edge of the border is widening, and the geopolitics are becoming less precise day by day" (2). What Gómez-Peña calls for then is a "response from artists" of the border territories to construct "alternative realities" through interdisciplinary projects, through multicultural programs, and through internationalist dialogues.

Rosaldo's essay, "Ideology, Place, and People Without Culture" (1988), similarly attempts to theorize the border as a zone of "cultural visibility and cultural invisibility" (78). Rosaldo is particularly concerned in his essay with documenting "the case of the undocumented workers" in North America. Like Gómez-Peña, Rosaldo conceives of the border as "The site of the implosion of the Third World into the first" (78). Rosaldo searches for portraits of the cultural "border zones" and eruptions in popular mass media forms as well as in oppositional Chicano literary forms. He encourages the reader to watch "Miami Vice," for example, to understand how the program, with its "White zoot suits, high-tension mood music, and carefully chosen pastels," disguises itself as "affirmative action heaven, with blacks, Latinos, and whites all playing cops and robbers, vibrantly policing and trafficking drugs together" (86, 85). According to Rosaldo, "Miami Vice" plays out for American viewers how Latin American drugs are "invading" North America and how Latino drug traffickers are "infesting" middle-class white neighborhoods. To be sure, the edge of the border is widening, but for Rosaldo, "Miami Vice" also informs middle-class Americans about the wave of immigrants from the south invading the north, while it helps to explain how "new immigration" bills in Congress are boosted and how the electorate passes such English-only initiatives as the recent one in California.

In addition to seeing the border as the site of "spatial stereotypes," Rosaldo also views the border as a zone for ludic artistry. In a revisionist reading of José Montoya's classic 1960s poem, "El Louie," Rosaldo characterizes the protagonist in the poem as postmodern before his time. Louie Rodriguez, Rosaldo contends, "seeks out incongruity, unlikely juxtapositions [in American culture]: Cagney, El Charro Negro, Bogart, and Cruz Diablo" (86). Louie Rodriguez is not a tragic hero, as many Chicano critics have argued, but rather a liminal Chicano character "playing the role, the cat role, just playing" (86). In brief, "El Louie" epitomizes the border as "a culturally distinct space"; it is at once a poem betwixt and between Chicano and Anglo-American cultural traditions and a work of art where Montoya "celebrates polyphony in its polyglot text, and heterogeneity in

To be sure, the edge of the border is widening, but for Rosaldo, "Miami Vice" also informs middle-class Americans about the wave of immigrants from the south invading the north, while it helps to explain how "new immigration" bills in Congress are boosted and how the electorate passes such English-only initiatives as the recent one in California.

making Anglo, Chicano, and Mexican elements move together in the dance of life" (86).

Finally, Anzaldúa argues convincingly in *Borderlands/La Frontera: the New Mestiza* (1987) that an autonomous, internally coherent, patriarchal universe no longer seems tenable in our postcolonial world on the border. Like Rosaldo's border zones, Anzaldúa's "la frontera" is a space, consciousness, and eruption where "*Los atravesados* . . . [the] squint-eyed, the perverse, the queer, the troublesome, the mongrel, the mulatto, the half-breed, [and] the half-dead" reside (3).

Like Cherríe Moraga's feminist narrative, *Loving in the War Years* (1983), Anzaldúa's narrative experiments with postmodernist and radical feminist textual forms (testimony, autobiography, poetry, and theory). Unlike Moraga's book, however, Anzaldúa's text meditates on the relationships of one Chicana lesbian with her homophobic south Texas border community. In a direct refutation of Moraga's narrative, Anzaldúa begins a local debate in Chicana feminisms by writing: "I feel perfectly free to rebel and to rail against my culture. I fear no betrayal on my part because, unlike Chicanas and other women of color who grew up white or who have recently returned to their native cultural roots, I was totally immersed in mine [on the border]" (21).

What is experimental in Anzaldúa's *Borderlands/La Frontera* is the author's effort to explore *mestiza* conventions, idioms, and myths, what she calls the "Shadow Beast" within herself. At the heart of Anzaldúa's dissent from racialist purity and patriarchal postmodernity is her deep hostility to the process of late capitalism. For Anzaldúa, multinational capital and agribusiness have an impact on the physical world of the borderlands that is just as devastating as their effects on Chicana workers and landowners. In the chapter entitled "The Homeland/Aztlán," for example, she describes how for the white agribusinessmen in south Texas, nature—and the borderlands— exists solely as commodity. On Anzaldúa's native farmlands in Hidalgo County, the use value of natural objects has been consumed by their exchange value. Moreover, she shows this destruction of nature actually coming to pass through the speculations of Anglo farmers and ranchers who almost literally carry the border landscape off to market: "In the 1950s, I saw the land cut up into thousands of neat rectangles and squares, constantly being irrigated" (9).

As Anzaldúa's description of agribusiness practices on the landscape makes clear, her quarrel with multinational capitalism is in large measure represented in a nationalist allegorical mode. In *Borderlands,* she exposes the primordial crime of capitalism: not so much wage labor but the primal displacement of the older forms of collective life from a borderland now seized and privatized. As Fredric Jameson stresses in his essay, "Third World Literature in the Era of Multinational Capitalism" (1986), "It is the oldest of modern tragedies, visited on Native Americans yesterday, on the Palestinians today" (84). This "oldest of modern tragedies" is significantly reintroduced by south Texas writers such as Anzaldúa and Hinojosa, where native borderlands were seized and privatized by Anglos, their Texas Rangers, and the lawyers. As Anzaldúa tells us, her grandmother "Mama Locha . . . lost her *terreno.* For a while we got $12.50 a year for the mineral rights of six acres of cemetery, all that was left of the ancestral lands. Mama Locha had asked that we bury her there beside her husband. . . . But there was a fence around the cemetery, chained and padlocked by the ranch owners of the surrounding land" (8). Anzaldúa's national border allegory determines a remarkable generic transformation of the author's experimental narrative: suddenly, at the beginning of her life history, we are no longer in a prototypical conversion, autobiographical confession mode, but in ritual. Anzaldúa's *Borderlands/La Frontera* foretells the utopian deconstruction of patriarchy in south Texas even as it reaches back to touch the oldest of modern tragedies on the border.

4

This essay has been concerned with border visions and practices. As we have seen, the cultural work of Hinojosa, Gómez-Peña, Rosaldo, and Anzaldúa challenges the authority and even the future identity of monocultural America. Contemporary cultural studies appears in several forms, traditional and innovative, postmodernist, and gendered. As an academic practice, cultural studies, like Hinojosa's use of the observer-participant in *Claros Varones de Belken,* is simply about diverse ways of thinking and writing about cultures. In this expanded sense, writers like Hinojosa, Gómez-Peña, and Anzaldúa are resounding ethnographers who also happen to be what social scientists call "native informants." Finally, cultural studies, a border zone of conjunctures, must aspire to be regionally focused and broadly comparative, a form of living and of travel in our global borderlands.

Notes

I am indebted to the following for their comments and interventions: Héctor Calderón, James Clifford, Susan Gillman, José Limón, and Renato Rosaldo.

1. Rolando Hinojosa's *Klail City Death Trip* series is comprised of the following books: *Estampas del Valle y Otras Obras*; *Klail City y sus alrededores*, subsequently published in a bilingual edition in the US as *Generaciones y semblanzas*; *Korean Love Songs*; *Mi querido Rafa*; *Rites and Witnesses*; *The Valley*; *Dear Rafe*; *Partners in Crime: A Rafe Buenrostro Mystery*; *Claros Varones de Belken/Fair Gentlemen of Belken County*; and *Klail City: A Novel*.

2. For the traditional view of the seditionists and Texas Rangers confrontation, see Webb 471–516.

Works Cited

Anzaldúa, Gloria. *Borderlands/La Frontera: The New Mestiza*. San Francisco: Spinsters/Aunt Lute, 1987.

Baker, Houston. "The LimIts of the Border." *Chicano Literary Criticism: New Essays in Cultural Studies and Ideology*. Ed. José David Saldívar and Héctor Calderón. Durham: Duke UP. Forthcoming.

Bakhtin, Mikhail M. *The Dialogic Imagination: Four Essays*. Ed. Michael Holquist. Trans. Caryl Emerson and Michael Holquist. Austin: U of Texas P, 1981.

Broyles, Yolanda Julia. "Rolando Hinojosa's *Klail City y sus alrededores*: Oral Culture and Print Culture." Saldívar, *Reader* 109–32.

Calderón, Héctor. "On the Uses of Chronicle, Biography, and Sketch in Rolando Hinojosa's *Generaciones y semblanzas*." Saldívar, *Reader* 133–42.

Cervantes, Lorna Dee. *Emplumada*. Pittsburgh: U of Pittsburgh P, 1981.

Clifford, James. *The Predicament of Culture: Twentieth-Century Ethnography, Literature and Art*. Cambridge: Harvard UP, 1988.

———, and George E. Marcus, eds. *Writing Culture: The Poetics and Politics of Ethnography*. Berkeley: U of California P, 1986.

Gómez-Peña, Guillermo. "Border Culture: A Process of Negotiation Toward Utopia." *La Linea Quebrada* 1 (1986): 1–6.

Fischer, Michael M. J. "Ethnicity and the Post-Modern Arts of Memory." *Writing Culture: The Poetics and Politics of Ethnography*. Ed. James Clifford and George E. Marcus. Berkeley: U of California P, 1986. 194–233.

Hall, Stuart. "Cultural Studies and the Centre: Some problematics and problems." *Culture, Media, Language*. Ed. Dorothy Hobson Hall, Andrew Lowe, and Paul Willis. London: Hutchinson, 1980. 15–47.

Hinojosa, Rolando. *Claros Varones de Belken/Fair Gentlemen of Belken County*. Tempe, AZ: Bilingual P, 1986.

———. *Estampas del Valle y Otras Obras*. Berkeley: Quinto Sol Publications, 1973.

———. *Klail City: A Novel*. Houston: Arte Público P, 1987.

———. *Klail City y sus alrededores*. Havana: Casa de las Américas, 1976.

———. *Korean Love Songs*. Berkeley: Editorial Justa, 1978.

———. *Mi querido Rafa*. Houston: Arte Público P, 1984.

———. *Partners in Crime: A Rafe Buenrostro Mystery*. Houston: Arte Público P, 1985.

———. *The Rolando Hinojosa Reader: Essays Historical and Critical*. Ed. José David Saldívar. Houston: Arte Público P, 1985. 18–24.

Jameson, Fredric. "Third World Literature in the Era of Multinational Capitalism." *Social Text* 15 (1986): 65–88.

Johnson, Richard. "What is Cultural Studies Anyway?" *Social Text* 16 (1986–87): 38–80.

Lipsitz, George. "Cruising Around the Historical Bloc — Postmodernism and Popular Music in East Los Angeles." *Cultural Critique* 5 (1986): 157–77.

Monda, Bernadette. "Interview With Lorna Dee Cervantes." *Third Woman* 2 (1984): 103–07.

Montejano, David. *Anglos and Mexicanos in the Making of Texas, 1836–1986*. Austin: U of Texas P, 1987.

Moraga, Cherríe. *Loving in the War Years: lo que nunca pasó por sus labios*. Boston: South End P, 1983.

Paredes, Américo. *"With His Pistol in His Hand": A Border Ballad and Its Hero*. Austin: U of Texas P, 1958.

Pulgar, Fernando del. *Claros Varones de Castilla*. Ed. Robert Brian Tate. Oxford: Clarendon, 1971.

Rosaldo, Renato. "Politics, Patriarchs, and Laughter." *Cultural Critique* 6 (1987): 65–86.

———. "Ideology, Place, and People Without Culture." *Cultural Anthropology* 3 (1988): 77–87.

———. *Culture and Truth: The Remaking of Social Analysis*. Boston: Beacon, 1989.

Saldívar, José David, ed. *The Rolando Hinojosa Reader: Essays Historical and Critical*. Houston: Arte Público P, 1985.

———. Lecture. "Chicano Border Narratives As Cultural Critique." Stanford Center for Chicano Research. Stanford University. April 1987.

Sánchez, Rosaura. "From Heterogeneity to Contradiction: Hinojosa's Novel." Saldívar, *Reader* 76–100.

Wallerstein, Immanuel. *The Modern World System I: Capitalist Agriculture and the Origins of the European World-Economy in the Sixteenth Century*. New York: Academic P, 1974.

Webb, Walter Prescott. *The Texas Rangers: A Century of Frontier Defense*. Boston: Houghton, 1935. Austin: U of Texas P, 1965.

White, Hayden. *The Content of the Form: Narrative Discourse and Historical Representation*. Baltimore: Johns Hopkins UP, 1987.

The Black Arts Movement and Its Critics

David Lionel Smith

Professional critics of the 1980s and 1990s generally hold writing of the Black Arts Movement in low esteem. Though the literary output by black writers of the 1960s and early 1970s was substantial, there is a paucity of scholarly literature on this body of work. Various characteristics common to Black Arts writing make it unappealing to many literary scholars: it often confuses social theory with aesthetics, failing to articulate the complex relationship between the two; much of it is predicated upon crude, strident forms of nationalism that do not lend themselves to careful analysis; and too often the work is marred by the swaggering rhetoric of ethnic and gender chauvinism. The extremes of this writing are so egregious that we may come to equate all the work of the movement with its worst tendencies.

By "paucity" I do not mean that the scholarly literature is weak or that there simply needs to be more of it. I mean, rather, that even the most rudimentary work in this area is yet to be done. We do not have a single book, critical or historical, scholarly or journalistic, devoted explicitly to the Black Arts Movement. Carolyn Fowler's extensive bibliography on the movement is a valuable research tool, but it was published privately in an edition that is available only directly from the author. A fair amount has been written on Black Arts theater; many articles and several books have been written on the work of Amiri Baraka. Yet except for Eugene B. Redmond's useful, albeit sketchy, history of black poetry, *Drumvoices* (1976), Reginald Martin's intriguing monograph, *Ishmael Reed and the New Black Aesthetic Critics* (1988), and a few notable articles, the Black Arts Movement remains unresearched. A review of the *MLA Bibliography* for the past 10 years gives the clearest picture of this dearth. Under the cross-indexed headings "Black Aesthetic," "Black Arts Movement," and "Black Poetry Movement," one finds seldom more than three or four listings in any given year. Because roughly a third of those articles have appeared in European or Australian journals, in most years there are only a couple of articles under these headings that one can easily obtain through normal channels. Furthermore, many of the movement's basic documents, such as *Black Fire* (edited by LeRoi Jones and Larry Neal) and *The Black Aesthetic* (edited by Addison Gayle, Jr.), are now out of print. The work of some poets, such as Haki Madhubuti (Don L. Lee) and Sonia Sanchez, remain available from small presses, but books by Carolyn Rodgers and many others are long out of print. Thus, even the materials for studying the movement are increasingly scarce.[1]

Basic questions about the Black Arts Movement — such as when did it begin and end, which writers and styles did it include and exclude, what were its cultural origins and characteristic tendencies, who were its factions, and how were its works developed and disseminated — await serious discussion. And clearly, a single, authoritative answer to such questions will not suffice. Instead, we need an ongoing critical discourse around these issues. Scholarship, after all, is a process of learned critical discussion, not merely a series of unconnected publishing events. At present, the silence regarding the Black Arts Movement is deafening.

I want to identify some of the basic issues raised by Black Aesthetic literary theorists and to suggest a continuing influence of Black Aesthetic theory in the work of some current theorists of black literature. I also want to indicate certain inadequacies in Black Aesthetic theory. The Black Arts Movement suggested exciting creative possibilities that have not yet been fully realized, but it also fostered certain habits of thinking which we would do well to abandon. My purpose here is to describe both tendencies and to note the role of several critics in the development of these ideas.

1. What is the Black Aesthetic?

The concept of "the Black Aesthetic" has been integrally linked with the Black Arts Movement, yet even at the height of that movement, there was no real agreement about the meaning of this term. In his introduction to one of the central documents of the movement, *The Black Aesthetic* (1971), Addison Gayle remarked: "The Black Aesthetic, then, as conceived by this writer, is a corrective — a means of helping black people out of the polluted mainstream of Americanism, and offering logical, reasoned arguments as to why he [sic] should not desire to join the ranks of a Norman Mailer or a William Styron" (xxii). For Gayle, the Black Aesthetic is an ideological tonic that cures misguided assimilationist tendencies.

By contrast, Hoyt Fuller, in the lead essay, defines the Black Aesthetic in terms of the cultural experiences and tendencies expressed in artists' work. He notes: "In Chicago, the Organization of Black American Culture has moved boldly toward a definition of a black aesthetic. In the writers' workshop sponsored by the group, the writers are deliberately striving to invest their work with the distinctive styles and rhythms and colors of the ghetto, with those peculiar qualities which, for example, characterize the music of a John Coltrane or a Charlie Parker or a Ray Charles" (9). Interestingly, when Fuller elaborates on what he means by black style, he does so by quoting several paragraphs from an essay by a white writer, George Frazier, who grudgingly praised black style in an essay he wrote for *Esquire.*

By focusing on rhythm and style as the essential aspects of a black literary aesthetic, Fuller identifies themes central to discussions of what is distinctive about black expression. Nonetheless, his essay reveals certain peculiarities. Though he does not follow Gayle in defining aesthetics as a form of political enlightenment, Fuller's account takes musicians as models for literary expression. Furthermore, though he stresses "styles and rhythms and colors of the ghetto," none of these musicians grew up in "the ghetto." Coltrane was from North Carolina, Parker from Kansas City, and Charles from Georgia. Fuller's long quotation from Frazier cites musicians, athletes, dancers, politicians, but not a single writer. This reflects a common problem among Black Aesthetic theorists in finding literary precedents for Black Arts Movement writing. Indeed, many of these critics asserted that no prior writing existed that deserved to be called "black writing." But the greatest irony here is that Fuller resorts to a white writer—a writer whom he identifies as hostile to "the likes of LeRoi Jones" (10)—in order to illustrate the quintessence of black style.

The difficulties these writers experience in defining the Black Aesthetic exemplify a dilemma that writers of that movement never resolved, one which, I argue, could not be resolved. The concept of "blackness" was—and is—inherently overburdened with essentialist, ahistorical entailments. An adequate account of African-American aesthetic practices would call the concept of "blackness" into question, and the failure to question this concept would inevitably lead to muddled theories. The nature of the problem can be readily illustrated in semantic terms.

Consider the difference between "the Black Aesthetic" and "Black Aesthetics." The former suggests a single principle, while the latter leaves open multiple possibilities. The former is closed and prescriptive; the latter, open and descriptive. The quest for one true aesthetic corresponds to the notion of an essential "blackness," a true nature common to all "black" people. This is the logic of race, a logic created to perpetuate oppression and not to describe the subtle realities of actual experience. The choice of "the Black Aesthetic" rather than "Black Aesthetics" represents a fundamental theoretical failure of the Black Arts Movement. Yet erroneous or not, this is the choice that Black Aesthetic theorists made, nor is it difficult to understand why, given the social imperatives of the time. Nevertheless, while we must assess the historical record as it stands, we might consider what it means to envision the African-American cultural tradition as plural, not singular. After all, most current theories of black culture are just as singular as "the Black Aesthetic," though less forthrightly political. A black pluralist historiography remains to be explored.

The problem of historical understanding is a central issue for Black Aesthetic critics. How writers conceive themselves in relation to their literary antecedents is important for several reasons. It defines what they explicitly embrace and reject, but even more important, it defines that broader field of works which they feel an obligation to know—in other words, the basis of their literary education. Both writers and critics of the Black Arts Movement frequently articulated the notion that they had few if any antecedents. For them, past black writing was mostly a chronicle of evasions: failures or refusals to discover and express authentic black consciousness. In *The Way of the New World* (1975) Addison Gayle concludes his discussion of early black fiction by declaring: "The inability of the black novelist to build upon the foundation laid down by [Martin] Delany meant that no viable literary tradition was possible until after *Native Son*" (29). For Gayle, "viable" black writing is that which expresses rage at and rejection of white people. Consequently, except for Delany, the first century of black fiction was entirely an exercise in false consciousness. A critic or writer who holds such a view is unlikely to learn much from those generations of writers whom he has dismissed. In effect, such an attitude embraces historical ignorance as a critical premise.

The consequence of such thinking is egregiously apparent in LeRoi Jones's essay, "The Myth of a Negro Literature." First published in 1962, this essay is an important articulation of

Both writers and critics of the Black Arts Movement frequently articulated the notion that they had few if any antecedents. For them, past black writing was mostly a chronicle of evasions: failures or refusals to discover and express authentic black consciousness.

Jones's early aesthetic thinking. He begins with a stark declaration: "From Phyllis Wheatley to Charles Chesnutt, to the
present generation of American Negro writers, the only rec-
ognizable accretion of tradition readily attributable to the black
producer of a formal literature in this country, with a few notable exceptions, has been of an almost agonizing mediocrity"
(*Home* 105). Jones proceeds to dismiss subsequent black writers
as well, with a sneering condescension: "[O]nly Jean Toomer,
Richard Wright, Ralph Ellison, and James Baldwin have managed to bring off examples of writing, in this genre, that could
succeed in passing themselves off as 'serious' writing, in the
sense that, say, the work of Somerset Maugham is 'serious'
writing. That is, serious, if one has never read Herman Melville
or James Joyce. And it is a part of the tragic naiveté of the
middle class (brow) writer, that he has not" (107). According
to Jones, all Negro writers ("with a few notable exceptions")
have aspired to middle-class respectability, which he sees as a
quest for mediocrity. It is furthermore a rejection of these writers' own black identity and of their honesty in rendering their
own experience, because the black middle class has always
spurned honesty as pernicious to its hopes of being accepted by
white people. "High art," Jones declares, "must issue from *real*
categories of human activity, *truthful* accounts of human life,
and not fancied accounts of the attainment of cultural privilege
by some willingly preposterous apologists for one social 'order'
or another" (*Home* 109).

The claim to be a defender of truth against a horde of liars
is most interesting for how such a posture uses ideas about race
as a grounding for aesthetic claims. Jones's black neoromantic
equation of art, truth, and beauty entails two conceptual problems. First, Jones defines middle-class experience as inherently
dishonest. Hence, any art, no matter how accomplished, dealing
with middle-class experience would be false and mediocre.
Among other things, this formulation reveals a wholly inadequate understanding of the class perspective of the writers Jones
claims to admire. Second, Jones equates black with lower class.
Hence, by Jones's prescription, for middle-class black writers
to produce "high art," they must repress the truth of their own
actual experience and write instead as though they were lower
class. Though Jones claims that his aesthetic is a rejection of
class bias in favor of truth, it is in fact a rejection of one class-
perspective in favor of another. Needless to say, fair-haired,
white-skinned, upper-class African Americans like Chesnutt
and Toomer cannot become more authentic as artists by mas-
querading as Lightnin' Hopkins. What Jones really articulates

here is the familiar posture of the bohemian, who always flees from class origins in quest of an aesthetic realm perceived as the margins of society.[2]

In this gospel according to Jones, black writers have failed because they have not been blues people. That is, they were doomed to fail by being real African Americans, not idealized exotic Negroes, and by being writers, not musicians. Interestingly, Jones does not acknowledge the efforts of writers such as Langston Hughes and Sterling Brown—one of his teachers at Howard—who did in fact embrace the folk and the blues. Perhaps they rank among his unnamed "notable exceptions," though, actually, his comment appears to refer to himself. In any case, the most conventional racial notion in Jones's argument is the assumption of black inferiority. Negro writing, he argues, is inferior writing. Negro writers are not honest, and, furthermore, they are ignorant. American racial discourse makes assertions of Negro ignorance inherently credible. Still, how could anyone read the first 10 pages of *Invisible Man* and claim that Ellison has not read Melville and Joyce? How could any reader of *Cane* dismiss it as a defense of middle-class values? Jones's comments suggest that he probably had not read the work of these authors. In accusing them of ignorance, he reveals his own, but to be ignorant of Negroes is no sin in our culture. After all, we assume Negroes to be unworthy of serious attention. Being black does not necessarily exempt us from the condescending modes of race thinking.[3]

Quite the contrary, race thinking exists to perpetuate hierarchical claims to privilege. These claims of superiority to "the Negro" are available to anyone who participates in this discourse, regardless of race. Thus, much of Jones's self-vindication in this essay depends upon his claim to be an exception to the Negro rule. Though Gayle and Jones are distinct individuals, they are splendid examples of the tendency in the Black Arts Movement to dismiss the accomplishments of previous black writers and to define blackness as a quality that other blacks have failed to realize.

Black Arts theorists consistently refused to acknowledge literary antecedents, and this refusal is closely linked to the movement's peculiar tendency to cite nonliterary (mostly musical) models as antecedents in a tradition of authentic black expression. In one sense, the movement's theorists correctly observed that black musical forms such as the blues and jazz are more profound expressions of black particularity than most black writing has been. But their attempts to explain why have usually depended upon claims, in one form or another, that black writers have erred in attempting to be white or to use white models. This argument is inadequate for many reasons—most of all because it fails to distinguish between quite different aesthetic modes and to consider the social means of producing, communicating, and perpetuating particular aesthetic forms.[4]

Black music is a strong aesthetic force because it belongs to a tradition many centuries old, imported directly from Africa and developed continuously in the New World. Unlike writing, music is accessible to virtually anyone in a culture, without a requirement of formal education, though certainly learning to perform requires training, and appreciation exists at various levels of sophistication. The black musical tradition is thoroughly incorporated into the social lives of black people as a vehicle of self-expression, worship, dance, socializing, artistic performance, and entertainment. Music is an integral part of African cultures and of African-American cultures as well. It is as fundamental and as ubiquitous to black people as speech.[5]

Though writing has existed in Africa at least as long as in Europe, probably longer, the culture of the book has been, until this century, more important for Europeans than for Africans. In any case, an African book culture certainly did not survive the Middle Passage, and even if it had, slaveholders would have extirpated it. Consequently, if we speak of black literature, we must necessarily speak of a tradition based on European models. Therefore, it makes no sense at all to compare black literature to black music, because the two have different social origins and different histories. Black literature must necessarily be a mixed mode, growing out of European language and European literary models. The example of the spirituals, which derived largely from European hymns, should indicate to us that authentic black models can develop from European models. Similarly, Sidney Bechet, Coleman Hawkins, Parker, and Coltrane took the instrument patented by the Frenchman Antoine-Joseph Sax in 1846 and made it into an instrument that is now inseparably associated with jazz. Black musical expression is not limited to forms or instruments created in Africa, and this need not be the case for black literature either.

If we take African music as the quintessential form of black cultural expression, one interesting implication seems clear. The aesthetic implied in the relationship between the music and the people is a very egalitarian, participatory one. The model does not stress roles of performer and audience but rather of mutual participation in an aesthetic activity. How such an African participatory aesthetic might be transferred to the realm of literature is a challenging problem. And perhaps the impulse to approximate such an aesthetic helps to explain why the creative energy of the Black Arts Movement was directed disproportionately into theater; for community-based writers' workshops, such as OBAC in Chicago and The Watts Writers' Workshop, and the emphasis on live performances of poetry, and on publishing broadsides and chapbooks were products of this spirit of inclusiveness. Although we cannot pursue here the social history of the movement, it should be clear that such a participatory aesthetic is radically at odds with the essentially modernist, elitist, and exclusionary aesthetic promoted by Jones and other black bohemians. Of course, Jones soon changed his name and modified his rhetoric. Whether that transformation led to a more African aesthetic remains a matter of contention.

Among the Black Arts theorists, Larry Neal was perhaps the most discerning about the implications of "the Black Aesthetic."[6] Neal was willing to declare explicitly that literature as we know it is inadequate to the requirements of a black aesthetic. He remarks in his afterword to *Black Fire*:

> Black literature must become an integral part of the community's life style. And I believe that it must also be integral to the myths and experiences underlying the total history of black people. New constructs will have to be developed. We will have to alter our concepts of what art is, of what it is supposed to "do." The dead forms taught most writers in the white man's schools will have to be destroyed, or at best, radically altered. We can learn more about what poetry is by listening to the cadences in Malcolm's speeches, than from most of Western poetics. Listen to James Brown scream. Ask yourself, then; Have you ever heard a Negro poet sing like that? Of course not, because we have been tied to the texts, like most white poets. The text could be destroyed and no one would be hurt in the least by it. The key is in the music. Our music has always been far ahead of our literature. Actually, until recently, it was our only literature, except for, perhaps, the folktale. . . . Our music has always been the most dominant manifestation of what we are and feel, literature was just an afterthought, the step taken by the Negro bourgeoisie who desired acceptance on the white man's terms. And that is precisely why the literature has failed. It was the case of one elite addressing another elite. (Jones and Neal 653–4)

Like Gayle, Jones/Baraka, and others, Neal sees almost nothing of value in past black writing, and he goes a step farther to assert that "poets must learn to sing, dance, and chant their works" (Jones and Neal 655).[7] Up to this point the propositions of music as a paradigm for literature have been treated as misguided; and indeed, such formulations do pose serious conceptual as well as practical problems. Nonetheless, Neal's work allows us to consider this aspect of Black Aesthetic thinking in a different light. Neal obviously recognizes the issues at stake in his call for a new kind of literature. Gayle and Jones both argue, with different ideals in mind, that previous black writers have erred in choosing the wrong literary models. For Neal, literature as we know it is an unsatisfactory form.

What, then, would this mean as a mandate for writers? Most obviously, it emphasizes performance. Neal wants poets to sing or to scream like James Brown. In addition to music, he proposes oratory ("Malcolm's speeches") as another paradigm. The emphasis on vernacular performance implies that literature should become an immediate, communal form to be experienced in public, contrary to the private experience of reading a text. Indeed, much of Black Aesthetic theorizing, especially Neal's, seems to want to replace reading as the dominant mode of literary reception with listening. Theater and poetry readings, once again, represent movement in this direction. Consequently, writers attempting to take "the Black Aesthetic" seriously would be inclined to reject formalist aesthetics and to think most seriously about the sound of their work and its effect upon a listening audience. They would be more concerned with rhythm than with stanzaic form, more with rhyme sound than with the formal pattern of rhyme, and, in particular, they would be concerned with diction based upon conversational norms rather than upon literary conventions. The use of allusion as a device would not vanish from such an aesthetic, but its focus would shift away from bookish references and into the realm of black historical experience and popular culture. An obvious area for literary exploration would be modes in which verbal effect and narrative converge. A striking example of the latter kind of innovation is Baraka's ritual drama, *Slave Ship*.[8] Thus, if Black Aesthetic theorizing proscribed writers' use of existing literary traditions, it also opened up exciting new possibilities of artistic experimentation, and it sought to redefine the relationship between writer and audience. In effect, this meant both liabilities and opportunities for writers, audiences, and critics. Neither the liabilities nor the innovations have been adequately understood. Regardless, the commitment to ground literature in black vernacular culture was a definitive characteristic of Black Aesthetic theory.

2. The Black Aesthetic Critics

The relationship of criticism to the Black Arts Movement is complicated. Some of the most knowledgeable and discerning critics of the movement, such as Neal, are also important figures within the movement. This is true even of many academically oriented critics, such as Stephen Henderson. On the other hand, some influential recent black critics have been openly hostile to the Black Arts Movement—most conspicuously Henry Louis Gates, Jr. The activists of a movement are not necessarily the ideal persons to assess the actual achievements of that movement, though their comments can be illuminating. Similarly, the ideological opponents of a movement are not the most reliable sources of careful and dispassionate analyses. Unfortunately, most criticism regarding the Black Arts Movement has been deeply partisan, for or against. The fierce polemics surrounding the movement have discouraged careful and balanced scholarship. Yet without such scholarship, the achievements and failures of the movement can never be clearly understood.

A conspicuous difference between Black Arts writing and the work of previous black writers such as Wright and Baldwin is that Black Arts writing directly addresses a black audience. Thus, it immediately demands of its reader (or listener) a sympathy and familiarity with black culture and black idioms—and in many cases, with black nationalist cultural politics as well. In particular, since such writing addresses common black people, it demands that the critic be familiar with the common experiences of black people—or more precisely, that the critic share the kind of knowledge that such an audience would likely possess. Finally, since the Black Aesthetic claims to reject European literary models, it requires the writers to develop new forms, new techniques, and new conventions. Therefore, the critic must be prepared to recognize, understand, and assess these new literary forms and experiments. Needless to say, an education in conventional literary studies does not prepare a critic to face these challenges. Consequently, a critic who wishes to study Black Arts Movement writing must be prepared to move beyond university training, which can entail both establishing new criteria and rejecting established ones. (Given the familiar set of incentives, rewards, and punishments within the academy, such boldness could prove very costly to a member of an English department—especially an untenured one.)

Poetry presents the most varied and difficult challenges, and Henderson's work is unique in its attempt to provide new terms for understanding "the new black poetry." The long introduction to his aptly named textbook, *Understanding the New Black Poetry,* provides the most detailed attempt to establish a black critical vocabulary. This work is illuminating in both its strengths and its weaknesses. Moreover, Gates's negative commentary on Henderson's work clearly illustrates several sharp critical disagreements generated by the Black Aesthetic.

The essential spirit of Henderson's work is tellingly expressed in the opening lines of his essay " 'Survival Motion': A Study of the Black Writer and the Black Revolution in America":

> To write black poetry is an act of survival, of regeneration, of love. Black writers do not write for white people and refuse to be judged by them. They write for black people and they write about their blackness, and out of their blackness, rejecting anyone and anything that stands in the way of self-knowledge and self-celebration. . . . The poets and the playwrights are especially articulate and especially relevant and speak directly to the people. (Cook and Henderson 65)

" 'Survival Motion' " was written in tumultuous 1968, shortly after the assassination of Martin Luther King, Jr., and while it offers many insightful comments on the relationship between jazz and poetry and on particular effects achieved by the poems under discussion, it is an elegiac essay, deeply preoccupied with the themes of death and survival. It is an eloquent meditation on how music and poetry express the capacity of black people to endure with style and with "soul" what they have suffered in violent, racist America.

Henderson's introduction to *Understanding the New Black Poetry* (1972) is much more technical. He begins by explaining what he considers the inadequacy of previous anthologies and what he hopes this one will achieve:

> Black poetry in the United States has been widely misunderstood, misinterpreted, and undervalued for a variety of reasons—aesthetic, cultural, and political—especially by white critics; but with the exception of the work of a few established figures, it has also been suspect by many Black academicians whose literary judgments are self-consciously "objective" and whose cultural values, while avowedly "American," are essentially European. . . . [A]n attempt should be made in which the *continuity* and the *wholeness*

of the Black poetic tradition in the United States are suggested. That tradition exists on two main levels, the written
and the oral, which sometimes converge. (3)

Unlike those polemical Black Aesthetic theorists who consider
earlier black writing to be worthless, Henderson is careful to
develop a historical account stressing "the continuity and the
wholeness of the Black poetic tradition." Though his anthology
focuses on black writing of the 1960s, he includes selections of
folk songs and rhymes and poetry by writers ranging from Paul
Laurence Dunbar to Gwendolyn Brooks. He also includes blues
lyrics by Ma Rainey, Leadbelly, and others. These inclusions
are important for Henderson, because in his view a literary
tradition develops out of a whole way of life. Since that way of
life is also expressed in nonliterary forms, those forms can be
used both as sources and as heuristic models.

The significance of this becomes clearer as Henderson explains his terms for understanding black poetry. He specifies
three critical categories: theme, structure, and saturation.
"Theme" refers to the characteristic subject matter of black
poetry, which for Henderson means reflections on the experience of being black in America. "Structure" is his most decep-
tive term, for it refers to the sources from which the work is
derived and not to the "form" of the work. The two essential
sources, according to Henderson, are "Black speech and Black
music" (31). In this section he gives eight categories of poetic
devices based on characteristics of black speech, along with
examples of each, and ten ways in which black music is often
used in poems. "Structure," then, refers to the poetic use of
vernacular models. Finally, "saturation" means "(a) the communication of Blackness in a given situation, and (b) a sense of
fidelity to the observed and intuited truth of the Black Experience" (62). This may seem no different from "theme"; but as
one reads Henderson's brief discussion of this category, it becomes clear that what he means is the *authenticity* with which
a work conveys "the black experience." This is what he apparently intends to underscore later when he comments: "[W]hat
we are talking about then is the *depth* and *quality* of experience
which a given work may evoke. We are also speaking about
saturation as a kind of *condition*" (64).

Henderson's conclusion demonstrates his commitment to
link his critical project with a political agenda of black cultural
nationalism. The purpose of his essay is to send readers back
"to the poems themselves and to the people who make them":
"This is the great challenge of our poets as they incessantly

proclaim their miraculous discovery that Black people are poems. What this means for the teacher and the student and the critic is that, like the poets, they must not separate themselves or their work, whatever it is, from the concerns of the people. . . . Black people are moving toward the Forms of Things Unknown, which is to say, toward Liberation, which, however I have stammered in the telling, is what it is all about" (69). Clearly, Henderson differs fundamentally from conventional academic critics regarding the function of criticism. This difference leads Gates to caricature the Black Arts critics as "race and superstructure" critics, taking Gayle, Henderson, and Houston Baker as the movement's chief exemplars.

Gates faults Henderson for failing to distinguish between poetic language and ordinary speech, for failing to acknowledge that much of what he says about black poetry is true of all poetry, and for making the tautological error of assuming "blackness" in order to make claims about "blackness." Gates's remarks on the "ultimate tautology," or "saturation," exemplify his general rancor regarding Black Arts critics: "[P]oetry is 'Black' when it communicates 'Blackness.' The more a text is saturated, the 'Blacker' the text. One imagines a daishiki-clad Dionysus weighing the saturated, mascon lines of Countee Cullen against those of Langston Hughes, as Paul Laurence Dunbar and Jean Toomer are silhouetted by the flames of our own black Hades. The blacker the berry, the sweeter the juice" (*Figures in Black* 35).[9] This is Gates's entire discussion of "saturation." He concludes that he has "belabored" Henderson's theory not because it is the weakest of the three arguments but rather because Henderson's "is by far the most imaginative of the three and has, at least, touched on areas critical to the explication of black literature." The others, by implication, have not. Gates's conclusion that "his examination of form is the first in a race and superstructure study and will most certainly give birth to more systematic and less polemical studies" (35) constitutes faint praise, indeed.

Gates's harsh tone reflects the bitter conflict between movement critics and conventional academics. Arguing from the latter perspective, Gates describes a conference sponsored by the MLA at Yale in the summer of 1977. He remarks: "[T]he conference itself, in short, represented an attempt to take the 'mau-mauing' out of the black literary criticism that defined the 'Black Aesthetic Movement' of the sixties and transform it into a valid field of intellectual inquiry once again" (*Figures* 44). Gates clearly sees his work as implicated in a struggle for authority—a struggle to displace Black Aesthetic critics as the dominant authorities on black literature.[10]

In a very direct sense, Gates's difference with the Black Aesthetic critics is summed up in his comment: "[W]e write, it seems to me, primarily for other critics of literature" (*Figures* 56). This expresses the conventional, academic understanding of criticism as the specialized discourse of a professional elite, in direct opposition to the Black Arts vision of a populist, communal discourse. Though Gates often assaults Black Aesthetic critics for having an ideological agenda, the real struggle is between one ideology that rejects the institutional status quo and another that embraces it.

Despite this antagonism, Gates's own criticism has been deeply influenced by Black Aesthetic theory. When Neal wrote his afterword to *Black Fire,* he titled it "And Shine Swam On," beginning the essay with a quotation from an urban toast called "The Titanic." Shine is a modern, urban equivalent of the Signifying Monkey, a figure Gates has adopted as the signature of his own critical theory. Furthermore, Gates's acknowledgement of influences in the preface to *Signifying Monkey* includes an homage to Baker: "[M]y reading of his manuscript convinced me that in the blues and in Signifyin(g) were to be found the black tradition's two great repositories of its theory of itself, encoded in musical and linguistic forms" (x). This, needless to say, is a conviction that Neal, Henderson, and other Black Aesthetic critics have long shared.

Baker's *Modernism and the Harlem Renaissance* (1987) might be understood as a new evolutionary development of cultural nationalist premises. With its emphasis on "family history" ("family" meaning both immediate family and race), "sound" (the authentic style of black expression), "mastery of form" (performative skill), and "deformation of mastery" (turning the tables on the white oppressor), this book returns to the fundamental themes of the Black Aesthetic critics. Its manner, however, clearly reflects Baker's painstaking study of post-structuralist critical traditions. In Baker's work, deconstruction has not displaced cultural nationalism. Rather, the Black Aesthetic has absorbed deconstruction.

Though one might voice many misgivings about *Modernism and the Harlem Renaissance* as a general model for literary historiography, it is a fascinating and moving performative work, one that dramatizes the process of one critic's emotional and intellectual coming to terms with black cultural traditions and contemporary critical theory. It is perhaps even erroneous and unfair to read this book as a work of literary history. Baker has tried to create an altogether new genre of writing, and in those terms, this book makes powerful claims on its readers. His study seems profoundly important because it represents a kind of writing that becomes possible by pursuing certain Black Aesthetic premises to their logical conclusions. Baker has written a book not for other critics, with their academic preconceptions of what a scholarly book should be, but rather for "the family," in celebration of the family's own survival, style, and traditions. This book exemplifies the continuing importance of the Black Arts Movement and of the intellectual and aesthetic opportunities and challenges it has created (see Smith, "Black Figures").

3. Conclusion

Since the turn of the century many black artists have envisioned the development of new aesthetic forms based on black vernacular culture. Nor has this vision been exclusive to black artists. In the nineteenth century Antonín Dvořák chided American composers for not utilizing African-American musical resources, and his *New World Symphony* stands as a monumental rebuke to Euro-American ethnochauvinism. White American writers of the 1920s such as Carl Van Vechten and Dubose Heyward, while rejecting the racist traditions of dialect writing, also regarded black vernacular culture as a rich aesthetic source. Among black writers, James Weldon Johnson and Langston Hughes made pioneering efforts both to incorporate black vernacular materials into their work and to create new forms based on black culture. Black Aesthetic writers and critics often claimed that they were the first generation to embrace black vernacular culture, but in fact, they simply represented the triumph of a consensus that had been developing throughout the century. We need to understand Black Aesthetic theory and aesthetic forms in this historical context.

Though I have concentrated on the relationship of critics to Black Aesthetic theory and on certain entailments of that theory, the most compelling questions pertain to the art of the movement. At one historical end, we need more study of the movement's origins, not only in "the African-American tradition" but also in "the European-American tradition." To what extent did the Beat movement, with its emphasis on jazz as an aesthetic model, influence the Black Arts Movement— especially through poets such as Ted Joans, David Henderson, and Jones? What was the role of the black surrealist poet Bob

Kaufman in this process? In the other historical direction, to what degree did the movement shape the literary sensibilities of female writers such as Alice Walker and Ntozake Shange? Can the form and language of Shange's theater pieces be understood without reference to Black Arts theater? And most intriguing of all, how would our assessment of the Black Arts Movement be affected if its developments in literature, theater, music, and the visual arts were all taken into account?

When we think of the Black Arts Movement, its polemics and excesses are what we often remember. We regard it as something that happened and ended in the efflorescent '60s. Perhaps it is time to reconsider the substantive achievements of the movement. Perhaps they are more significant, enduring, and influential than we commonly acknowledge. It is certain, in any case, that this movement poses a great opportunity and challenge for literary and cultural historians. Though understanding this particular movement and its place in our national history is the immediate issue, meeting this scholarly challenge may well lead us to create new ways of understanding our collective past. If we do, our view of the present cannot stand unaltered.

Notes

1. Baker's *Journey Back* is probably the best starting point for a scholarly assessment of the movement. Lee's *Dynamite Voices* was written as a general introduction to black poets of the 1960s, but it remains useful—not least as an expression of the critical ideas of one of the movement's leading poets. Volume 41 of *Dictionary of Literary Biography* offers detailed discussions of most poets considered by Lee plus many others. Chapter 6 of *Propaganda and Aesthetics,* by Abby and Ronald Johnson, called "Black Aesthetic Revolutionary Little Magazines, 1960–1976," is unique for the insight it provides into the ideological debates and factions within the movement. Aside from the anthologies discussed in the body of this essay, two others are notable: Brooks's *A Broadside Treasury* and Parks's *Nommo: A Literary Legacy of Black Chicago.* The latter is the only anthology of writers from the OBAC Writers Workshop. Baraka's cultural nationalist essays are collected in (Jones's) *Raise Race Rays Raze,* and his more recent views on the movement are presented at length, often hilariously, in *The Autobiography of LeRoi Jones.* The recent publication of Neal's selected writings in *Visions of a Liberated Future* is a valuable addition to the available writings of and about the Black Arts Movement.

2. Jones's class-based aesthetics is most fully developed in his book *Blues People.* Sollors's study of Baraka is especially useful for its discussion of Baraka's relationship to modernist and bohemian ideas.

3.   Baraka's literary essays of the 1970s and 1980s demonstrate that he has discovered earlier black writers. Some of these essays are virtual annotated bibliographies of a tradition that he previously alleged did not exist. His more recent essays and poems, collected in *The Music*, adopt a celebratory tone toward the black tradition. I have discussed some of this latter work in my essay "Amiri Baraka and the Politics of Popular Culture."

4.   As a preferable model for cultural analysis, I am thinking of the example provided by Williams in his later books, such as *Marxism and Literature*.

5.   See Levine's pioneering study of the central role of music and folklore in African-American culture. In a more recent book, Stuckey provides a striking illustration of how one music-dance-worship ritual (the "ring shout") has sustained itself from its African origins to become a familiar feature of black religious tradition in America. Unfortunately, black literary historiography has never approached the sophistication of such work in history, anthropology, and religious studies.

6.   Neal died in 1981 at the age of 44. A special issue of *Callaloo* (8.1[1985]) was devoted to Neal and his work, providing the most thorough discussion we have of this important figure.

7.   Neal later moderated this view. See, for example, his essay "Ellison's Zoot Suit" in *Visions*.

8.   Neal's comments on this play are astute. See Gayle *Black Aesthetic* 268–69.

9.   "Mascon" is Henderson's term. It refers to the "massive concentration" of black experience in particular words or images.

10.   Baker offers his own account of this critical history in chapter 2 of *Blues*.

Works Cited

Baker, Houston A., Jr. *Blues, Ideology, and Afro-American Literature.* Chicago: U of Chicago P, 1984.

———. *The Journey Back: Issues in Black Literature and Criticism.* Chicago: U of Chicago P, 1980.

———. *Modernism and the Harlem Renaissance.* Chicago: U of Chicago P, 1987.

Baraka, Amiri. *The Autobiography of LeRoi Jones.* New York: Freundlich, 1984.

———. *The Music: Reflections on Jazz and Blues.* New York: William Morrow, 1987.

Brooks, Gwendolyn, ed. *A Broadside Treasury: 1965–1970.* Detroit: Broadside, 1971.

Cook, Mercer, and Stephen E. Henderson. *The Militant Black Writer.* Madison: U of Wisconsin P, 1969.

The Dictionary of Literary Biography. Vol. 41: Afro-American Poets Since 1955. Ed. Trudier Harris and

Thadious Davis. Detroit: Gale Research Co., 1985.

Fowler, Carolyn. *Black Arts and Black Aesthetics: A Bibliography.* N.p.: n.p., 1981.

Gates, Henry Louis, Jr. *Figures in Black: Words, Signs, and the 'Racial' Self.* New York: Oxford UP, 1987.

———. *The Signifying Monkey: A Theory of African-American Literary Criticism.* New York: Oxford UP, 1988.

Gayle, Addison, Jr., ed. *The Black Aesthetic.* Garden City: Doubleday-Anchor, 1971.

———. *The Way of the New World: The Black Novel in America.* Garden City: Doubleday-Anchor, 1976.

Henderson, Stephen. *Understanding the New Black Poetry: Black Speech and Black Music as Poetic References.* New York: William Morrow, 1973.

Johnson, Abby Arthur, and Ronald Maberry Johnson. *Propaganda and Aesthetics: The Literary Politics of Afro-American Magazines in the Twentieth Century.* Amherst: U of Massachusetts P, 1979.

Jones, LeRoi. *Blues People.* New York: William Morrow, 1963.

———. *Home: Social Essays.* New York: William Morrow, 1966.

———. *Raise Race Rays Raze: Essays Since 1965.* New York: Random, 1971.

Jones, LeRoi, and Larry Neal, eds. *Black Fire: An Anthology of Afro-American Writing.* New York: William Morrow, 1968.

Lee, Don L. *Dynamite Voices: Black Poets of the 1960's.* Detroit: Broadside, 1971.

Levine, Lawrence W. *Black Culture and Black Consciousness.* New York: Oxford UP, 1977.

Martin, Reginald. *Ishmael Reed and the New Black Aesthetic Critics.* New York: St. Martin's, 1988.

Neal, Larry. *Visions of a Liberated Future: Black Arts Movement Writings.* Ed. Michael Schwarz. New York: Thunder's Mouth P, 1989.

Parks, Carole, ed. *Nommo: A Literary Legacy of Black Chicago (1967–1987).* Chicago: OBAhouse, 1987.

Redmond, Eugene B. *Drumvoices: The Mission of Afro-American Poetry.* Garden City: Doubleday-Anchor, 1976.

Smith, David Lionel. "Amiri Baraka and the Politics of Popular Culture." *Politics and the Muse.* Ed. Adam Sorkin. Bowling Green: Popular Press, 1989. 222–38.

———. "Black Figures, Signs, Voices." *Review* 11 (1989): 1–36.

Sollors, Werner. *Amiri Baraka/ LeRoi Jones: The Quest for a Modernist Populism.* New York: Columbia UP, 1978.

Stuckey, Sterling. *Slave Culture.* New York: Oxford UP, 1987.

Williams, Raymond. *Marxism and Literature.* New York: Oxford UP, 1977.

Reassembling Daisy Miller

Lynn Wardley

> *There is only one way to improve ourselves, and that is by*
> *some of us setting an example which the others may pick up*
> *and imitate till the new fashion spreads from east to west.*
> *Some of us are in more favorable positions than others to set*
> *new fashions. Some of us are more striking personally, and*
> *imitable, so to speak. But no living person is sunk so low as*
> *not to be imitated by somebody.*

William James (142)

When, at the end of the nineteenth century, critics of the
"New Woman" discovered in her the features of the androgyne —
the person who "flirted with hermaphroditism" — their description might have applied just as well to the person who grew up
alongside her, the male or the female adolescent (Smith-Rosenberg 260). In this essay I argue that Henry James's "Daisy
Miller: A Study" (1878) figures forth in Daisy the androgynous
body constructed in popular nineteenth-century accounts of
adolescence. If, as Frederick Winterbourne sees it, Daisy Miller
oscillates between masculine and feminine identifications, she
also oscillates between American and alien, savage and citizen,
parvenu and natural aristocrat. Set in Switzerland and in Rome,
"Daisy Miller" chronicles the behavior of Americans abroad.
But it also depicts a displaced landscape of North American
immigration and the nativist's anxiety about the American girl's
intimacy with a handsome Italian. Although Daisy's "archetypal" (Welter 3), near "mythic" (Fiedler 298–300) influence
has long been recorded, as has her migration from *nouvelle* to
etiquette manual, no study has sufficiently accounted for her
staying power as an American type.[1] Part One of this essay
begins to reinterpret Daisy Miller's impressive reach by suggesting that her story be read in light of certain transformations
in education in the postbellum and post-Darwinian US. Part
Two attempts a more detailed explication of "Daisy Miller" to
show that as Winterbourne steps in to reeducate the flirtatious

Daisy, she elicits anxieties about cultural difference (with "her mystifying manners"), sexual difference ("and her queer adventure"), and the integrity of the "American Man" (*DM* 93, 7). Part Two begins with the controversy surrounding female flirtation into which James's "pretty perversion" was received (*Art* 269).

1

Although William and Henry James agreed that the way to educate the American character was to become a person whose example works "contagiously in *some* particular," they appear to have disagreed over the methods of their own childhood education (William James 143). In *A Small Boy and Others* (1913), Henry compares the flood of random impressions "picked up" while roaming unchaperoned among the "society, manners, type, characters, possibilities and prodigies and mysteries of fifty sorts" in Paris to the supervised Swiss schooling he was to receive in Geneva.

> Such were at any rate some of the vague processes—I see for how utterly vague they must show—of picking up an education; and I was, in spite of the vagueness, so far from agreeing with my brother afterwards that we didn't pick one up and that that never *is* done, in any sense not negligible, and also that an education might, or should, in particular, have picked *us* up, and yet didn't—I was so far dissentient, I say, that I think I quite came to glorify such passages and see them as part of an order really fortunate. (*Autobiography* 199)

Henry's autobiographical reflection, like William's description of the psychology of imitation from his *Talks to Teachers* (1892) above, has its place within a greater transformation in the model of education in the US, a transformation chiefly associated in the antebellum period with the philosophy of Horace Mann, but strongly informed at a later date by the evolutionary science and social thought characteristic of the fin de siècle. As the education historian Lawrence Cremin reminds us, virtually every field of knowledge came under the influence of science in general and Darwinism in particular at the century's end, and pedagogy was no exception (*Transformation* 90–91). Having abandoned the Calvinist doctrine of innate depravity and its emphasis on conversion, and having adopted a meliorist vision of the plastic character of children, progressive pedagogical reformers incorporated neurological and physiological accounts of human evolution into their studies of the effects of nurture, instruction, and the environment on the developing child. In *The Child and the Republic,* Bernard Wishy identifies Jacob Abbott's best-selling *Gentle Measures in the Management and Training of the Young* (1871) as a transitional text, one exemplifying specific changes in nurture books between 1860 and 1880 and legitimating child study by marshaling what seemed to be the "impressive evidence of evolution" (95). While "bad tendencies" in children might stem from hereditary predispositions, "bad habits of action" followed from inadequate or unwholesome training (Abbott, qtd. in Wishy 96). According to the neo-Lamarckian evolutionary doctrine informing much of the optimistic nurture literature, proper habits instilled in children through proper training would gradually be organized as instincts, ultimately passing by transmission to the next generation as permanent improvements.[2] The nature of the child's future — and the perfectibility of "the race" — hinged on the process of the child's development, and no student of that process could now overlook either the body's inheritance or what, more crucially, the "young of the human species . . . first a young animal . . . then a young human" picked up (Gilman, *Home* 234).

Abbott's *Gentle Measures* precipitated many systematic and highly specialized institutional studies of the child. The psychologist G. Stanley Hall, perhaps best known for his two-volume study of adolescence (1904), published the pamphlet *The Study of Children* in 1883, the popularity of which helped to foster local child-study clubs which gradually expanded into organizations like the National Congress of Mothers (1897) (Wishy 107). A national "child-saving movement," identified by at least one historian as a middle-class moral crusade (Platt), extended the child-reformer's power outside of the private home to rescue and restore "the spirit of youth" sapped by "the city streets" (Addams). The child-savers, Anthony Platt informs us, whose targets were the "urchins," "wayward waifs," and "problem children" of the urban environment, borrowed from the medical profession the "imagery of pathology, infection, immunization and treatment," and constructed the categories of juvenile "dependency," "delinquency," and "deviance" with the assistance of the pseudoscience of nineteenth-century American criminology (18).

The rhetoric of the child-saving movement drew attention to the role of the body in contracting the "contagion of character" (Haller 1). But the physical image of character-building as contagion carried within it certain liabilities, among them the possibility that those who are "effectively contagious," those in a position to "inoculate seventy millions of people with new standards," may mistakenly pick up a "vicious fashion or taste" (William James 143, 142). James's protestation to his brother Henry that an education should "have picked *us* up" reveals his reliance on the intervention of the sufficient, and the sufficiently charismatic, model. Abbott too had already recorded that it was "not the arguments" that affected the impressible child "but the person who led them" (qtd. in Wishy 97)—the person, progressive philosophers G. H. Mead and John Dewey would later agree, the child "wished to resemble" (Wishy 97). But, as Karen Halttunen points out, undesirable individuals were no less infectious or imitable than those considered proper models; "evil influence" was publicized by some antebellum moralists as endemic to urban settings and so potent "that a young man could be contaminated merely walking the streets" (5). By the end of the century, analogies drawn from medical science offered an "increasingly plausible idiom in which to formulate . . . almost every aspect of an inexorably modernizing world," from prolonged exposure to industrialization to the effects of immigration (Charles Rosenberg 7). William James and his colleagues concluded that modern American subjects had unprecedented opportunities to form "bad habits," "bred of custom and example, born of the imitation of bad models"— like the bad habits that had already produced in "our characteristic national type" an appalling "absence of repose" (William James 140). Prescribing an antidote to the "wear and tear and fatigue" of American life, James also offers his more general formula for the mechanism of social evolution in the absence of desirable models: "*Become the imitable thing*" (139, 143). If calm is your ideal, and if you seek "harmony, dignity and ease," then "individually achieve calmness and harmony in your own person." If you do, then "you may depend upon it, that a wave of imitation will spread from you, as surely as the circles spread outward when a stone is dropped into a lake" (142).

But the kind of orderly human improvement psychologists like James were describing suddenly faced a more unpredictable obstacle in the impressible students themselves, more specifically, adolescents. Although Hall's two-volume work *Adolescence: Its Psychology and Its Relations to Physiology, Anthropology, Sex, Crime, Religion and Education* (1904) was, his biographer reminds us, probably the first systematic study of puberty in the modern world, the components of *Adolescence*

were already considered commonplace at the time of its publication (Ross 333). If childhood was characterized by a great
plasticity in psyche and physiology, a self "susceptible to drill
and discipline," adolescence was considered a volatile stage of
development, a stage Hall associated with the changes determined by evolution (1: ix). While in Hall's recapitulationist
scheme the child "comes from and harkens back to a remoter
past," and between ages nine and twelve relives an "old and
relatively perfected stage of race maturity," adolescence (from
about fourteen to twenty) interrupts this time in "paradise" (2:
61; see also Russett 59). The adolescent is "neo-atavistic," and
in him or her not only do the "later acquisitions of the race,"
like the social instincts, "slowly become prepotent" (1: xiii), but
male and female within an individual body and psyche "struggle
for prepotency" (2: 117).

   This process has a peculiar resolution with startling implications: where boys pass through puberty, girls never entirely
leave adolescence — or its gender struggle — behind. Woman, "at
her best, never outgrows adolescence," and, in turn, adolescence
is so identified with femininity as to be classified the "feminine
stage" (Hall 2: 625). Arrested in her development, a woman is
something of an immature man; this, Hall believed, links her
to the members of the "adolescent races," for example, Indians
and blacks, who "in most respects, are children, or, because of
sexual maturity, more properly, adolescents of adult size" (2:
649). Adolescence is ineluctable, but this does not mean that
it always unfolds according to plan; the storm and stress of
female periodicity in particular, understood in terms of dis-
equilibrium and physiological crisis, demanded special surveillance. Thus Hall contributed his influential voice to an argument favoring sexual segregation in education and a unique
curriculum for girls that took the dynamics of the menstrual
cycle into account. He also called for the rehabilitation of maternal care and supervision, having noted that the American
daughter has been left to pick up "her cue" on her own (2: 575,
573). Criticizing mothers and daughters both, Hall addressed
at least three historical changes in modern American life: the
increasing presence of mature, native-born, middle-class wom-
en in extra-familial occupations and professions; the demand
for identical educational opportunities for the sexes; and the
novel appearance of adolescents as an independent social group
in urban environments, a group whose members posed a challenge to their elders' authority.[3] As historian Joseph Kett observes, the group typically embodying the greatest threat to the
established order was a group of adolescent boys ("lads from

fourteen to twenty-one" are the "busiest instigators" of lawless conduct [anonymous, qtd. in Kett 89]). Yet much attention was paid to the potential of wayward female adolescents to jeopardize the future of "the race," which inherits its tendencies from them.

Studies like William B. Forbush's *The Boy Problem: A Study in Social Pedagogy* (1902) or *The Boy and his Gangs* (1911), by J. Adams Puffer, (two texts introduced by Hall) do reveal a vocational investment on the part of child-savers—particularly the so-called boys-workers—in the psychodynamics of the masculine experience of adolescence.[4] Yet at least part of this interest remained in the *feminization* implicit in the adolescent process, a feminization suffered by "street arabs" and the James brothers alike (Hall 1: 361). At stake in the James brothers' debate about the methods of their own European education is the issue of the dangers posed to unsupervised males at the stage in their development when "cohesions between the elements of the personality loosened" and "perversions multiplied" (Hall 1: ix; Cremin, *American Education* 306). What risks are run when the evolving human male himself passes through adolescence, the "feminized stage" of development? What consequences are imagined, for Henry James, in pursuing an education in Paris "splendidly 'on my own'" (*Autobiography* 199)? If Richard Poirier is right that William James's advocacy of culturally marginalized subjects (mystics, mental patients, saints) reflects the psychologist's attempt to "release himself, and the rest of us, from any settled, coherent idea of the human" (qtd. in Posnock 7), we might ask how the figure of an unsettled, incoherent gender identity complicates this attempt.[5] Or, as it is expressed in "Daisy Miller: A Study" (1878), how does an adolescent American flirt affect an American man, who, in attempting to reeducate her, is reacquainted with the marks of a familiar struggle?

The itinerary of Daisy, who explicitly "'picks up'" not only a "good-looking Roman, of vague identity" (*Art* 267) but also a particularly "terrible case of the *perniciosa*" (*DM* 91) as she travels unchaperoned in Rome, dramatizes the "vague processes of picking up an education" that the novelist recollects, and his brother repudiates. A product of his boyhood schooling in Geneva and now a resident alien of that city, the "American man" Frederick Winterbourne determines that the "name" of American flirts of the Daisy variety is "incoherence" (7, 72). "She was composed," he notes, "of charming little parts that didn't match and that made no *ensemble*" (10–11). Daisy Miller is alternately "innocent," "ignorant," "uncivilized," and "crude." She suffers from a "want of finish," but Winterbourne flatters himself that she comes to Europe, and to him, as to a finishing school (11). Daisy's little brother Randolph, an "urchin of nine or ten," must also be saved (5). Although with his "pale complexion" and "poor little spindle-shanks" Randolph resembles an urban beggar—" 'Will you give me a lump of sugar?' he asked in a small sharp hard voice"—Randolph is not a criminal but a victim (5, 6). Like his sister's, Randolph's education has been unsystematic and peripatetic; he has been subjected to a broken string of "foreign" tutors when he has not been left to get his lessons "in the cars" (14). With a voice "immature, and yet somehow not young," the small boy exhibits all the symptoms of an unwholesome precocity (6). With a mother who embodies a "very different type of maternity" from that of the matrons to whom Winterbourne is accustomed, the uncivilized Miller children are metonymically linked to a number of types he regards as sinister—the parvenu, the alien, the savage, to name only three—and they possess strange manners and customs (35). But as long as he reads in even "so 'strong' a type" as Daisy not intractable difference but negligible training ("it was only her habit, her having no idea whatever of form . . ."), he remains committed to the project of Daisy's improvement (16, 11). When he concludes that Daisy is, after all, perverse, and of a "perversity" pathogenically represented as a "black little blot," he retreats to Geneva (86).

The potential illegibility of cultural or national or class affiliation makes characters like Winterbourne anxious. He is introduced in the promiscuous international setting of a comfortable Swiss resort that could pass for an inn at Saratoga, where German waiters resemble "secretaries of legation," Russian princesses mingle with Polish tourists, and he himself is mistaken for a German by Daisy, unpersuaded that he is a " 'real American' " (3–4, 12). But it is less the apparent portability of class or national or ethnic characteristics—the possibility that anybody, even the ignorant Daisy, can pick an identity up and assume it in masquerade—than the instability of gender that confuses the American man. Daisy's European tour is the rite de passage of an aspiring young woman of her class. This rite of conspicuous acculturation loses none of its significance as a passage into adult sexuality: for not only does the tour prepare her, like a regimen of etiquette lessons, for a well-made match, but Daisy's itinerary also obliquely represents what Freud would later describe as the "difficult development

But it is less the apparent portability of class or national or ethnic characteristics—the possibility that anybody, even the ignorant Daisy, can pick an identity up and assume it in masquerade—than the instability of gender that confuses the American man.

to femininity"—before the libido, that is, has "taken up final positions" (135). To suspect that Daisy Miller is as yet incoherent or incomplete is to suspect that the "charming little parts that didn't match and that made no *ensemble*" are not only the parts of her dress or speech. "We may not know exactly what sex is," Havelock Ellis would conclude, "but we do know that it is mutable, with the possibility of one sex being changed into the other sex, that its frontiers are often uncertain, and that there are many stages between a complete male and a complete female" (225). Winterbourne's suspicions help to explain his "odd attachment" to the "little capital of Calvinism" and his ultimate preference for a hermeneutics in which a "perversity" of Daisy's order can have no ambiguous gray "shades" (5, 86).

Daisy's physiological riddles and contradictions are complemented by her "fearful, frightful" flirtations (71). In Daisy's particular case, the oscillations and indirections of flirtation correspond to what Ruth Bernard Yeazell refers to as the "imagined indirections of female desire," moving always, in Ellis's words, "in a zigzag or a curve" (qtd. in Yeazell 46). According to Yeazell, the courtship plot that structures certain nineteenth-century English novels also informs the findings of Charles Darwin and Ellis, who would discover "inscribed in Nature a familiar narrative of courtship—a narrative about female resistance and female choice" (34). For Darwin and Ellis, Yeazell explains, feminine courtship behavior is dictated by the "sexual modesty of the female animal," a modesty rooted in her "sexual periodicity" and expressive of the (biological) fact that the "time for love is not now" (qtd. in Yeazell 35). If we leave behind momentarily the sexologists' evolutionary explanation to seek a more local motivation for Daisy's oscillations, one presents itself not in the organic changes in the maturing female body but in the cultural demands those changes occasioned in the nineteenth-century US. Barbara Welter has already recognized in Daisy the "archetype of American adolescent girls" reluctant to submit to the initiation into adult womanhood sometimes referred to as " 'breaking the will' of the wayward tomboy" by curbing her behavior and "calming her down" around the time of menarche (3, 203n; see also Habegger 182–83). Poised, like Louisa May Alcott's Jo March, on a liminal threshold, Daisy Miller resists the forfeiture of an unchaperoned autonomy as a single American girl for what she suspects is the "dreadfully pokey time" of a married American woman (70).

But in Winterbourne's eyes, Daisy oscillates not so much between two gendered roles as between two gendered bodies.

It is to sexual difference or, more properly, the failure of sexual difference that Winterbourne's gaze returns, reinforcing Alexis de Tocqueville's observation that gender is the linchpin of the social and political, as well as the psychical, organization of the democracy, a preventive of promiscuous mergings. In studying Daisy (he was "addicted to noting, and, as it were recording, her nose, her ears, her teeth" [11]), Winterbourne adds to, as he himself evinces, a "girl fetish" in the postbellum US (Welter 3), the widespread cultural project Martha Banta has defined as "imaging American women." There is of course more to this project than fetishism. But in responding to Daisy's adolescent incoherence by attempting to assemble her "charming little parts," Winterbourne does seem to seek reassurance that his own coherence—imagined as a final sexed subjectivity—is unassailable. " 'It is well for the world,' " William James noted, " 'that in most of us, by the age of thirty, the character has set like plaster and will never soften again' " (qtd. in Posnock 11). Mr. Winterbourne, Daisy says of the twenty-seven-year-old man, has "no more 'give' than a ramrod" (83). His completeness is here marked, as I have said, by a fixed sexed subjectivity. But to begin to question that fixity, as the mere appearance of the apparently mutable Daisy seems to, is to begin unsettling his identity with respect to more than sex. As Randolph Miller vivaciously inquires, " 'Are you an American man?' " (7).

With the publication of "Daisy Miller: A Study," Henry James contributed indirectly to changing conceptions of education in the US by emphasizing both the role of the evolving body in the educational process and the volatile character of the adolescent experience. "Daisy Miller" is of course better remembered for its contribution to the controversy surrounding the cultural practice of flirtation in modern urban environments. As "Daisy Miller" dramatized the pedagogical problem of picking up influential, imitable models, Daisy Miller was appropriated by numerous social critics as a negative model of the American girl who flirts with "any man she can pick up" (*DM* 64). Flirtation, like education, operates in the manner of contagion, as Daisy "picks up" a lethal case of Roman Fever along with Mr. Giovanelli. Flirtation puts the body at risk of exposure to noxious influences, literalized in the malaria ("bad air") to which Giovanelli is immune. Although it takes place in Europe, James's narrative of 1878 offers a setting for examining the cultural conditions in the metropolitan US, when the opportunities for multiethnic or interracial affiliation and amalgamation—expressed in Daisy's presumed flirtation and eventual "intimacy" with the Roman man—radically increased.[6] So, too, in the context of the Woman Movement, did the opportunities for public exercises of a potentially autonomous feminine will. It was not that coquetry had been previously unequivocally regarded or that it was not perceived to have (sometimes fatal) consequences. It was, rather, that near the end of the nineteenth century the imagined content of those consequences changed, and female flirtation, like female education, became a subject worth studying.

2

In the early twentieth century, sociologist Georg Simmel considered flirtatious behavior a form of power and devoted an essay ("On Flirtation," 1909) to flirtation's contemporary significance. Simmel cites an anonymous French sociologist who argues that flirtation might derive from the "ancient . . . phenomenon of 'marriage by abduction,' " or it might be the novel product of the "advance of culture," wherein the "large increase in the number of provocative phenomena"

> [has] produced an erotic repression in men. It is simply not possible to possess all of the attractive women — whereas in primitive times, such as [sic] abundance of attractive phenomena just did not exist. Flirtation is the remedy for this condition. By this means, a woman could give herself — potentially, symbolically, or by approximation — to a large number of men, and in this same sense, the individual man could possess a large number of women. (139–40)

Men engage in flirtation, but to flirt means to be able to refuse and concede at once, and "refusing and conceding are what women, and only women, can do in a consummate fashion." After Darwin, we can understand flirtation as the "consummation of the sexual role that belongs to the female throughout the animal kingdom: to be the chooser" (140). The "oscillating impulses" of the female of the species betray her reluctance to close the deal, for in the act of making the deal women are, momentarily, the "masters." This mastery is temporary and its contradictory logic — "saying no and saying yes" — is a kind of temporizing. For when a woman flirts, Simmel writes, she flirts with freedom and power: "[O]nce she has decided, in either direction, her power is ended" (141).

Simmel's "On Flirtation" contributed to an ongoing conversation about the place of flirtation in the history of female oppression, a conversation sustained in part by feminist intellectuals. In one view, flirtatious female behavior strategically resisted, however temporarily, male prerogatives; from another vantage point, flirtation indicated a pernicious social condition. Charlotte Perkins Gilman's 1898 evolutionary analysis of the white middle- and leisure-class woman's "sexuo-economic" position assumes that flirtation and self-ornamentation—women's speech, body language, and dress—are the products of our "peculiar inversion in the usual habit of species," in which the "males compete in ornament and the females select" (*Women and Economics* 54–55). Flirtation is not the mark of the female's role as the chooser, but an indication that her role has been usurped. Where once men and women were equals in the economic relation, women are now kept by their mates. Coquetry, outré self-ornamentation, even the fetishization of such body parts as the ankle and foot—these are all the means to the female's end of attracting the male on whom she relies for her very survival. Gilman's commitment to Lamarckian evolutionary thought led her to the conclusion that the feminine weaknesses which arose from these conditions would pass through maternal transmission to the next generation, gradually degrading the entire race. Gilman's solution was economic independence for the female of the human species, her full participation in the industrial market outside the "painfully inadequate limits" of the private home (*Home* 21). It would follow from this that the self-supporting female of the future would redefine femininity itself. Thus the women of the utopian landscape of Gilman's *Herland* (1915) baffle the visiting bachelors who find them not at all "provocative"; their ornamentation and dress, the male narrator notes, "had not a touch of the come-and-find-me element" (128).

Daisy Miller's behavior exhibits either the self-determination of the flirt (" 'I've never allowed a gentleman to dictate to me or to interfere with anything I do' " [57]) or the illusory nature of her mastery. James's study of the "specimen" Daisy appeared to some grateful advice-givers to be prescriptive; it inoculated "innumerable" American girls, who "learned more from it than they would through a volume of well-intentioned maxims" (Mrs. Sherwood, qtd. in Stafford 130). Although William Dean Howells notes with regret that by 1880 Henry James had wiped all the charming Daisys off the face of Europe ("In 1870 you saw and heard her everywhere on the European continent; in 1880 you sought her in vain." [164–76]), the author of *Good Manners for All Occasions,* Mrs. Sherwood, was unsentimentally relieved to report two decades later that Daisy Miller is "almost an extinct species" (qtd. in Stafford 130).

But identifying Daisy's genus and educating by her bad example was not the only cultural work "Daisy Miller" performed; it also offered instruction in the classification of other differences as readers studied along with Daisy something like an ethnography of human types. In her salon Mrs. Walker collects "several specimens of diversely-born humanity" to serve as the "text-books" in Daisy's training, in hopes that the American girl will soon "instinctively discriminate" against the "unmistakeably low foreigners" among whom she now ignorantly selects (67, 58). If Daisy hears Winterbourne refer to Giovanelli as "that thing," the reader knows the Italian as an "it"—"it had a handsome face, a hat artfully posed, a glass in one eye and a nosegay in its buttonhole"—or sees him segmented, almost zoologically, into parts: "flashing teeth, all manners and a wonderful moustache" (56). But here the naturalist's voice is interrupted by the language of manufacture; so consciously assembled are the Italian's traits that he can be "set . . . in motion," as if wound by a key: "[H]e curled his moustaches, and rolled his eyes, and performed all the functions of a handsome Italian at a dinner party" (69). Like ethnic markers, the grammar of class seems easy to read; the description of Daisy's garrulous mother owes something to the phrenological system, and it anticipates Thorstein Veblen: her "unmistakeable forehead" is "decorated with thin, much-frizzled hair" perched above a "dead waste of temples," and she wears "enormous diamonds" in her ears (31, 67). Daisy is introduced to the arcane and silent symbolics of the ladies of Mrs. Costello's expatriate Protestant tribe. Mrs. Costello's sick-headache and Mrs. Walker's cold shoulder are daily lessons: " 'They'll show you the cold shoulder,' " Winterbourne explains. " 'Do you know what that means?' " (83). The reader is initiated immediately into an anthropological approach to a character's subjectivity through Winterbourne's tutelage: " 'How pretty they are! ' " he says to himself when he first spots the solitary American girl (8). But if his habit of scanning bodies for the marks of their national or class or even species specificity is a defense against accidentally mingling with alien life forms, his totalizing gaze is ultimately disconcerting. To record Daisy's teeth, well-shaped ear, and habits of speech, or Giovanelli's eyeglass, motions, and moustache, can only reflect the arbitrary assembly of the American's own identity and unmask its prosthetic quality.

In an environment in which identifying marks are easily

discarded, adopted, or traversed, sexual difference guarantees distinctions. But even sexual difference is less reliable than it first seems, at least during the polymorphic stages of adolescence. Sexual difference is legible only as it manifests itself (and is thereby shored up) in traditionally gendered forms of social conduct. As Hall observes in *Adolescence,* "both sexes have within them the germs of the other's quality," and this fact "makes it incumbent on each to play its sex symphony with no great error." Thus it is an "important office of convention, custom and etiquette to preside over this balance between the relationship of the sexes at large" (2: 118). Modesty, for example, fulfills this important office neatly, for modesty is "at root mode, and woman is its priestess" (2: 118). In identifying modest behavior with femininity, Hall echoed the findings of contemporary sexologists who concluded, as, again, Yeazell reminds us, that modesty had its evolution in an instinctual response rooted in the sexual periodicity of the female, who could be judged "her own duenna" and trusted to "venture out into the world alone" (34, 36). This may help us to explain Leslie Fiedler's peevish intuition that Daisy Miller is "innocent by definition, *mythically* innocent" (298–300), but it renders unaccountable Daisy's explicit *immodesty*–the fact that she makes a spectacle of herself, as Mrs. Costello puts it, or that Daisy, like the rest of her family, is "bad enough to blush for" (46). But Hall answers this contradiction readily: "while boys in general are more prone to the overt forms of showing off, they often incline in early adolescence toward modesty, and girls, usually a little more retiring at this period, now become for a time less so." This "initial forwardness of girls may be a rudiment of the age when woman was the active agent in domesticating man and developing the family father" (2: 372). A young woman's immodesty may be explained away as an atavism, the exception that proves the rule of a characteristic female modesty. But the reappearance of such a rudimentary trait calls for careful guidance through the adolescent passage, for not only is the individual female's acquisition of a proper gender identity at stake, but so too is the balance between the sexes at large. Daisy's crash course in manners, morals, and modesty, then, is meant as an inducement to play her "sex symphony with no great error" (2: 118).

But the expression of modesty, understood at once to articulate and to guarantee sexual difference, also prevented undifferentiation of other kinds. Daisy Miller engages in what a few American social critics called "public flirtation," about which public opinion was divided: while such flirting constituted

an "innocent promiscuity" by most US standards, one observer
records with disapproval that in "Barnum's Museum couples
strolled around the galleries with their arms intertwined; and
in the small dark museum theatre they could be observed em-
bracing" (Banner 80, 81). Like Barnum's immodest couples,
Daisy and Giovanelli exhibit in the dusky spaces of St. Peter's
and the secluded nooks of the Doria Palace a liaison better
reserved for the interiors of private homes. Mrs. Walker is
alarmed at the education Randolph Miller is imbibing from his
sister's intrigue, as if her conduct might excite in him a dangerous precocity (64). Daisy threatens to erode the distinctions
between private and public spaces further when she elects to
"walk about the streets of Rome" or, rather, as she protests to
Winterbourne, about the Pincio, which " 'ain't the streets' "
(70). To walk, or as the ironically named Mrs. Walker tellingly
puts it, to "prowl" unchaperoned at twilight will ruin Daisy's
reputation (53). In so saying Mrs. Walker echoes a turn-of-the-
century rule of thumb among members of her class that a "lady
was simply not supposed to be seen aimlessly wandering the
streets in the evening or eating alone," that such acts were in
themselves potentially fatal forms of exposure (Vicinus 297,
218).

In the US, debates about the need for chaperones revolved
around the perception that "the innate propriety of the American woman and the chivalrous nature of the American man"
no longer erected a barrier against strangers who "might be
wolves in sheep's clothing" (Schlesinger 45). This perception
responded to the appearance of the confidence man in modern
urban settings, but it also evoked the image of the alien species
(the wolf disguised as a sheep) or "foreigner," as the American
colonists in Rome insist on referring to natives like Giovanelli.
Thus the American girl's blithe interaction with "third-rate
Italians" also conjures the picture of cross-cultural or interracial
mixing, of undifferentiation of a vaguely criminal kind. This
displaced American spectacle helps account for the expatriates'
repeated anxiety that Daisy Miller will be "carried off" or "carried away" by the wonderfully moustachioed Giovanelli, a
phrase suggestive of a marriage by abduction or a selling into
white slavery, as well as of Daisy's own " 'lawless passions' "
(59).

It is explicitly in terms of an immigrant appropriation of
the American woman, a woman figured as the "conservative
storehouse" of a homogeneous American culture (Brooks 160),
that Henry James addressed the members of the graduating
class of Bryn Mawr in 1904, appealing to each to fortify herself

against the incursions of alien cultures and the temptation to pick up alien ways. Her best protection rests in resisting any such innovations by learning to emulate instead the "proper" speech, manners, and customs of former models until they are acquired as a "second nature" (*Question* 51). In this commencement address (later published as "The Question of Our Speech") and in the essays assembled in *The Speech and Manners of American Women* (1905), James betrays his suspicions not only about the heterodox mixing of cultures and customs at the turn of the century but also about the seemingly unstable nature of female character, as I have argued elsewhere. Daisy's desire to walk the streets links her to another nineteenth-century female "lost to modesty," the urban prostitute (Harris, qtd. in Ryan 72). More American men than American women reported themselves the victims of street crime (Ryan 69–74). Thus, it seems less for the sake of female education than for that of male protection, when, as if paraphrasing his brother William's "Talks to Students," James urges his women listeners to transform themselves into models who transmit a "beneficent contagion" (*Question* 51), like the "early Victorian and mid-Victorian [governess] of English girlhood" (*Speech* 34). The English governess is extinct, but the modern woman can become like her in becoming a "closed vessel of authority," closed against "sloppy leakage" (*Speech* 74). But this image is remarkable even for James, who ends his address at Bryn Mawr invoking martyrdom and heaven, suggesting that there is something costly, because moribund, in so thorough an internalization. Under its terms, the model woman resembles Mrs. Costello, constantly smelling camphor in order to stem contamination from others. The model metropolis looks like the Protestant cemetery near the wall of Imperial Rome, the ultimate cordon sanitaire between American and foreign bodies (91).

It is not the familiar foreign body, however, that threatens American integrity; Giovanelli, as Mrs. Walker proves, is easily studied. Not so the unfamiliar, adolescent American girl, whose polluting powers, and whose vitality, are aptly articulated by the color red. Daisy's debut in Vevey is heralded by Randolph, who precedes his sister dressed in red stockings and a "brilliant red cravat" (5). When Winterbourne first reunites with Daisy in Rome, she is once again associated both with the small boy who precedes her and with a shade of red: "An instant later his pretty sister crossed the threshold" of a "little crimson drawing-room" (47).[7] Although Daisy's coming to Italy and coming of age initially strike Winterbourne as the right occasions on which to exert a kind of tribal claim on the "pretty young daughter of English race," Daisy's arrival arouses in Mrs. Costello an almost apotropaic response (54). To her, Daisy Miller is a "little abomination" (44), and Mrs. Costello's vigilance in keeping herself out of Daisy's pernicious orbit carries within it the authority of taboo: " 'I wouldn't if I hadn't to, but I have to' " (23). If the American colony must cordon itself off from the adolescent, it is less because Daisy's intimacy with Giovanelli flirts with the possibility of mixture than it is because she already plays host to apparently incompatible categories and identities. As if taking their cue from Mrs. Costello, James's readers generally agree that Daisy, or "Annie P. Miller," as it says on her cards, is the "improbable sister to the hard-riding, hard-shooting, sometimes cigar-smoking heroines of the dime novel, related through Molly Wopsus of Joaquin Miller to Annie Oakley" (Fiedler 299). Crossing the threshold into Mrs. Walker's salon, the girl from "that land of dollars and six-shooters" crosses the border between genres, between the American western and the Continental *nouvelle*. Perhaps in this gesture James's story also suggests that the pedagogical authority of Mrs. Walker's well-mannered agenda, and of the novel of manners behind it, is about to succumb.

But perhaps "Daisy Miller" works instead to alert its audience to the different disciplinary requirements of the adolescent, in whom male and female "struggle for prepotency" (Hall 2: 117). Assessing the symptoms of the urchin Randolph's inadequate training—his sleeplessness, his craving for sweets, his spotty schooling—Winterbourne's attention eventually fastens on the small boy's peculiar likeness to his big sister. Randolph, a precocious nine-year-old, and Daisy, about eighteen, are together in the adolescent struggle. More than the color red links brother to sister—she also shares his phallic traits. Where Randolph thrusts his "long alpenstock" into the "flowerbeds" or "trains of ladies dresses," Daisy flaps the "largest fan [Winterbourne] ever beheld" as she pokes her nose into numerous houses (5–6). Put simply, Randolph is his sister's "telltale appendage" (12), and in a vision capturing Daisy's erotic androgyny, even her polymorphic perversity, Winterbourne watches her descend a staircase while "squeezing her folded parasol against her pretty figure" (39).

As if to orchestrate Daisy's femininity in the midst of such confusion, "Daisy Miller" resuscitates a familiar nineteenth-century plot, even to its sentimental conclusion of the (perhaps voluntary) death of the young woman betrayed in love. As the suggestions of both seduction and miscegenation develop, Daisy assumes an unambiguously gendered place in a plot generically inflected by the captivity narrative and the gothic novel. Daisy seems "carried away," whether in a cabinet of the Doria Palace seated not only with Giovanelli but also, as if the cabinet were a confessional, in the "papal presence" of Innocent X, or on her visit to the Palace of the Caesars, where Giovanelli "glowed as never before with something of the glory of his race" (79, 82). Observing the couple in this setting, Frederick Winterbourne "inhaled the softly humid odors and felt the freshness of the year and the deep antiquity of the place reaffirm themselves in deep interfusion" (81). The "deep interfusion" of Old World and New is apparently sealed later one evening in the "villainous miasma" of the Colosseum, where the American again encounters the immodest twosome (85). Although he had admitted to shifting visions of Daisy's nature, Winterbourne now sees merely a "black little blot," an image expressive of the peculiarly Calvinist account of the soul, the indication of a pathology, and the mark of amalgamation (86). The rush to get Daisy, like Cinderella, home before midnight suggests her imminent physical transformation.

Daisy Miller's death, arguably the result of her association with the Roman Catholic Giovanelli, paradoxically certifies the certain "indispensable fineness" she was assumed all along to lack and admits her to the elect Protestant colony, albeit by way of the Protestant cemetery (59). It will take a final confession from Giovanelli that Daisy was "naturally! the most innocent young lady" he ever knew to persuade Winterbourne that he had misinterpreted Daisy's behavior and that perhaps she might, as he modestly puts it, have returned the American's "esteem" (92, 93). Perhaps Daisy's black little blot is actually the diacritical mark of the blind spot in Winterbourne's reading of the pretty American flirt and not the sign of her innocence lost, like the "X" that follows the notorious Innocent's name. But in light of the ambiguity in Giovanelli's confession (how innocent is the "most innocent" young lady in his acquaintance?) and in the context of the cultural conditions out of which James drew his study, the conditions not only of "Daisy Miller" but also of *The Golden Bowl,* we might argue instead that this story ends by underscoring Winterbourne's blindness—blindness to the mixture inherent in any past or future construction of American identity, even that of his own settled and coherent ensemble. It follows, then, that Winterbourne's suggestive characterization of Daisy's burial mound, a "raw protuberance" in a bed of flowers, reassuringly reflects the firmness of his own subject position as an American man (93). Or that, on second glance, her grave is to him a prosthetic specter, and he was well counseled to ward her off.

3

She looked at him a moment, and then let it renew her amusement. "I like to make you say those things. You're a queer mixture!" (41)

Daisy Miller suggests to Frederick Winterbourne the possibility of his own androgyny and of his own assembled or reassembled identity as an American man. When, with Mrs. Costello, he questions Daisy's virtue—"It was impossible to regard her as a wholly unspotted flower" (59)—it is a way of stressing as well Daisy's far from unspotted genealogy, her hybrid or mongrel identity.[8] For Mrs. Costello, no less than for her nephew, Daisy is a revenant reminder that the "deep interfusion" against which she protects herself has already long taken place—perhaps not only in North American history but also, as her surname suggests, in the course of Mrs. Costello's own life. Her discomfort in Daisy's presence stems not from the fact that the girl is incorrigible but rather that she learns only too easily how to emulate and to replicate the likes of Mrs. Costello: the speech, fashions and customs, the manners and morals, of Mrs. Costello's hierarchically organized and tidily transplanted Forty-Second-Street clan. Indeed, Mrs. Costello quickly grasps the American girl's capacity to pick up and repeat Winterbourne's little lessons (31, 57), when she remarks to her nephew that Daisy possesses " 'that charming look they all have. I can't think where they pick it up. And she dresses in perfection; no, you can't know how well she dresses' " (23–24). We might go so far as to say that " 'dying to be exclusive' " in the manner of Winterbourne's irreproachable aunt, Daisy proves a quick study when she enters the Protestant colony near the wall of Imperial Rome (28). It is less Daisy's difference from than it is her uncanny ability to resemble Mrs. Costello that requires the aunt's almost ritualistic response, adding a gothic dimension to James's comedy of manners. For even Mrs. Costello's own granddaughters, as it turns out, are rumored to be " 'tremendous flirts' " (26). What looks at first like difference—the differences among the "specimens of diversely-born humanity" studied in Mrs. Walker's salon—looks, on closer inspection, like family.

This essay has focused, with Mrs. Costello, on the numerous dangerous individual bodies Daisy Miller comes to resemble in the course of her flirtatious passage though James's narrative of 1878. But my focus exposes its own blind spot to the emergence of a very different body both on the Continent and in the US, what we might call the collective body of the coalition. The public spectacle of an organized labor force would have been impossible to ignore after 1877, the year of the Great Strikes. This is not to conclude that Daisy Miller is the figure of the union organizer—not a Molly Wopsus, after all, but a Molly Maguire. But it is to suggest that what might be at stake in Daisy's flirtations—flirting with anyone she can pick up—is the possibility of affiliation across the constructed borders of race, ethnicity, gender, and class, with or without the relaxation of bodily boundaries. Mrs. Costello had seen immigrants in New York, the nouveau riche in Swiss resorts, and even American Girls in Rome before, and she knew one when she saw one. But she had never seen coalitions of interests, and if she refused to learn to recognize them, maybe they would all go away.

Notes

1.   See Schlesinger 45; Stafford; Banner 80–81; Helsinger, Sheets, and Veeder 171–92.

2.   For an informative account of the influence of Lamarckian doctrine on American science and social thought at the turn of the century, see Stocking 234–69; for some of the implications of Lamarckian thought for women, see Russett 158–60.

3.   See Rosalind Rosenberg 1–27, 95–103; Russett 49–77, 119–25. Demos and Demos argue that the adolescent group was a new phenomenon on the late nineteenth-century urban scene. In his analysis of L. Frank Baum's *Oz* series, Culver describes the mature modern woman as an especial threat to G. S. Hall (28–37). I thank Culver for sharing with me his work on Baum.

4.   Mailloux has examined the role of fiction in the socialization of boys. He reads Mark Twain's *Adventures of Huckleberry Finn* not only within the literary tradition of the bad-boy book but also within the larger nexus of cultural practices concerning male juvenile delinquency (100–29). See also Kett 86–108, 215–44 for discussions of conduct-of-life literature for boys and of male adolescence and deviance.

5.   Posnock's persuasive interpretation of the contrasting temperaments of William and Henry James begins with a description of William's preference for action over what he called " 'thought oscillating to and fro' " (1). Posnock suggests that William's "first exposure to the virus of 'pure theoretic con-

templation' occurred as an adolescent strolling the streets of Paris and London with his brother Henry, who somehow seemed immune to the sickness" (1). I agree with Posnock's thesis that the components of the James brothers' relationship are inseparable from their interest in "forms of being that resist normalization" (3), but I count women and adolescents among these seemingly resistant forms to add that an anxiety about feminization is attached to William's fear of the loss of action. Posnock's discussion of William's famous abulia, the "near suicidal paralysis of will that plagued him in the late 1860's" (4), is interestingly complicated by Smith's analysis of the connection between abulia and the construction of male homosexuality in the sexological science of the fin de siècle.

6. For a pertinent account of the so-called "new immigration" (characterized as consisting of populations from southern and eastern Europe, especially Italians and Poles) and of nativists' responses, see Higham 12–67. Although the new immigrants were described as ill suited for assimilation, I am suggesting that what motivates Mrs. Costello's anxiety is her suspicion that the alien is all too adept at incorporating "American" culture.

7. The color red (associated with the so-called savage instincts, with the loss of virginity, and with menarche) also plays a part in another narrative of an American girl's coming of age, Crane's story of that "rare and wonderful production of the tenement district," Maggie, in *Maggie, a Girl of the Streets* (16). The adolescent Maggie, who "blossomed in a mud puddle," abruptly attracts the attention of the "young men of the vicinity" (16, 17). Her little brother Jimmy occupies himself on street corners, where he "dreams blood-red dreams of the passing of pretty women" (14). See Lévi-Strauss on the significance of red "as the supreme presence of colour" (65). See also Cappetti for an acute discussion of the early sociology of female deviance and the construction of literary types.

8. Describing " 'Miss Baker's, Miss Chandler's—what's her name?—Miss Miller's intrigue,' " Mrs. Costello calls attention to Daisy's class background (76). But "Miller" itself raises the question of Daisy's respectability, insofar as mill work was thought incompatible with virginity (Siegel 87). See also Denning (185–200); Peiss. I thank Shelley Fisher Fishkin for helping to shape my reading of Mrs. Costello.

Works Cited

Addams, Jane. *The Spirit of Youth and the City Streets.* New York: Macmillan, 1930.

Banner, Lois. *American Beauty.* Chicago: U of Chicago P, 1983.

Banta, Martha. *Imaging American Women: Idea and Ideals in Cultural History.* New York: Columbia UP, 1987.

Brooks, W. K. *The Law of Heredity.* Baltimore, 1883.

Cappetti, Carla. "Deviant Girls and Dissatisfied Women: A Sociologist's Tale." Sollors 124–57.

Crane, Stephen. *Maggie, a Girl of the Streets.* 1895. New York: Bantam, 1988.

Cremin, Lawrence A. *American Education: The Metropolitan Experience, 1876–1980.* New York: Harper, 1988.

———. *The Transformation of the School: Progressivism in American Education, 1876–1957.* New York: Knopf, 1961.

Culver, Stuart. "Growing Up in Oz: L. Frank Baum and the Progressive Fairy Tale." Unpublished ms., 1990.

Demos, John, and Virginia Demos. "Adolescence in Historical Perspective." *Journal of Marriage and the Family* 31 (1969): 632–38.

Denning, Michael. *Mechanic Accents: Dime Novels and Working-Class Culture in America.* London: Verso, 1987.

Ellis, Havelock. *The Psychology of Sex.* New York: Ray Long and Richard R. Smith, 1933.

Fiedler, Leslie. *Love and Death in the American Novel.* New York: Criterion, 1960.

Freud, Sigmund. "Femininity." *The Standard Edition of the Complete Psychological Works.* Vol. 22. Trans. James Strachey. London: Hogarth P, 1953. 24 vols. 1953–73.

Gilman, Charlotte Perkins. *Herland.* New York: Pantheon, 1979.

———. *The Home: Its Work and Influence.* Chicago: U of Illinois P, 1972.

———. *Women and Economics.* New York: Harper, 1966.

Habegger, Alfred. *Gender, Fantasy, and Realism in American Literature.* New York: Columbia UP, 1982.

Hall, G. Stanley. *Adolescence: Its Psychology and its Relations to Physiology, Anthropology, Sex, Crime, Religion and Education.* 2 vols. New York: D. Appleton, 1909.

Haller, Newell. *The Contagion of Character.* New York: n.p., 1911.

Halttunen, Karen. *Confidence Men and Painted Women: A Study of Middle-Class Culture in America, 1830–1870.* New Haven: Yale UP, 1982.

Harris, Thomas L. *Juvenile Depravity and Crime in our City: A Sermon . . . Preached in the Stuyvesant Institute . . . Jan. 13, 1850.* New York, 1850.

Helsinger, Elizabeth, Robin Lauterbach Sheets, and William Veeder. *The Woman Question: Science and Literature in Britain and America, 1837–1883.* Vol. 3. Chicago: U of Chicago P, 1983. 3 vols.

Higham, John. *Strangers in the Land: Patterns of American Nativism, 1860–1925.* 1955. New Brunswick: Rutgers UP, 1988.

Howells, William Dean. *Heroines in Fiction.* New York: Harper, 1901.

James, Henry. *The Art of the Novel: Critical Prefaces.* New York: Scribner's, 1948.

———. *Autobiography.* Ed. Frederick W. Dupee. Princeton: Princeton UP, 1983.

———. *Daisy Miller, Pandora, The Patagonia, and Other Tales.* Vol. 18 of *The Novels and Tales of Henry James.* New York Edition. New York: Scribner's, 1909. 26 vols. 1907–17.

———. *The Question of Our Speech and the Lesson of Balzac: Two Lec-*

tures. 1905. Folcroft, PA: Folcroft P, 1956.

———. *The Speech and Manners of American Women.* Ed. J. S. Riggs. Lancaster, PA: Lancaster House P, 1973.

James, William. *Talks to Teachers on Psychology; and to Students on Some of Life's Ideals.* New York: Norton, 1958.

Kett, Joseph. *Rites of Passage: Adolescence in America, 1790 to the Present.* New York: Basic Books, 1977.

Lévi-Strauss, Claude. *The Savage Mind.* Chicago: U of Chicago P, 1966.

Mailloux, Stephen. *Rhetorical Power.* Ithaca: Cornell UP, 1989.

Peiss, Kathy. *Cheap Amusements: Working Women and Leisure in Turn-of-the-Century New York.* Philadelphia: Temple UP, 1986.

Platt, Anthony. *The Child Savers: The Invention of Delinquency.* Chicago: U of Chicago P, 1977.

Posnock, Ross. "William and Henry James." *Raritan* 8.3 (1989): 1–26.

Rosenberg, Charles. *No Other Gods: On Science and American Social Thought.* Baltimore: Johns Hopkins UP, 1976.

Rosenberg, Rosalind. *Beyond Separate Spheres: The Intellectual Roots of Modern Feminism.* New Haven: Yale UP, 1982.

Ross, Dorothy. *G. Stanley Hall: The Psychologist as Prophet.* Chicago: U of Chicago P, 1972.

Russett, Cynthia Eagle. *Sexual Science: The Victorian Construction of*

Womanhood. Cambridge: Harvard UP, 1989.

Ryan, Mary P. *Women in Public: Between Banners and Ballots.* Baltimore: Johns Hopkins UP, 1990.

Schlesinger, Arthur. *Learning How to Behave: A Historical Study of American Etiquette Books.* New York: Macmillan, 1946.

Siegel, Adrienne. *The Image of the American City in Popular Literature, 1820–1870.* Port Washington, NY: Kennikat P, 1981.

Simmel, Georg. *On Women, Sexuality and Love.* Trans. and ed. Guy Oakes. New Haven: Yale UP, 1984.

Smith, John H. "Abulia: Sexuality and Diseases of the Will in the Late Nineteenth Century." *Genders* 6 (1989): 102–24.

Smith-Rosenberg, Carroll. *Disorderly Conduct: Visions of Gender in Victorian America.* New York: Knopf, 1985.

Sollors, Werner, ed. *The Invention of Ethnicity.* New York: Oxford UP, 1989.

Stafford, William James. *James's "Daisy Miller": The Story, the Play, the Critics.* New York: Scribner's, 1963.

Stocking, George. *Race, Culture and Evolution: Essays in the History of Anthropology.* Chicago: U of Chicago P, 1982.

Vicinus, Martha. *Independent Women: Work and Community for Single Women, 1850–1920.* Chicago: U of Chicago P, 1985.

Wardley, Lynn. "Woman's Voice, Democracy's Body, and *The Bostonians*." *ELH* (1989): 639–65.

Welter, Barbara. *Dimity Convictions: The American Woman in the Nineteenth Century.* Athens: Ohio UP, 1976.

Wishy, Bernard. *The Child and the Republic: The Dawn of Modern American Child Nurture.* Philadelphia: U of Pennsylvania P, 1968.

Yeazell, Ruth Bernard. "Nature's Courtship Plot in Darwin and Ellis." *Yale Journal of Criticism* 2.2 (1989): 33–59.

Good-bye, Columbus?
Notes on the Culture of
Criticism

Henry Louis Gates, Jr.

*"We must remember that until very recently Nigeria was
British," said Miss Spurgeon. "It was pink on the map. In
some old atlases it still is." Letty felt that with the way
things were going, nothing was pink on the map any more.*

Barbara Pym, *Quartet in Autumn*

1

I recently asked the dean of a prestigious liberal arts college
if he thought that his school would ever have, as Berkeley has,
a majority nonwhite enrollment. "Never," he replied candidly.
"That would completely alter our identity as a center of the
liberal arts."

The assumption that there is a deep connection between
the shape of a college curriculum and the ethnic composition
of its students reflects a disquieting trend in American education. Political representation has been confused with the "representation" of various ethnic identities in the curriculum, while
debates about the nature of the humanities and core curricula
have become marionette theaters for larger political concerns.

The cultural right, threatened both by these demographic
shifts and by the demand for curricular change, has retreated
to a stance of intellectual protectionism, arguing for a great and
inviolable "Western tradition" which contains the seeds, fruit,
and flowers of the very best that has been thought or uttered
in human history. The cultural left demands changes to accord
with population shifts in gender and ethnicity (along the way
often providing searching indictments of the sexism and racism
that have plagued Western culture and to which the cultural
right sometimes turns a blind eye). Both, it seems to me, are
wrongheaded.

As a humanist, I am just as concerned that so many of my
colleagues, on the one hand, feel that the prime motivation for

a diverse curriculum is these population shifts as I am that those opposing diversity see it as foreclosing the possibility of a shared "American" identity. Both sides quickly resort to a grandly communitarian rhetoric. Both think they're struggling for the very soul of America. But if academic politics quickly becomes a *bellum omnium contra omnes,* perhaps it's time to wish a *pax* on both their houses.

What *is* multiculturalism, and why are they saying such terrible things about it? We've been told it threatens to fragment American culture into a warren of ethnic enclaves, each separate and inviolate. We've been told that it menaces the Western tradition of literature and the arts. We've been told it aims to politicize the school curriculum, replacing honest historical scholarship with a "feel good" syllabus designed solely to bolster the self-esteem of minorities. As I say, the alarm has been sounded, and many scholars and educators—liberals as well as conservatives—have responded to it. After all, if multiculturalism is just a pretty name for ethnic chauvinism, who needs it?

Well, there is, of course, a liberal rejoinder to these concerns, which says that this isn't what multiculturalism is—or at least, not what it ought to be. The liberal pluralist insists that the debate has been miscast from the beginning and that it's worth setting the main issues straight.

There's no denying that the multicultural initiative arose, in part, because of the fragmentation of American society by ethnicity, class, and gender. To make it the culprit for this fragmentation is to mistake effect for cause. Mayor Dinkins's metaphor about New York as a "gorgeous mosaic" is catchy but unhelpful, if it means that each culture is fixed in place and separated by grout. Perhaps we should try to think of American culture as a conversation among different voices—even if it's a conversation that some of us weren't able to join until recently. Perhaps we should think about education, as the conservative philosopher Michael Oakeshott proposed, as "an invitation into the art of this conversation in which we learn to recognize the voices," each conditioned, as he says, by a different perception of the world. Common sense says that you don't bracket 90% of the world's cultural heritage if you really want to learn about the world.

To insist that we "master our own culture" before learning others only defers the vexed question: what gets to count as "our" culture? What makes knowledge worth knowing? There's a wonderful bit of nineteenth-century student doggerel about the great Victorian classicist Benjamin Jowett which nicely sums up the monoculturalist's claims on this point.

> Here I stand, my name is Jowett
> If there's knowledge, then I know it.
> I am the master of this college:
> What I know not, is not knowledge.

Unfortunately, as history has taught us, an Anglo-American regional culture has too often masked itself as universal, passing itself off as our "common culture" and depicting different cultural traditions as "tribal" or "parochial." So it's only when we're free to explore the complexities of our hyphenated American culture that we can discover what a genuinely common American culture might actually look like. Is multiculturalism un-American? Herman Melville—canonical author and great white male—didn't think so. As he wrote in *Redburn,* "We are not a narrow tribe, no. . . . We are not a nation, so much as a world." Common sense (Gramscian or otherwise) reminds us that we're *all* ethnics, and the challenge of transcending ethnic chauvinism is one we all face.

Granted, multiculturalism is no magic panacea for our social ills. We're worried when Johnny can't read. We're worried when Johnny can't add. But shouldn't we be worried, too, when Johnny tramples gravestones in a Jewish cemetery or scrawls racial epithets on a dormitory wall? It's a fact about this country that we've entrusted our schools with the fashioning and re-fashioning of a democratic polity: that's why the schooling of America has always been a matter of political judgment. But in America, a nation that has theorized itself as plural from its inception, our schools have an especially difficult task.

The society we have made simply won't survive without the values of tolerance, and cultural tolerance comes to nothing without cultural understanding. In short, the challenge facing America in the next century will be the shaping, at long last, of a truly common public culture, one responsive to the long-silenced cultures of color. If we relinquish the ideal of America as a plural nation, we abandon the very experiment that America represents.

2

Or so argues the liberal pluralist. But it's a position that infuriates the hard left as much as the conservative rhetoric of exclusion distresses the liberal pluralist. The conservative (these are caricatures, and I apologize), extolling the achievement of something narrativized under the rubric "Western civilization," says: "Nobody does it better." We liberal reformists say: "Do unto others as you would have them do unto you . . . and hope for the best." The hard left says: "Let's do unto you what you *did* unto Others and then see how you like that."

For the hard left, what's distasteful about the ideology of pluralism is that it disguises real power relations while leaving the concept of hegemony unnamed—that it presents an idyllic picture of coexistence that masks the harsh realities. Pluralism, for them, fails to be adequately emancipatory; it leaves oppressive structures intact.

There are at least two things to notice here. First, if the hard left is correct, then the hard right has nothing to worry about from the multicultural initiative. Second, the hard left distinguishes itself from the liberal pluralist position in its frank partisanship; it subsists on a sharp division between hegemons and hegemonized, center and margin, oppressor and oppressed, and makes no bones about which side it's on.

Finally, there is something more puzzling than it first appears about the more general objective: the redistribution of cultural capital, to use the term made familiar by Pierre Bourdieu (see Bourdieu and Passeron). I think it's clarifying to cast the debate in his terms, and faithful to what's at the core of these recent arguments; I also think there's a reason that participants in the debate have been reluctant to do so. Again, let me enumerate.

First, the concept of "cultural capital" makes an otherwise high-minded and high-toned debate sound a little . . . sordid. The very model of cultural capital—by which the possession of cultural knowledge is systematically related to social stratification—is usually "unmasked" as an insidious mechanism; it's held to be the bad faith that hovers over the "liberal arts." You don't want to dive into this cesspool and say, "I want a place in it, too."

Second, a redistributionist agenda may not even be intelligible with respect to cultural capital. Cultural capital refers us to a system of differentiation; in this model, once cultural knowledge is redistributed so that it fails to mark a distinction, it loses its value. To borrow someone else's revision of Benjamin, this may be the work of reproduction in an age of mechanical art (Appadurai 17). We've heard, in this context, the phrase "cultural equity," a concept that may well have strategic value, but that is hard to make sense of otherwise, save as an illicit personification (the transferral of equal standing from people to their products). What could confer "equity" on "culture"? The phrase assumes that works of culture can be measured on some scalar metric—and decreed, from some Archimedean vantage point, to be equal. The question is why anybody should care about "culture" of this sort, let alone fight for a claim upon its title.

Third, the question of value divides the left in two. On the one hand, the usual unself-conscious position is to speak in terms of immanently valuable texts that have been "undervalued" for extrinsic reasons. On the other hand, the more "theorized" position views the concept of "value" as essentially mystified. That position has shrewdly demonstrated that our usual *theories* of value are incoherent, unintelligible, or otherwise ill-founded; the only error it made was to assume that our *practices* of evaluation should, or could, fall by the wayside as well, which is surely a non sequitur. Indeed, the minute the word "judgmental" became pejorative, we should have known we had made a misstep. This is not for a moment to concede that anybody actually stopped judging. Literary evaluation merely ceased to be a professionally accredited act.

In the end, neither left nor right escapes the dean's dilemma. In short, we remain mired in the representation quandary.

3

The interplay between the two senses of the word "representation" has, indeed, been foundational to the now rather depleted argument over the "canon." On the one hand, it has dawned on most of us that the grand canon—this fixed repository of valuable texts—never existed, which is why it was such a pushover. On the other hand, more scholars have come to see that the conflation of textual with political representation fueled a windily apocalyptic rhetoric that had nowhere to go when its putative demands were granted. (It tended to sponsor a naively reductionist mode of reading as well: Alice Walker as the black Eternal Feminine on two legs.) As John Guillory, perhaps our most sophisticated scholar of canon formation, has remarked,

> this sense of representation, the representation of groups by texts, lies at a curious tangent to the concept of political representation, with which it seems perhaps to have been confused, a confusion which is the occasion of both the

> impasse of cooptation and the very cachet of the non-
> canonical, contingent as it is upon the delegitimation of
> the canon. . . . The work of recovery has for the most part
> been undertaken as though the field of writing were a *ple-
> num,* a textual repetition of social diversity. In fact, as is
> quite well known, strategies of exclusion are employed his-
> torically most effectively at the level of access to literacy.
> ("Canonical" 484–85)

But the tension between the two senses of "representation" isn't
restricted to arguments about the canon; in the minority context, the same issues resurface as an issue about the "burdens
of representation" of the black artist. If black authors are primarily entrusted with producing the proverbial "text of blackness," they become vulnerable to the charge of betrayal if they
shirk their duty. (The reason that nobody reads Zora Neale
Hurston's *Seraph on the Suwannee* isn't unrelated to the reason
that everybody reads *Their Eyes Were Watching God.*) Isaac
Julien and Kobena Mercer, the black British filmmaker and
media theorist, have focused on the tension "between representation as a practice of depicting and representation as a
practice of delegation. Representational democracy, like the
classic realist text, is premised on an implicitly mimetic theory
of representation as correspondence with the 'real' " (4). (As
one of a small number of black filmmakers, Julien has felt the
pressure to be in some sense "representative," so that his theoretical objections have an additional polemical edge.)

And while most of us will accept the point, I think many
of us haven't appreciated the significance of this breach when
it comes to the highly mediated relation between critical debates
and their supposed referents.

Indeed, with the celebrated turn to politics in literary studies in the past decade, there's been a significant change in the
register of reproach. Pick up any issue of *Modern Philology* in
the 1950s, and turn to the review section. You'll find that in
those days, one would typically chastise a study for unpardon-
able lapses in its citations or for failing to take full account of
the insight yielded by other scholarship, and judge the author
to be a slipshod ignoramus. Today, for equivalently venial offenses, the errant scholar can be reproached as a collaboration-
ist—accused of unwitting complicity with the ideologies and
structures of oppression, of silencing the voice of the Other, of
colluding with perpetrators of injustice: "Thus Heywood's study
only reinstates and re-valorizes the very specular ideologies it
appears to resist. . . ." The culprit, some fresh-faced young ac-

ademic from the Midwest, stands exposed for what she is, a collaborator and purveyor of repression, a woman who silences entire populations with a single paragraph, who, in view of fatal analytic conflations, has denied agency to all the wretched of the earth.

Politics never felt so good.

It's heady stuff. Critics can feel like the sorcerer's apprentice, unleashing elemental forces beyond their control. But we know, on some level, that it's mostly make-believe—that the brilliant Althusserian unmasking of the ideological apparatus of film editing you published in *October* won't even change the way Mike Ovitz treats his secretary, let alone bring down the house of patriarchy.

I suppose that's why these levels of criticism often get mixed up. I've seen readers' reports on journal manuscripts that say things like: "Not only does so-and-so's paper perpetuate a logic internal to the existing racist, patriarchal order, but footnote 17 gives page numbers to a different edition than is listed in the bibliography." Well, we can't have that, now can we?

The dilemmas of oppositional criticism haunt the fractured American academic community. The 1980s witnessed not only a resurgence of what I'll call the New Moralism, but the beginnings of its subsidence. And this, too, is very much bound up with the problematic of representation, such that the relation between the politics of theory and the politics of politics became a question to be indefinitely deferred or finessed.

Seventies-style hermeneutics killed the author; eighties-style politics brought the author back. The seventies sponsored a hedonic vocabulary of "free-play," *jouissance,* the joys of indeterminacy. The eighties brought back a grim-faced insistence on the hidden moral stakes: New Historicist essays on the English Renaissance, for instance, regularly turned out to be about Indians and empire.

Oppositional criticism in the early seventies offered us a sort of "wacky packs" version of literary history as a procession no longer of laureled heads but of clay feet. Later critiques of the canon went on to dispute its patterns of inclusion and exclusion. And, as Guillory has also pointed out, the reason the debate over the canon entailed the resurrection of the author was simply that it required representatives of a social constituency: The debate over canon formation was concerned, in the first instance, with *authors,* not texts ("Canon" 40).

And we "minority" critics came to play a similar role in the marionette theater of the political that I referred to earlier. We shouldn't wonder at the accompanying acrimony. Edward

Said has indicted what he describes as the "badgering, hectoring, authoritative tone" that persists in contemporary cultural studies, adding, "The great horror I think we should all feel is toward systematic or dogmatic orthodoxies of one sort or another that are paraded as the last word of high Theory still hot from the press" (182). Is it merely the uncanny workings of the old "imitative fallacy" that account for the authoritarian tonalities of scholarship and professional intercourse where issues of domination are foregrounded?

Again, I want to stress the way in which minority criticism can become a site for larger contestations. Robert Young, an editor of the *Oxford Literary Review,* ventured an intriguing proposition in a recent paper entitled "The Politics of 'The Politics of Literary Theory.'" He notes that literary Marxism in contemporary America (as opposed to that in Britain) has "few links with the social sciences or with a political base in the public sphere. You can make almost any political claim you like: you know that there is no danger that it will ever have any political effect." "At the same time," he continues, "the pressure of feminism, and more recently Black Studies, has meant that today the political cannot be ignored by anyone, and may be responsible for the white male retreat into Marxism. Marxism can compete with feminism and Black Studies insofar as it offers to return literary criticism to its traditional moral function, but can, more covertly, also act as a defence against them . . ." (137). The elided social referent of struggle returns, but now it is merely a struggle for the moral high ground. And I think you could argue that this return to a gestural sort of politics reflects a moralizing strain in contemporary criticism that has lost faith in its epistemological claims. If we can't tell you what's true and what's false—the thought goes—we'll at least tell you what's right and what's wrong. What's wrong? Racism, colonialism, oppression, cultural imperialism, patriarchy, epistemic violence. . . . So we lost facts, and we got back ethics—a trade-in, but not necessarily an upgrade.

4

One problem is, as I've suggested, that the immediate concern of the "politics of interpretation" is generally the politics of interpreters. Another is that we tend to equivocate between, on the one hand, what a text *could* mean—the possibilities of its signification, the "modalities of the production of meaning," as de Man has it—and on the other hand, what a text *does*

mean—the issue of its actual political effectivity. Political criticism usually works by demonstrating the former and insinu-
ating the latter. Now, the pleasurable political frisson comes
from the latter, the question of reception and effects (as an old
newsroom slogan has it, if it bleeds, it leads). But critics are
reluctant to engage in actual sociology: it isn't what they were
trained to do; it's not what they were raised to value. Still, as
political critics, we usually *trade* on that ambiguity.

Let me give you an example of a now familiar version of
such political reading. In the course of elaborating a theory of
the "corporate populist," a recent critical essay accused the
filmmaker Spike Lee of being responsible, though perhaps indirectly, for the death of black youths.[1] The chain of causality
begins with Spike Lee, who makes television commercials promoting Air Jordans; it ends with the inner city—devastated by
crack and consumerism—and a black youth with a bullet through
the brain, murdered for his sneakers. All because Spike said
that he's gotta have it. You think Mars Blackmon is funny?
Those commercials have a body count.

I want to insist that this was not an aberration, but a state-
of-the-art critical essay, one that represents the impasse we've
reached in the American academy. This is how we've been
taught to do cultural politics: you find the body; then you find
a culprit. It's also where the critique of the commodity will lead
you. This is an old phenomenon on both the right and the left—
and certain kinds of Marxism can be very theological on this
point: commodification is a kind of original sin, and any cultural
form it touches is tainted. These critiques, to be sure, are usually
anchored to semi-organicist notions of authenticity.

The old leftist critique of the commodity has a usefully
confining tendency: it sets up a cunning trap that practically
guarantees that the marginalized cultures it glorifies will remain
marginalized. They knew just how to keep us in our place. And
the logic was breathtakingly simple: If you win, you lose.

And that's because it's just a fact about what we quaintly
label the "current conjuncture" that if a cultural form reaches
a substantial audience, it has entered the circuits of commodification. What Paul Gilroy calls "populist modernism" stays
in good ideological standing so long as it doesn't get too popular.
And one of the most important contributions of a younger breed
of cultural theorists has been a critique of the old critique of
the commodity form. Mercer, for example, explores ways in
which commodity forms have been expressively manipulated
by the marginalized to explore and explode the artificiality of
the identities to which they've been confined.

I want to propose that it's worth distinguishing between morality and moralism, but I do so with trepidation. As Logan Pearsall Smith has observed: "That we should practise what we preach is generally admitted; but anyone who preaches what he and his hearers practise must incur the gravest moral disapprobation." At the same time, I worry that the critical hair shirt has become more of a fashion statement than a political one.

A friend of mine suggested that we institutionalize something we already do implicitly at conferences on "minority discourse": award a prize at the end for the panelist, respondent, or contestant most oppressed; at the end of the year, we could have the "Oppression Emmy" Awards.[2] For what became clear, by the end of the past decade, was that this establishment of what J. G. Melquior calls an "official marginality" meant that minority critics are accepted by the academy, but in return, they must accept a role already scripted for them: once scorned, now exalted. You think of Sally Field's address to the Motion Picture Academy when she received her Oscar. "You like me! You really, really like me!" we authorized Others shriek into the microphone, exultation momentarily breaking our dour countenances. (We can, of course, be a little more self-conscious about it and acknowledge our problematic positionality: "You like me, you really, really like me—you racist patriarchal Eurotrash elitists!") But let's face it. It takes all the fun out of being oppositional when someone hands you a script and says, "Be oppositional, please—you look so cute when you're angry."

What feel-good moralism had to confront was the nature of commodified postmodern ethnicity—which we could describe as the Benetton's model. "All the colors of the world": none of the oppression. It was a seductive vision: cashmere instead of power relations.

And it *was* a change. Usually, the Third World presented itself to us as the page people turn when the *Time* magazine ad says, "You can help little Maria or you can turn the page." It was a tropological locale of suffering and destitution. Now little Maria's wearing a purple Angora scarf and a black V-neck sweater, and the message is: "You can have style like Maria and shop at Benetton's—or don't you even care about ethnic harmony?"

To be sure, the Benettonization of culture was not without its ironies: in New York, as Patricia J. Williams has pointed out, the shops may not buzz you in if you actually look like one of those "ethnic" models. But as the eighties came to a close, a nagging doubt began to surface: was academic politics finally a highbrow version of what *Women's Wear Daily* would call the "style wars"? I think that too easily lets us off the hook of history; I want to talk about the ways we've been betrayed by our two-decade-long love affair with theory. Oscar Wilde once quipped that when good Americans die, they go to Paris. I think in Paris, when good theories die, they go to America.

In retrospect, it was easy to point to blunders, some of which I've mentioned. Righteous indignation became routinized, professionalized, and in so doing, underwent an odd transformation. Back in the 1930s, a magazine editor wondered aloud if there was a typewriter at the *Partisan Review* with the word "alienation" on a single key. At the moment, I'm on the lookout for a typewriter that has "counter-hegemonic cultural production" on a single key.

5

And one of the most interesting developments in the past decade took place when theoretically sophisticated minority scholarship parted company with its left-theoretic mentors. I want to take my example here not from literature, but law, and the field of critical legal studies in particular. The participants include the legal scholars Maria Matsudo, Richard Delgado, and Patricia J. Williams, and the philosopher Cornel West.[3] What was revealed was a principled distrust of a "radically utopian strain" in CLS. West took to task American leftism for its undialectical, purely antagonistic relation to liberalism: If you don't build on liberalism, he argues, you build on air. In this vein the minority legal scholars pointed out that those rudiments of legal liberalism—the doctrine of rights, for example, formality of rules and procedures, zones of privacy—that CLS purists wanted to demolish as so much legalistic subterfuge was pretty much all they had going for them. So the irony was, when all the dust had cleared (I'm oversimplifying of course, but not hugely), that the left minority scholars had retrieved and reconstituted liberalism. Some may well dismiss this as just another example of "uneven theoretical development," the minoritarian resistance to universalizing theory. It is, in fact, one of the most telling intellectual twists of recent memory.

And one that also points to the way in which critical theory has failed to keep pace with the larger world. The very notion of an ethical universal—for years dismissed as hopelessly naive—is beginning to make a comeback in the works of a number of feminist theorists. We had so much fun deconstructing the liberal ideology of "rights," for example, that we lost sight of how strategically—humanly—valuable the notion proved in, for example, much Third World politics (as Francis Mading Deng, Abdullahi Ahmed An-Na'im, and others have shown).

Turning a baleful eye to its fellow disciplines, literary criticism has spent the last two decades singing, "Anything You Can Do, I Can Do Better" rather like a scratched Ethel Merman recording, which makes the difficulty literary critics have had in grasping some elementary ideas rather poignant. What was once a resistance to theory has turned into a resistance to anything not packaged as theory.

The oppositional style of criticism has failed us, failed us in our attempt to come to grips with an America that can no longer be construed as an integral whole. What Richard Hofsteader famously called the "paranoid style" of American politics has become the paranoid style of American studies.

None of this is of recent vintage, of course. In 1930, Lionel Trilling could write, "There is only one way to accept America, and that is in hate; one must be close to one's land, passionately close in some way or other, and the only way to be close to America is to hate it. . . . There is no person in the United States, save he be a member of the plutocratic class . . . who is not tainted, a little or much, with the madness of the bottom dog, not one who is not in sympathy of disgust and hate with his fellows." For these are "the universally relevant emotions of America" (29, 32; see also Krupnick 40–46).

Today, success has spoiled us, the right has robbed us of our dyspepsia, and the routinized production of righteous indignation is allowed to substitute for critical rigor.

Today, success has spoiled us, the right has robbed us of our dyspepsia, and the routinized production of righteous indignation is allowed to substitute for critical rigor.

And nothing more clearly marks our failure to address the complexities of the larger world than the continuing ascendancy, in contemporary criticism, of what could be called the colonial paradigm. Colonialism, more as metaphor than as a particularized historical phenomenon, has proven astonishingly capacious; Fanon is blithely invoked to describe the allegedly "colonizing" relation between English departments and history departments. The irony is that, in the meantime, the tendency in subaltern studies has been to pluralize the notion of "colonization," to insist on the particularity of its instances and question the explanatory value of the general rubric. So too with the concept of "neocolonialism," which is increasingly regarded as both exculpatory of despotic Third World regimes and, 30 years after independence, too vague to be helpful in characterizing the peculiarities of these states in the world economy.[4]

But the sovereign-colony relation is simply another instance of the spatial topography of center and margin on which oppositional criticism subsists. And it is just this model that, I want to suggest, has started to exhaust its usefulness in describing our own modernity.

6

Let me say at once that I do not have in mind what some people have trumpeted as the new Pax Americana. In his recent "reflections on American equality and foreign liberations," David Brion Davis remarks, apropos of the recent decline of Eastern bloc communism, that "[n]othing could be more fatuous than to interpret these developments . . . as a prelude to the Americanization of the world." He reminds us of Marx's view that capitalism itself is "permanently revolutionary, tearing down all obstacles that impede the development of productive forces, the expansion of needs, the diversity of production and the exploitation and exchange of natural and intellectual forces" (Davis 6). But to view recent events as a triumph of American corporate capitalism, which has failed to abate the immiseration of the so-called underclass in its own backyard, is simply to misread history. (The Chinese students at Tianenman Square quoted Locke and Jefferson, not Ayn Rand or Lee Iaccocca.) At the same time, I think Davis establishes that the historiographical tradition that depicts America univocally as a force of reaction in a world of daisy-fresh revolutionary ferment reduces a history of complex ambivalence to a crude morality tale.

A great deal of weight has been assigned to the term "cultural imperialism": I do not know that much time has been spent thinking about what the phrase should mean. Should the global circulation of American culture always be identified as imperialism, even if imperialism by other means? In an era of transnational capital, transnational labor, and transnational culture, how well is the center-periphery model holding up?

The distinguished anthropologist Arjun Appadurai has drawn our attention to that "uncanny Philippine affinity for American popular music": "An entire nation," he writes, "seems to have learned to mimic Kenny Rogers and the Lennon sisters, like a vast Asian Motown chorus" (3). All this, in a former US colony racked by enormous contrasts of wealth and poverty, amounting to what he felicitously describes as "nostalgia without memory." And yet the usual remarks about "cultural imperialism" fail to acknowledge the specificity of cultural interactions. An American-centered view of the world blinds us to the fact that America isn't always on center stage, whether as hero or as villain. As Appadurai writes,

> [I]t is worth noticing that for the people of Irian Jaya, Indonesianization may be more worrisome than Americanization, as Japanization may be for Koreans, Indianization for Sri Lankans, Vietnamization for the Cambodians, Russianization for the people of Soviet Armenia and the Baltic Republics. Such a list of alternative fears to Americanization could be greatly expanded, but it is not a shapeless inventory: for polities of smaller scale, there is always a fear of cultural absorption by polities of larger scale, especially those that are nearby. One man's imagined community is another man's political prison. (5–6)[5]

What we are beginning to see, in work that proceeds under the rubric of "public culture," is that, as Appadurai concludes, "the new global cultural economy has to be seen as a complex, overlapping, disjunctive order, which cannot any longer be understood in terms of existing center-periphery models (even those which might account for multiple centers and peripheries)" (6). Again, I want to suggest that the spatial dichotomies through which our oppositional criticism has defined itself prove increasingly inadequate to a cultural complex of traveling culture. Once more, the world itself has outpaced our academic discourse.

Melville's America retained a strong sense of its marginality vis-à-vis its former sovereign and colonizer, and yet his assertion that we are "not a nation, so much as a world" has *become* true, as a geopolitical fact. As a result, the disciplinary enclave of American studies is surely the proper site to begin a study of both the globalization of America and the Americanization of the globe; but, equally, the resistance bred by both of these trends. I think this is a project worth pursuing even if it does not come without a price. Surely it is clear to us all that the ritualized invocation of Otherness is losing its capacity to engender new forms of knowledge, that the "margin" may have exhausted its strategic value as a position from which to theorize the very antinomies that produced it as an object of study.

Or as Audre Lorde writes in her poem "Good Mirrors are Not Cheap,"

It is a waste of time hating a mirror
or its reflection
instead of stopping the hand
that makes glass with distortions

But I've been misunderstood in the past, so I want to be very clear on one point. While I may be taken to have argued for the retrieval of liberalism, however refashioned, as a viable, reformable agenda, I distrust those—on the left, right, or center—who would erect an opposition between leftism and liberalism. West has rightly argued that a left politics that can imagine only an agonistic relation to real-world liberalism is a bankrupt politics, but the converse is true as well; a rights-based liberalism unresponsive to radical (and conservative) critiques is an impoverished one indeed. So let me make it clear that my remarks are primarily aimed at those massively totalizing theories that marginalize practical political action as a jejune indulgence. It's a critique I made a few years back about Luce Irigaray—that her conception of the amazing fixity of patriarchy, the complete unavailability of any external purchase, is more likely to send us to the margins of Plato, Freud, and Lacan than to encourage anything so vulgar as overt political action. The embrace of systematicity—and this is something common to a certain structural/functional tradition of social thought, a tradition whose grand paranoias have made it particularly seductive to literary criticism—rules out humble amelioration (see Gates, "Significant Others"). And while some of the masters of grand totalizing theory will concede the need to struggle for such unglamorous things as "equal wages and social rights," the fact that they feel obliged to make the (rather left-handed) concession indicates the difficulty; their Olympian, all-or-nothing perspective cannot but enervate and diminish the arena of real politics. In short, my brief—and that of many minority intellectuals today—is against the temptations of what I call Messianic pessimism.

Nor, however, can we be content with the multiplication of authorized subjectivities, symbolically rewarded in virtue of being materially deprived. Perhaps we can begin to forgo the pleasures of ethnicist affirmation and routinized ressentiment in favor of rethinking the larger structures that constrain and enable our agency. In an increasingly polycentric world, our task may be to prepare for a world in which nothing is pink on the map.

Notes

1. "For Lee to deny the potential connection between the indiscriminate hawking of shoes and a climate of indiscriminate crime is incredibly to render his advertising as the commercial version of the Air Force's vaunted surgical strike," Jerome Christensen maintains (593).

2. I don't think this is much of an extrapolation. In an issue of *Screen,* for instance, Yvonne Rainer, a distinguished avant-garde filmmaker, helpfully listed her conferential Others: "Starting with the most victimised (alas, even the most noble fantasy of solidarity has its pecking order), they were: blacks, Lesbians, Latina women, Asians, and gay men." (She apologized that Latino men "got lost in the shuffle" [Reynaud and Rainer 91–92].)

3. "There simply is no intellectually acceptable, morally preferable, and practically realizable left social vision and program that does not take liberalism as a starting point," West argues. "I find it ironic that as a black American, a descendant of those who were victimized by American liberalism, I must call attention to liberalism's accomplishments. Yet I must do so. . . . Liberalism is not the possession of white male elites in high places, but rather a dynamic and malleable tradition. . . . In this regard, liberalism signifies neither a status quo to defend . . . nor an ideology to trash . . . but rather a diverse and complex tradition that can be mined in order to enlarge the scope of human freedom" ("Colloquy" 757); see also Williams 146–65; Delgado 301; and the selection presented in *Minority Critiques.* Cf. my "Contract Killer."

4. For a more extended discussion of the colonial paradigm, see my "Critical Fanonism."

5. Further, as Appadurai argues, "the simplification of these many forces (and fears) of homogenization can also be exploited by nation-states in relation to their own minorities, by posing global commoditization (or capitalism, or some other such external enemy) as more real than the threat of its own hegemonic strategies" (6).

Works Cited

Appadurai, Arjun. "Disjuncture and Difference in the Global Cultural Economy." *Public Culture* 2.2 (1990): 1–24.

Bourdieu, Pierre, and Jean-Claude Passeron. *Reproduction in Education, Society and Culture.* Trans. Richard Nice. London: Sage, 1977.

Christensen, Jerome. "Spike Lee, Corporate Populist." *Critical Inquiry* 16.2 (1990): 438–65.

Davis, David Brion. *Revolutions: Reflections on American Equality and Foreign Liberations.* Cambridge: Harvard UP, 1990.

Delgado, Richard. "The Ethereal Scholar: Does Critical Legal Studies Have What Minorities Want?" *Harvard Civil Rights-Civil Liberties Law Review* 22 (1987): 301–22.

Gates, Henry Louis, Jr. "Contract Killer." *Nation* 10 June 1991: 766–70.

———. "Critical Fanonism." *Critical Inquiry* 17 (1991): 457–70.

———. "Significant Others." *Contemporary Literature* 29 (1988): 606–24.

Guillory, John. "Canon, Syllabus, List: A Note on the Pedagogic Imaginary." *Transition* 52 (1991): 36–54.

———. "Canonical and Non-canonical: A Critique of the Current Debate." *ELH* 54 (1987): 483–527.

Julien, Isaac, and Kobena Mercer. "Introduction—De Margin and De Centre." *Screen* 29.4 (1988): 2–10.

Krupnick, Mark. *Lionel Trilling and the Fate of Cultural Criticism.* Evanston: Northwestern UP, 1986.

Lorde, Audre. "Good Mirrors Are Not Cheap." *From a Land Where Other People Live.* Detroit: Broadside, 1973. 15.

Melville, Herman. *Redburn, His First Voyage.* Ed. Harold Beaver. Harmondsworth, NY: Penguin, 1976.

Minority Critiques of the Critical Legal Studies Movement. Spec. issue of *Harvard Civil Rights–Civil Liberties Law Review* 22 (1987): 297–447.

Oakeshott, Michael. *The Voice of Liberal Learning: Michael Oakeshott on Education.* Ed. Timothy Fuller. New Haven: Yale UP, 1989.

Reynaud, Bérénice, and Yvonne Rainer. "Responses to Coco Fusco's 'Fantasies of Oppositionality.'" *Screen* 30.3 (1989): 79–99.

Said, Edward, and Raymond Williams. "Media, Margins, and Modernity." *The Politics of Modernism: Against the New Conformists.* Ed. Tony Pinkney. London: Verso, 1989. 177–97.

Smith, Logan Pearsall. *All Trivia.* New York: Ticknor & Fields, 1984.

Trilling, Lionel. "The Promise of Realism." *Speaking of Literature and Society.* Ed. Diana Trilling. New York: Harcourt, 1980. 27–33.

West, Cornel. "Between Dewey and Gramsci: Unger's Emancipatory Experimentalism." *Northwestern University Law Review* 81 (1987): 941–51.

———. "Colloquy: CLS and a Liberal Critic." *Yale Law Journal* 97 (1988): 757–71.

Williams, Patricia J. *The Alchemy of Race and Rights.* Cambridge: Harvard UP, 1991.

Young, Robert. "The Politics of 'The Politics of Literary Theory.'" *Oxford Literary Review* 10.1–2 (1988): 131–57.

The Last Real Man in America: From Natty Bumppo to Batman

David Leverenz

In the summer of 1989, one of the glossiest men's magazines appeared with a picture of Sean Connery on the cover. Dressed in a creamy ivory tuxedo, standing with arms folded against a beige background, visible only to the waist, he embodied elegance, sensuality, and virility. The caption proclaimed him "The Last Real Man in America."

Why should the Last Real Man in America be a British actor? The taunting ambiguity implies that no American can claim true manliness anymore; to see it at all is to see it vanishing. Only a working-class Scotsman who secured his international image as James Bond, an Englishman equally skilled in civility and violence, can temporarily import virility to American shores. Yet the pleasurable visual framing of his face as white on white on beige seems curiously reassuring. Connery represents the last, best hope, the master of everything not quite seen, dark, and below the belt. He can protect a civilized, yet effete Us from a barbaric though enviably violent Them.

The July cover of *Gentleman's Quarterly* slipped from my mind until late August, when I was standing in a checkout line at a Florida supermarket and noticed the September cover of *Celebrity Plus,* a decidedly downscale fan magazine. This cover featured Harrison Ford in a woodsy setting, with a yellow blurb announcing, "Rare Interview! The 'Last' Real Man."[1] Faced with such a flagrant intertextual rip-off, I began wondering: in what other country could variations on that come-on sell magazines? To ask the question exposes the strange mixture of bravado, anxiety, and nostalgia in the motif. Male readers in more traditionally patriarchal cultures might well feel insulted. Why did I feel a bit wistful, even teased? The motif has a beleaguered quality to it, as if urban, yuppie, corporate, feminist America had become intrinsically emasculating.

Nineteen eighty-nine was the summer in which Batman, the Last Real Man in Gotham City, galvanized the highest short-term gross in movie history in part by dramatizing a double myth of man-making. To save hapless bourgeois cosmopolitans from their high-tech powerlessness, Bruce Wayne becomes half beast and descends into the underclass, a downward mobility that also gives steel and grit to his aristocratic boyishness. The year before, another sweetly bumbling Bruce Wayne patrician had managed to step into Ronald Reagan's manly image and position by banishing what a *Newsweek* cover story had labeled "The Wimp Factor" with two brilliantly chosen counterimages. Willie Horton, the underclass rapist, evoked the powerlessness of middle-class voters as well as the spinelessness of liberal officials. With a more subliminal audacity, George Bush secured his mythic transformation into an electable manly image by choosing Robin as his running mate. The war with Iraq confirmed that new image so completely that cartoonist Pat Oliphant "temporarily retired" Bush's purse (see Gamarekian). Collectively, the war enacted a drama of national remasculinization in which the "humiliation" of Saddam Hussein avenged the still-festering humiliation of Vietnam.

As I write in March of 1991, the number one best-seller for the past few weeks has been *Iron John: A Book About Men.* Robert Bly's book speaks to many mid-life American men who look into themselves and find mostly rubbery adaptations. The movement Bly has inspired depends less on a recoil against feminists than on a widespread need to struggle beyond workplace-generated norms for fathering and male friendships. Many men want to feel both "wild" and strong yet emotionally open and vulnerable with other men, beyond the capitalist constraints enforcing competitiveness, mobility, and self-control. Astutely repackaging psychoanalytic confessions in Native-American patriarchal trappings, Bly's movement offers Indian tribal ceremonies as initiation rites and mentoring support groups for remasculinization, in ways quite continuous with turn-of-the-century, middle-class lodge rituals. Under this patriarchal cover, as Mark Carnes has argued for Masonic ceremonies (*Secret Ritual*), men can express their hidden nurturing side as well as their anger and grief about inadequate fathering, without feeling feminized or weak (see also Jeffords).[2]

The first Last Real Man in America, Cooper's Natty Bumppo, dramatizes a similar white flight from civilized unmanliness to Native-American traditions of patriarchal comradeship. Especially in *The Last of the Mohicans* (1826), the novel-romance that established Natty's image as heroic frontiersman, an elegiac nostalgia suffuses Cooper's portraits of red and white heroes alike. As a variety of critics have demonstrated, Cooper simultaneously replicates and displaces expansionist conflicts by subsuming a collective story of manifest destiny in an elegy for primitive manly character.³ Fleeing civilization and progress, "Hawkeye" or "La Longue Carabine"—almost his only names here—finds his soul mate in Chingachgook, the first "gook" to inhabit the enduring white myth of the self-subordinating man of color. When the reader meets Natty and Chingachgook, however, the two characters are vehemently arguing over why white people have any right to take the Indians' land.

At first Natty claims that the whites are just doing what the Indians used to do to each other. But it does seem unfair, he acknowledges to himself, that white men have bullets. Worse, modern white men no longer publicly shame the " 'cowardly' " and acclaim the brave; they " 'write in books' " instead of telling their deeds in their villages, Natty says in disbelief, and they spend their " 'days among the women, in learning the names of black marks,' " instead of hearing the deeds of the fathers and feeling " 'a pride in striving to outdo them' " (35). Eventually the two friends agree to blame the whole problem on the Dutch, who gave the Indians firewater (37). But the solution seems patently inadequate to the tensions raised by the protracted argument. Or rather, the solution allows them to feel that their friendship can evade history, much as Natty frequently proclaims his uncontaminated white identity, " 'a man without a cross,' " while plunging further and further into crossover liminal realms of mixture.⁴ At the end, when Chingachgook's son Uncas dies and the father himself ironically becomes the Last of the Mohicans, the "self-command" of both grieving friends gives way to bowed heads and "scalding tears" (414). Childless, facing death, and bonded with natural manly feeling, the two embody a double elegy for a vanishing patriarchal simplicity.

Why would Cooper write a book to mourn the passing of a manliness that scorns the womanish writing of books? Because he and his civilized male readers could condescend to this "Natural Bumpkin" yet long for the manliness that Natty Bumppo represents. Ostensibly devising a paternalistic narration to harmonize civilized and savage life with principles of moral conduct, as the 1850 preface to the Leatherstocking Tales sententiously claims, Cooper fortunately brings stress-points and contradictions out into the open. He reserves his most pointed mockery for the maladapted transplant from high civilization, David Gamut, the musician in the wilderness. On the frontier, where traditional class status seemingly yields to a hierarchy of natural manliness, psalm-singing David Gamut begins at the bottom. He cannot even manage his mare.

The hapless male musician has been a contrasting foil in

various Real Man myths since the time of Hercules, who as a boy knocked his music teacher dead with his lyre. It was an accident, as the Greek myth tells it; the little lad just did not know his own strength. Benvenuto Cellini begins his swaggering autobiography by recounting how he pleaded, fought, and fled from his doting father, who so desperately wanted Benvenuto to play the flute. The most recent American version of this myth comes from *Trump: The Art of the Deal*: "Even in elementary school, I was a very assertive, aggressive kid. In the second grade I actually gave a teacher a black eye—I punched my music teacher because I didn't think he knew anything about music and I almost got expelled. I'm not proud of that, but [!] it's clear evidence that even early on I had a tendency to stand up and make my opinions known in a very forceful way. The difference now is that I like to use my brain instead of my fists" (71–72).[5] At least Cooper presents Gamut with amused respect for his civilized "gifts." Moreover, by the end of *Last of the Mohicans* Gamut has ascended the scale of manliness. He demonstrates fortitude and integrity where other men display villainy and cowardice. He also helps to harmonize their beleaguered group, much as Cooper's narrative seeks to blend civilized and savage virtues through a traditionally patriarchal rhetoric of mutual respect and honor.

Like any conception of manhood, an emphasis on honor functions ideologically, which is to say, as a social fiction constructed by empowered constituencies to further their power, yet felt as a natural and universal law. It shames individual deviance to protect the group, making men more fearful of losing the respect of other men than of losing their lives in battle. Cooper vividly dramatizes a ritual of public, tribal shaming in contrasting the stoic self-command of Uncas with the abject behavior of Reed-that-bends, both captured by the Hurons. Soon the Huron chief proclaims the unflinching, haughty stranger as someone who has " 'proved yourself a man' " (286). Shortly thereafter, the father of Reed-that-bends publicly disowns his son in the "bitter triumph" of a stern "stoicism" over a father's "anguish" (293). If Chingachgook, Colonel Munro, and the aged Tamenund cannot protect their children or their people from kidnapping and carnage, they take solace in their rigid adherence to a traditional manly code of honor and shame.

If manhood is not forever, its seemingly ageless durability has less to do with testosterone than with social constructions of male shaming to protect the social unit.[6] In that respect, capitalism's great change has been to destabilize small-scale patriarchy, in which rituals of honoring and shaming depend on a long-term, knowable audience for their effectiveness. Natty Bumppo's characterization preserves traditions of patriarchal honor yet exposes their flimsiness, by presenting him as a man of fixed integrity who is always on the move, forever estranged from stable community. Writing for an audience of strangers in an emerging mass market, Cooper depicts Natty as an embodiment of patriarchal honor without the patriarchy, entrepreneurial mobility without the entrepreneur. An incipient clash between two social constructions of identity yields to an idealization of cross-color male chumship in an ahistorical mode. Yet Cooper taunts civilized readers with a vague sense of the shamefulness inherent in the white march westward—not, paradoxically, with the guilt from exercising oppressive power but with the shame from accommodating to a large-scale nation-state. As domestic intimacy and career advancement supersede traditional manliness, Natty's image takes on the status of a compensatory simplification—a myth of mourning the fathers, not of emulating them.

Baffled by what he hears of the settlements, Natty wonders if it could be true that these new ways of living offer something " 'which binds man to woman closer than the father is tied to the son' " (315). Urbane readers could indulge his naïveté yet feel the twinge of loss. How silly: Natty feels neither sexual desire nor delight in home companionship. How sad: no civilized white man feels the fabric of father-son bonds as Natty does. Once again Cooper forces his readers into contradictions evaded by Natty's portable manliness. His hero seems unnaturally asexual, yet more natural than men of the settlements, many of whom found their homes defined by their women and the marketplace defined by their competitive solitude, without communal or paternal anchors.

That rhetoric, too, bespeaks a sentimental mystification. The instant success of *Last of the Mohicans* depended in part on Cooper's ability to recast emerging power relations as elegiac nostalgia. Fatherly yet childish, the Indians are vanishing into the cultural museum of literature by their own choice and accord. Besides, runs the implicit fantasy, so long as lower-class vagrants like Natty help to dispossess the red men for the better sort, some of his best friends can be Indians, and he can call his readers women or bookish or even married. Cooper's double elegy for patriarchal manhood, red and white, veils a postpatriarchal set of power relations based initially on class and racial dominance, driven ultimately by capitalist modes of circulation, which unsettle all modes of collective, stable identity except those based on the nuclear family and specialized skills in the corporate workplace.[7]

In Shakespeare's day, "pioner" meant the basest manual laborers in the army, the men who dug trenches and mines. At the onset of his frenzy, Othello tells Iago,

> I had been happy if the general camp,
> Pioners and all, had tasted her sweet body,
> So I had nothing known.

(III.iii.342–44)

Something of that baseness carries over to Cooper's portrait of his garrulous, illiterate hero. Yet a new myth of manly heroism also begins to emerge in Natty, situated as he is midway between preindustrial hierarchies of the honorable versus the base and a new, more diffusely fluid circulation of entrepreneurial middle-class energies.

As Kenneth Cmiel's *Democratic Eloquence* emphasizes, traditions of "character" could not hold against a democratization which blurred the boundaries separating genteel from vulgar, high from low. A new "middling culture" mixed formal and folksy speech to redefine proper public language and self-presentation. Along with a pervasive push for upward mobility came a premodernist sense of role-playing, offering "numerous identities . . . a multitude of expressive choices" (Cmiel 92, 58). Other historians, notably Stuart M. Blumin, analyze the paradox of a new middle class whose male members experience identity as competitive individualism, with class consciousness applied only to those at the top and bottom (269–92).[8]

If middle-class male constructions of "self" become linked to roles and competitive upward mobility in an increasingly professionalized workplace, "class" becomes either a genteel self-refashioning or a depth into which no capitalist climber must fall. Horatio Alger's most successful novel, *Ragged Dick* (1868), presents a Bowery urchin who rises to middle-class respectability not simply by pluck, luck, and entrepreneurial industry but also by continually telling tall tales about himself. He extravagantly fictionalizes his classy connections to play linguistic dress-up. Ragged Dick knows he will be capitalized by his genteel mentors only as he embraces both the speculative mobility of voice and the Protestant work ethic produced by capitalism.

In that context, a new myth of manly heroism takes on the self-divisions and psychic mobility fostered by a marketplace beyond small-scale ideological controls. An avenging hero, half animal and half human, fusing beast and patrician, descends into an evil underclass to save a helpless bourgeois civilization. From Tarzan to Batman, the myth expresses the paradox of a collectively empowered middle class in which men feel personally powerless or unmanly except as they compete in the workplace. Simultaneously, the mass-market myth appeals to a fantasy of working-class remasculinization through often sadistic violence, diffusely directed against black men, gay men, and women.

The paradox has its contradictory sources in the Jacksonian era, when both Cooper's works and the Davy Crockett myths begin to exploit the beast-man motif, though without the later patrician incorporation. In Carroll Smith-Rosenberg's analysis, the Davy Crockett stories voice a widespread sense of being "powerless in the face of massive and unremitting social transformation" (90). Challenging but not overthrowing the bourgeois struggle for legitimacy, Crockett's adventures represent several kinds of liminality: male and female adolescence, a society in transition from patriarchal communities to industrial capitalism, and crossovers between dominant and marginal groups. The tall tales of young, violent males taking on the bestiality of their animal or subhuman opponents celebrate individual freedom and personal control while dehistoricizing capitalist forces of change and inverting bourgeois sexuality (100–07). Dramas of incessant personal dominance and humiliation seek to recast these dynamics in the preindustrial interpretive framework of honor and shaming.[9]

In *The Last of the Mohicans,* Cooper edges Natty toward beast-man status, especially in the last third of the story, where Natty infiltrates an Indian village by dressing up as a bear. There, however, Cooper does almost nothing with the tensions latent in such a crossover. Fifteen years later, in *The Deerslayer* (1841), Cooper at last plunges toward the new myth, as readers learn for the first time how Natty got that strange animal name of "Hawkeye."

In chapter 7, Natty becomes a man by killing his first Indian. Instead of taking a scalp, Natty takes a new name as his trophy—a name bestowed on him by his victim. Behaving with traditional honor, Natty had refrained from shooting the Indian unfairly. But honor cannot protect him against a "savage" whose body betrays his sneaky bestiality: his eyes rage like a "volcano," and his nostrils dilate "like those of some wild beast" (108). Fortunately, just as the Indian crouches like a "tiger" in the bushes to shoot, Natty senses danger, whirls, cocks his rifle, aims, and fires, all before the Indian's tightening finger quite pulls the trigger. This is the kind of woodsmanship that Mark Twain so gloriously debunks in "Fenimore Cooper's Literary Offenses."

The mythic transformation begins after the shooting. Prone though still conscious, the victim watches Natty "as the fallen bird regards the fowler," while the lad feels "melancholy" as he stands over the "black" eyes of the " 'riptyle' " (110–11). Then the Indian dies like a man. With "stoicism," "firmness," and "high innate courtesy," the Indian raises his hand to "tap the young man on his breast." The red man's dying words rechristen the white man: " 'eye sartain—finger lightning—aim, death—great warrior soon. No Deerslayer—Hawkeye—Hawkeye—Hawkeye. Shake hand' " (113–14).

One could argue that this mutual mythic transformation relieves white readers of guilt for the pleasures of Indian killing. While a red man threatens, the narrative depicts him as a snaky beast. After he ceases to be dangerous, he becomes a man so that he can bless the suitably empathetic killer with a new identity: Deerslayer becomes Manslayer. But the naming goes the other way, from Deerslayer to Hawkeye. A bird's soaring, predatory quickness dignifies and sharpens Natty's rightful yet brutal dominance. Here is a new myth of American manhood in the making: to be civilized and savage in one composite, self-divided transformation. The myth dramatizes a potential for downward mobility on the liminal frontier, to save the manhood of upwardly mobile men in the settlements.[10]

By the turn of the century, the new myth shapes a multitude of texts, from Frederick Jackson Turner's frontier thesis to Frank Norris's *McTeague* (1899) and Jack London's *Call of the Wild* (1903). Norris's tale of a brute-man's downward mobility from petit-bourgeois aspirations to theft and murder has grotesque violence to women at the center of McTeague's descent. If the dentist's hapless ambitions can be blamed on his mother and his wife, who goad him out of his natural niche as a miner to compete in a profession requiring intelligence and dexterity, McTeague takes his "ape-like" revenge by killing his wife after nearly biting her fingers off. Throughout, Norris's patronizingly self-conscious genteel narration simultaneously relishes McTeague's brutality while exposing McTeague as a figure of urban powerlessness, helpless against complexity, rivals, or his own desires. Lashing out whenever he is made to " 'feel small,' " this Last Real Man in America ends his life as a comic butt, handcuffed to a pursuer's corpse in the desert, where he stares stupidly at a bird cage. Incapable of the chameleonic self-transformations required for capitalist success, McTeague represents a cautionary tale of the brute inherent in all real men and the monstrous desires that have to be masked in the upward march to genteel decorum.[11]

For London, the Last Real Man in America is a dog who turns into a wolf. London's *Call of the Wild* mocks the silliness of self-absorbed, hysterical Mercedes (the only woman who ventures onto the arctic tundra), especially when she tries to talk about theater and art. As she vanishes into an ice hole, the narrative all but says good riddance. Buck's allegorical manliness also survives his chumship with John Thornton, who saves and cherishes Buck with a "genuine passionate love" (74), climaxing in an ecstasy of penetration and talking dirty, from which the onlookers discreetly withdraw.[12] But Thornton, too, is only human, with a capitalist lust for gold, and is therefore powerless when confronted by the arctic underclass, the sub-human Yeehats. In avenging Thornton's death and tasting human blood for the first time, Buck enacts Deerslayer's rite of initiation with a hint of comic reversal: the dog "had killed man, the noblest game of all" (98). Now he can fulfill the "pride" of his downwardly mobile call of the wild by taking over the leadership of a wolf pack.[13]

In human society, however, Buck too is powerless. As the first sentence declares, "Buck did not read the newspapers." He cannot understand why he is being bought and sold. The arbitrary buying and selling of Buck that structures the plot takes on meanings beyond his comprehension, yet obvious to those who can read: men need to carry the news, men want to find gold. Unlike Norris, London unambivalently contrasts Buck's natural leadership with the degeneracy of such men. Nevertheless, ideal manliness thrives in Buck only because he becomes less and less human, more and more wild, while his admiring narrator—like Cooper—writes a "wild" book about him for boy-men readers who feel trapped in their maturation and long for exotic virility.

Like tales of musician bashing, the beast-man myth is as old as the dawn of storytelling. Its transformation into late nineteenth-century myths of vanishing American manhood also draws on age-old myths of a hero's descent into the underworld and on the cross-cultural bourgeois myth of an aristocratic hero who makes himself inhuman in order to become superhuman, for example, the Count of Monte Cristo. Ultimately, as Victoria Kahn suggests for Machiavelli's rhetorical finale in *The Prince,* where manly *virtù* beats womanly Fortuna into submission, all myths of manliness may seek allegorical stabilization to ward off the perception that "the individual is not at all in control of his behavior" (78).[14] The special American quality lies in the new myth's exaggerated emphasis on frontier liminality, in the contradictory class mobilities, and in the incipient note of mourning. In a world in which both class and gender start to feel like nostalgic props, upwardly mobile readers relish stories with downwardly mobile heroes and with narrative voices divided between class loyalty and gender urgency.

To read Turner's "The Significance of the Frontier in American History" (1893) in the context I am sketching here exposes his fascination with redemptive manly savagery and belligerence. For Turner, the frontier is "the meeting point between savagery and civilization" and therefore becomes a crucible for "rapid and effective Americanization." Stripping a man of his European manners, the frontier "takes him from the railroad car and puts him in the birch canoe. . . . Before long he has gone to planting Indian corn and plowing with a sharp stick; he shouts the war cry and takes the scalp in orthodox Indian fashion. In short, at the frontier the environment is at first too strong for the man" (38–39). Unlike Cooper, Turner relishes the prospect of such assimilation. The strong man "transforms the wilderness" only after the wilderness has transformed him. A hybrid, both savage and civilized, he is no longer ridden by class-linked, European manners; "here is a new product that is American" (39).

Not until 1920, when Turner at last expanded his brief essay into a book, do the gender issues become flamboyantly manifest. Climaxing his vision of the frontier as a natural factory for producing American manhood, Turner all but lets out a war whoop when the New World produces Andrew Jackson. Outrageously casting Thomas Jefferson as a frontier prophet, "the John the Baptist of democracy" (qtd. in Berky and Shenton 470), Turner's revised version presents Jackson as democracy's incarnation, explicitly "Moses" and implicitly Christ. Above all, Jackson stands forth as the First Real Man in America. Why? Because when Jackson tried to speak on the floor of the Senate, his rage blocked his words. Turner exultingly quotes Jefferson, without a hint of Jefferson's patrician recoil: " 'When I was President of the Senate he was a Senator, and he could never speak on account of the rashness of his feelings. I have seen him attempt it repeatedly and as often choke with rage' " (qtd. in Berky and Shenton 471).

What Ishmael finds both appalling and fascinating in Ahab, Turner celebrates in Jackson without reservation: "At last the frontier in the person of its typical man had found a place in the Government. This six-foot backwoodsman, with blue eyes that could blaze on occasion, this choleric, impetuous, self-willed Scotch-Irish leader of men, this expert duelist, and ready fighter, this embodiment of the tenacious, vehement, personal West, was in politics to stay. . . . The men of the 'Western World' turned their backs upon the Atlantic Ocean, and with a grim energy and self-reliance began to build up a society free from the dominance of ancient forms" (qtd. in Berky and Shenton 471–72). To be aggressive, rebellious, enraged, uncivilized: this is what the frontier could do for the European clones on the East Coast, still in thrall to a foreign tyranny of manners.[15]

If Turner's bull-in-the-china-shop image of manliness covertly empowered his own assault on an overbearing Eastern establishment, it also empowered the emerging profession of American history.[16] Just as with Norris and London, however, a diffuse sense of civilized powerlessness lurks at the margins of his text. The frontier is closed now, he reemphasizes at the end; the days of democratic man-making seem to be over. Now, to challenge the new " 'manufacturing aristocracy,' " he finds not frontier fire-eaters but only inequality, poverty, and labor unions. Turner's muted ending evokes a baffled Lone Ranger surrounded by Marxists and plutocrats. As he concludes, the frontier has been a safety valve postponing the conflict between capital and labor: "But the sanative influences of the free spaces of the West were destined to ameliorate labor's condition, to afford new hopes and new faith to pioneer democracy, and to postpone the problem" (qtd. in Berky and Shenton 473).

As if waiting in the wings to seize the image of bully-boy patrician leading the nation away from class conflicts toward a renewal of collective virility on international frontiers, the man who most successfully exploited the emerging myth of the cross-class beast-man was Theodore Roosevelt, not Eugene V. Debs.[17] Roosevelt epitomized manly zest for the new imperial nation in part because of his jaunty energy, but also because his image brought together both aspects of the new myth: the top rung of the ladder of social aspiration and the gladiatorial animal arena sensed at the bottom. In what other advanced industrial country could a former president, an asthmatic child of old money, make a serious run for his country's top office under the banner of "The Bull Moose Party"?[18] Later in 1912, after his quixotic drive for national leadership failed, Roosevelt accepted the solace of another presidency, from the American Historical Association, as fitting reward for his various books about manliness on the western frontier.

Like Turner, Roosevelt both celebrates and mourns the frontier as a crucible of man-making whose time has passed. *Ranch Life and the Hunting-Trail* (1888), for instance, begins with an epigraph from Browning: " 'Oh, our manhood's prime vigor! . . .' " The book depicts the "daring and adventurousness" of stockmen (7) and the reckless, "defiant self-confidence" of cowboys (9) in Cooper-like terms, as "a primitive stage of existence" which is now "doomed, and can hardly outlast the century" (24). Here "[c]ivilization seems as remote as if we were living in an age long past. The whole existence is patriarchal in character: it is the life of men who live in the open . . . who call no man master" (6). Written self-consciously to Easterners, the book carefully differentiates among the exotic frontier types while warning that the West "is no place for men who lack the ruder, coarser virtues and physical qualities, no matter how intellectual or how refined and delicate their sensibilities" (10). For those who can take it, the frontier brings out mutual honor and self-respect—not "the emasculated, milk-and-water moralities" but "the stern, manly qualities that are invaluable to a nation" (56). Cowboys are "much better fellows and pleasanter companions" than men on small farms, Roosevelt declares, "nor are the mechanics and workmen of a great city to be mentioned in the same breath" (10).

Roosevelt had an immense personal impact on the two writers who inaugurated the most enduring twentieth-century myths of American manliness. In Owen Wister's *The Virginian* (1902), dedicated to Roosevelt, an urbane Eastern narrator quickly discovers that the ungrammatical but self-possessed hero from old Virginia (never named) embodies the essence of true gentlemanliness as well as bravery. Wister had been a David Gamut in the making. A summa cum laude graduate in music from Harvard, who had played privately for Franz Liszt on the European tour preparing him as an opera composer, he suffered his first nervous breakdown in 1884 and went to Wyoming at the suggestion of his doctor, the ubiquitous S. Weir Mitchell. Over the next two decades, Wister and his friend Frederic Remington together created the myth of the cowboy at the moment of the cowboy's obsolescence. Both men cherished Roosevelt's example and friendship.[19] In the second edition of *The Virginian* (1911), Wister's "Rededication" hails Roosevelt as an inspiring "benefactor" who brought "sincerity" back to public men after "nigh half-a-century of shirking and evasion" (vii). Earlier, as president, Roosevelt had praised exactly what Wister had intended in crafting his cowboy myth: *The Virginian* fused frontier democracy with chivalric aristocracy, joining gentlemanly ideals of honor and rhetorical wit with frontier ideals of manliness.[20]

As Wister's first preface acknowledges, however, his book is an elegy for a rough nobility that must inevitably fade in the transition to what has become "a shapeless state . . . of men and manners" (xi). Beyond the domestic comedy, in which the hero's "rhetorical aplomb" brings schoolteacher Molly Stark Wood to accept his patriarchal dominance despite his lower social status (Mitchell 70–71, also 73–74), Wister's enduring contribution has been the genre of the American Western, where the plot culminates in a face-to-face shoot-out between good and evil. That drama has shaped and simplified national self-perceptions from the Virginian versus Trampas to General Schwarzkopf versus Saddam Hussein. Giving closure to the recurrent saga of triumph and humiliation, a man of honor who is also a man of violence stands tall and alone against the darkening sky, as elegiac counterpoint to the sunset of self-reliance and the rise of the corporate state.

Perhaps not surprisingly, the writer who codified the Last Real Man myth by fusing beast with patrician had been rejected by Roosevelt's Rough Riders. Published in the year of the Bull Moose Party, 1912, Edgar Rice Burroughs's *Tarzan of the Apes* presents a benignly self-divided hero. Tarzan, or Lord Greystoke, an orphan child of British aristocrats who is raised by African apes, enacts the age-old drive for dominance over other males—but only as an ape. When his equally age-old gentlemanly instincts are aroused, he turns chivalric, especially with Jane, who shares his double self. In the novel's most mythic moment, having saved Jane from Terkoz, an ape-ravisher, Tarzan first "did what no red-blooded man needs lessons in doing. He took his woman in his arms and smothered her upturned, panting lips with kisses." Jane's primal self responds; her civilized self recoils. So "Tarzan of the Apes did just what his first ancestor would have done. He took his woman in his arms and carried her into the jungle" (156–57).

As Marianna Torgovnick emphasizes, however, Tarzan immediately feels great confusion about what a man ought to do. To rape, as Terkoz would? Yet he is a man, not an ape; how should a Real Man act? (52). Having carried her off against her (civilized) will, Tarzan resolves to "act as he imagined the men in the books would have acted" (166). These are the books in his parents' cabin that he is teaching himself to read, though as yet he can speak not a word. Giving Jane a locket, "like some courtier of old . . . the hall-mark of his aristocratic birth"

(168), he sleeps outside her bower to make her feel protected from him as well as by him. By the end of the book, when Tarzan first speaks to her, he is bilingual and can drive a car.[21]

Burroughs's myth transforms Cooper's Hawkeye to a Rooseveltian pince-nez strong man. Tarzan the aristocrat lets another man claim Jane in marriage, since no gentleman would think of asking a lady to break a promise, while Tarzan the ape posts a terse warning on his parents' cabin door: "THIS IS THE HOUSE OF TARZAN, THE KILLER OF BEASTS AND MANY BLACK MEN. DO NOT HARM THE THINGS WHICH ARE TARZAN'S. TARZAN WATCHES. TARZAN OF THE APES" (103). No one notices Tarzan's casual equation of beasts and blacks or his presumption of property rights, Eric Cheyfitz comments. What everybody wants to know about is his name, which means "White Skin." Only mother-love is exempted from the novel's pervasive racism. African blacks represent an evil worse than apes, except perhaps on the generically male side. Equally brutish are the ship's low-class mutineers.[22] If Tarzan's character divides Natty Bumppo's harmony of civilized and savage gifts, the plot fulfills almost every civilized white fantasy of class and race domination.

So, more desperately, does *Batman*'s plot, which begins with Batman fighting urban muggers and ends with the hero on a tower fighting first a black man and then the Joker, his trickster double, the "artist of homicide." In *Batman,* human powerlessness is everywhere. Cooper's patriarchal controls vanish in the first scene, as Daddy takes his family down the wrong street toward urban danger, much as Tarzan's father led his family into African violence. Neither these fathers nor the city fathers can stop the seeping evil represented by "Axis Chemicals" and the Joker. "Axis," of course, is not accidental. Anton Furst's sets not only evoke the awed helplessness induced by Nazi architecture but also call attention to themselves *as* sets, making moviegoers half aware of their own presence as dwarfed spectators. Everyone sits in the dark, watching the flickering lights, wondering where the sun went, and passively awaiting the next random spectacle of mutilation.

Only a superhero could save this civilization of victims. After the Joker challenges Batman, via the TV screen, to a "*mano-a-mano*" combat, he dispenses money and poison gas to the greedy, faceless, Depression-era masses, along with cynical words about the uselessness of their ordinary lives. Enacting again and again the only drama he knows, he sadistically exposes everyone's loss of face. He disfigures the women he dominates, he turns underworld rivals into skulls, and he defaces himself with his ceaselessly inhuman smile, the inverse of the Batman symbol. Nor can Lord Greystoke's aristocratic instincts serve Bruce Wayne as a source of chivalric power. Stripped of his dress-up costume, the hero seems all too human and adolescent, to the initial disgust of Batman fans who expected a version of the *Dark Knight* comic book.

Here, in fact, the moviemakers may have been more attuned to their mass-market audience than sophisticated reviewers have allowed. If "Me Tarzan, you Jane" is Tarzan of the movies, simplifying Lord Greystoke's double self into a noble savage primitivism, Burroughs's novel voices a contradictory fusion of savage violence with a comedy of manners. This double drama of man-making mixes brutal dominance and humiliation with civilized self-control. From a very different perspective, the postmodern uses of psychoanalytic doubling and gender crossover in Frank Miller's *Batman: The Dark Knight Returns* and Alan Moore's *Batman: The Killing Joke* (both of which influenced the movie) jettison the contradictory myth, replacing it with a noble deconstructionist.

In the adult comics, a battered, aging Bruce Wayne desperately tries to ward off the contemporary chameleonism, cynicism, and even psychosis that the Joker gleefully welcomes. "You have a Bad Day once, am I right?" says Joker to Batman. "Why else would you dress up like a flying rat?" (Moore n.p.). Everyone has been driven crazy; it's even crazier to pretend that it makes sense to keep on struggling. Where these comic books dramatize the story of an agonized, mid-life consciousness on the verge of self-deconstruction in a world unraveling toward relentless urban violence and moral nihilism, the movie draws on similar images of futility while telling the story of a young near-Fauntleroy, whose salvational mission redeems the world, assuages his pain, and makes him a man.

Like Sherman McCoy in Tom Wolfe's *Bonfire of the Vanities* (1987), another rich boy-man who yearns to be "King of the Jungle" and "Master of the Universe," Bruce Wayne seems to have it all yet does not even know how to manage his first date with Vicki Vale. Their comic awkwardness at opposite ends of his enormous dining room table resolves into speedy downward mobility to the butler's kitchen, where they can get to know each other like kids on a sleep-over. Wolfe's cynical narration has no such endearing touches. Readers meet Sherman McCoy on his knees, trying to put a leash on his dachshund before walking to his mistress's apartment. More than 600 pages later, unleashing the Bernhard Goetz inside himself, the real McCoy feels a climactic rush that comes not from sex or money, but only from punching a tall black man in the solar plexus. "'You cold-cocked him!'" a friend says, astonished (651–52). Vitalized at last, McCoy wants to do it "*again*" and "*again*" (656). While the people around him wonder if he has become a lunatic, he shows his teeth and "let[s] out a short harsh red laugh" as the band of demonstrators retreats "down the marble halls" (656). With that bestial surge, the book ends. This is the urban context for *Batman*'s more cross-class appeal. Both plots offer what Richard Slotkin has called the frontier fantasy of "regeneration through violence" as a restoration of manliness, overcoming diffuse fears of shameful ordinariness lurking below the ostensible fears of random muggings.[23]

Bruce Wayne's double drama of man making occurs at the level of cosmopolitan gender stereotypes as well as beast-man myth. The Gatsby-like boy-man becomes a Real Man, in human terms, when he visits Vicki Vale to tell her his half-human identity. Angry because she thinks he has stood her up on a date, she starts to voice her outrage. "'Shut up,'" he explains, and pushes her down on the couch. Accepting that move without a murmur, the Pulitzer Prize–winning photographer waits expectantly. Ahhhh, viewers should feel; we can relax. He *is* a real man after all. He *can* carry her off into the jungle, or the Bat Cave. Besides, what a typically feminine trivialization, to reduce all the horrors of what the Joker tried to do to her in the museum to being stood up on a date. Part of the scene's comedy, as Bruce reverts to inarticulate stumbling in attempting to tell her about himself, is Vicki's immediate inference that he must be gay. But viewers now know better: the anxious rich kid will be a gentleman of force, not another lost or vicious urbanite, of whatever sexual persuasion.

Thereafter, despite Vicki Vale's fast-track city career, their dialogue updates *Tarzan*'s traditionally gendered comedy of manners while the plot enacts sadistic fantasies of man-making and humiliation. In Vicki's apartment as in the Bat Cave, it is much more important for a man to talk about his work than for a woman to talk about her feelings. When Vicki at last insists on bringing up love, Bruce-Batman responds with an almost parodic imitation of the credo, "Later—a man's got to do what a man's got to do." From then on, Vicki becomes a marginal drag on and support for Batman's work identity. She never seems annoyed that he stole her potentially prizewinning photographs of him. Instead, she becomes a traditional help-meet, who lies a little about her weight and shows courage to aid his career. At the very end, Vicki makes the ultimate, self-degrading sacrifice to help her man triumph. She goes down on

Bruce Wayne's double drama of man making occurs at the level of cosmopolitan gender stereotypes as well as beast-man myth.

the Joker, slowly and unmistakably sliding down his body and off the screen, to divert his attention.

As beast-patrician and fair young damsel are chauffeured away into their snug seclusion, one could imagine a feminist ending. Vicki Vale will return to her career with exclusive Batman photos, win a second Pulitzer Prize, and move on up to become the first female anchor of a prime-time news show. Meanwhile Bruce Wayne will have retired from his dangerous, adventurist, and unpaying job to become a contented house husband, managing the friendly servants who do the child care, the laundry, and the dishes.

On balance, however, it seems more likely that Vicki Vale's voluptuous presence as faithful sidekick functions primarily to remove the threat of homosexuality from the Batman myth, not to awaken hopes of a feminist swerve.[24] Several years before the movie was made, Batman fans responded to a poll by vigorously demanding that Robin be dumped. He seemed too wimpy and twerpy; some used gay-baiting terms. Yet much of the movie's power comes from its playing with the adolescent ambiguities in Michael Keaton's role as Batman. He could have become a Robin, or a homosexual, or an effete impotent snob, or a faceless husband to a strong career woman. Instead, he can masculinize himself, in a world that seems hell-bent on robbing every man of a father and virility. The fact of Kim Basinger's casting looms larger than her stereotypic gendering to empower the hero as yet another Last Real Man in America.

I draw six conclusions from this sketch of a changing myth. First, ideologies of manhood have functioned primarily in relation to the gaze of male peers and male authority. Suppressing complexities of feeling often involving women, such ideologies produce good workers, competitors, and fighters in the public sphere. Here I differ from Eve Kosofsky Sedgwick, who argues in *Between Men* and elsewhere that "homosocial desire" builds on homophobia and misogyny to perpetuate patriarchal oppressions. It is amply understandable that many women and gays feel unempowered in or erased from hierarchic structures of male rivalry. Not homosexual panic or desire, however, but the construction of male roles to serve the social unit fosters a male preoccupation with measuring self-worth in the eyes of one's workplace peers.

In theory, the workplace could be gender-neutral. In practice, as Daniel Gilmore concludes in *Manhood in the Making,* a society's preoccupation with manhood "directly correlates with male-role stress," especially "when men are conditioned to fight" (221). Gilmore intriguingly suggests that both male codes of combative or stoic assertiveness and female codes of self-sacrifice have to be learned, but that men need ritual and ideological socialization because they are more "atomistic," whereas women are "normally under the control of men" (221), especially in precapitalist societies. In capitalism, too, fathering and competition play roles at least as central in male self-construction as any forms of sexual desire or ambivalence about mothering, in large part because competitiveness drives the energy of any market economy.

What changes is how the respect of peers and authority is constituted. In preindustrial, small-scale societies, whether in Native-American villages or Greek and Italian city-states, manhood connotes honor, fatherhood, citizenship, sexual prowess, and bravery in battle as well as pride of craftsmanship and primacy as family provider. In modern economies, especially in the United States, where as Alfred Chandler argues, capitalism has taken an exceptionally competitive form, patriarchy has given way to a more amorphous mixture of collaboration, rivalry, and role-playing to give upward mobility in the professionalized marketplace.[25] The evolving beast-patrician myth of man-making incorporates a mid-nineteenth-century image of entrepreneurial individualism with turn-of-the-century class extremes to stabilize a violent yet hypercivilized compensatory fantasy.

Second, the myth has become both more homophobic and more ambiguously playful about sexual identity. Not one of Cooper's contemporary readers would have dreamed of calling for a Kim Basinger to replace Chingachgook, though it is fun to imagine what Natty would do. Cooper half tried once, and egregiously failed, in *The Pathfinder* (1840). On the other hand, *Batman*'s social comedy flirts with Bruce Wayne's potential gayness, while his animal cross-dressing evokes Mark Seltzer's label for Jack London's heroes, "Men in Furs" (153).

Third, the myth continues to idealize, marginalize, and mutilate women. Though Jane and Vicki Vale are a good deal more respectably sexy than shrinking Alice Dunham or intrepid Judith Hutter in *The Deerslayer,* women continue to function as adjuncts to a man's remasculinization, providing emotional supports and physical targets.

Fourth, the incipient theme of effete, feminized urbanity in Cooper becomes an explicit rejection of high-society manners in Turner and London, an attempt at amalgamation in Wister and Burroughs, then a cross-class dramatization of civilized powerlessness in *Batman*. In that sense, "woman" may be a token signifier for a larger, stranger issue, present also in *Tarzan* and *McTeague,* where spirited modern heroines become helpless victims: why should the power of bourgeois civilization breed such fantasies of middle-class male powerlessness?

Fifth, I see three stages in the progression of the new myth. In the "Hawkeye" stage, Natty's lateral mobility and chumship with Chingachgook complement a nostalgic mourning for precapitalist patriarchy and a covert fantasy that frontier bumpkins can rid the civilized world of Indians. In the turn-of-the-century stage, McTeague, Buck, and Turner's Andrew Jackson dramatize a downward mobility from lower-class status into savagery to redeem or shock effete Eastern gentility. Norris, in particular, seems to have written *McTeague* as a manly riposte to the feminized tea-party "realism" of Howell's *The Rise of Silas Lapham* (1885).[26] A relish for violence to women surfaces in Norris, London, and Burroughs, becoming a fascination with grotesque mutilations in *Batman.* In the third, post–Teddy Roosevelt stage, the hero seems comfortably (Tarzan) or uncomfortably (Bruce Wayne) divided between an old-money class identity and a role as bestial avenger, while urban civilization seems faceless and impotent, and class itself seems stereotypically inadequate to empower any sense of self.

Sixth and finally, an ambivalence about the powers of the female body saps the strength yet girds up the loins of these Last Real Men. As he leads his pack after a rabbit, Buck feels "an ecstacy" of blood-lust, "a complete forgetfulness that one is alive," like an inspired "artist" or a "war-mad" soldier, "sounding the deeps of his nature . . . going back into the womb of Time. He was mastered by the sheer surging of life, the tidal wave of being" (London 49). Ape-man McTeague feels insensibly reborn in his manliness as he reaches the mountains, where Mother Nature is not "cosey, intimate, small, and homelike, like a good-natured housewife"—or the woman he has murdered—but "a vast, unconquered brute of the Pliocene epoch, savage, sullen, and magnificently indifferent to man" (Norris 212–13). With a simpler dichotomizing, Batman becomes invulnerable in his womb-like Batmobile and Bat Cave, though instantly vulnerable in his all too fragile and phallic Batplane, shot down by a single blast from the Joker's ridiculously long toy gun.

Here manliness seems regenerated not by violence but by umbilical connection. Perhaps, to apply Carnes's argument about overtly patriarchal lodge rituals again, all the masks of machismo hide and license a male maternalism: Tarzan feeds, shelters, and holds Jane just as Kala mothered him (see Carnes 139–50; Torgovnick 64–69). Or perhaps the womb-surge is even more basic. If Tarzan makes inarticulate sounds and howls in ecstasy while his blood pounds like a tidal wave, if Batman feels like sleeping upside down before careening toward the moon, it is not that a nice young gentleman suddenly has rape and murder on his mind. The Last Real Man in America is just having his period.[27]

Such fantasies empower women only tangentially and metaphorically, legitimating violence with a traditional sex role polarity: within every macho brute hides a good mother. The claim belies the ugliness always latent in the Real Man myth. For me that darkness became most visible in a $10 Batman shirt, a spin-off from the movie: not the Michael Keaton boy-man who plays protective urban terrorist, but Batman for the skinhead market. Under a blood-orange moon, his teeth gleam over dark, random corpses. By his left foot lies a prone, sallow, agonized face, of a person whose spiky Mohawk haircut am-biguously brands him as a dying Indian or street gang member, with a gun pointing aimlessly upward behind his shoulder. By his right foot, with a manacled arm reaching up Batman's cloak in a curious gesture—a prisoner? a slave? a homoerotic invi-tation?—lies a burr-headed black man. Other scattered bodies and a litter of guns, knives, chains, and eerily disconnected limbs sprawl about his feet, evoking an American landscape filled with skulls and crossbones, urban muggers, and frontier vio-lence. Above it all, collapsing American history into an image of the beast-man, stands Batman-Dracula, master of the uni-verse and vampire bat, about to drink their blood. Here is the psychic landscape lurking below Sean Connery's white-on-white cover of *Gentleman's Quarterly.*

The skinhead Batman glories in the racist violence on which the myth of the Last Real Man in America has fed, from Coop-er's Indian wars to Buck's killing of the Yeehats to Tarzan's killing of African blacks. Part of the myth's pleasure lies in what James Bond called the hero's "license to kill," a license helping to make the myth so serviceable in the international arena. A more basic pleasure lies in the ritualistic arena of *"mano-a-mano"* rivalry, where women and other complex states of being are out of sight and out of mind.

The myth of a Last Real Man depends on its equal and opposite myth, that of a subhuman underclass, to generate ceaseless dramas of dominance and humiliation. These ahis-torical dramas of self-empowerment express and evade both the felt facelessness of the upwardly mobile and the diffuse resentments of the immobilized. So long as corporate capitalism structures male identity primarily through role-playing and

The myth of a Last Real Man depends on its equal and opposite myth, that of a subhu-man underclass, to generate ceaseless dra-mas of dominance and humiliation.

workplace competition, the craving for Real Man myths will continue despite the entry of women into management positions. In a world where Sherman McCoys at the top and their fast-lane counterparts at the bottom measure worth only as supremacy in the cash-flow game, the men at the top will talk of "hemorrhaging money" (Wolfe 330) while the men at the bottom hemorrhage violence. Batman embodies an intimate circulation of old money and new blood.

But capitalism's opening beyond small-scale patriarchal stabilizings to diversified international markets also encourages the circulation and exchange of more heterogeneous energies. A currently intractable impasse between capitalism's production of material abundance and its production of a useless urban underclass fosters much of the anxious urgency invested in the ideology of upward mobility. If you are not rising, as a person or a corporation, you must be powerless or falling—into what? Yet the competitive pluralism intrinsic to any large-scale market checks and challenges anyone's will to power, while marketing itself enforces a continuous reassessment of otherness and difference among potential buyers. Equally to the point, the corporate workplace encourages collaborative as well as competitive energies, often beyond the imagination of academic artisans and entrepreneurs. Moreover, as countless recent movies about male mid-life crises have dramatized, people with money can find various cushions for relaxing into life as well as hyperventilating about achievement. What may be nice for the middle class, however, is not so nice from below. An unemployable underclass remains the bourgeois bogeyman and cautionary tale, the demonized other for middle-class fears of falling.

Ideologies die operatic deaths, and individualism's deflection of class contradictions into manliness has led to an exceptionally long aria—165 years and counting. From the beginning, the myth of the Last Real Man in America fuses idealizations of high civility with increasingly brutalized representations of lower-class violence. From the beginning, too, the myth has subsumed an elegiac simplification of history, grieving for the passing of frontier self-reliance and patriarchal dominance. In the cosmopolitan perspectives of another 160 years or so, the myth may well be set beside the grandfather clock and the Model T Ford as another example of persistent yokelism.

On the other hand, the myth's tenacity signals the vitality of capitalist paradoxes. Perhaps on a multinational stage, Real Man myths will even expand their market: the Last Real Man in Czechoslovakia, the Last Real Man in Argentina. If there will eventually be more gender-neutral stories to tell, myths of self-empowering will still mix elegance with violence to tease people away from thinking about what makes them feel unreal.

Notes

Earlier versions of this essay were presented at a conference on masculinities organized by John R. Gillis at Rutgers University in 1989 and at Northwestern University in 1991.

1. The *Celebrity Plus* cover presents Ford as, in smaller print, a "Crusader" who "Shoots From The Hip In This Candid Talk." The story simply depicts him as a man at ease with himself, living in Wyoming with his family, remembering his hard knocks, and fishing instead of playing Hollywood games. The *Gentleman's Quarterly* essay, by Diane K. Shah, entitled "All Together Now: Sean Connery Is an Icon," bears a similarly tangential relation to the "Last Real Man" packaging on the cover.

2. As Michaels has pointed out for D. H. Lawrence's forays into New Mexico and classic American literature, such remasculinization through wildness depends on the previous extinction of the Indians, to transform them from a social threat into an assimilable cultural resource ("Vanishing American" 236–37). Lears and many others emphasize connections between turn-of-the-century feelings of powerlessness and fantasies of hypermasculinity.

3. Kaplan applies this argument to turn-of-the-century chivalric romances of imperialism. My discussion of manliness on the frontier also builds on well-known studies by Fiedler and Slotkin.

4. In "No Apologies for the Iroquois," ch. 4 of *Sensational Designs,* Tompkins emphasizes the crossover liminalities throughout Cooper's narrative.

5. Trump goes on to talk with pride about stealing his younger brother's blocks and going to military school, where he found teachers he could admire, particularly a former marine drill sergeant, "the kind of guy who could slam into a goalpost wearing a football helmet and break the post rather than his head." This Real Man would "go for the jugular if he smelled weakness," but he would treat you "like a man" if you "finessed" him with respect (72–74). Trump's autobiography shares several characteristics with Cellini's: both seem to have been dictated, both celebrate competitive prowess, and both show considerable relish for outstripping their fathers, though each pays ostentatious respect to his father as well.

6. Gilmore takes a cross-cultural approach to the social construction of masculinities, arguing that traditional manly codes of stoicism, physical strength, sexual prowess, and bravery function to protect the social unit. Gilmore's useful and unpretentious survey concludes that the " 'Ubiquitous Male' " criteria of " 'Man-the-Impregnator-Protector-Provider' " function in "either dangerous or highly competitive" social situations to force men beyond their longing to retreat to "childish narcissism" (222–24), a state repeatedly linked to Melville's Bartleby (109, 174–75). My own book argues

that all ideologies of manhood draw on male fears of being humiliated and, more diffusely, of being seen by other men as weak and vulnerable (72–73). Pericles's "Funeral Oration" to the Athenians is the most eloquent summation of precapitalist manliness I have run across; he explicitly links honor in battle to a man's fear of humiliation and the desire to have the respect of one's fellow men.

7.   I am drawing here on Greenblatt's idea of individual identity as a "way station on the road to a firm and decisive identification with normative structures" (75–76), structures that he elsewhere discusses as masks and mobile improvisations whose instabilities themselves are part of power's circulations. Cf. also a fine review-essay by McGraw, reassessing the Berle-Means thesis about American capitalism's tendency toward industrial concentration and the separation of ownership from control. McGraw speaks of the sociology of executives: their "submergence in a corporate culture obsessed with competitive market performance, their keen identification of self with company" (586). Chandler contrasts American competitive corporate capitalism with England's more family-based capitalism and Germany's more collaborative capitalism.

8.   As Blumin notes, the middle class's "individualistic, competitive values ... were those most at odds with sustained, explicitly class-based organization" (257), despite "the increasingly distinctive three-class structure of daily social life" (288), especially in the cities, where "class segregation" increased (284) and an accelerating suburbanization of the middle class exacerbated class divisions. Blumin also suggests that middle-class values gained such ideological hegemony because the preindustrial upper class gave way to "more specialized celebrities" at the top (296), while manual workers had enough money to define themselves as middle-class consumers. Ryan recurrently discusses the new middle class's fear of falling into the new working class—a more fundamental motive for upward mobility, in her view, than the drive for competitive success (184, 210, 238). See my notes to ch. 3 of *Manhood*; also Cmiel on the "polysemic" diversity of language and self that accompanied the triumph of "middling" oratory over elite traditions of refined language and character. Cmiel also notes that, paradoxically, after the Civil War, class divisions hardened while elite symbols diffused into mass culture (145–47).

9.   In addition to Smith-Rosenberg's *Disorderly Conduct,* a recent anthology of essays edited by Carnes and Griffen, *Meanings for Manhood,* historicizes masculine gender constructions more complexly than I can do here. See especially Rotundo's essay (15–36) and Griffen's speculative overview (183–204). Filene (69–93) surveys late nineteenth-century American male anxieties, especially in relation to women and domestic roles.

10.   My emphasis on the inversions of upward/downward mobility differs here from Slotkin's quasi-Jungian sense of the frontier beast-man myth as a mythic initiation into soul-archetypes, where manhood becomes a sacred marriage through violence with the anima and natural fertility goddess (*Regeneration* 156, 539, 543). In *Fatal Environment,* especially when discussing General Custer, Slotkin's more sociological focus for myths of manhood could complement Cmiel's and my own sense of entrepreneurial role-playing. Slotkin argues (377) that the masculine imperatives of self-assertion

and stern command, with their feminine inversions, lead to a double bind: self-reliant, yet subordinate to authority, a subordination that Custer split as masculine and feminine. Slotkin also emphasizes Custer's resolution of this split through role-playing and self-dramatization (378, 383).

11.   Cf. Michaels, *The Gold Standard*, which situates McTeague's desire in relation to American anxiety about money circulation (148–54) and more profound insatiabilities of desire generated by capitalism. Howard comes closer to my view in framing Norris's contradictions about masculinity as part of "inconsistent fears" ranging from genteel nervousness about proletarianization to petit bourgeois feelings of entrapment "between the working class and the corporation" (95–96). The issues resolve into a diffuse powerlessness projected onto a monstrously empowered Other, which Howard links to manly brutality in both Norris and London (51–63, 117–25, 140).

12.   London 85–86: "Thornton fell on his knees beside Buck. Head was against head, and he was shaking him back and forth. Those who hurried up heard him cursing Buck, and he cursed him long and fervently, and softly and lovingly. . . . Buck seized Thornton's hand in his teeth. Thornton shook him back and forth. As though animated by a common impulse, the onlookers drew back to a respectful distance, nor were they again indiscreet enough to interrupt."

13.   Wilson notes the subtle undertone of satire created by adopting Buck's limited point of view concerning human desires (102–04). Wilson is also astute on the complex links between professionalism and narcissistic masculinity emerging at the turn of the century (xiv, 197–99). Seltzer uses London's *Sea-Wolf* to culminate his complex argument about the machine-like disciplining of men's bodies as represented in various texts—"an erotics of discipline" yet a promiscuous transgression of boundaries, including the natural and the unnatural (155–56).

14.   I am indebted here to discussions with Brandy Kershner. See also Kershner's fine interpretive survey of European fantasies about degeneration. Kahn's essay brilliantly teases out the differences between prince-like and subject-like readings of the Agathocles-Borgia contrast—if we are taken in by humanistic morality, we are unreflective subjects—before exposing "the essential emptiness of the concept of *virtù*" (77).

15.   Rogin speculates about the psychodynamics of Jackson's rage and his relish for killing Indians. Turner's 1893 essay keeps Jackson's rage offstage, stressing more palatable aspects of individualism such as "coarseness and strength . . . buoyancy and exuberance" ("Significance" 61).

16.   A great many studies in the last 15 years have emphasized the rise of the professions after the Civil War. Wiebe deftly sketches the complex tensions empowering an emphasis on class and a resolution through the professions, with residual ethnic and racial ways of voicing a profound sense of uprooting; see especially ch. 5. Cronon notes Turner's fear that without the frontier, immigrants could not escape class conflict (167), but misses Turner's insistence on man-making as the goal of environmental interaction.

17.   See Wiebe 132; also Nick Salvatore on Debs's appeal to native artisan traditions of American manliness rather than to European traditions of socialism.

18.   McCullough's study of Roosevelt's childhood, especially 90–108, speculates that Roosevelt unconsciously used his asthma attacks to gain days alone with his father. "[F]ather and the out of doors meant salvation" (108). Ostensibly Roosevelt's National Progressive Party, formed in June 1912 after he had been humiliated at the Republican convention, was given its nickname by the newspapers because he told reporters he felt as fit as a bull moose. The manly response to wounding caught the nation's fancy.

19.   See Knight 55, also 72 on Roosevelt the literary critic (as president!), especially a 1907 essay criticizing London's *White Fang* for depicting a fight between dog and wolf that is " 'the very sublimity of absurdity.' " Knight situates Roosevelt's image and impact in the context of American imperialism (50–59, also 6–12).

20.   On rhetorical play in *The Virginian* and its uses for dominating the independent, equality-minded heroine, see Mitchell. On the sometimes vexed Wister-Remington friendship, see Vorpahl, which also thoughtfully sketches their lives and works. Wister had three serious breakdowns, a second in 1895 (171) and the last in 1909 (323), which he cured with another trip to Wyoming. On Wister's music background, see 9–10. Remington was a Yale football player whose drawings for Roosevelt's *Ranch Life* helped to establish his journalistic career (26), while his famous painting of Roosevelt's Rough Riders charging up San Juan Hill (a fiction) helped to launch his friend into national politics. Remington's letters to Wister about the Cuban invasion are flagrantly racist in their indiscriminate contempt for "a lot of d— niggers" (221), "the Dagoes or the Yaps" (225, also 223). Remington's burly machismo contrasts with Wister's more guarded gentility throughout, e.g., Remington, fresh from the success of the Spanish-American War, asking about Wister's recent marriage: "How do you get on with your wife—who is boss? or haven't you had time to settle that yet. I believe that sometimes takes several campaigns. Annexation is attended with difficulties" (279). I am indebted to Carl Bredahl for this reference.

21.   Speaking French and (haltingly) English, Tarzan drives Jane away from a forest fire in Wisconsin before he relinquishes her to her fiancé, the presumed Lord Greystoke.

22.   Cheyfitz links Burroughs's narrative to US imperial expansion. Torgovnick explores the tensions in various Tarzan books between the doubt-filled Tarzan, who can fleetingly imitate maternal modes and learn from blacks, and the macho Tarzan required by the nearly all-male audience, gradually suppressing the character who dares ask, "what does a man do?" (70; 68–71). See Bederman on the gender struggle in churches at this time.

23.   See also Green, who argues rather simply that the American tradition of manly adventure is imperialist, while oddly claiming that it constitutes the finest aspect of American literature. Torgovnick also links *Bonfire* with *Tarzan* (259).

24.   See Wertham for a 1950s psychoanalytic (and homophobic) assault on Robin. Miller's *Batman* plays with Robin as a crossover gender figure.

25.   On traditional societies, see Gilmore, though he implies the codes and ideologies have not changed much. On capitalism, see Chandler; Cmiel. Lears voices a hesitant admiration for religious and masculinist stances in opposition to inchoate modernization, e.g., 138, on the "eloquent" and "admirable" manly stoicism of combat, regretfully assimilable to modern nihilism, or 258–59, on the "softened" quality of " 'male' " and " 'female' " ideals through therapeutic secularism rather than transcendent religion, yet the potential "heroism" of religious-based protest and dissent (181, 260). Lears's conscious ambivalence about the loss of manly strength and religious transcendence gives his book its own complex eloquence. Davis links the turn-of-the-century fascination with the "strenuous life" to the breakdown of traditional Protestant bonds between material success and spiritual salvation; stress-seeking man "became an embodiment of sheer vitality in a limitless void" (72).

26.   See Norris, "A Plea for Romantic Fiction" (1901): "Realism is minute, it is the drama of a broken teacup . . . the adventure of an invitation to dinner" (*McTeague* 314).

27.   See, for instance, Jeffords, who argues that the Vietnam War reestablished patriarchal bonding as an alternative to women's reproductive powers. Jeffords's book can be juxtaposed with Sheehan's *A Bright Shining Lie,* which explores how John Paul Vann transformed himself from the illegitimate child of a prostitute into an extraordinary leader, an exemplary American in Vietnam, yet also a rapist and a compulsive womanizer. See esp. 389–90, 397–423 on Vann's childhood; 433–34 on the freedom of army respectability; and 487–92 on rape allegations and Vann's ability to fool the lie detector.

Works Cited

Bederman, Gail. " 'The Women Have Had Charge of the Church Work Long Enough': The Men and Religion Forward Movement of 1911–1912 and the Masculinization of Middle-Class Protestantism." *American Quarterly* 41 (1989): 432–65.

Berky, Andrew S., and James P. Shenton. *The Historians' History of the United States.* Vol. 1. New York: Capricorn, 1966.

Blumin, Stuart M. *The Emergence of the Middle Class: Social Experience in the American City, 1760–1900.* Cambridge: Cambridge UP, 1989.

Bly, Robert. *Iron John: A Book About Men.* Reading, MA: Addison-Wesley, 1990.

Burroughs, Edgar Rice. *Tarzan of the Apes.* 1912. New York: Ballantine, 1983.

Carnes, Mark C. *Secret Ritual and Manhood in Victorian America.* New Haven: Yale UP, 1989.

Carnes, Mark C., and Clyde Griffen, eds. *Meanings for Manhood: Constructions of Masculinity in Victorian America.* Chicago: U of Chicago P, 1990.

Chandler, Alfred D., Jr. *Scale and Scope: The Dynamics of Industrial Capitalism.* Cambridge: Harvard UP, 1990.

Cheyfitz, Eric. "*Tarzan of the Apes*: U.S. Foreign Policy in the Twentieth Century." *American Literary History* 1 (1989): 339–60.

Cmiel, Kenneth. *Democratic Eloquence: The Fight over Popular Speech in Nineteenth-Century America.* New York: William Morrow, 1990.

Cooper, James Fenimore. *The Deerslayer or The First War-Path.* 1841. Garden City: Dolphin-Doubleday, n.d.

———. *The Last of the Mohicans: A Narrative of 1757.* 1826. New York: Signet, 1980.

Cronon, William. "Revisiting the Vanishing Frontier: The Legacy of Frederick Jackson Turner." *Western Historical Quarterly* 18 (1987): 157–76.

Davis, David Brion. "Stress-Seeking and the Self-Made Man in American Literature, 1894–1914." Rpt. in *From Homicide to Slavery: Studies in American Culture.* New York: Oxford UP, 1986. 52–72.

Fiedler, Leslie A. *Love and Death in the American Novel.* 1960. Rev. ed. New York: Stein and Day, 1966.

Filene, Peter G. *Him/Her/Self: Sex Roles in Modern America.* 2nd ed. Baltimore: Johns Hopkins UP, 1986.

Gamarekian, Barbara. "The Cartoonists' Art: Nothing Is Too Sacred." *New York Times* 19 Mar. 1991: B2.

Gilmore, David D. *Manhood in the Making: Cultural Concepts of Masculinity.* New Haven: Yale UP, 1989.

Green, Martin. *The Great American Adventure: Action Stories From Cooper to Mailer and What They Reveal About American Manhood.* Boston: Beacon, 1984.

Greenblatt, Stephen. *Shakespearean Negotiations: The Circulation of Social Energy in Renaissance England.* Berkeley: U of California P, 1988.

Howard, June. *Form and History in American Literary Naturalism.* Chapel Hill: U of North Carolina P, 1985.

Jeffords, Susan. *The Remasculinization of America: Gender and the Vietnam War.* Bloomington: Indiana UP, 1989.

Kahn, Victoria. "*Virtù* and the Example of Agathocles in Machiavelli's *The Prince*." *Representations* 13 (1986): 63–83.

Kaplan, Amy. "Romancing the Empire: The Embodiment of American Masculinity in the Popular Historical Novel of the 1890s." *American Literary History* 2 (1990): 659–90.

Kershner, R. B., Jr. "Degeneration: The Explanatory Nightmare." *Georgia Review* 40 (1986): 416–44.

Knight, Grant C. *The Strenuous Age in American Literature.* Chapel Hill: U of North Carolina P, 1954.

Lears, T. J. Jackson. *No Place of Grace: Antimodernism and the Transformation of American Culture*

1880–1920. New York: Pantheon, 1981.

Leverenz, David. *Manhood and the American Renaissance*. Ithaca: Cornell UP, 1989.

London, Jack. *The Call of the Wild and White Fang*. 1903; 1906. Toronto: Bantam, 1981.

McCullough, David. *Mornings on Horseback*. New York: Simon, 1981.

McGraw, Thomas K. "In Retrospect: Berle and Means." *Reviews in American History* 18 (1990): 578–96.

Michaels, Walter Benn. *The Gold Standard and the Logic of Naturalism: American Literature at the Turn of the Century*. Berkeley: U of California P, 1987.

———. "The Vanishing American." *American Literary History* 2 (1990): 220–41.

Miller, Frank, with Klaus Janson and Lynn Varley. *Batman: The Dark Knight Returns*. Intro. Alan Moore. New York: DC Comics, 1986.

Mitchell, Lee Clark. " 'When You Call Me That . . .': Tall Talk and Male Hegemony in *The Virginian*." *PMLA* 102 (1987): 66–77.

Moore, Alan. *Batman: The Killing Joke*. Illus. Brian Bolland. Lettered by Richard Starkings. Colored by John Higgins. Ed. Denny O'Neil. New York: DC Comics, 1988.

Norris, Frank. *McTeague: A Story of San Francisco*. 1899. Ed. Donald Pizer. New York: Norton Critical Edition, 1977.

Pericles. "Funeral Oration." *History of the Peloponnesian War*, Bk. 2, by Thucydides. Trans. Rex Warner. Harmondsworth, Eng.: Penguin, 1972. 143–51.

Rogin, Michael Paul. *Fathers and Children: Andrew Jackson and the Subjugation of the American Indian*. New York: Knopf, 1975.

Roosevelt, Theodore. *Ranch Life and the Hunting-Trail*. 1888. Ann Arbor: University Microfilms, 1966.

Ryan, Mary P. *Cradle of the Middle Class: The Family in Oneida County, New York, 1790–1865*. Cambridge: Cambridge UP, 1981.

Salvatore, Nick. *Eugene V. Debs: Citizen and Socialist*. Urbana: U of Illinois P, 1982.

Sedgwick, Eve Kosofsky. *Between Men: English Literature and Male Homosocial Desire*. New York: Columbia UP, 1985.

Seltzer, Mark. "The Love-Master." *Engendering Men: The Question of Male Feminist Criticism*. Ed. Joseph A. Boone and Michael Cadden. New York: Routledge, 1990. 140–58.

Sheehan, Neil. *A Bright Shining Lie: John Paul Vann and America in Vietnam*. 1988. New York: Vintage, 1989.

Slotkin, Richard. *The Fatal Environment: The Myth of the Frontier in the Age of Industrialization 1800–1890*. New York: Atheneum, 1985.

———. *Regeneration Through Violence: The Mythology of the American Frontier, 1600–1860*. Middletown, CT: Wesleyan UP, 1973.

Smith-Rosenberg, Carroll. *Disorderly Conduct: Visions of Gender in Victorian America*. New York: Oxford UP, 1985.

Tompkins, Jane. *Sensational Designs: The Cultural Work of American Fiction 1790–1860.* New York: Oxford UP, 1985.

Torgovnick, Marianna. *Gone Primitive: Savage Intellect, Modern Lives.* Chicago: U of Chicago P, 1990.

Trump, Donald J., with Tony Schwartz. *Trump: The Art of the Deal.* New York: Warner, 1987.

Turner, Frederick Jackson. "The Frontier in American History." Berky and Shenton 462–73.

———. "The Significance of the Frontier in American History." Rpt. in *Frontier and Section: Selected Essays of Frederick Jackson Turner.* Ed. Ray Allen Billington. Englewood Cliffs, NJ: Prentice, 1961. 37–62.

Vorpahl, Ben Merchant. *My dear Wister—: The Frederic Remington–Owen Wister Letters.* Palo Alto: American West, 1972.

Wertham, Frederic. *The Seduction of the Innocent.* New York: Rinehart, 1954.

Wiebe, Robert H. *The Search for Order 1877–1920.* New York: Hill and Wang, 1967.

Wilson, Christopher P. *The Labor of Words: Literary Professionalism in the Progressive Era.* Athens: U of Georgia P, 1985.

Wister, Owen. *The Virginian.* 1902. New York: Grosset and Dunlap, 1929.

Wolfe, Tom. *The Bonfire of the Vanities.* New York: Farrar, 1987.

Emily Dickinson and Class

Betsy Erkkila

Nowhere is the controversy over the relative merits and limits and possible interdependence of class and gender as categories of historical and cultural analysis more evident than in recent work on Emily Dickinson.[1] From Rebecca Patterson's early emphasis on Dickinson's erotic relationships with women in *The Riddle of Emily Dickinson* (1951), to Adrienne Rich's important essay "Vesuvius at Home: The Power of Emily Dickinson" (1975), to more recent work by Sandra Gilbert, Joanne Feit Diehl, Barbara Mossberg, Vivian Pollak, and Wendy Martin, among others, feminist critics have overturned traditional representations of Dickinson as sentimental recluse, "Belle of Amherst," unrequited lover, or sublimated neurotic. But through an almost exclusive focus on gender, psychosexuality, and patriarchy as the only oppression, feminist critics have also tended paradoxically to take Dickinson out of history, (re)privatizing her in the space of the home and the psyche, and subsuming the particularity and difference of Dickinson's life and work into a repeat across time of the same familial romance: the story of the daughter's revolt against a perpetually demonized and transhistorical patriarch and her desire to return to a preoedipal and prehistorical mother.[2]

In this essay, I would like to problematize the historical grounds of these polarizations by (re)situating Dickinson as fully and complexly as possible in relation to the social, political, and cultural struggles of her times. While it is certainly true to say that Dickinson was not an overtly political poet in the same sense that Whitman was, it is simply not true to say that she had no politics and no ideological investment in a particular order of power. Dickinson was, in fact, born into a more publicly active and politically engaged family than Whitman: her grandfather, Samuel Fowler Dickinson, helped to found Amherst Academy (1814) and later Amherst College (1821); her father, Edward Dickinson, and her brother, Austin, were actively involved in public projects and in the institutional ordering and administration of church, college, and town over many years. As William Tyler writes in his *History of Amherst College* (1873), Edward Dickinson "has been so long and so fully identified with the town, the first parish and the College, that the history of either of them cannot be written without writing the principal events of his life" (539). Following the panic of 1837, Edward Dickinson also served two terms (1838–40) as a state representative in the Massachusetts General Court and later as a state senator (1842–44) and a member of the Governor's Council (1845–47). In 1852, at a time of intensified struggle over the issue of slavery, he was elected representative to Congress from the Tenth District of Massachusetts. Later, in 1873, only a year before his death, he was elected again to serve in the Massachusetts General Court.

But politics is not only or always an active involvement or concern with the governance of the state; politics is also the entire network of power relations ordering a society. If Dickinson was a more private poet than Whitman, the metaphysical and linguistic space of her poems is nonetheless traversed by her ideological assumptions and presumption as a member of New England's political—and Whig—elite. In this essay, I shall seek to "de-naturalize" and make visible the historical and specifically class formation of Dickinson's life and work.[3]

"In the family," Engels wrote, the man "is the bourgeois, the woman represents the proletariat" (89).[4] Yet Dickinson's sister, Lavinia, described the economy of the Dickinson household in terms that suggest that Dickinson was not at all a proletarian in any modern or Marxist sense of the term: "As for Emily, she was not withdrawn or exclusive really. She was always watching for the rewarding person to come, but she was a very busy person herself. *She had to think*—she was the only one of us who had that to do. Father believed; and mother loved; and Austin had Amherst; and I had the family to keep track of" (Bingham 413–14; emphasis added). While father "believed" and worked as a lawyer in the Amherst community, mother "loved," and Lavinia managed the house, Dickinson *thought*; meanwhile, the Dickinson household, stable, and grounds were supported and maintained over many years by a number of Irish immigrant servants, including, at the time of Dickinson's death in 1886, six Irish workmen who carried her body across the fields to the family plot (Dickinson, *Letters* 3: 959–60).

As the privileged daughter of the town squire, Dickinson did not, like some of her middle-class New England sisters, have to enter the factory system that was then emerging locally. Nor did she, like some of the poorer women and children of Amherst, have to "put out" straw hats for David Mack's hat factory. Within the domestic economy of the Dickinson household, as in the larger political economy of nineteenth-century America, Dickinson was the "lady" and the intellectual whose leisure, freedom, and space "to think" were made possible by the manual labor and proletarianization of others.

If in relation to the larger social and industrial transformation of the US in the nineteenth century, the Dickinson household appears to represent the interests and economy of an emergent middle class, in the Amherst community, it enjoyed the status and rank of an aristocratic and feudal estate. Amherst residents consistently referred to the Dickinson house as the "Homestead" and the "Mansion," terms that reveal a typically American slippage between farmhouse and manor, yeoman and aristocrat, an agrarian American order and an older English feudal order. Like his father Samuel Fowler Dickinson, Edward Dickinson was the local squire, which meant technically that he was a justice of the peace, but which gave him the status of an English country gentleman and linked him with an older New England order of rule by a landed squirearchy of wealth and royal entitlement.[5] Edward Dickinson, wrote his niece Clara Newman Turner in 1894, "was a grand type of a class now extinct—An Old-School-Gentleman-Whig!" (Sewall 60).

Both within and outside the Dickinson family the sense of class consciousness and the potentially dangerous permeability of class boundaries was so strong that when, in 1856, Austin Dickinson married Sue Gilbert, whose father was a local tavern owner, he was looked upon as having married beneath his class. "The whole situation was another illustration of the impossibility of a marriage between different grades of society ever becoming a perfect fusion," wrote Clara Newman, who, along with her sister Anna, came to live with her uncle in 1852, and who lived with Austin and Sue after their marriage in 1856. "Sue's father was a 'tavern keeper' of decidedly convivial habits, and Austin's father was a dignified gentleman, a lawyer of the old school," Newman noted. "The two could hardly have known of each other's existence, mentally, at least. In those early days the democratic mixing of upper and lower classes was, to be sure, much more easily accomplished than in these later and stricter days of preserving family and training. And Sue always made a point of associating principally with daughters of the better class" (Sewall 282).[6] Newman's comments suggest that the famous "War between the Houses" of Emily and Sue was, in part, a class war, rooted in the socioeconomic differences between Sue Gilbert as the orphaned, mobile, and socially aspiring daughter of an Amherst tavern owner and Emily Dickinson as the privileged, homebound, and socially endowed daughter of the town squire. Unlike Sue, Dickinson could exercise the class privilege of choosing to stay at home and ultimately not to marry, reproduce, or circulate, either herself or her poems.

The ways Dickinson's sense of identity and status became bound up with the Dickinson property and her own fear of a "democratic mixing" of classes are suggested by a dream she had when she was a student at Mount Holyoke. In October 1847, she wrote to Austin: "Well, I dreamed a dream & Lo!!! Father had failed & mother said that 'our rye field which she & I planted, was mortgaged to Seth Nims.' I hope it is not true but do write soon & tell me for you know 'I should expire with mortification' to have our rye field mortgaged, to say nothing of it's falling into the merciless hands of a loco!!!" (*Letters* 1: 48–49). In addition to registering a more general Whig fear that the Democrats were censoring the mails, Dickinson's dream registers her protest against the Jacksonian democratization of the civil service and her personal anxiety that the Dickinson property and class position were under siege by the leveling spirit of Jacksonian democracy represented locally by the locofoco postmaster Seth Nims.

In the same letter, Dickinson half-humorously protested the expansionist and nationalist Democratic policies of President Polk, policies that had led to the Mexican War and that seemed to endanger Dickinson's own sense of identity, status, and place in rural New England. "Has the Mexican war terminated yet & how?" she asked her brother. "Do you know of any nation about to besiege South Hadley? If so, do inform me of it, for I would be glad of a chance to escape, if we are to be stormed" (*Letters* 1: 49).

Dickinson's fear of downward mobility was not completely unfounded. Her childhood and adolescence had been marked by the panic of 1837 and a depression in the economy from which the country did not fully recover until the mid-forties. During these years, the privileged socioeconomic status of the Dickinson family was not at all secure. Samuel Fowler built the Dickinson "Mansion" in 1813, at a time of rapid growth in manufacturing, agriculture, and the service industries in the Amherst community. After 1830 and particularly following the panic of 1837, however, as Amherst shifted from self-sufficiency to dependence on outside markets and control of manufacturing moved from independent household production to the factory, the town began to lose manufacturing strength and population both to the large-scale industrial development of eastern cities and to the expansion of settlement westward (see Taylor; Clark;

Brown). In 1830, the year of Emily Dickinson's birth, her father had to buy half of the family "Mansion" on Main Street from her grandfather because the latter had lost the family fortune by overinvesting his time and money in public projects such as the founding of Amherst College.[7] In 1833, Samuel Fowler Dickinson departed for Ohio in financial ruin, and his half of the "Mansion" was sold to an outsider, General David Mack, who came to Amherst to set up a factory for the manufacture and sale of straw hats (Fig. 1).

Fig. 1. 1840 lithograph of Main Street provides earliest glimpse of Dickinson homestead (center background), with David Mack & Son Straw Works in foreground. (The Jones Library Special Collections, Amherst, MA.)

Left with half a house, a failing law practice, and his father's debt, Edward Dickinson experienced a sense of panic that he was losing status and ground to a new breed of entrepreneurs. "I must make money in some way," he wrote to his wife on 7 September 1835. "To be shut up forever 'under a bushel' while hundreds of mere Jacanapes are getting their tens of thousands & hundreds of thousands, is rather too much for my spirit—I must spread myself over more ground—half a house, & a rod square for a garden, won't answer my turn" (Leyda 1: 30).[8] During his tenure as a representative in the Massachusetts state legislature from 1838 to 1840, his personal fortunes do not appear to have improved much. By 1840, Mack's prosperous hat business enabled him to buy the entire Dickinson mansion. The Dickinson family moved to a house on North Pleasant

Fig. 2. 1858 lithograph by Bachelder of the family homestead, which Edward Dickinson repurchased in April 1855 from Samuel Mack. (The Jones Library Special Collections, Amherst, MA.)

Street where they lived until 1855, when an improvement in their finances enabled them to repurchase the "Old Homestead" from Mack (Fig. 2).[9]

As an "Old-School-Gentleman-Whig," Edward Dickinson embodied the paradox of the Whig position at a time when an older New England elite of landed wealth and social status was eroding under the pressure of an ascendant capitalist economy of money and individual enterprise. For all his aspiration to be an English country gentleman, his entitlement in the US was neither natural nor hereditary but grounded in his possession of a certain amount of land and, increasingly, large amounts of money. Edward Dickinson's fear of being "shut up forever 'under a bushel'" while hundreds of mere Jacanapes are getting their tens of thousands & hundreds of thousands" represents a moment of socioeconomic crisis when the traditional New England ruling class realizes that it is about to be displaced not only by the so-called "self-made men" of the Jacksonian era but by the entrepreneurial and progressive logic of Whig economic policy itself.

During the fifties, as the Whig party dissolved under the pressure of the slavery controversy and Edward Dickinson held to the conservative party faith of Daniel Webster, even as many of his friends joined the newly formed Republican party, Emily Dickinson sought to resist the forces of democratic, commercial, industrial, and nationalist transformation by enclosing herself in ever smaller social units—first within Amherst, then within her house, and ultimately within her room and the space of her own mind. Not only did she set herself against the abolitionist, reformist, and democratizing energies of the times, she also set herself against the public and political engagement of her father. When he was serving as a representative in Congress between 1852 and 1854, Emily Dickinson resented the fact that he, like her grandfather, neglected the family for the public interest. "Caesar [Father] is such 'an honorable man,' " she wrote Austin in arch protest against the rhetoric of republicanism, "that we may all go to the Poor House, for all the American Congress will lift a finger to help us" (*Letters* 1: 275).

Moreover, while her father was instrumental in bringing the Belchertown Railroad to Amherst in 1853, she looked upon the railroad as an intrusion from abroad that quickened the pace of life and thrust Amherst into the grip of outsiders and the "almighty dollar." "Our house is crowded daily with the members of this world," she wrote Austin; "the 'poor in this world's goods,' and the 'almighty dollar,' and 'what in the world are they after' continues to be unknown—But I hope they will pass away, as insects on vegetation, and let us reap together in golden harvest time—that is you and Susie and me and our dear sister Vinnie" (*Letters* 1: 257).

Although Dickinson's acts of self-enclosure were at least in part a means of protecting her artistic creation, they were also class acts, manifesting her desire to define herself against and distinguish herself from the potentially polluting incursions of the democratic multitude. Dickinson was driven by a "suppressed and ungratified desire for distinction," wrote her childhood friend Emily Fowler Ford. "She wore white, she shut herself away from her race as a mark of her separation from the mass of minds" (Todd 132). It was this same separation from the "common daily strife" of the masses that Ford emphasized in a poem to Dickinson published in the *Springfield Republican* on 11 January 1891: "Nor will you touch a hand, or greet a face,— / For common daily strife to you is rude" ("Eheu! Emily Dickinson"). Although Ford may be merely an-

Although Dickinson's acts of self-enclosure were at least in part a means of protecting her artistic creation, they were also class acts, manifesting her desire to define herself against and distinguish herself from the potentially polluting incursions of the democratic multitude.

gry because Dickinson had refused to see even her in 1882, her characterization corresponds with Dickinson's own representation of herself and others in her letters and in her poems.

As a student at Mount Holyoke in 1847, Dickinson wrote her friend Abiah Root: "When I left home, I did not think I should find a companion or a dear friend in *all the multitude.* I expected to find *rough & uncultivated manners*" (*Letters* 1: 55; emphasis added). This sense of social difference, and the urge to define herself against and apart from the "rough & uncultivated" multitude, is a recurrent theme of Dickinson's poems (poem numbers cited are in *Poems*):

> The Soul selects her own Society—
> Then—shuts the Door—
> To her divine Majority—
> Present no more—
>
> Unmoved—she notes the Chariots—pausing—
> At her low Gate—
> Unmoved—an Emperor be kneeling
> Upon her Mat—
>
> I've known her—from an ample nation—
> Choose One—
> Then—close the Valves of her attention—
> Like Stone— (#303)

Whether referring to an act of self-enclosure or enclosure within a specific class, what Dickinson describes in a monarchical language of emperors, chariots, and divine right is a rigidly stratified social order of rank, exclusion, and difference in which the "Door" of one's "own Society" is closed to all but a select few chosen from an "ample nation."

Similarly, in *"One Life* of so much Consequence!" and "The Soul's Superior instants," the poet sets herself omnipotently above and beyond the "thick" and "dense" multitude, identifying with a monarchical and privileged elite *"perceptible— /* Far down the dustiest Road!" (#270). Even Dickinson's poems of romantic entrapment, including "Mute thy Coronation," "I met a King this afternoon!" "The *Sun—just touched* the Morning," "The Court is far away—," and "He put the Belt around my life—," are enacted as scenes of submission to superior men—dukes, masters, wheeling kings, and even God himself as "a distant—stately Lover—." In fact, in Dickinson's most anthologized poem, "Because I could not stop for

Death—," Death himself comes courting as an aristocratic gentleman with horses and carriage to take the lady of "Gossamer" and "Tulle" for an "immortal" ride.

Like nineteenth-century Whig political rhetoric, the language of Dickinson's poems slips between the old and the new, between an aristocratic language of rank, royalty, and hereditary privilege, and a Calvinist language of spiritual grace, personal sanctity, and divine election, in which the aristocratic ideals of hierarchy and social subordination are displaced from the secular to the divine arena. Although Dickinson never converted to Calvinism, its terms continued to shape the language, imagery, and conceptual framework of her poems. For her, as for other conservative New England Whigs, the notion of a divinely elected spiritual aristocracy predestined to power served ultimately to support a hierarchical social order against the more public, egalitarian rhetoric of the time. In fact, until the nineteenth century, in New England at least, the Calvinist notion of an aristocracy of the spirit had never existed apart from the fact of an economic elite who actually did rule politically, socially, and culturally.

Thus, in the poem "Mine—by the Right of the White Election!" Dickinson deploys a simultaneously aristocratic and Calvinist language of rank, royal entitlement, and divine right:

> Mine—by the Right of the White Election!
> Mine—by the Royal Seal!
> Mine—by the Sign in the Scarlet prison—
> Bars—cannot conceal! (#528)

Setting the speaker's own right to possession against the claims of some unnamed antagonist, the poem inscribes the social and territorial as well as racial imperatives of New England's ruling class. Although the poet speaks the language of Revelations, here as in "A solemn thing—it was—I said— / A woman—white—to be—" and other Dickinson poems, the language of the "Right" of "White Election" cannot finally be separated from nineteenth-century debates about the racial hegemony of the white race and of New Englanders in particular.

Dickinson's elitism is evident in her almost complete silence on the major social issues of her time, and, when she did speak, in her phobic and seemingly genocidal attitude toward foreigners and the masses. "Vinnie and I say masses for poor Irish boys souls," she wrote to her brother Austin in 1851, when he was having trouble disciplining his Irish students as a teacher in the Boston schools. "So far as *I* am concerned I should like

to have you kill some—there are so many now, there is no room
for the Americans" (*Letters* 1: 113). Dickinson's xenophobia
was shared by her brother, who later became active in the
Know-Nothing party. Austin was "aristocratic, contemptuous," remembered Millicent Todd Bingham, "the spare old
Squire who despised the common herd" (Sewall 297; 299).

In her letters and poems, Dickinson assumes an aristocratic
order of rank and difference as part of the natural order of
things. Writing to her friends Josiah and Elizabeth Holland in
November 1858, she referred to one of her father's workmen
as a "serf" as she reflected on the democratic blurring of social
bounds brought by death as the great leveler. "I buried my
garden last week—our man, Dick, lost a little girl through the
scarlet fever," Dickinson wrote, in a passage that disturbs not
so much because she equated the loss of her garden with the
loss of a workman's child, but because she placed her own loss
an aristocratic and "purple" notch above the loss of the "serf's
child." "Ah! dainty—dainty Death! Ah! democratic Death!"
Dickinson exclaimed, "Grasping the proudest zinnia from my
purple garden,—then deep to his bosom calling the serf's child!"
"Say, is he everywhere? Where shall I hide my things?" (*Letters*
2: 341), she asked, as her psychic and metaphysical fear of
"democratic Death" begins to merge with a material and historical fear of losing the Dickinson property, goods, and name
to the disruptive Jacksonianism represented by the "loco" postmaster Seth Nims.

This assumption of a natural social order of class and race
informs several poems, including most notably "Color—Caste—
Denomination—," which turns on the ironic contrast between
a hierarchical and time-bound order of race and class difference,
in which dark is subordinated to light, "Umber" to "Chrysalis
of Blonde," and a "diviner" and timeless order in which these
marks of social distinction will be erased by Death's "Democratic fingers":

Color—Caste—Denomination—
These—are Time's Affair—
Death's diviner Classifying
Does not know they are—

As in sleep—All Hue forgotten—
Tenets—put behind—
Death's large—Democratic fingers
Rub away the Brand—

If Circassian—He is careless—
If He put away
Chrysalis of Blonde—or Umber—
Equal Butterfly—

They emerge from His Obscuring—
What Death—knows so well—
Our minuter intuitions—
Deem unplausible— (#970)

Although the poem gestures toward a "large" and essentially utopian social order in which "All Hue" will be "forgotten," the speaker suggests that in time, at least, democracy is impossible. Any democratic "Obscuring" of the time-bound "Brand" of race and class difference, she concludes, "Our minuter intuitions— / Deem unplausible—." What the poem suggests finally is that the speaker's "minuter intuitions" have led her to "deem" democracy "unplausible" and indeed rather horrifying not only within but beyond social time.

"The Malay—took the Pearl—" assumes a similarly unchangeable social order of race and class difference and subordination:

The Malay—took the Pearl—
Not—I—the Earl—
I—feared the Sea—too much
Unsanctified—to touch—

Praying that I might be
Worthy—the Destiny—
The Swarthy fellow swam—
And bore my Jewel—Home—

Home to the Hut! (#452)

The poem appears to use the language of racial and class difference to represent an essentially egalitarian spiritual order in which all—blacks as well as whites, "Swarthy" fellows as well as the "Earl"—have access to the "Jewel" of God's grace. Feminists have also read the poem as an articulation of a specifically female anxiety about "the primitivism of male dominance" and the fear of "homosexual conquest" (Pollak 156). But these readings gloss over the fact that the "The Malay" is a dark man of a lower social order and that the entire poem turns on the irony that "The Swarthy fellow," who is assumed to be less worthy, "took the Pearl" which the speaker as "the Earl" implicitly deserves. Indeed, the "Pearl" that the Malay "took" is not his at all; it is "my Jewel," belonging originally, it would seem, to the white and aristocratic speaker.

Read this way, the "Jewel" assumes a more specifically material and historical significance as a sign perhaps of social plenitude, possession, and the fulfillment of earthly desire. The poem—which was written at the time of the Civil War—appears to describe a historical situation in which others, specifically black others, are making gains, while the speaker, an aristocrat, is being "undone." In fact, the speaker's sense of deprivation and loss interestingly parallels Dickinson's father's sense that "mere Jacanapes" were "getting their tens of thousands & hundreds of thousands" while he was losing ground (Leyda 1: 30) and Emily Dickinson's own anxiety that the family might be losing ground amid large-scale social changes in ownership and power.

Dickinson manifested little concern about the problems of slavery, industrialism, the urban poor, and the dispossession of American Indians that sent other New England women to fight publicly against social injustice. Even when Dickinson does appear to address the social problems of her time, in a poem such as "The Beggar Lad—dies early—," she seems removed from the subject; the "Beggar Lad" becomes a mere vehicle for a conventional spiritual allegory about the ultimate redress of God.[10] Defining herself against not only the lower orders, but against certain categories of middle-class women, including the Christian benevolent model of true womanhood represented by Mary Lyons at Mount Holyoke and such female proponents of Whig ideology as Catharine Beecher and Sarah Josepha Hale, Dickinson could be quite hard-hearted about the masses being dispossessed and impoverished by the same forces of socioeconomic transformation that threatened her own status in rural Amherst.[11] In an 1850 letter to her friend Jane Humphrey, Dickinson mocked the benevolent notion of women as the feeders, caretakers, and reformers of the world represented by the local sewing society to which she refused to belong: "Sewing Society has commenced again—and held its first meeting last week—now all the poor will be helped—the cold warmed—the warm cooled—the hungry fed—the thirsty attended to—the ragged clothed—and this suffering—tumbled down world will be helped to it's feet again—which will be quite pleasant to all. I dont attend—notwithstanding my high approbation—which must puzzle the public exceedingly. I am already set down as

one of those brands almost consumed—and my hardhearted-
ness gets me many prayers" (*Letters* 1: 84).

To Dickinson and her sister, the labor abuses, accidents,
and increasing loss of lives brought by industrial transformation
became a form of sensational entertainment for the gleeful consumption of the leisure class: "Who writes those funny accidents, where railroads meet each other unexpectedly, and gentlemen in factories get their heads cut off quite informally?"
Dickinson asked Samuel Bowles, the editor the *Springfield Republican,* which she read every night. "The author, too, relates
them in such a sprightly way," Dickinson noted, "that they are
quite attractive. Vinnie was disappointed to-night, that there
were not more accidents—I read the news aloud, while Vinnie
was sewing" (*Letters* 1: 264).

"She's tearful—if she weep at all— / For blissful Causes,"
Dickinson later wrote in the poem "She's happy, with a new
Content—," satirizing the reformist energies of her New England sisters (#535). Similarly, in the poem "What Soft—Che-
rubic Creatures— / These Gentlewomen are—," Dickinson satirized the pious and pure model of true womanhood associated
with middle-class women who were, as Gerda Lerner observes,
aspiring "to the status formerly reserved for upper-class wom-
en" (25–26). But while Dickinson mocked what she called the
"Dimity Convictions" of the Angel in the House, she could
also write such lines of pure domestic—and Whig—sentiment
as "If I can stop one Heart from breaking / I shall not live in
vain" (#919). Moreover, by enclosing herself in the traditionally
female space of the home, she ends by enforcing the sexual
division of labor and the division of public and private spheres
that was at the base of the new bourgeois social order she seeks
to resist and protest in her life and work.

Within the Dickinson household and in her poems, Dickinson was in some sense the spokesperson and representative
of older ruling class interests.[12] In setting herself against Whig
commercial interests and her father's initiative in bringing the
Belchertown Railroad to Amherst, Dickinson identified herself
with the "country party" tradition of the eighteenth century
and the more specifically Federalist, anticommercial, and ruling
class heritage of John Adams and later John Quincy Adams.[13]
In fact, Dickinson's fears about the train's arrival in Amherst
were borne out by its ultimately debilitating effects on the Amherst community. If it brought business, goods, and what Dickinson called the "almighty dollar" to Amherst, it also linked
the town with large-scale and mechanized national and international markets, destroyed its nascent manufacturing econo-

my, and eroded Amherst's population growth and status as an educational center by carrying young people out of the town to points east and west in search of their fortunes (see Taylor).

Although Dickinson contested Whig economic policies, she subscribed to an essentially Whig moral economy that fostered a personal and social regime of self-renunciation, hierarchy, and control, particularly control of a potentially unruly body. "I do not care for the body," Dickinson wrote Abiah Root in 1850, "the bold obtrusive body—Pray, marm, did you call *me?*" (*Letters* 1: 103). Figuring the body as a servant of the lower class, Dickinson registers her experience of the body as a site not only of her oppression, the place where female nature, and in particular the female capacity for reproduction, can be made to serve the needs of man and race; the body is also the site of her identification with and potential invasion by the "rough & uncultivated" desires she associated with the lower class.

Over and over in her poems, from "I dreaded that first Robin, so, / But He is mastered, now," to such erotic dream poems as "I started Early—Took my Dog—" and "In Winter in my Room," to more explicitly didactic poems such as "Renunciation—is a piercing Virtue—," Dickinson registers a fear of being overwhelmed by and a corresponding desire to retreat from the body, sexuality, and the specifically corporeal dimensions of experience. On a fundamental level, Dickinson's poems are about disciplining rather than unleashing sexual and social desire; they are about policing, mastering, and controlling the body within the regime of the mind, the soul, and the imagination. This dread of physical experience and the corresponding desire for social control are, I would argue, bound up not only with a fear of the body as a site of female colonization but with an essentially conservative Whig distrust of the body of the democratic masses.

"How do most people live without thoughts," Dickinson once asked, in a comment that suggests her own superior sense that "most people" lived on the level of the body "without thoughts" (*Letters* 2: 474). Within the political order of Dickinson's verse, the multitude and the democratic masses are consistently demonized. In "The Popular Heart is a Cannon first—" and "The Ditch is dear to the Drunken Man," the masses are associated with intemperance, criminality, and an explosive violence without past or future. The poem "I'm Nobody! Who are you?" appears to parody the politics of title and place:

> How dreary—to be—Somebody!
> How public—like a Frog—
> To tell your name—the livelong June—
> To an admiring Bog! (#288)

From a gender point of view, the poet's lack of settled identity as "Nobody" represents a form of liberation from the structures of social authority that define and limit a woman's life. But this seemingly democratic "Nobody" masks an aristocrat who refuses to be defined in and through the demonized body of the democratic masses figured as "an admiring Bog."

Like de Toqueville in *Democracy in America,* Dickinson was critical of the dull conformity of democratic and majority rule. " 'George Washington was the Father of his Country'— 'George Who?' That sums all Politics to me," she wrote toward the close of her life (*Letters* 3: 849), registering her protest against the process of democratization and national political integration that led, in the post-Civil War period, to the enfranchisement of ignorant masses who did not even know the fundamentals about American heritage. If Dickinson's poems bear traces of the antiauthoritarian political rhetoric of her times, that rhetoric is translated not into a dream of democracy but into a royalist dream of rule by hereditary and divine right. Thus, in the poem "I'm ceded—I've stopped being Their's—," Dickinson deploys the politically charged language of secession, but the secession she imagines is not in favor of a sovereign republican self or state. Rather, "With Will to choose, or to reject," she secedes into an essentially monarchical order in which she will be "Queen."

Within the context of nineteenth-century American democratic culture, Dickinson's poetry becomes particularly—and politically—interesting, for it articulates an aristocratic social ideal that had been suppressed in the more public political rhetoric of the Whig party. Whereas Douglass, Thoreau, Whitman, and Melville, and many of the women writers of her age, including Stowe, Fuller, Child, and Jacobs, embraced the democratic language of republican ideology even as they turned that language to a critique of the actual practice of the American government, Dickinson returned to a pre-Revolutionary and aristocratic language of rank, titles, and divine right to assert the sovereignty of her self as absolute monarch. Not only does she set herself against what F. O. Matthiessen calls "the possibilities of democracy" invoked by other writers of her age (ix), but at a time when a woman, Victoria, was the queen of England, Dickinson's royalist language also bears witness to the political irony that it is under an aristocratic order of hereditary and divine right rather than under a democratic order of contract and inalienable rights that a woman was entitled to political power and to rule.

Considered within the context of their social moment, at a time when the old rhythms of gentry and rural life were being disrupted by rapid transformations in the socioeconomic landscape of nineteenth-century America, even Dickinson poems that seem most resistant to a historical, and specifically class, reading begin to assume a more than merely personal resonance.[14] The strongly elegiac tone of Dickinson's verse and her constant return to the subjects of time, change, loss, mortality, and death, represent a response not only to the death of this or that person, but to change itself as the overwhelming social and economic fact, even in rural Amherst.

In Dickinson's poems, the garden as a site of social abundance is continually threatened by the leveling forces of time, change, and democratic death. In the poem "A loss of something ever felt I—" the poet articulates her sense of loss in explicitly social terms. "As one bemoaning a Dominion / Itself the only Prince cast out—" she experiences her bereavement as the loss of an entire way of social being associated with an aristocratic and essentially monarchical past. Exiled and "cast out" of her princely heritage, she longs for a restoration of her lost rank and estate, signified in the poem by her "Delinquent Palaces" (#959). Even in poems of seemingly "pure" imagination, such as "There is a morn by men unseen" or "I taste a liquor never brewed," the poet expresses her desire to retreat from social time into some "remoter green" of ease and stability protected from historical change. Thus, in the poem "Dare you see a Soul *at the White Heat*?" the "finer Forge" within becomes a way of securing the speaker against the fact that real forges and real blacksmiths were being dispossessed as the country came increasingly under the control of money, markets, and what Dickinson called "the Mighty Merchant" (#365).

As if in response to the increasing valuation placed on money and material possessions as opposed to ascribed status in the new marketplace economy, Dickinson's poems return almost obsessively to the problem of money, or rather, the poet's lack of it. During the depression of 1856–57, the *Hampshire and Franklin Express* commented on the plan to bring a good lecturer to Amherst every few weeks: "A half dozen of our young men, determined upon varying the monotony of the hard times by something that should remind us that we have minds and tastes too as well as pockets, formed themselves into a club, pledging each other for a first class lecture here as often as once a fortnight" (Leyda 1: 350). The cultural note suggests an underlying strategy of Dickinson's work. Whereas Edward Dickinson sought to secure his social position through the acquisition of more money and more land, Dickinson sought to secure the declining status of both her gender and her class through the accumulation of cultural and spiritual capital, what she called "My Soul's *entire income*" (#270). Over and over again, Dickinson's poems assert the ultimate and real value of an interior, mental, and spiritual economy against the instability of the new marketplace economy of wages, prices, contracts, merchants, securities, stocks, and reversals. "Reverse cannot befall / That fine Prosperity / Whose Sources are interior—" the poet says, setting an inner "Prosperity" against the "Adversity" and "Misfortune" of an international marketplace dependent on the happenings "In far—Bolivian Ground—" (#395). Similarly, in the poem "Some—Work for Immortality— / The Chiefer part, for Time—" the immediate compensation of the marketplace, "The Bullion of Today—," is set against the cultural and spiritual "Work" of the poet as the "Currency / Of immortality": "One's—Money—One's—the Mine," she says (#406).

In a lithograph of Amherst dated 1886, two hat factories and a train appear in the foreground and the Homestead and the Evergreens appear in the background in a pictorial representation that sets rural past against industrial future, figuring how an older order of landed wealth, rank, and privilege was giving way to a new economic order of industry, entrepreneurs, and money as the ultimate measure of distinction and value (Fig. 3). Read within the context of the declining status of her social class, Dickinson's poems might be said to represent that historical moment when the values of an old aristocracy of established rank and power were being translated from the public and political to the literary and artistic realm, forming a kind of new cultural aristocracy. For Dickinson, as for the club of young men who determined to bring "first class" lecturers to Amherst during the depression of 1856–57, "mind and taste" became a means of compensating for the real losses of the "pocket," as a new cultural elite sought to perpetuate the values of stability, order, and degree against the debased imperatives of commercial marketplace and democratic masses.

Dickinson's refusal to publish was marked by a similar aristocratic resistance to the twin forces of democratization and commercialization. In 1843, a reviewer for the prestigious, Whig-oriented *North American Review* expressed anxiety about the

ЯМЂЕЂSТ, МЯSS.
1886.

Fig. 3. 1886 lithograph of Amherst, with hat factories and train in foreground and the Dickinson homestead and the Evergreens just behind factories. (The Jones Library Special Collections, Amherst, MA.)

increasing commercialization and democratization of literature as the written word and authorship itself became subject to the laws of a marketplace economy. "Literature begins to assume the aspect and undergo the mutations of trade," he noted. "The author's profession is becoming as mechanical as that of the printer and the bookseller, being created by the same causes and subject to the same laws. The nature of the supply seems likely to be as strictly proportioned to the demand, as in any other commercial operation" ("The Works of Alexander Dumas").

In "Myself was formed—a Carpenter—," Dickinson registers a similar anxiety about the literary marketplace. At a time when the traditional artisan economy of craft and handwork was being reduced to wage labor, Dickinson imagines herself as an artisan whose craft is under siege by the marketplace values of speed, cost, and efficiency:

> Myself was formed—a Carpenter—
> An unpretending time
> My Plane—and I, together wrought
> Before a Builder came—
>
> To measure our attainments—
> Had we the Art of Boards

Sufficiently developed—He'd hire us
At Halves— (#488)

Representing herself as a Christ-like figure, Dickinson responds "Against the Man" that she is engaged in another, more immortal kind of work: "We—Temples build—I said—."

Dickinson offered a similar response "Against the Man" in refusing to let her "Mind" be published and put to "use" by the male publishing world. In 1862, she wrote to Thomas Higginson: "Two Editors of Journals came to my Father's House, this winter—and asked me for my Mind—and when I asked them 'Why,' they said I was penurious—and they, would *use it for the World*—" (*Letters* 2: 404; emphasis added).[15] The terms of Dickinson's refusal to publish are inscribed in poem #709:

Publication—is the Auction
Of the Mind of Man—
Poverty—be justifying
For so foul a thing

Possibly—but We—would rather
From Our Garret go
White—Unto the White Creator—
Than invest—Our Snow—

Deploying a highly charged political language in which the rhetoric of antislavery protest intersects with the rhetoric of protest against wage labor as a new form of human enslavement, Dickinson pleads against the "Auction" block of commercial publication: "Reduce no Human Spirit / To Disgrace of Price—."

When in 1872, Dickinson was approached by a "Miss P" (perhaps Elizabeth Stuart Phelps, the editor of the *Women's Journal* and author of *The Gates Ajar* [1868], a popular novel that materialized heaven as a middle-class, female-centered household complete with pianos), she responded with an irony that verged on hostility. "Of Miss P—I know but this, dear," she wrote her cousin Louise Norcross. "She wrote me in October, requesting me to aid the world by my chirrup more. Perhaps she stated it as my duty, I don't distinctly remember, and always burn such letters, so I cannot obtain it now. I replied declining. She did not write to me again—she might have been offended, or perhaps is extricating humanity from some hopeless ditch . . ." (*Letters* 2: 500).

Dickinson explicitly mocks and, in effect, "burns up" the

middle-class notion of women's writing as an extension of women's domestic role—the missionary idea that it is her "duty" to "aid the world by my chirrup more." Her choice of *chirrup* underlines the trivialization of women's songs and puns on the literary domestic notion that it is the woman writer's role to "cheer-up" the world rather than, in Dickinson's terms, to make it "see" complexly, oppositely, and at times somberly. She also takes a parting shot at women reformers, aimed perhaps at Miss P[helps]'s involvement in temperance reform and the work of "extricating humanity from some hopeless ditch. . . ."

In her own writing Dickinson appears to have been more interested in being immortal than in being merely useful, helpful, dutiful, or moral. Adhering to an essentially aristocratic and Carlylean notion of literature as the production of mind and genius for eternity, she set herself against not only the new commercialization and democratization but against the sentimental women writers of her time who had gained money and fame in the American marketplace. At a time when the traditionally productive space of the home and traditional female housework were being devalued, Dickinson also appears to have been engaged in reclaiming the home and women as producers of valuable and enduring work. Sometime in the late fifties she began arranging and sewing her poems into groupings that Mabel Loomis Todd called "fascicles." Among Dickinson's manuscripts, there are 39 groupings that have been threaded and bound together and 25 other groupings that have not been sewn. Although Dickinson may have been preparing her poems for eventual publication, her attitude toward the literary marketplace makes it more likely that she was engaged in a private form of publication.

Folding, sewing, and binding four to five sheets of paper together in groupings of eighteen to twenty poems, Dickinson, in effect, converted traditional female thread and needle work into a different kind of housework and her own form of productive industry. She appears to have been engaged in a kind of home or cottage industry, a precapitalist mode of manuscript production and circulation that avoided the commodity and use values of the commercial marketplace. Along with the manuscripts that she produced, threaded, and bound herself, Dickinson also engaged in a private, essentially aristocratic form of "publication" by enclosing and circulating her poems in letters to her friends. The irony, of course, is that while Dickinson contested the values of the capitalist marketplace in her life and work, by retreating from historical time and social representation toward writing as a subjective, private, and aestheticized act, she, like other Romantic poets, ended by enforcing the separation of art and society and the corresponding feminization, trivialization, and marginalization of art in the new bourgeois aesthetics.

In *The Madwoman in the Attic,* Sandra Gilbert and Susan Gubar argue that upper-class women "were denied the economic, social, and psychological status ordinarily essential to creativity" and "denied the right, skill, and education to tell their own stories with confidence" (71). I have been suggesting that, on the contrary, it was precisely Dickinson's upper-class economic, social, and psychological status that enabled in fundamental ways her poetic creation and the seeming radicalism of her vision. If Dickinson challenged the masculine orders of authority in home and family, church and state, it was an assault launched from within the confines and class privilege of her "Father's house." If from the point of view of gender her refusal to marry, to publish, and to circulate might be read as a radical act, from the point of view of class that refusal was paradoxically grounded in the privilege of her status as the daughter of a conservative Whig squire. In fact, Dickinson's decision not to marry was underwritten by her father, whose reluctance to have his daughters leave his house may well have been related to a desire to keep family and class position intact against the potentially corrosive—and democratizing—influences of the time. It was because Dickinson had the economic privilege to choose to stay at home that she could finally refuse to go to market. "Poverty—be justifying / For so foul a thing / Possibly," she wrote in "Publication—is the Auction," apparently oblivious to the fact that other writers, including her friend Helen Hunt Jackson, really did have to write and to publish for money and survival.

At about the same time Dickinson began writing her poems, the Seneca Falls Convention of 1848 was calling upon women to organize for women's rights, women's suffrage, and real political power; Margaret Fuller was enjoining women to redeem the lost political ideals of America and pay for what she called "Isabella's jewels" in *Woman in the Nineteenth Century* (1845); and other women writers, including most notably Harriet Beecher Stowe and Harriet Jacobs, were celebrating the networks among black and white women as a powerful means of subverting and contesting the slave system. Although Dickinson's recognition of the oppression she shared with other women had the effect of politicizing that experience, the bonds of assistance and resistance she formed with her women friends lacked any larger political reference. She never conceived of taking her struggle into the public sphere.

"If women have a role to play," says Julia Kristeva in "Oscillation between Power and Denial," "it is only in assuming a *negative* function: reject everything finite, definite, structured, loaded with meaning, in the existing state of society. Such an attitude places women on the side of the explosion of social codes: with revolutionary movements" (166). If Dickinson was on the side of revolution, for her, as for Kristeva, it was a revolution located not in the political and economic but in the linguistic sphere. Like Kristeva and other French feminists, including Hélène Cixous and Luce Irigaray, Dickinson showed little concern with politically transforming the material conditions of women's lives. Her revolution was enacted on the level of language by rupturing "everything finite, definite, structured, loaded with meaning" and thus challenging a metaphysical order and an entire way of knowing and signifying grounded in the transcendent power of the Word as Logos and Father.

Insofar as language is the symbolic structure that constitutes the social order, Dickinson's disruption of language and syntax might, as Kristeva suggests in *Revolution in Poetic Language,* register or anticipate a revolutionary transformation in the political sphere. But while Dickinson's poetic assault on the patriarchal orders of language parallels the more public agitation for a change in woman's social, economic, and legal status in the US, it is unclear how her poetic revolution might become an agent of political change. As Catherine Clément notes in *The Newly Born Woman,* in a comment on the distinction between Hélène Cixous's notion that language can be a vehicle of historical transformation through the writing of female desire and a more traditional Marxist notion of language and history as seemingly different realms of struggle: "There is imagination, desire, creation, production of writing . . . and then somewhere else, on another level of reality, there is class struggle, and within it, women's struggle. There are missing links in all that, which we should try to think in order to succeed in joining our two languages" (Cixous and Clément 159).

The "missing links" between Dickinson's revolutionary poetics and the revolutionary struggles of blacks, women, and workers that marked her time suggest a potential problem and contradiction in the current theoretical—and feminist—emphasis on language as the site of political transformation. Not only does Dickinson's revolutionary poetic practice appear to be unconnected with any real transformation in woman's historical status as object and other in a system of production and exchange controlled by men, but as in the work of James Joyce, Antonin Artaud, and other celebrated modern poetic "revolutionaries," her radical poetics was conjoined with an essentially conservative and in some sense reactionary and Know-Nothing politics. If on the level of language Dickinson might be celebrated as a kind of literary terrorist—a "loaded Gun" and dancing "Bomb"—who blew up the social and symbolic orders of patriarchal language, it is also important that we recognize that her poetic revolution was grounded in the privilege of her class position in a conservative Whig household whose elitist, antidemocratic values were at the very center of her work.

Notes

1.   For the debate between Marxists and feminists about class and gender as categories of analysis, see, for example, Robinson; MacKinnon; Moi; Lentricchia; and Gilbert and Gubar, "The Man on the Dump."

2.   This ahistoricism in Dickinson studies is by no means limited to feminist critics. Commenting on the underlying vision of Dickinson's work in *Emily Dickinson,* Richard Chase observes: "Emily Dickinson's eschatological cast of mind, on the whole a departure from New England Puritanism, was entirely a personal vision of life and has no direct historical or social implications" (186). In *Beneath the American Renaissance,* David Reynolds argues that it is precisely in transcending politics that Dickinson becomes a major woman artist (387–437).

3.   Ideology, writes Terry Eagleton, is "that complex structure of social perception which ensures that the situation in which one social class has power over the others is either seen by most members of the society as 'natural', or not seen at all" (5).

4.   Feminists are less certain about the relation and relevance of class in the history of women. In *The Second Sex,* Simone de Beauvoir argues that women are dispersed among men and divided from other women along class lines: "If they belong to the bourgeoisie, they feel solidarity with men of that class, not with proletarian women; if they are white, their allegiance is to white men, not to Negro women" (xix). In *Sexual Politics,* on the other hand, Kate Millett rejects class altogether as a significant category of analysis, arguing that patriarchy is the fundamental system of domination, independent of capitalism or any other mode of production. Whereas American feminist historians, most notably Gerda Lerner and Elizabeth Fox-Genovese, have tended to follow de Beauvoir in emphasizing the class and race divisions among women in the US, American feminist literary critics have tended to follow Millett in emphasizing the communality of interests among women across race, class, and cultural bounds.

5. For a study of New England squirearchy, see Gross.

6. For an opposing view of class, see Pessen, *Jacksonian America* and *Riches, Class, and Power*. He argues that far from being an age of equality and "the democratic mixing of upper and lower classes," the antebellum decades featured an inequality among classes that surpassed anything that came afterward.

7. In *History of Amherst College,* William S. Tyler says of Samuel Fowler Dickinson: "His business which was so large as to require all his time and care, suffered from his devotion to the public. He became embarrassed and at length actually poor. And in his poverty he had the additional grief of feeling that his services were forgotten" (121).

8. Edward Dickinson's marriage in 1828 to Emily Norcross, who came from a family of wealthy entrepreneurs who had made much money in land speculation, may itself have been linked with his attempt to secure his social position against the impending losses of his father. For a discussion of the socioeconomic background of the Norcross family, see Bernhard, who notes: "At a time when the Dickinson family fortunes were in jeopardy, the Norcross family resources were secure as a result of Joel [Norcross]'s business acumen" (376).

9. On 20 April 1855, the *Franklin and Hampshire Express* noted under "SALE OF REAL ESTATE": "The elegant place where the late venerable Dea. Mack resided for upwards of twenty years, has been recently sold by his son, Samuel E. Mack, of Cincinnati, to the Hon. Edward Dickinson, whose father, Samuel F. Dickinson, formerly owned the place. Thus has the worthy son of an honored sire the pleasure of possessing the 'Old Homestead'" (Leyda 1: 331). How Edward Dickinson obtained the money to repurchase the "Old Homestead" is open to question. His wife, Emily Norcross Dickinson, may have received an inheritance from her father's estate. However, Barton Levi St. Armand and Cynthia Griffin Wolff both argue that Edward Dickinson embezzled from his nieces, Clara and Anna Newman, who came to live with the Dickinson family in the early fifties.

10. For a discussion of the relation between Dickinson and other more socially engaged women writers of her time, see Dobson (78–98).

11. Beecher defended the home as the site of national renewal in such books as *The Duty of American Women to Their Country* (1844). Hale was the editor of *Godey's Lady's Book* (1837–77) and the author of several humanitarian works, including the antislavery *Northwood: A Tale of New England* (1827).

12. In "Ideology and Ideological State Apparatuses," Louis Althusser comments on the relation between the state and what he calls "Ideological State Apparatuses" such as the church, the family, the educational system, and the arts. These institutions are, he argues "not only the *stake,* but also the *site* of class struggle, and often bitter class struggle" because "the former ruling classes are able to retain strong positions there for a long time" and because "the resistance of the exploited classes is able to find means and occasions to express itself there" (147).

13. For a discussion of the "country party" tradition as it was embodied in such figures as John Quincy Adams, see Howe and Thornton.

14. In *The Decline of American Gentry,* Stow Persons argues that "the destruction of gentry leadership and the emergence of a mass society in which powers were dispersed to a degree hitherto unknown constituted perhaps the greatest social transformation in American history" (4).

15. The two editors to whom Dickinson refers may be Samuel Bowles and Josiah Holland, the editors of the *Springfield Republican.*

Works Cited

Althusser, Louis. "Ideology and Ideological State Apparatuses." *Lenin and Philosophy and Other Essays.* New York: Monthly Review, 1971. 127–86.

Beauvoir, Simone de. *The Second Sex.* Trans. H. M. Parshley. New York: Knopf, 1953. Trans. of *Le Deuxième Sexe.* 1949.

Bernhard, Mary Elizabeth. "Portrait of a Family: Emily Dickinson's Norcross Connection." *New England Quarterly* 40 (1987): 363–81.

Bingham, Millicent Todd. *Emily Dickinson's Home: Letters of Edward Dickinson and His Family.* New York: Harper, 1955.

Brown, Richard D. "The Emergence of Urban Society in Rural Massachusetts." *Journal of American History* 61 (1974): 29–51.

Chase, Richard. *Emily Dickinson.* New York: Sloane, 1951.

Cixous, Hélène, and Catherine Clément. *The Newly Born Woman.* Trans. Betsy Wing. Minneapolis: U of Minnesota P, 1986. Trans. of *La jeune née.* 1975.

Clark, Christopher. "The Household Economy, Market Exchange and the Rise of Capitalism in the Connecticut Valley, 1800–1860." *Journal of Social History* 13 (1979): 169–90.

Dickinson, Emily. *The Poems of Emily Dickinson.* Ed. Thomas H. Johnson. 3 vols. Cambridge: Belknap-Harvard UP, 1955.

———. *The Letters of Emily Dickinson.* Ed. Thomas H. Johnson. 3 vols. Cambridge: Belknap-Harvard UP, 1960.

Diehl, Joanne Feit. *Dickinson and the Romantic Imagination.* Princeton: Princeton UP, 1981.

Dobson, Joanne. *Dickinson and the Strategies of Reticence: The Woman Writer in Nineteenth-Century America.* Bloomington: Indiana UP, 1989.

Eagleton, Terry. *Marxism and Literary Criticism.* Berkeley: U of California P, 1976.

Engels, Friedrich. *The Origin of the Family, Private Property, and the State.* New York: International, 1942.

Fox-Genovese, Elizabeth. "Placing Women's History in History." *New Left Review* 133 (1982): 5–29.

Gilbert, Sandra. "The American Sexual Poetics of Walt Whitman and Emily Dickinson." *Reconstructing American Literary History*. Ed. Sacvan Bercovitch. Cambridge: Harvard UP, 1986. 123–54.

Gilbert, Sandra, and Susan Gubar. *The Madwoman in the Attic: The Woman Writer and the Nineteenth-Century Literary Imagination*. New Haven: Yale UP, 1979.

———. "The Man on the Dump versus the United Dames of America; or, What Does Frank Lentricchia Want?" *Critical Inquiry* 14 (1988): 386–406.

Gross, Robert A. "Squire Dickinson and Squire Hoar." *Massachusetts Historical Society Proceedings* 101 (1989): 1–23.

Howe, Daniel Walker. *The Political Culture of the American Whigs*. Chicago: U of Chicago P, 1979.

Kristeva, Julia. "Oscillation Between Power and Denial." *New French Feminisms*. Ed. Elaine Marks and Isabelle de Courtivon. Amherst: U of Massachusetts P, 1980. 165–67.

———. *Revolution in Poetic Language*. Trans. Margaret Walker. New York: Columbia UP, 1984. Trans. of *La Révolution du langage poétique*. 1974.

Lentricchia, Frank. "Andiamo!" *Critical Inquiry* 14 (1988): 407–13.

———. "Patriarchy Against Itself—The Young Manhood of Wallace Stevens." *Critical Inquiry* 13 (1987): 743–86.

Lerner, Gerda. "The Lady and the Mill Girl: Changes in the Status of Women in the Age of Jackson." *The Majority Finds Its Past: Placing Women in History*. New York: Oxford UP, 1979. 15–30.

Leyda, Jay. *The Years and Hours of Emily Dickinson*. 2 vols. New Haven: Yale UP, 1960.

MacKinnon, Catharine. "Feminism, Marxism, Method, and the State: An Agenda for Theory." *Signs* 7 (1982): 515–44.

Martin, Wendy. *An American Triptych: Anne Bradstreet, Emily Dickinson, Adrienne Rich*. Chapel Hill: U of North Carolina P, 1984.

Matthiessen, F. O. *American Renaissance: Art and Expression in the Age of Emerson and Whitman*. New York: Oxford UP, 1941.

Millett, Kate. *Sexual Politics*. Garden City, NY: Doubleday, 1970.

Moi, Toril. *Sexual/Textual Politics: Feminist Literary Theory*. New York: Methuen, 1985.

Mossberg, Barbara. *Emily Dickinson: When a Writer is a Daughter*. Bloomington: Indiana UP, 1982.

Patterson, Rebecca. *The Riddle of Emily Dickinson*. Boston: Houghton, 1951.

Persons, Stow. *The Decline of American Gentility*. New York: Columbia UP, 1973.

Pessen, Edward. *Jacksonian America: Society, Personality, and Politics*. Chicago: Dorsey, 1969.

———. *Riches, Class, and Power Before the Civil War*. Lexington, MA: Heath, 1973.

Pollak, Vivian. *Dickinson: The Anxiety of Gender*. Ithaca: Cornell UP, 1984.

Reynolds, David. *Beneath the American Renaissance: The Subversive Imagination in the Age of Emerson and Melville.* New York: Knopf, 1988.

Rich, Adrienne. "Vesuvius at Home: The Power of Emily Dickinson." 1975. *On Lies, Secrets, and Silence: Selected Prose 1966–1978.* New York: Norton 1979. 157–83.

Robinson, Lillian. "Dwelling in Decencies: Radical Criticism and the Feminist Perspective." 1970. *Sex, Class, and Culture.* New York: Methuen, 1986. 3–21.

St. Armand, Barton Levi. *Emily Dickinson and Her Culture: The Soul's Society.* New York: Cambridge UP, 1984.

Sewall, Richard. *The Life of Emily Dickinson.* New York: Farrar, 1974.

Taylor, George R. "The Rise and Decline of Manufacturers and Other Matters." *Essays on Amherst's History.* Amherst: Vista Trust, 1978.

Thornton, Tamara Plakins. *Cultivating Gentlemen: The Meaning of Country Life Among the Boston Elite, 1785–1860.* New Haven: Yale UP, 1989.

Todd, Mabel Loomis, ed. *Letters of Emily Dickinson.* New York: Harper, 1931.

Tyler, William S. *History of Amherst College During Its First Half Century.* Springfield, MA: Clark W. Bryan, 1873.

Wolff, Cynthia Griffin. *Emily Dickinson.* New York: Knopf, 1986.

"The Works of Alexander Dumas." *North American Review* 56 (1843): 110.

The Borderlands of Culture: Américo Paredes's *George Washington Gómez* and Chicano Literature at the End of the Twentieth Century

Ramón Saldívar

The Caribbean revolutionary, writer, and theoretician C. L. R. James once noted that "[o]ver a hundred years ago, Hegel said that the simplest reflection will show the necessity of holding fast . . . the affirmation that is contained in every negation, the future that is in the present" (161).[1] Doing "cultural studies" before the term, with all of its current proprietary implications, was in common use, James has much to say about questions of culture, writing, and politics, issues of vital concern today. James's analyses are particularly instructive in the way they consider issues of cultural production in relation to personal consciousness and across national boundaries and historical eras.

The last few years, however, have been marked less by speculation on the future than by what Fredric Jameson has called "an inverted millenarianism . . . in which premonitions of the future, catastrophic or redemptive, have been replaced by senses of the end of this or that (the end of ideology, art, or social class; the 'crisis' of Leninism, social democracy, or the welfare state, etc., etc." ("Postmodernism" 53). Given the recent, astonishingly sudden, collapse of Communism in the Soviet Union and in Eastern Europe, an event that Robin Blackburn has called "sufficiently comprehensive to eliminate [Communism] as an alternative to capitalism and to compromise the very idea of socialism" (5), one might understandably be tempted to add to this list, in premature gesture of dismissal, the end of Marxism, or of revolution. "Taken together," maintained Jameson in 1984, "all of these [endings] perhaps constitute what is increasingly called postmodernism" ("Postmodernism" 53).

If in the wake of these millennial endings we are indeed on the threshold of something like George Bush's fabled "new world order," the beginning of the post–cold war era has shown us that we are also still very much in the depths of an old *dis*order. The social, economic, political, and psychic crises that were momentarily elbowed into the background by the recent, short-lived euphoria accompanying the end of hot and cold wars now seem again to characterize the present. We are left still to wonder what a truly "new world order" might look like in a post–cold war, post-Marxian, postcolonial, postmodern, indeed, "postcontemporary" era.

Resisting the temptation to prognosticate, I wish to return to James's notion of the "future in the present" as a way of reading a recent Chicano novel for what it might teach us about the processes of cultural and subjective formation in our "postcontemporary" age, and for a hint of what affirmations might sublate present negations. Situated on the time-space border between North American and Latin American world experiences, Chicano and Chicana discourse generally is a prime instance of what has recently been termed "border writing," that kind of postcontemporary discourse that, according to Emily Hicks, exhibits a "multidimensional perception and nonsynchronous memory" (xxiii). The multidimensionality and nonsynchronicity of "border writing" emerge from its capacity to see from both sides of one border and configure a concept from within two cultural contexts. "Multidimensionality" and "nonsynchronicity" are thus differential variations of James's dialectical "future in the present." Since Chicana scholars, artists, and writers have been in the avantgarde of the recent flowering of Chicano literary, visual, and performance arts, I will address momentarily the issue of gender in relation to Chicano cultural studies.[2] In light of James's argument concerning the future in the present, however, I wish to focus on a writer who is now widely recognized as having articulated the terrain of Chicano cultural studies and established the very ground for "border writing": Américo Paredes.[3]

Paredes's best-known contribution to American cultural history is perhaps *"With His Pistol in His Hand"* (1958), a study of ballads of US-Mexican border conflict.[4] In late 1990, Paredes furthered his study of the border by publishing a novel, *George Washington Gómez*. Written between 1935 and

1940, the novel lay deferred by the pressures of everyday life for 50 years before its appearance.[5] Set at the beginning of the century, written near mid-century, but published at the end of the century, Paredes's novel addresses as a curiously polytemporal text the central social issues of our era. As a product of the Great Depression, it speaks from the past to the present. Paradoxically, it also expresses from that past the constitution of the present ethnic subject and the formation of what Norma Alarcón has recently termed "ethno-nationalism," issues that James had already characterized as elaborations of the future in the present. Bordered by dissymmetries of space and dispersed in nonsynchronous stages of material history, the Chicano subject's "identity" and the patterns of its formation as a subject may be seen, as Paredes's novel shows, as effects of the discontinuous network of strands made up by the discourses and practices of politics, ideology, economics, history, sexuality, and language itself. In *George Washington Gómez,* we thus have a prefigurative instance of the state of Chicano literature and the Chicano subject at the end of the twentieth century. Paredes's novel offers "the future in the present" in ways that both prepare for his own future ethnographic and literary historical work and also anticipate the links between the sociopolitical and ethicosubjective in contemporary borderlands representations of identity. The novel pulls from the residual elements of traditional culture the patterns that conceive the subject and interrogates those patterns in the light of its dominant, modern formation to suggest other, as yet untried, designs for imagining a new ethnic consciousness.

The novel pulls from the residual elements of traditional culture the patterns that conceive the subject and interrogates those patterns in the light of its dominant, modern formation to suggest other, as yet untried, designs for imagining a new ethnic consciousness.

In an essay on "The Problem of Identity in a Changing Culture," Paredes maintains that the material, nonessential nature of the transformative Chicano consciousness is a by-product of the real "conflict—cultural, economic, and physical—[which] has been a way of life along the border between Mexico and the United States" (68). Following Paredes, anthropologist Renato Rosaldo reminds us that borders are hardly innocent spaces but rather "sites where identities and cultures intersect" (149). Gloria Anzaldúa, in sharp addition to both, notes that "[t]he U.S.-Mexican border *es una herida abierta* [is an open wound] where the Third World grates against the first and bleeds. And before a scab forms it hemorrhages again, the lifeblood of two worlds merging to form a third country—a border culture" (3). Rosaldo and Anzaldúa thus agree with Paredes that in those borderland contact zones between conflicting cultures, identity becomes a central problematic, linked explicitly to racial and economic, as well as to psychological and ethical, categories.

This scene of conflict and the narratives of its resolution have their special place in American history. Because of their historical and geopolitical positioning as the easternmost outpost, first of colonial New Spain, and then of the newly independent Republic of Mexico, the people of the present-day South Texas region—people of Mexican culture—argues Paredes, experienced first the conflict with Anglo-American culture that would soon affect all of the Mexican borderland settlements of the Southwest, prefiguring the history of New Mexico, Arizona, Colorado, and California. In Texas by 1835, the Anglo-Texan fight for independence from Mexico had left Mexican Texans dispossessed foreigners on their own native land, culturally Mexican, politically American, in reality not quite either. Like their ancestors sent to settle the South Texas region in 1749 to fill the gap between the central Mexican seat of government to the south and the far-off Anglo-Texan colonies to the north, the inhabitants of the present Lower Rio Grande Valley came to live, and experience their everyday lives as inhabiting, "an in-between existence" (Paredes, "The Problem of Identity" 73).

After 1835, this sense of being caught in the middle intensified and became a hallmark of Mexican-American identity. Paredes's "*With His Pistol in His Hand*" was a study of the border ballad tradition—the *corrido* tradition—that arose chronicling this history of border conflict and its effects on Mexican-American culture. Paredes there noted that "[b]orders and ballads seem to go together, and their heroes are all cast in the same mold. . . . During the Middle Ages there lived in some parts of Europe, especially in border areas, a certain type of men whose fame has come down to us in legend and in song. . . . People composed ballads about men like these; legends grew up about them, and they became folk heroes to be studied and argued about by generations of scholars" (xii). As the oral folk history of nineteenth-century Mexican-American resistance to Anglo-American political and cultural power, affecting both subjective and collective identity construction, the Mexican-American *corrido* functioned as an ideological expression of what Raymond Williams, in another idiom, calls the "residual" cultural order. "The residual, by definition," says Williams, "has been effectively formed in the past, but it is still active in the cultural process, not only and often not at all as an element of the past, but as an effective element of the present. Thus certain experiences, meanings, and values which cannot be expressed or substantially verified in terms of the dominant culture, are nevertheless lived and practised on the basis of the residue—cultural as well as social—of some previous social and cultural institution or formation" (122). These lived "experiences, meanings, and values" of traditional Mexican-American communities (effectively formed in the past, but still active in the present cultural process) expressed in nineteenth-century and early twentieth-century *corridos* centered on folk heroes who represented the community's collective resistance to the new dominant Anglo power. Typically in the *corrido* of intercultural conflict, a hard-working, peace-loving Mexicano is goaded by Anglo outrages into violence, causing him to defend his rights and those of others of his community against the *rinches,* the border Spanish rendering of Texas "Rangers."[6]

Paredes's novel, *George Washington Gómez,* is set against this history of cultural-political conflict chronicled in the US-Mexican border ballad. It takes especially as its moment the 1915 uprising in South Texas by Mexican Americans attempting to create a Spanish-speaking republic of the Southwest.[7] Dismissed as "Mexican bandits" by Anglo historians, the *sediciosos* ("seditionists"), as they came to be known, were acting under a carefully considered revolutionary manifesto, the "Plan de San Diego," that called for a union of Texas Mexicans with American Indians, African Americans, and Asian Americans to create an independent border republic of the Southwest. Answering deep-seated feelings of anger and frustration over Anglo oppression and injustice, the seditionist movement of 1915 was an early expression of the feelings evoked later by the Chicano Movement of the 1960s and an early enunciation of coalition politics among internal Third World groups in the US.

In 1915, bands of armed men under the leadership of Aniceto Pizaña and Luis de la Rosa raided Anglo military posts, ranches, railroad lines, and depots throughout South Texas. In the end, the seditionists were overwhelmed by the American military forces brought in to quell the uprising. Resistance was followed swiftly by terror, as the Texas Rangers set out to enact reprisals against the entire Mexican-American population of South Texas. In the aftermath of the seditionist uprising, hundreds of innocent Mexican-American farmers and ranchers were slaughtered by Texas Rangers, summarily executed without trial at even the smallest hint of possible alliance with, or even sympathy for, the seditionists.[8] The result was that South

Texas was virtually cleared of landholding Mexican Americans, making feasible the Anglo development of the region into its capitalist agribusiness formation in the 1920s. Paredes's novel situates us in the midst of this historical scenario, taking its tone, however, not from the celebration of the tragic *corrido* hero, doomed to honorable but certain defeat with his pistol in his hand, but from the pathos of those innocents from whom was exacted the cost of defeat.

Richard Johnson has claimed that one may arrive at a functional definition of that slippery term "culture" indirectly by focusing on related key words, such as "consciousness" and "subjectivity" (45). "Identity" is, of course, linked to these terms as well, as the signifier of differentiation within consciousness and subjectivity. "When we name things," says Paredes, "we give them a life of their own; we isolate them from the rest of our experience. By naming ourselves, we affirm our own identity; we define by separating ourselves from others, to whom we give names different from our own" ("The Problem of Identity" 78).

The issue of identity is raised from the first pages of the novel, as Gumersindo and María Gómez, María's mother, and her brother, Feliciano Garcia, discuss the naming of the child who has been born to them in the midst of the seditionist uprising and its bloody aftermath:

> The baby . . . was feeding greedily at his mother's breast. Born a foreigner in his native land, he was fated to a life controlled by others. At that very moment his life was being shaped, people were already running his affairs, but he did not know it. Nobody considered whether he might like being baptized or not. Nobody had asked him whether he, a Mexican, had wanted to be born in Texas, or whether he had wanted to be born at all. The baby left the breast and María, his mother, propped him up in a sitting position. She looked at him tenderly. "And what shall we name him?" she wondered aloud. (15)[9]

The answer to her question exemplifies one version of Chicano subject formation in the American West and Southwest, an American postcolonial variant of the "processes of subjectification" that Homi K. Bhabha has identified with colonial discourse and the formation of the colonial subject in general. We already know the literal answer to her question: the baby is the title character. Positioned as a subject by the material actions and symbolic rituals of the community into which he has been born, the child also has a figural present and a prefigural future in the present underwritten by the relations of class and race in which he will live his life, as Paredes's previously published work suggests. Indeed, the process of subjectification that we witness at the beginning of his story only makes concrete the abstract process of categorization that has configured the child even before his birth.

The other characters, María's husband, mother, and brother, offer her a variety of names for the child, each pointing toward an alternative narrative within which the child's destiny might be played out: first, "Crisósforo," a name of grandiose and idiosyncratic proportions, is considered as a sign of his singularity; "José Angel," a name serving as a sign of the continuity of traditional religious value, follows; "Venustiano" and "Cleto," names alluding to the Mexican revolutionary leader Venustiano Carranza and to one of the leaders of the ongoing sedition, are suggested as signs of revolutionary commitment; and even the father's own name, "Gumersindo," as sign of genealogical continuity, is considered but, oddly, rejected like the rest. Finally, the child's mother speaks: " 'I would like my son . . . ' she began. She faltered and reddened. 'I would like him to have a great man's name. Because he's going to grow up to be a great man who will help his people.' " Gumersindo responds playfully, saying, "My son . . . is going to be a great man among the Gringos . . . " and then adds in sudden inspiration, "A Gringo name he shall have! . . . Is he not as fair as any of them?" (16), introducing into this moment of subject formation the issues of race and color. We might see this moment as an exemplary instance of Althusserian interpellation (174), the process whereby an "individual" is "appointed as a subject in and by the specific familial [and political] ideological configuration in which it is 'expected' once it has been conceived" (176). Once appointed as a subject, the configured individual may then respond to the pressures of ideology by functioning within the category of the subject. At issue immediately in the novel, then, are questions of "identity," "subjectivity," and "consciousness," especially as these concepts relate to "culture."

Trying to recall what "great men" the Gringos have had, Gumersindo considers before exclaiming: "I remember . . . Wachinton. Jorge Wachinton" (16). The grandmother's attempt to say the strange name "Washington" comes out as: "Gualinto. . . . Gualinto Gómez" (17). And so the name sticks. The clash of identities that is the substance of Gualinto Gómez's life is instantiated at this originary moment where the various discourses that might have ordered his life are signaled to us. The story of this child, a "foreigner in his native land," will follow the commandments implicit in the ideologies unconsciously projected in his "very good name," ideologies that will position him as a subjected representation of the imaginary relations to the real conditions of existence in the early twentieth-century borderlands of South Texas.

Each of the names, those considered and rejected, as well as the one chosen and immediately transformed into its dialectal equivalent, signals a different set of speech genres and promises to inscribe the child into a particular discursive history. As Mikhail Bakhtin points out, speech genres, certain combinations of forms of utterances, underwrite permissible locutions in lived life and, more importantly, serve as normative restraints on our most intimate intentions; they form the legitimate borders of what we can say and not say. The textual instance at hand represents two sets of such speech genres at work: on the one hand are represented the utopian hopes and dreams of the father and mother, who optimistically project a future of reconciled differences with their crossed references to the child's promised Mexican and American destinies. On the other hand are the historically validated misgivings of the child's uncle concerning these crossed destinies. As he leaves the scene of ritual naming, Feliciano, soon to be the child's surrogate father, sings some verses from one of the most famous of the *corridos* of border conflict, "El Corrido de Jacinto Treviño": "*En la cantina de Bekar, se agarraron a balazos*" ("In Baker's saloon, some shots rang out").[10] Prefiguring the violent murder of Gumersindo by Texas Rangers in the very next chapter, the song activates an entirely different speech genre to guide the interaction between the child's Mexican nurturing and American enculturing. The dialectics between these binary oppositions move the novel's ideological plot but in decidedly unforeseeable patterns.

The instability of this ideological plot is signaled throughout the remainder of the novel by the continuing instability of the title character's name. In crucial early scenes, before he enters the American schools, the child is Gualinto Gómez, with a name he and his uncle like to explain is "Indian." These idyllic preschool years will later serve as the Edenic counterpoint, the largely untroubled duration of no time before the fall into history, that might ironically reemerge to save him for history. In the narrated present, however, once the child enters school, his heart and mind become the battleground for cultural hegemony:

So, . . . [Gualinto] began to acquire an Angloameri-
can self, and as the years passed, . . . he developed simultaneously in two widely divergent paths. In the school-
room he was an American; at home and on the playground
he was a Mexican. Throughout his early childhood these
two selves grew within him without much conflict, each
an exponent of a different tongue and a different way of
living. The boy nurtured these two selves within him,
each radically different and antagonistic to the other,
without realizing their separate existences.

It would be several years before he fully realized that
there was not one single Gualinto Gómez. That in fact
there were many Gualinto Gómezes, each of them double
like images reflected on two glass surfaces of a show window. The eternal conflict between two clashing forces
within him produced a divided personality, made up of
tight little cells independent and almost entirely ignorant
of each other, spread out all over his consciousness,
mixed with one another like squares on a checkerboard.
(147)

To raise the question of "identity" as this passage does is
not to celebrate it or fix it as something that is knowable, and
known, a priori. What follows instead in the course of the narrative of Gualinto's history is a systematic exploration of the
attempted standardization of the notion of "identity," as much
by the American school system that attempts to pass off ideology in the guise of truth as by the economic system that com-
modifies complex differences of identity by reflecting a single
specular image in the "glass surfaces of a show window" in the
marketplace. Equally operative, even if repressed from the
conscious levels of the narrative, is the fixation of Mexican
gender ideology that identifies Gualinto as a belated heir to the
tradition of armed resistance represented most starkly by his
uncle Feliciano. Given this interplay of determining discourses, figured in this passage by the cubist image of the "checkerboard" of a modernist consciousness, from this point on,
"identity" will not be available except in the form of a mediation, one that includes the existential materials of daily life
along with those psychological ones in which the identity-
form is imprinted in the early versions of twentieth-century
mass culture. The catoptric theater of reflecting showcase windows, as Walter Benjamin has argued in another but related
context, is not accidental but symbolic, a representational
stratagem. The magic mirrors of the marketplace are contrived

to confound identity and the subject's relation to commodities mingled with its reflected selves in the object world.

As Paredes's narrator later puts it: "Consciously [Gualinto] considered himself a Mexican. He was ashamed of the name his dead father had given him, George Washington Gómez. He was grateful to his Uncle Feliciano for having registered him in school as 'Gualinto' and having said that it was an Indian name. . . . The Mexican national hymn brought tears to his eyes, and when he said 'we' he meant the Mexican people. . . . Of such matter were made the basic cells in the honeycomb that made up his personality" (147). This initial characterization turns out to be romantically, not to say sentimentally, incomplete. It implies that we might be able later to read the identity of the subject in relation to its experience of the Mexican object world that fills its private, affective world. From this view, a particular experience of reality would determine the content of ideology; determining the position of the subject in the real would be enough to recognize the content of its ideology and its source. Paredes denies, however, that the identity of the subject may be understood solely by virtue of its "conscious" positioning for, as we learn, "[t]here was also George Washington Gómez, the American. He was secretly proud of the name his more conscious twin, Gualinto, was ashamed to avow publicly. George Washington Gómez secretly desired to be a full-fledged, complete American without the shameful encumberment of his Mexican race. He was the product of his Anglo teachers and the books he read in school. . . . Books had made him so" (147–48). Gualinto's "identity" and his constitution as a subject may be seen, then, as an effect of an immense network of strands that includes the state school and its lists of required readings but that may be termed more generally "politics, ideology, economics, history, sexuality, language" (Spivak, "Subaltern" 13). These other colonial contexts and revolutions crowd in those instilled by the oral tradition of the border *corrido,* dispelling the possibility of positing a single, homogeneous, and authentically determining cause for this subject. Still, Gualinto's American self is not to be read simply as a latent repression of the Other ready to break through from unconscious levels of the psyche to overwhelm the manifest Mexican identity of his conscious self. The mediation between the terms is infinitely more complex than the classical scenario of "true" and "false" consciousness might imagine: "In school Gualinto/George Washington was gently prodded toward complete Americanization. But the Mexican side of his being rebelled. Immigrants from Europe can become Americanized in one

generation. Gualinto, as a Mexicotexan, could not. Because . . .
he was not an immigrant come to a foreign land" (148).

Without the security of knowing or even of feeling that he
will encounter what he already knows, Gualinto, like "other
Mexicotexan children" (148), lacks even the advantage of his
parents, who, as combatants in a racial and class struggle
against an invariable enemy, knew who they were. The narrative of the parents' identity, troubled and painful as it might be,
is nonetheless determinate, reinforced in the icons of Mexican
material culture and especially in the expressions of folklore:
jokes, popular sayings, legends, and songs. In the traditional
corrido, for example, the most formalized expression of the organic patriarchal discourse that names this identity, the fate of
the individual and of the community are not separate. Rather,
they are bound together in a unitary structure, like the various
stanzas of the *corrido.* For the parents, conceptions of identity
and subjectivity imparted by the traditional social environment
are contained, as Antonio Gramsci has noted, in "language itself," "common sense," "popular religion," and therefore also
"in the entire system of beliefs, superstitions, opinions, ways
of seeing things and of acting, which are collectively bundled
under the name of 'folklore'" (323).

For the children, however, now "gently prodded toward
complete Americanization," rather than violently repressed for
being Mexican, subjected to the interpellative work of both
traditional Mexican folklore and the American ideological
state apparatus, identity both is and is not what it seems to be.
Both the American ideological apparatus and the Mexican
folkloric enculturing networks acquire causal status by seeming to produce the effect of a primary, active subject. Gualinto
the American would thus be seen as the product of a pluralist
American melting pot ideology, while Gualinto the Mexican
would be the shaped product of a sustaining traditional world.
But as Paredes brilliantly shows, the apparently homogeneous,
deliberative subject of borderland cultures emerges less as either a sovereign and causal, or dependent and effected, consciousness than as the doubly crossed "subject-effect" (Spivak, "Subaltern" 12) of both American ideological and
Mexican folkloric systems.

These double Mexican and American culture systems
each acquire within their own spheres a presumed priority by
virtue of their apparent production of a formed subject. But
this subject is then also taken to be an active causal agent, itself
willfully capable of producing and reproducing the effects of
both the American ideological and Mexican folkloric configu-

rations within which its own singular fate is said to evolve. Hence, what might initially have been conceived of as a double cultural systemic *cause* must now be regarded as the dual *effects* of a (bifurcated) sovereign subject. Yet simultaneously, the presumed sovereign *subject* remains the effected *object* of ideology and tradition. Within these doubly crossed catachrestic negations the sovereign Chicano subject, initially conceived as a formed effect and then as a forming agent, now appears instead as "the effect of an effect, and its positing a metalepsis, or the substitution of an effect for a cause" (Spivak, "Subaltern" 13). This metaleptic ground demarcates the social space of the bordered subject, encompassing both the figural construction of willed behaviors and the elaboration of ideological processes of subjectification. Now, if in the wake of this double deconstruction the category of the subject is to remain viable, it must be seen as a category at once essential and provisional, sovereign and bifurcated, a compelling form of what Spivak terms the "strategic use of positivist essentialism in a scrupulously visible political interest" ("Subaltern" 13). This doubly crossed figure is Paredes's decisive proleptic rendering of the bordered subject of contemporary Chicano narrative.

Other types of national narratives constructed to provide the etiologies of identity, such as narratives of the immigrant experience, for instance, simply will not apply to the situation of such bordered, *trans*cultured subjects. Standing in the borderlands of culture, these metaleptic figures exist on a much more problematic and unstable ground of heterogeneous determinations and crisscrossed negations: "Hating the Gringo one moment with an unreasoning hatred, admiring his literature, his music, his material goods the next. Loving the Mexican with a blind fierceness, then almost despising him for his slow progress in the world" (150). The rest of Gualinto's story is concerned with what it would take, materially and psychologically, to imagine a new identity, how one could conceptualize what one can by definition not yet imagine since it has no equivalent in current experience. The novel attempts meticulously to imagine, in other words, the affirmation that is contained in every negation, in short, the future in the present. The conceptualization of identity that we are offered at novel's end can thus in no way be taken as a precritically ideal one, even though it does remain, to a disturbing degree, sociologically and dialectically problematic.

Following these metaleptic, symbolic, and material transformations, identity now becomes in Paredes's novel something akin to Juan Flores and George Yudice's description of Latino identity in general, "a fending off of schizophrenia, of that pathological duality born of contending cultural worlds and, perhaps, more significantly, of the conflicting pressures toward both exclusion and forced incorporation" (60). As Paredes's narrator remarks: "The Mexicotexan has a conveniently dual personality. When he is called upon to do his duty for his country he is an American. . . . But while there are rich Negroes and poor Negroes, rich Jews and poor Jews, rich Italians and Poles and poor Italians and Poles, there are in Texas only poor Mexicans. Spanish-speaking people in the Southwest are divided into two categories: poor Mexicans and rich Spaniards" (195–96). The narrator elsewhere claims that "[t]he word Mexican had for so long been a symbol of hatred and loathing that . . . it had become a hateful and loathsome word" (118). Through a process of metonymic association whereby a descriptive signifier, *Mexican,* becomes a pejorative stigmata, middle-class sectors, anxious to dissociate themselves from the American denigration of the word and the culture, now became *Spanish.* This figural transformation obliquely suggests the continuing ideological dissimulation of Anglo-American hegemonic racial categories. By "conveniently" dividing "Spanish-speaking people" into two categories, "poor Mexicans and rich Spaniards," dominant historical narratives encourage a particular social hierarchy. History and knowledge are not in this case, however, the disinterested production and representation of essential facts. They are instead the decidedly interested elements of "a subject-constituting project" (Young 159). In the face of such practices, a concrete manifestation of what Gayatri Spivak describes as the "epistemic violence" ("The Rani of Sirmur" 130) enacted on the colonized subject, the formation of the dual identity, Mexican and American and yet not either, is clearly not tied simply to coercive power structures or to essential features of race, class, or ethnicity alone. It is linked as well to vested constructions of specifically represented objects, with no existence or reality outside of their discursive representation. One is thus either "a rich Spaniard" or "a poor Mexican," independent of biological or historical factors, for as social constructions the terms may not cross.

This confluence of subject-determining forces is ultimately forcefully represented to the eponymous hero when a former Texas Ranger says to him: "They sure screwed you up, didn't they, boy? . . . You look white but you're a goddam Meskin. And what does your mother do but give you a nigger name. George Washington Go-maize" (284). Straddling the multicultural ground proves to be too much for Gualinto Gómez, who attempts to resolve these ambivalences by finally changing his name legally. He now forswears the bewildering unreality of his former composite names: the American "George Washington," with all of its own now-mixed ethnic signals, alluding as the old Texas Ranger understands, not to the Founding Fathers, but to other, ethnic Washingtons, like George Washington Carver. And he rejects as well the American Indian sounding "Gualinto," with all of its associations with familial, cultural, and local history. He takes instead the simpler, if not quite neutral, "George G. Gómez."

In the wake of this scene of identity negotiation, Paredes offers one last dramatization of Chicano/Latino responses to the steering mechanisms of American society. Gualinto's efforts first to resist the homogenizing pressures of the American school system and then to embrace his parents' original dream that he be a "leader of his people" are both subverted when he becomes in the days just before World War II an officer in Army counterintelligence whose job is, ironically, "border security" (299): spying on newly emerging political organizations formed by his childhood friends. But this disowning of his family's and his people's history is achieved within a specific horizon of blurred personal and social experience. At novel's end, Gualinto is curiously troubled by a recurring dream, which itself is a return of repressed boyhood daydreams. In the dream, he imagines himself leading a victorious counterattack against Sam Houston's army at the decisive battle of San Jacinto in 1836, which had led to the creation of an independent Anglo Republic of Texas. In his dream, Gualinto rewrites history. With Santa Anna hanged and all traitors dispatched, in the dream "Texas and the Southwest . . . remain forever Mexican" (281): "He would imagine he was living in his great-grandfather's time, when the Americans first began to encroach on the northern provinces of the new Republic of Mexico. Reacting against the central government's inefficiency and corruption, he would organize *rancheros* into a fighting militia and train them by using them to exterminate the Comanches. . . . In his daydreams he built a modern arms factory at Laredo, doing it all in great detail, until he had an enormous, well-trained army that included Irishmen and escaped American Negro slaves" (282). On the verge of quite self-consciously losing himself as a pre-movement *mexicano* into the American melting pot, Gualinto's political unconscious in the form of the collective memory instantiated by the sense of self mod-

eled by his father's, his uncle's, and his mother's lives, returns
to offer an alternative ideology and self-formation. In this return of the repressed (not of the classical unconscious but of
historicity), the buried memories and daydreams of childhood
erase Gualinto's apparently resolved identity by reinscribing
over that presumed identity the provisional quality of its instrumental form.

As we have seen, the discursive speech genres of birth
certificates, educational degrees, career dossiers, service
records, marriage licenses, or legal records bind Gualinto institutionally to a formidable identity discourse. But now the
simpler structures of a precritical utopian dream emerge from
the repressed to trouble the stability of his newfound bourgeois
self. Gualinto's self-formation is powerfully formed by the
public American sphere he has chosen to embrace. He continues to be authored as well, however, by experiences and discourses of experience that by now have retreated into the unconscious fantasy structures of his life. At the point of
complete denial of his Mexican past, Gualinto can thus in the
aftermath of his daydreams and fantasies

> end up with a feeling of emptiness, of futility. Somehow,
> he was not comfortable with the way things ended. There
> was something missing that made any kind of ending fail
> to satisfy. . . . Lately, however, now that he was a grown
> man, married and with a successful career before him,
> scenes from the silly imaginings of his youth kept pop-
> ping up when he was asleep. He always woke with a feel-
> ing of irritation. Why? he would ask himself. Why do I
> keep doing this? Why do I keep on fighting battles that
> were won and lost a long time ago? Lost by me and won
> by me too? They have no meaning now. (282)

Flores and Yudice have argued that Latino "[s]elf-formation is
simultaneously personal and social (or private and public)
because the utterances and acts through which we *experience*
or gain our self-images are reaccentuated in relation to how
genres have institutionally been made sensitive or responsive
to identity factors such as race, gender, class, religion, and so
on" (65). In times of crisis, such as in the crisis of stability indicated by the name "postmodernity," "'private' identity factors
or subject positions may become unmoored from institutionally bound generic structures" (65). But in this case perhaps the
issue has less to do with the stylistics and formalisms implied
by "postmodernity" than with the configurations of identity put

at stake by the shifting relations of material and cultural production on the US-Mexican border in the first decades of this century. This "unmooring" of the subject position from the bonds of institutional ideology that might be more profitably associated with "modernity" and projects of modernization could explain why Gualinto's present "childish daydreams" and "silly imaginings" leave him "with a feeling of emptiness, of futility." It is for good reason that Theodor Adorno has claimed that "identity is the primal form of ideology" (148). Situated in the sphere of intimacy, these "daydreams" fuel a decidedly discomfiting "primal," utopian self-formation that stands against the one that he has consciously "chosen" under the various signs of his interpellation. That is to say, the fantasy structures of the unconscious return, bringing a historical memory that has the practical function of designating an alternative, even if deeply latent and tenuous, content to the formed subject of history. As Jameson has noted, "Fantasy," in this sense, "is no longer felt to be a private and compensatory reaction against public situations, but rather a way of reading those situations, of thinking and mapping them, of intervening in them, albeit in a very different form from the abstract reflections of traditional philosophy or politics" ("On Negt" 171). These alternative public spheres remain potential for Gualinto, situated as they are within knowledges formed by the anxiety of the clash between the everyday real and utopian fantasy. However, the fact of their continued existence, even if in such an attenuated form as daydream and fantasy, signals the possibility of other interventions in more opportune historical eras.

At least as significant as the precritical utopian impulse that emerges at novel's end, disrupting any reading that attempts to forge a simple, Manichaean relationship between true and false consciousness, between resistance to or assimilation into Anglo-American culture, is one other latent emplotment, concerning the question of gender. In Paredes's novel gender is articulated through and through with questions of identity formation and the creation of stable subject positions. A fully gendered reading would be concerned not only with the separate fates of Gualinto's mother, María, and his sisters, Carmen and Maruca, as they fulfill their familial roles as mother, daughters, sisters, nieces, and wives; it would also be concerned with how that fate is legislated by Mexican-American patriarchal ideology, expressed most starkly in the guiding speech genre of the text, the *corrido*.

Rosaldo, Anzaldúa, Alarcón, and others have rightly pointed out that the *corrido* expresses a specific construction of male mastery, linking ideologies of resistance and historical agency with ideologies of masculinity. Margot Backus and JoAnn Pavletich argue that the gender-coded icons and images that predominate in these songs help produce a male-gendered space that creates "only secondarily and by supplementarity a grieving female space occupied by women and children." The weight of male icons and images is such that "the moments of greatest cultural, political, and aesthetic weight are, simultaneously, the most powerfully gendered" (7). As a socially symbolic act, the *corrido* both draws from and adds to the patriarchal constitution of Chicano culture. As gender-coded discourse, it identifies the Mexican-American community and represents it in monologically male terms.

Paradoxically, that same symbolic importance also enables an interrogation of the patriarchal constitution of traditional Chicano culture. So while the *corrido* links patriarchy and resistance, it also unconsciously joins patriarchal authority and defeat, since in the songs of border conflict the hero is invariably killed, captured, or exiled from his home (Backus and Pavletich 11). Reading Paredes's novel as gendered discourse points to the ways this new dialectic, not now between patriarchy and resistance but between patriarchy and defeat, emerges in Paredes's novel as historical inevitability, in the emplotted form of disillusion and loss. One might well argue, therefore, that given the single-mindedly, implacably male-dominated articulation of resistance in the *corrido* and *corrido*-inspired narratives, the characters represented in them could not but be defined by these ethical and political limitations. We come up against the borders of male-gendered discourse throughout the novel, but perhaps nowhere more poignantly than in the failed utopian vision at the narrative's end. This link between the Mexican patriarchal discourse of the *corrido* and a certain political vision is surely one reason for the decline of the *corrido* as a viable resistance form in the 1930s and the rise of other genres that do not constrain themselves so readily by failing to interrogate patriarchal ideology.

With the end of the historical moment of armed struggle after the sedition of 1915, the interventions of resistance permitted in the symbolic, cultural sphere become all the more crucial. But to the extent that these emergent acts of symbolic social resistance continue to be articulated with uncritical, male-dominant, gendered discursive systems, and hence burdened by the limits of such systems, their own viability as enunciations of liberation will remain equally in doubt. The present flowering of Chicana writings, which in exciting and sometimes troubling ways attempts to critique articulations of race, class, and gender, corroborates the bankruptcy of patriarchally invested Chicano social texts that fail to interrogate the procedures by which an authentically determinative subject-effect is produced. Gender factors, no less than those of class and race, create a heterogeneous field that problematizes the general notion of an undifferentiated Chicano subject.

Formulated as a potential for a future reconstruction in more self-consciously gendered narratives, the undoing of "George G. Gómez"'s apparently stable subject position at novel's end marks the boundaries of the cultural borderlands that Chicano literature is at times problematically traversing at century's end. In *George Washington Gómez,* this potential certainly remains precariously fragile. Fantasy might as easily serve to dissipate practice and undermine its intent; gender remains latent and repressed, the traces of its course deferred and displaced; and the unsettled quality of our hero's identity marks the present unavailability of unified solutions. Still, the sublimation of the possibility of historical agency into the political unconscious at novel's end does not represent the end of praxis but only its transference. Though we may not be able, finally, to specify in satisfyingly concrete terms through the figure of George Washington Gómez the nature of a completed Chicano subject position, we may at least articulate some features of its subject-effects. Through these effects we also glimpse the heterogeneous arenas through which future Chicano subjectivities might yet emerge into the realm of history. The ending represented in Paredes's novel is thus hardly apocalyptic, nor even prefigurative of an "inverted millenarianism"; it is, rather, an early expression of the now widely explored complexities of Chicana and Chicano subject identity. As such an expression, Paredes's novel works powerfully as a sign of the state of Chicano literature at the end of the twentieth century. It depicts the possibility of wresting, from within the realm of necessity, the hope of freedom, which is but another way of articulating the future in the present.

Notes

1. Despite a resurgence of interest in James, many considerations of "cultural studies" continue to ignore his centrality for the present development of cultural criticism. American cultural studies has been particularly negligent of this important figure, preferring to focus instead on those versions of cultural studies that do not raise the difficult question of race.

2.   See Alarcón; Calderón and Saldívar; J. Saldívar; and R. Saldívar. In addition to the works of these cited scholars, one should consult the now-voluminous bibliography on Chicana cultural production. See the bibliographies in R. Saldívar, *Chicano Narrative,* and Alarcón, "Chicana Writers."

3.   In 1989 Paredes was honored as one of five Americans selected as the first recipients of the Charles Frankel Prize of the National Endowment for the Humanities for lifelong achievement in the humanities. In 1991 he was named as one of the first Mexican-American recipients of the *Orden de la Aguila Azteca,* Mexico's highest award given for efforts in human rights and the preservation of Mexican culture. Later that year, he was also honored by the Texas Historical Association for his exemplary contributions to the understanding of the Western and Southwestern frontier experience. Having devoted his scholarly life to researching the folk life and popular culture of greater Mexico and the American Southwest, Paredes has done ethnographic and literary critical work now being described as definitive on the folk poetry, folktales, and folk theater as well as on the proverbs, jests, legends, and riddles of the Mexican-American people.

4.   Paredes's latest work includes a volume of selected essays, *Folklore and Culture on the Texas Mexican Border*; a new study of Mexicotejano jokes, jests, and oral narratives, *Uncle Remus con Chile*; and a volume of poetry, *Between Two Worlds.*

5.   The novel was written and completed, although not circulated for publication, during the period that Paredes worked as a newspaper reporter in Brownsville, Texas. Drafted into the Army during the war, Paredes served first as a political writer and then as political editor of *Stars and Stripes,* covering the end of the war in the Pacific, the occupation of Japan, the Chinese Revolution, and the beginnings of the Korean War. In 1950, Paredes returned to Texas to take the BA, MA, and PhD degrees in English at the University of Texas at Austin. After a year teaching in El Paso, Paredes joined the faculty of the University of Texas as an assistant professor of English. In these tumultuous and hectic years, the manuscript of the novel lay untouched. When Paredes retired from the University, he finally found respite from his many research, teaching, and professional duties to take up several unfinished projects, including the novel *George Washington Gómez.* I first saw the text of the novel in manuscript copy in 1986. The novel was accepted for publication with Paredes's stipulation that it appear in unedited form, precisely as he had left it in 1940. From personal interviews with Paredes, July 1990. For further biographical information on Paredes, see Limón, "Américo Paredes" and *Mexican Ballads.*

6.   On the aesthetics of Mexican-American border ballads, see Limón, *Mexican Ballads,* and R. Saldívar, *Chicano Narrative.*

7.   For a full discussion of this history of conflict, see Montejano.

8.   The viciousness of the Texas Rangers is well documented in both nineteenth-century sources by Anglo historians and by twentieth-century Chicano revisionist historians. See Oates; Samora; and Montejano. The myth of the Texas Ranger as the lone source of civilized order was a product of the

jingoistic histories written by J. Frank Dobie and Walter Prescott Webb and consolidated by Hollywood.

9.   An interesting counterpoint to Paredes's narrative is Hart Stilwell's 1945 novel *Border City*, which chronicles the same region in the same historical era from an old left, proletariat perspective. Paredes, who worked as a newspaper reporter under Stilwell, editor of the *Brownsville Herald* at the time, appears as a minor character in Stilwell's novel. Conversations with the author, July 1991.

10.   "El Corrido de Jacinto Treviño" tells the story of a violent confrontation between the representatives of the old Texas-Mexican and the new Anglo-Texan power structures. Since the outcome of the struggle is preordained, the ends of the struggle are less important than the fact of its occurrence and the manner in which the Texas-Mexican figure enacts it. Feliciano sings verses from this song periodically to punctuate his own private resistance to cultural change. For text and analysis of this *corrido,* see Paredes, *A Texas-Mexican* 32, 69–70.

Works Cited

Adorno, Theodor. *Negative Dialectics.* Trans. E. B. Ashton. New York: Continuum, 1973.

Alarcón, Norma. "Chicana Writers and Critics in a Social Context: Towards a Contemporary Bibliography." *The Sexuality of Latinas. Third Woman* 4 (1989): 169–78.

———. "Traddutora, Traditora: A Paradigmatic Figure of Chicana Feminism." *Cultural Critique* 13 (1989): 57–87.

Althusser, Louis. "Ideology and Ideological State Apparatuses: (Notes Toward an Investigation)." *Lenin and Philosophy and Other Essays.* New York: Monthly Review, 1971. 127–86.

Anzaldúa, Gloria. *Borderlands/La Frontera: The New Mestiza.* San Francisco: Spinsters/Aunt Lute, 1987.

Backus, Margot, and JoAnn Pavletich. "Helena Maria Viramontes and the Corrido: Re-articulating Opposition." Unpublished manuscript.

Bakhtin, Mikhail. *Speech Genres and Other Late Essays.* Trans. Vern W. McGee. Ed. Caryl Emerson and Michael Holquist. Austin: U of Texas P, 1986.

Benjamin, Walter. *Charles Baudelaire: A Lyric Poet in the Era of High Capitalism.* London: NLB, 1975.

Bhabha, Homi K. "The Other Question: Difference, Discrimination and the Discourse of Colonialism." *Out There: Marginalization and Contemporary Cultures.* Ed. Russell Ferguson et al. New York: New Museum of Contemporary Art; Cambridge: MIT P, [c. 1990]. 71–87.

Blackburn, Robin. "Fin de Siècle: Socialism after the Crash." *New Left Review* 185 (1991): 5–66.

Calderón, Héctor, and José D. Saldívar. *Criticism in the Borderlands: Studies in Chicano Literature, Culture, and Ideology.* Durham: Duke UP, 1991.

Flores, Juan, and George Yudice. "Living Borders/Buscando America: Languages of Latino Self-Formation." *Social Text* 24 (1990): 57–84.

Gramsci, Antonio. *Selections from the Prison Notebooks.* Ed. and trans. Quintin Hoare and Geoffrey Nowell Smith. New York: International, [c. 1971].

Hicks, D. Emily. *Border Writing: The Multidimensional Text.* Minneapolis: U of Minnesota P, 1991.

James, C. L. R. "Dialectical Materialism and the Fate of Humanity." *The C. L. R. James Reader.* Ed. Anna Crimshaw. Cambridge, MA: Blackwell, 1992. 151–81.

Jameson, Fredric. "On Negt and Kluge." *October* 46 (1988): 159–72.

———. "Postmodernism, or, The Cultural Logic of Late Capitalism." *New Left Review* 146 (1984): 53–92.

Johnson, Richard. "What Is Cultural Studies Anyway?" *Social Text* 16 (1986–87): 38–80.

Limón, José. "Américo Paredes: A Man from the Border." *Revista Chicano-Riqueña* 8.3 (1980): 1–5.

———. *Mexican Ballads, Chicano Poems: History and Influence in Mexican-American Social Poetry.* Los Angeles: U of California P, 1992.

Montejano, David. *Anglos and Mexicans in the Making of Texas, 1836–1986.* Austin: U of Texas P, 1987.

Oates, Stephen B. "*Los Diablos Tejanos*: The Texas Rangers." *The Mexican War: Changing Interpretations.* Ed. Odie B. Faulk and Joseph A. Stout, Jr. Chicago: Sage, 1973. 120–36.

Paredes, Américo. *Between Two Worlds.* Houston: Arte Público, 1991.

———. *Folklore and Culture on the Texas Mexican Border.* Ed. Richard Bauman. Austin: U of Texas P; Center for Mexican American Studies, 1992.

———. *George Washington Gómez: A Mexicotexan Novel.* Houston: Arte Público, 1990.

———. "The Problem of Identity in a Changing Culture: Popular Expressions of Culture Conflict Along the Lower Rio Grande Border." *Views Across the Border: The U.S. and Mexico.* Ed. Stanley R. Ross. Albuquerque: U of New Mexico P, 1978. 68–94.

———. *A Texas-Mexican "Cancionero": Folksongs of the Lower Border.* Urbana: U of Illinois P, 1976.

———. *Uncle Remus con Chile.* Houston: Arte Público, 1993.

———. "*With His Pistol in His Hand*": *A Border Ballad and its Hero.* Austin: U of Texas P, 1958.

Rosaldo, Renato. *Culture and Truth: The Remaking of Social Analysis.* Boston: Beacon, 1989.

Saldívar, José D. "Criticism in the Borderlands." Calderón and Saldívar 1–7.

Saldívar, Ramón. *Chicano Narrative: The Dialectics of Difference.* Wisconsin: U of Wisconsin P, 1990.

————. "The Politics of Culture." *Chicano Cultural Studies.* Ed. Mario García. Los Angeles: U of California P, forthcoming.

Samora, Julian. *Gunpowder Justice: A Reassessment of the Texas Rangers.* South Bend: U of Notre Dame P, [c. 1979].

Spivak, Gayatri Chakravorty. "In a Word. Interview: with Ellen Rooney." *Differences* 2 (1990): 124–56.

————. "The Rani of Sirmur." *Europe and its Others.* Ed. Francis Barker et al. Vol. 1. Colchester: U of Essex, 1985. 128–51. 2 vols.

————. "Subaltern Studies: Deconstructing Historiography." *Selected Subaltern Studies.* Ed. Ranajit Guha and Gayatri Chakravorty Spivak. New York: Oxford UP, 1988. 3–32.

Stilwell, Hart. *Border City.* New York: Doubleday, 1945.

Williams, Raymond. *Marxism and Literature.* New York: Oxford UP, 1977.

Young, Robert. *White Mythologies: Writing History and the West.* New York: Routledge, 1990.

George Whitefield, Spectacular Conversion, and the Rise of Democratic Personality

Nancy Ruttenburg

1

"I think I am never more humble than when exalted," wrote George Whitefield in his journal entry for Sunday, 21 January 1739 (*Journals* 194).[1] Ostensibly meant to invoke the conventional Christian belief in empowerment through meekness and yet perceptibly at odds with it, this sentiment is reiterated throughout the spiritual autobiography of the iconoclastic Anglican minister who between 1739 and 1770 undertook an enormously influential series of preaching "tours" in colonial America. By no means the first evangelical minister to enthuse an American audience—Jonathan Edwards had recorded a cluster of "surprising conversions" in the Connecticut River valley in 1735—Whitefield is yet widely credited with launching an intercolonial religious revival of unprecedented scope and duration, which many have argued definitively altered the state of social and political life in the colonies. Known as the Great Awakening, this grass-roots religious movement democratized American religion by shifting the balance of power between minister and congregation.[2] The deference traditionally accorded the Puritan clergy gave way to a spirit of popular criticism while the respectful silence customarily observed in Puritan churches was broken by the cries and groans of a congregation whose religious experience was, according to their conservative detractors, increasingly "enthusiastic." Both developments were legitimated if not explicitly sanctioned by prominent members of the "New Light," or evangelical, ministry. Many students of the Great Awakening and its aftermath have suggested its central role in the development of an American revolutionary ideology, a development enabled, I would argue, by Whitefield's strategic reconciliation of power and humility.[3]

Whitefield's evangelical energy was fueled by the steady current of opposition from the established ministries of England and America to his charismatic person and unorthodox methods—in particular, to his practice of preaching extempore and to his itinerancy. Endlessly circulating throughout the United Kingdom and the British-American colonies, he exulted in the opposition he so assiduously courted, claiming it as a sign of his professional efficacy that mandated in turn his transgressing the boundaries of established parishes and co-opting the prerogatives of settled pastors in order to gather a congregation of the newly regenerate that neither church wall nor parish line could contain. He augmented his far-reaching influence (for which the physical range of his voice was a fitting image) by traveling with an entourage of devotees who functioned as a press corps, advertising his itinerary and the remarkable success of his field sermons in local newspapers, and disseminating his journals and sermons through local publishing networks.[4] Initially from curiosity and later from conviction, crowds gathered in unprecedented numbers (the Boston Common sermon of 1740 attracted more than 20,000) in the fields, commons, and marketplaces of colonial America to hear the celebrated "Grand Itinerant" preach on the nature and necessity of conversion, or translation out of the limitations of the self and the achievement of a "new birth."

Offering himself to his audiences as a charismatic model of the "new man"—both an exemplary convert and a masterful converter of others—Whitefield used his "wonderful Power" to mobilize people in the name of a new vision of personal, spiritual, and community life. This vision entailed the establishment of a radical itinerant ministry in each of the major colonial denominations, and led consequently to a general fragmentation, or separation, of constituted parishes.[5] Separate institutions for training and licensing such ministers soon challenged the hegemony of Harvard and Yale along with the belief that the ability to interpret Scripture depended more on education than on "experiential knowledge of Jesus Christ and Him crucified" (Whitefield, *Journals* 38), a knowledge by definition available to anyone who sought it. As the young convert Timothy Allen, who abandoned Yale to study divinity at New London's Shepherd's Tent, put it, "I WANTED NOT HUMAN LEARNING, in order *to declare the will of GOD to the* World" (qtd. in Stout and Onuf 564).[6]

The growth of an itinerant ministry and the progress of separatism fostered in turn the emergence of a class of lay preachers—including women, people of color, and even children—who traversed the colonies to exhort others on the glories and the promise of regeneration, transmuting the evangelical impulse into a republican one in the decades before the Revolution.[7] Both the vocal, if inarticulate and even hysterical, "enthusiasm" of the revivalists' congregations (the seemingly irrepressible "roarings, agonies, screamings, tremblings, dropping-down, ravings" [Whitefield, *Works* 4: 160]) as well as the emergence of lay exhorters initiated the debate we normally associate with the Revolution concerning the people's voice—its provenance and the scope and nature of its representativeness.

Whitefield's enabling claim to have reconciled humility and power functioned as the core of his self-representation, both textual and performative: it asserts that the abasement of the self coincides with its exaltation or "enlargement," suggesting a humility—and corollary empowerment—independently achieved rather than mandated as the necessary prerequisite to a future exaltation.[8] But it functioned equally as the prescription for a model of authentic selfhood intended not simply to mold the behavior of his followers but to enable them to recognize and then legitimate their transformation into "new"—divinely translated—men and women. Whitefield enacted this regenerative—and revolutionary—conjunction of self-debasement and self-exaltation through a religious performance, the field sermon, an unorthodox form of public worship that I analyze in what follows as "spectacular conversion." The newborn self newly wrought at each step along the itinerant's route was at once integral, translatable, and transferable to others. Its dominant characteristic was the aggressive uncontainability of its speech, which was authorized not despite but because of the prohibitions of established authority: in short, democratic personality in its first American instantiation. In the following pages, I will examine both the extent and the limitations of Whitefield's role in fashioning an incipient American democratic polity.

Whitefield enacted this regenerative—and revolutionary—conjunction of self-debasement and self-exaltation through a religious performance, the field sermon, an unorthodox form of public worship that I analyze in what follows as "spectacular conversion." The newborn self newly wrought at each step along the itinerant's route was at once integral, translatable, and transferable to others. Its dominant characteristic was the aggressive uncontainability of its speech, which was authorized not despite but because of the prohibitions of established authority. . . .

2

The psychospiritual dynamic that Whitefield both expertly staged before his vast audiences and that he claimed underlay his own conversion and ministry was determined by his complex relationship to his opposition. As he explicitly stated, opposition was prerequisite not only to professional success but to his own peace of mind: "I never am so much assisted, as when persons endeavour to blacken me, and I find the number of my hearers so increase by opposition, as well as my own inward peace, and love, and joy, that I only fear a calm" (*Journals* 228). For Whitefield, to be was to be embattled: precisely this conviction encapsulated from the first his experience of "experimental" religion. This characteristic orientation was established in that period of his childhood when he became convinced that God had destined him to fulfill some special mission, having separated him "even from my mother's womb, for the work to which He afterwards was pleased to call me" (*Journals* 28). To illustrate his early conviction of his calling, he cited an incident that occurred in his boyhood. Having run from some neighborhood children who had been taunting him, he tearfully knelt in his room and "prayed over that Psalm wherein David so often repeats these words—'*But in the Name of the Lord will I destroy them*' " (*Journals* 28).

As the Lord's instrument and in His name, Whitefield was from this moment determined to "destroy" his opposers by "stopping their mouths," by forcing them "into an awful silence," only to resurrect them continually, at the site of each well-advertised sermon, as the vocally hostile crowd that alone could activate and then validate his divine instrumentality. The belligerence of Whitefield's childish prayer thus evolved into the aggressive circularity of his evangelism, whereby the opposers whom Whitefield, as God's agent, made it his business to destroy were uniquely capable of engendering and then legitimating his sacred agency through their very destruction. For this reason, Whitefield tirelessly courted opposition so that he could, by means of his "enlarged" self, overwhelm it, or more accurately, incorporate it, for upon this progressive incorporation his continual enlargement depended (*Journals* 239, 255).

The centrality of opposition to Whitefield's project is borne out by his description of the formative event of his years as a student at Oxford, which he was enabled to attend despite humble family circumstances (his widowed, then divorced, mother ran an inn) by acting as servitor to a number of wealthy students. Early in his Oxford career, the sight of Methodist students proceeding "through a ridiculing crowd to receive the Holy Eucharist at St. Mary's" struck him with the force of a revelation: it invigorated his mysterious, because apparently unmotivated, attraction to the outcasts by stimulating in him an irresistible compulsion "to follow their good example" (*Journals* 36). As soon as a plausible excuse afforded him the opportunity, he contacted the mentor of the Oxford Methodists, Charles Wesley.

His association with Wesley and the Methodist students fatefully altered the expected course of his college studies; it "taught me to die daily," he wrote, referring not simply to the work of conversion or rebirth, but more pointedly to the private religious exercises in humility he publicly undertook in order to become "a new creature" and which soon turned him into an object of general derision (*Journals* 41). With his cooperation, reluctant at first, Whitefield's private life was converted into public spectacle, but one whose structure of signification was withheld from its audience, Oxford's "polite students." This unsuspected power to make oneself the sign of an unsuspected meaning or value—to secrete spiritual treasure in full view of one's adversaries on the private stage of the self—Whitefield describes as the enviable prosperity of the Methodists, who "never prospered so much in the inward man, as when they had all manner of evil spoken against them falsely without" (*Journals* 39).[9]

So conceived, the process of rebirth was achievable only through the constant circumambient pressure of willful misrepresentation, so necessary to Whitefield, but which rigorously confined the inward man to his inwardness. For Whitefield, however, the measured satisfaction of this secret prosperity was too modest a prize. Not content with his power to flaunt his possession of spiritual treasure before the blind eyes of natural men, Whitefield would transgress the Methodist model of the self to realize what was only implicit in it: the fundamentally dramatic nature of conversion and hence its potential as spectacle.[10] This discovery allowed him to exploit the paradoxical centrality of the outcast in order to stimulate in his hostile spectators a desire for such spiritual currency as he alone possessed and whose disbursement he alone could control.

Unlike the Methodists, then, conversion was for Whitefield not a private moment of grace that invisibly refigured one's orientation to the things and people of this world, but rather a public event, an act of revelation that necessarily mobilized a spectatorship, a novel (and potentially revolutionary) social configuration. From the moment he declared his allegiance to the life of the spirit by associating with Wesley and the Methodists, Whitefield would differentiate his "inward sufferings" from those of his fellows who outwardly suffered with him the daily death of their "fair reputations." His sufferings, he claimed, partook of "a more uncommon nature," in that Satan chose to mislead Whitefield by causing him to pursue "a state of quietism" ("he generally ploughed with God's heifer," Whitefield explained), tempting him with that which

Whitefield, of course, never coveted, the prospect of a wholly private privacy:

> [W]hen the Holy Spirit put into my heart good thoughts or convictions, [Satan] always drove them to extremes. . . . When Castaniza advised to talk but little, Satan said I must not talk at all. So that I, who used to be the most forward in exhorting my companions, have sat whole nights almost without speaking at all. Again, when Castaniza advised to endeavour after a silent recollection and waiting upon God, Satan told me I must leave off all forms, and not use my voice in prayer at all. (*Journals* 44)

But if Satan enjoined Whitefield to perfect silence, God would give precisely the opposite counsel to the future Grand Itinerar.t. On the day following his ordination as an Anglican minister at the precocious age of 21, Whitefield claimed to have received a divine directive: "The next morning, waiting upon God in prayer to know what He would have me to do, these words, 'Speak out, Paul,' came with great power to my soul. Immediately my heart was enlarged. God spake to me by His Spirit, and I was no longer dumb" (*Journals* 61).

The next Sunday, preaching "to a very crowded audience" drawn by curiosity to see the youthful minister, Whitefield found himself exhorting "with as much freedom as though I had been a preacher for some years" (61): "As I proceeded, I perceived the fire kindled, till at last, tho' so young, and amidst a crowd of those who knew me in my childish days, I trust, I was enabled to speak with some degree of Gospel authority. Some few mocked; but most for the present seemed struck: and I have since heard, that a complaint had been made to the Bishop, that I drove fifteen mad, the first sermon" (qtd. in Gillies 10). As his career advanced, Whitefield continued to promote the ritual kindling of the spiritual fires whose flames would inevitably, but nonetheless spectacularly, engulf the outermost ring of his audiences: those who came to dampen, but remained to burn, the opposition.

Whitefield's determination to occupy center stage through his perfection of a theatricalized humility raises the question of his early love for, and ostensible abandonment of, what he later called the "sin and folly" of the drama, both reading plays and playing roles, including the role of minister (*Journals* 54). His youthful ambition to act upon the stage remained an inextricable part of that "holy ambition" of his maturity: "to be one of those who shall shine as the stars for ever and ever" (qtd. in Gillies 207).[11] The centrality of the drama to Whitefield's self-conception fully survived his transformation from the idle adolescent, who spent all of his time "in reading plays, and in sauntering from place to place," to the Grand Itinerant (*Journals* 32).[12] This centrality is perhaps most starkly evident in that eminently dramatic moment when he forswore the pleasure of the drama once and for all. He had unthinkingly picked up a play to read when "God struck my heart with such power, that I was obliged to lay it down again; and, blessed be His Name, I have not read any such book since" (*Journals* 36). Indeed, as he represents it, his earliest intimation of his destiny came to him while reading a play aloud to his sister: he involuntarily interrupted himself to inform her that "God intends something for me which we know not of" (*Journals* 32).

Precisely such expressions of youthful messianism—which reveal an intense conviction of personal mission along with a striking ignorance of the object of that mission—form the basis of the study of "epochal" or historically significant personality undertaken by the cultural semiotician Lydia Ginzburg in *On Psychological Prose*. Although Ginzburg bases her theory of the relationship of self-invention to cultural-historical moment upon nineteenth-century personalities and events, it is remarkably relevant to the case of Whitefield, arguably the eighteenth century's most accomplished entrepreneur of the self.[13] According to Ginzburg, the construction of epochal personality is a self-conscious endeavor undertaken by certain individuals to organize the "inner self" into a portentous but easily purveyable image of a culture's hidden and unitary meaning and thus a prefiguration of its destiny (see esp. "Introduction" 3–24).[14] Self-represented and, if successful, received as a "new man," the epochal personality par excellence, one could argue, would be that of the convert, the individual wholly engaged in that process of self-translation by which the "new creature" emerges from the old and, in so doing, claims access to a universal meaning available only from a future perspective, that of the end of time.

Whitefield's achievement, then, in replacing the drama with his charismatic ministry was to replace what he experienced as his debased subjectivity, which impotently sought release through the imitation of a series of fictional selves, with the epochally significant personality of the convert, and to represent the attainment of epochal personality in and as the quintessential Whitefieldian spectacle, the field sermon. He did so not just by asserting but by enacting the fundamental difference between imitation and impersonation. Imitation involved a debased duplication of unworthy or unremarkable selves who, possessing no real field of action, can possess no real identity.[15] It is precisely this sense of existential emptiness that Whitefield's formidable detractor, Charles Chauncy, wished to convey when he characterized the Grand Itinerant's ministry as amounting to a mere *"prophane* Imitation" of Christ (*A Letter to the Reverend* 37). Whereas imitation might thus be associated with the sin of idolatry, impersonation would signify the *kenosis* or self-emptying that permits the incorporation of a transcendent Other. Whereas imitation leads to a depletion of the self, impersonation leads to self-fulfillment as well as to a legitimate sphere of activity, in a word, to a sanctified enlargement of the self.

So understood, conversion as Whitefield represented it in the journals and in the field involved an impersonation of God, such that the convert's every word, gesture. decision, and action would directly signify Him, Who would in turn irradiate these with irrefutable meaning and irresistible power. Having consecrated himself to God, Whitefield claimed to be so intimately affiliated with Him as to be for all practical purposes indistinguishable from Him. According to Whitefield's account of his rebirth, God had wholly subsumed him as an individual subject or agent, only to reconceive him as a pure instrument or agency, unalloyed with self, for the realization of His will or, more specifically, for the articulation of His Word. Impersonating God enabled Whitefield to claim that he exercised legitimately—that is, "innocently," because selflessly—"great boldness," "liberty," and "freedom of speech" (*Journals* 207, 211). Moreover, the confluence of God and Whitefield provided the occasion for another confluence, the remarkable assemblages of aspiring converts, and transferred those same privileges of bold speech to them.

The extraordinary sinuosity of Whitefield's public personality, his uncanny ability to choreograph its transfigurations with the inflections of his historical moment and indeed of each individual sermon, cannot be wholly accounted for by his self-representation as a pure instrument for the expression of the divine will. In what would appear to contradict this version of the self, as well as his account in his spiritual autobiography of his own instantaneously achieved regeneration, Whitefield elsewhere represented his conversion as an ongoing process in which God was continually undoing and reconstituting him, such that his character at any given moment had to be understood as both incomplete and, in the Bakhtinian

Whereas imitation might thus be associated with the sin of idolatry, impersonation would signify the kenosis or self-emptying that permits the incorporation of a transcendent Other. Whereas imitation leads to a depletion of the self, impersonation leads to self-fulfillment as well as to a legitimate sphere of activity, in a word, to a sanctified enlargement of the self.

sense, finalized. As we will see, these two seemingly incongruous aspects of his self-representation—self as pure agency and self as simultaneously incomplete and finalized—allowed Whitefield to claim the achievement of an artless, and therefore "innocent," mode of self-representation whose credibility rested precisely on the degree to which it offered itself as both an acknowledgment and a resolution of its constituent incompatibilities. The resolution of these two contradictory modes of self-representation was ensured by the topos of uncontainability central to both, which motivated not only his self-fashioning but also his theology and his evangelism.[16] Each aspect of the epochally significant personality of the convert will be examined in turn in the following sections.

3

Whitefield's project of positing a self that was less subject than the unambiguous signifier and instrument of divinity is most clearly discerned when he brings himself and Christ into the same closely circumscribed referential space. This practice earned him much criticism from his clerical adversaries who, like the Boston Congregationalist and vociferous opponent of the Great Awakening, Charles Chauncy, took him publicly to task in a letter of 1745 for his tendency to "magnify" facts, such as the circumstance of his birth in an inn, that were in themselves so "common" and "trivial" as to be hardly "worthy of particular and publick Notice" (*A Letter to the Reverend* 32). Chauncy considered such tactics far from Whitefield's greatest offenses, reprehensible as they were. In his letter, he cites two instances in which the Grand Itinerant exceeded the limits of mere bad taste. The first derived from the passage in Whitefield's spiritual autobiography in which he describes his conversion. In the throes of a prolonged agony of spirit, Whitefield wrote, he suddenly recalled that the crucified Christ had cried out, "I thirst! I thirst!" immediately before his death and delivery from suffering. Without hesitation, the young aspirant likewise threw himself down upon his bed in his Oxford garret exclaiming, "I thirst! I thirst!" and, as he represents it, rose from his bed reborn, "delivered from the burden that had so heavily oppressed me" (*Journals* 48). The moment of Christ's delivery is thus made to refer to the moment of Whitefield's.

Chauncy attributes Whitefield's extreme sinfulness here not to his putting himself "on a Level with *Jesus Christ,*" even though, Chauncy adds, he had been a repeat offender in this regard: "[T]his is not the only Instance, wherein your *Fancy* has formed a Kind of Resemblance between *your own,* and the Circumstances of Christ Jesus" (*A Letter to the Reverend* 36–37). Rather, Chauncy objects to Whitefield's insinuation of a relationship between himself and divinity far more intimate than mere resemblance: the conversion episode, he wrote Whitefield, "appeared to me very evidently to exhibit a *prophane* Imitation of the *Son* of *God* in his last Sufferings" (37). Through his profane appropriation of Christ's suffering, Whitefield sought to justify his claim to the authenticity of a communion that was in reality a shameful solipsism.

The second objectionable incident to which Chauncy refers in his letter extends his indictment of Whitefield's profanity. It concerns the case of a certain Mr. Barber, who had written a letter to Whitefield, evidently published, in terms so deferential as to constitute, for Chauncy, "an Act of downright gross Idolatry." To substantiate his accusation, Chauncy quotes from Barber's letter: "I shall omit writing any Thing, and only hereby present my hearty Love, and let you know that *I am waiting at the Post of your Door for Admission: Though I am unworthy, my Lord is worthy, in whose Name, I trust, I come"* (*A Letter to the Reverend* 29–30). Chauncy identifies Barber's words as an "evident Allusion to those Words of *Wisdom* (by whom is commonly understood the *Lord Jesus Christ,* the *Wisdom of God*), *Blessed is the Man that heareth me,—waiting at the Posts of my Doors,* Prov. 8.34." Given this source of Barber's address to Whitefield, Chauncy asks:

> [D]oes he not use the *same Form* of Words to encourage a Hope of Admission into *your Presence,* which is commonly used in Prayer when we approach before the great GOD? Are not *you,* in these Words, according to the literal and most obvious Meaning, the *final Object,* and the *great Saviour* the *Medium* of Access to you? . . . If Words can express it, *you* are the Person into whose Presence Mr. *Barber* wanted to come, and Christ is the *Medium* of Approach. (31)

Chauncy's outrage is here directed at the suggestion of a blasphemous typology in which Whitefield is the object and Christ the medium of access to that object; in which Christ is made to refer to Whitefield (as in the conversion account) rather than Whitefield to Christ; in which, finally, Whitefield represents himself less as a type of Jesus than Jesus a type of Whitefield, the latter having enjoyed more success than the former in converting the opposition.[17]

That Whitefield was aware of the blasphemous implications of his claims is suggested by the fact that his frequent hints of an equivalence between himself and God are almost invariably embedded in statements that explicitly assert their radical incommensurability. Just as St. Paul claimed (in 1 Cor. 15.10), "I labored more abundantly than they all, yet not I," Whitefield claimed that he exerted a "Divine attraction," "extraordinary authority," and "irresistible power" (*Journals* 234, 239, 269) that yet had no reference to self, but were instead "proofs" of God's ultimate authorship and control of self's appearances and success: "I have scarce known a time I have preached anywhere, but I have seen some effect of my doctrine. From the hearts of the Mighty the Word of the Lord hath not turned back, the Sword of the Spirit returned not empty. A proof this, I hope, that the words are not my own, and that God is with me of a truth" (*Journals* 104).

This denial of authorship—of one's words, of one's self-presentation, of one's self—and simultaneous claim to the status of pure instrumentality enabled Whitefield to enjoy surpassing rhetorical and vocational advantages. The rhetorically nuanced double referentiality of his experience at the mining town of Kingswood, for example, where he "went upon a mount, and spake to as many people who came unto me," allowed him to assert the incontestable propriety of the controversial practice of field preaching: "I believe I never was more acceptable to my Master than when I was standing to teach those hearers in the open field" (*Journals* 209). Similarly, Christ's approbation (for how could Christ disapprove that which he himself performed) also inheres in his decision to preach extempore, rather than from notes: as Whitefield explains to his readers, "I fear I should quench the Spirit, did I not go on to speak *as He gives me utterance*" (*Journals* 198; emphasis added). If here Whitefield may be understood to refer to the mode, rather than the substance, of speech, he unambiguously claims elsewhere that he and God cohabit a single voice, with God providing the intention and justification of the utterance, and Whitefield the fleshly apparatus necessary to speech.

The clerisy's objections to Whitefield's method were collectively centered upon his proclivity to trespass: to appropriate the attributes, and even the biography, of God, as well as the pastoral prerogatives of his clerical brethren through the practices of ministerial itinerancy and field preaching. He defended himself against such charges by denying, doctrinally as well as autobiographically, his possession of a self to defend. As his adversaries were painfully aware, the denial of self permitted Whitefield to assert the inevitability of his own words and actions, grounded as they were in the infallibility of the God he claimed to realize through the miraculous medium of his own "transparency," his own indefatigable body and the physical power of his voice. Whitefield's "innocence" in regard to his opponents' charges, in other words, derived from his self-proclaimed status as pure agency: what his adversaries saw as his carnal manipulations of press and pulpit to accomplish an unholy self-aggrandizement, he represented as an artless, because selfless, bringing forth of speech, a self-representation innocent of self.[18]

This innocence underwrote Whitefield's preeminently evangelical logic of uncontainability, which comprehended an ideal tautology of message, messenger, and receiver.[19] The delineation of references in the journals to that which cannot be contained—God, Whitefield, the Word, and the crowd amassed to hear it—ultimately comprises so totalizing a network of synonyms that to object to Whitefield is to object to God, and to object to Whitefield's project is to object to the project of evangelical Christianity. Just as Whitefield characterizes himself, after Christ and Paul, as having "no continuing city" (Heb. 13.14), so he characterizes God, for the edification of an opponent who had complained that by preaching in the fields, Whitefield preached on "unconsecrated ground," as "not now confined to places" (*Journals* 112, 305).[20] The uncontainability of God and Whitefield makes it impossible that "the Word of God should be bound, because some out of a misguided zeal deny the use of their churches" (*Journals* 202). The uncontainability of Whitefield and the Word of God, despite the closing of the churches, is registered in the uncontainability of the crowd drawn to hear them: "I now preach to ten times more people than I should, if I had been confined to the churches." Inherent in the crowd's unconfinability is itinerancy's equally irrepressible justification: "Now know I more and more that the Lord calls me into the fields, for no house or street is able to contain half the people who come to hear the Word" (*Journals* 256)—that is, who come to hear Whitefield. Ultimately, the logic of uncontainability, which is the logic of evangelical itinerancy, legitimates Whitefield's anti-institutionalism, his refusal to "place the Church . . . in the church walls" (421).[21] Uncontainability, in sum, epitomized the God-ness of God, and by extension of Whitefield; God's Word, and by extension Whitefield's words; and finally, God's true church, and by extension the reach of Whitefield's voice, both material and textual, as well as the range of his body. Ultimately, it guaranteed that Whitefield's peregrinations encompassed the whole "task of typology": "to define the course of the church ('spiritual Israel') and of the exemplary Christian life" (Bercovitch 36).

Whitefield's uncontainability was consummated in those moments when God's Word, transmitted to the assembled crowd by means of the preacher's palpable, audible transparency, hit its mark and delivered, as one of the Grand Itinerant's disciples put it, "a home stroke" (*Journals* 375). Although he describes many such instances in his journal, two seem particularly suggestive of a kind of phenomenology of Whitefieldian uncontainability. The first occurred in October of 1740, in Massachusetts, where Whitefield had enjoyed the support of Boston's first ministers as well as the highly visible patronage of Governor Jonathan Belcher. Belcher had personally accompanied him to the Boston Common, where over 20,000 souls had gathered to hear him preach, and had escorted him afterwards, with tears and fanfare, to the Charlestown ferry. Whitefield was "upon the mount, indeed." At his next stop, he wrote: "My soul was upon the wing. I was exceedingly enlarged, and was enabled, as it were, to take the Kingdom of God by force. Oh, what precious hours are those, when we are thus strengthened, as it were, to lay hold on God. Oh, that we should ever cast ourselves down from thence! God be merciful to me a sinner!" (*Journals* 477).

Here, Whitefield, self-described as a "Joshua . . . going from city to city, and subduing the devoted nations" (*Journals* 239), is sufficiently enlarged to imagine his successful attack upon the walls sealing off not Satan's kingdom but the Kingdom of God and his "laying hold" of its King.[22] For one heady, rhetorical moment, conquest and communion become indistinguishable. The ambiguity of Whitefield's position is made explicit in the passage's final two sentences, which transmit both his exhilaration at having successfully achieved, through his bold enlargement and irresistible appropriation of the prerogative of divinity, the status of man-god, translation out of the limitations of the natural self, as well as his temerity at his ambitious assault upon God's Kingdom. The increasingly aggressive uncontainability of Whitefield's trajectory—despite the opposition of a long-established ecclesiastical and civil order—here carries him to the acme of enlargement where, through the trumpeting of his voice, he brings down the walls that had from eternity sealed off mortal man's access to the heavenly Kingdom.[23]

The second passage suggests something like the people's responsive enlargement, in this instance so powerful as to threaten to overwhelm Whitefield's own. In a "desert place" outside a Pennsylvania hamlet, 12,000 had gathered to hear Whitefield preach. His audience was primed: no sooner had he spoken his first words than he "perceived numbers melting. As I proceeded, the influence increased, till, at last . . . thousands cried out, so that they almost drowned my voice." The audience's ecstatic agony of self-abandonment precipitated Whitefield's own self-translation or conversion, his own death and rebirth: "After I had finished my last discourse, I was so pierced, as it were, and overpowered with a sense of God's love, that some thought, I believe, I was about to give up the ghost. How sweetly did I lie at the feet of Jesus! With what power did a sense of his all-constraining, free, and everlasting love flow in upon my soul! It almost took away my life" (*Journals* 423). In this instance, the wall that falls is that which distinguished preacher from congregation; when all are dissolved in an ecstasy that seems to have no source and negates all distinctions, all "discourse" of necessity comes to an end.

Accompanying the collapse of the discursive structure that differentiated God and Whitefield, and Whitefield and the surrounding crowd, was that of the representative function the field sermons were intended to serve as occasions of public exhortation to sinners and public prayer to God. No longer need Whitefield serve as a channel for representing God's Word to humankind or humankind's words to God. Having rhetorically appropriated the divinity of God "by force" in one instance, and in the other having suffered himself, the people's "mouth unto God," to be swallowed up in the people's voice, Whitefield's self-as-agency, that embodiment of the doubled self's final moments before its unrepresentable resolution in a transcendent integrity, achieves its apotheosis in these twin moments of self-insemination. With the delivery of the "home stroke," self-as-agency attains such a degree of enlargement that it overwhelms itself as channel, floods its own banks, and submerges all surrounding it in its own element. This is the conversional moment: when the enlarged self of Whitefield converges, at the height of spiritual ecstasy, with the mimetically enlarged voice of the crowd, and the oppositional, divisive voice of the scoffers is reborn as the all-encompassing voice of the people.

4

Insofar as they bear a generic resemblance to all other conversion narratives, whose burden is to present as dramatically as possible a life trajectory whose teleology is well known, Whitefield's autobiographical writings characterize their subject as simultaneously incomplete and finalized. In the introduction to the account of his own conversion (first published in 1740 and prefixed, in expurgated form, to the 1756 edition of the collected journals that chronicle his ministry), he distinguishes two versions of himself, one past ("what I was by nature") and one present ("what I am by grace") (*Journals* 26). The distinction is a conventional one: as John Freccero has described it, the voice of the "poet" represents the valid and eternal self, and as such the possessor of the text's finalizing consciousness who evaluates the thoughts and activities of the "pilgrim"—the partial and obsolescent self—while narrating them.

The moment of conversion, when these two versions of the self come together, is narratologically the most problematic. As a New Light theologian, Whitefield rejected what he considered to be the Arminian notion of a preparationist conversion that would occur through what his great foe, Alexander Garden, approvingly called an "*Oeconomy* of Grace": "a *gradual co-operating* Work of the *Holy Spirit,* commencing at *Baptism,* and gradually advancing throughout the whole Course of the Christian Life" (11). Instead, Whitefield upheld the Pauline model of an instantaneous rebirth accomplished solely through the grace of God rather than human effort, however well intended. Practically and doctrinally considered, then, even taking the rationale of impersonation into account, Whitefield could not claim himself to have delivered the reconceiving blow. Instead, he used the conversion spectacle to reenact the original drama of his own rebirth, itself a reenactment of Jesus's passion.

The journals, too, by cataloging each successive performance, rehearsed a metamorphosis that was, by definition, entirely singular. Although the scenario remained eternally the same, each stop on Whitefield's itinerary possessed the undifferentiated specificity of a reenactment: an oppositional encounter for which success entailed further opposition which, predictably overcome, entailed success. The repeated threat of personal dissolution and the repeated thrill of divinely aided reconstitution contribute to the vitality of an autobiographical narrative in which all major details, actors, and events are revisited. Each event is both anomalous and reenacted, each sermon (as Ben Franklin noted in *The Autobiography*) both extemporaneous and rehearsed (180).

Whitefield's experience of illness aptly illustrates his ability to invest repetition with dynamism and drama. The physical rigors of the itinerant's life, especially in the vast, unsettled areas of the American colonies, perhaps suggested to him the representational possibilities of the overwhelming exhaustion he suffered immediately prior to his personal appearances. As he described it in his journals, his private struggle with bodily infirmity paralleled his public struggle with external adversity in the form of "natural men." Each paired episode features a nearly fatal encounter with the debilitating forces of negation, a last-ditch summoning of the supernal energy required to overwhelm the opposition and then, at last, victory, experienced as an incrementally achieved enlargement of the self. As an internalization of the spectacle of conversion, in which oppositional otherness was continually surmounted and overtaken by an ever-expanding self, Whitefield's failing health entered into each of his performances as its proem or prelude, integral to the powerful flow of words that followed.

The Pennsylvania incident recounted above was not unique in Whitefield's experience. After preaching to 20,000 souls on Kennington Common (near London), for example, Whitefield found himself enjoying a pleasure so profound it accomplished that which had foiled all his opponents and the devil himself—the stopping of Whitefield's mouth: "God was pleased to pour into my soul a great spirit of supplication, and a sense of His free distinguishing mercies so filled me with love, humility, and joy, and holy confusion, that I could at last only pour out my heart before Him in an awful silence. It was so full, that I could not well speak. Oh the happiness of communion with God!" (*Journals* 258). Aside from the fact that it chronicles a rare instance of Whitefield's submission to a power stronger than his will to speak, this passage is remarkable for its implicit characterization of speech as symptomatic of humankind's fallen condition. Above all, holy speech—prayer and sermon—is not exempt from this indictment of the true character of language as indicating the absence of fullness, for, as Whitefield puts it, if one is full, one cannot speak, and if humankind were not separated from God as a result of its own sinfulness, neither prayer nor exhortation would be necessary.

The moment of preaching was thus for Whitefield the most exalted and the most debased of moments. His unconquerable drive to speak ("it is hard work to be silent" [qtd. in Gillies 152]), through which he both realized (albeit temporarily) his aspiration to transcendent being and acknowledged the futility of such an aspiration, recalls in its poignancy Edward Taylor's poetic obsession with the need to accept the pathetic fragility of the linguistic enterprise as humankind's best hope. Speech is both the unique means to transcendence and precisely that human activity which transcendence reveals as "nought"; it is the means to communion and yet its absence is the truest sign that communion has occurred. Death, and particularly death in the pulpit, becomes Whitefield's oft-reiterated wish, as the only way in which the paradox of speech—as a metaphor for the miracle of conversion, which brings life out of death, exaltation out of humiliation—could, as it were, be consummated: "O that I had as many tongues, as there are hairs upon my head! the ever-loving, ever-lovely *Jesus* should have them all. Fain would I die preaching" (qtd. in Gillies 200). Only death in the pulpit would publicly seal Whitefield's achievement of an irreversible conversion, a passage in which he would be made, at last, "perfectly whole" (qtd. in Gillies 255).

As it was, however, Whitefield toiled unceasingly for 35 years to maintain the all-too-human, if formidable, ubiquity of itinerancy. Endlessly circulating throughout the American colonies and the United Kingdom, repeatedly overwhelming the opposition at each successive village, Whitefield was yet relieved from the limitations of the self only in the pulpit, in the space of a sermon. Only the timelessness and placelessness of preaching earned him moments of communion with others and with the divine; only the Sisyphean labor of preaching so consumed him as to extend the hope of effecting one day the longed-for, final translation into wordlessness.

For this reason, the pulpit was both the cause of and the sole cure for the "continual vomitings" he suffered between sermons. It was as if, for Whitefield, all of life was orality, and orality comprised but a single pair of alternatives: either holy speech issued from one's mouth or the noxious efflux of one's own mortality: "Fear not your weak body; we are immortal till our work is done. *Christ's* labourers must live by miracle; if not, I must not live at all; for God only knows what I daily endure. My continual vomitings almost kill me, and yet the pulpit is my cure, so that my friends begin to pity me less, and to leave off that ungrateful caution, 'Spare thyself' " (qtd. in Gillies 180).

To a remarkable degree, Whitefield segregated the two signifieds of speech—as a means to salvation and a sign of damnation—and then linked kenosis and emesis in a cycle such that when he stopped preaching he began to vomit, and when he wished to stop vomiting he preached. As with the medieval sufferers of "holy anorexia" recently described by Rudolph M. Bell, the death of the body represented the only possibility of release. More particularly, for Whitefield only death in the pulpit would break the cycle (as Hawthorne's Dimmesdale well knew) and bring about the apotheosis of holy speech as a pure product, untainted by the fetid breath of mortality. As it turned out, Whitefield's actual death, from an asthmatic attack in Newburyport, Massachusetts, in September 1770, was immediately preceded by the spasmodic production of much "phlegm and wind," which issued from him in lieu of words as he tried in vain to beg for air.[24]

The peculiar pathos of the vomiting/preaching cycle to which the concern of Whitefield's supporters testifies can also be discerned at the heart of his presentation of conversion as spectacle. Only rarely did the sermon experience procure for him that blessed silence in which the circularity of vomiting and preaching was replaced with a silent circulation of spirit, by which God "pour[ed] into" his supplicant's soul love, humility, and joy, and Whitefield, "filled" beyond satiety with this spirit, "pour[ed] out his heart . . . in an awful silence." More typically, for any given sermon, Whitefield's (or God's) ability or will to release and the congregation's (or Whitefield's) ability to receive and contain the full volume of the spiritual current were limited. These inevitable limitations were marked by the primacy of voice—Whitefield's and his auditors'—as the distinguishing feature of spectacular conversion.

The mass of newspaper accounts, published testimonials, and rumors that circulated in advance of Whitefield's individual appearances prepared the spectator to recognize in the minister a remarkable synesthesia of radical incompatibilities. For the space of a sermon, the body and voice of the itinerant seemed simultaneously occupied by divinity and mortality. Members of his audience bore witness to the fact that Whitefield was visibly accompanied by the "Presence of GOD" ("A Report" 23) and his preaching was imbued with an audible "divine power and energy" (qtd. in Gillies 65n). Chauncy disdainfully conceded that Whitefield was widely considered to be "no meer Man"; he reported to a correspondent in Scotland that when Whitefield "came to *Town* . . . he was received as though he had been an *Angel of God*; yea, *a God come down in the Likeness of Man*" (*A Letter from a Gentleman* 8, 6). The spectator thus anticipated the inherent drama of immortality inhabiting mortality, of immortality ventriloquizing mortality, articulating in the process an extraordinary syntax in which the transformation of the old man into the new was, miraculously, made representable.

Dominated by the exclusive, alternating imperatives of vomiting and preaching, Whitefield's body functioned as a sort of mobile arena in which mortal limitation struggled ceaselessly (and visibly) with divine inspiration to enact the conversional moment. This highly theatricalized moment was marked by the overtaking—the silencing—of the opposition, both externalized as skeptics and internalized as psychological resistance or bodily frailty. The opposition receding into the silence of obsolescence, the "new man," the convert as epochal personality, emerged out of and away from the oppositional old before the astonished eyes of the spectator. By dramatically prolonging the conversional moment, Whitefield could represent, in the staged experience of the exemplary convert, the coming-into-being of epochal personality. Through this representation, his audience was enabled to appropriate mimetically the conversion experience along with the character of the exemplary convert. The success of this double transaction was verifiable as the voice that emerged from the midst of the hitherto silent—unmeaning and characterless—crowd.

Although many testimonials of this transference exist, most explicitly those of Nathan Cole and John Marrant (see Crawford; Aldridge), a particularly straightforward example of a spectator's mimetic appropriation of Whitefield's character and voice is provided by an account "of a Reformation among some Gentlemen, at Boston," published in the English revival party's organ, *The Weekly History,* for 17 October 1741.[25] The writer tells the story of a wealthy Boston gentleman, "a great Hater of Religion, and especially Mr. *Whitefield*'s Preaching," who "one Day as he was walking in his Room . . . thought he heard Mr. *Whitefield*" in the process of concluding a prayer and beginning a sermon ("A Remarkable Account" 3). The voice sounded to the perplexed gentleman as if it were coming from somewhere in his house. Upon investigation, it turned out to be "one of his Negroes preaching" (4). No longer "pensive," but rather greatly amused at the success of his servant's imitation, the wealthy man the following day invited a group of friends to "an Entertainment": "*Come,*" he told his company, "*I'll entertain you with Mr. W's Preaching: For my Negroe can preach as well as he*" (4). The "Negroe," the writer reported, "had the very Phrases of Mr. *Whitefield*," and amidst the laughter of the company, began his exhortation:

I am now come to my Exhortation; and to you my Master after the Flesh: But know I have a Master even Jesus Christ my Saviour, who has said that a Man cannot serve two Masters. Therefore I claim Jesus Christ to be my right Master; and all that come to him he will receive. You know, Master, you have been given to Cursing and Swearing, and Blaspheming God's holy Name, you have been given to be Drunken, a Whoremonger, Covetous, a Liar, a Cheat, &c. But know that God has pronounced a Woe against all such, and has said that such shall never enter the Kingdom of God. (4)

The writer, who had himself heard the story from "an eminent Divine," concluded:

The Negroe spoke with such Authority that struck the Gentlemen to Heart. They laid down their Pipes, never drank a Glass of Wine, but departed every Man to his own House: and are now pious sober Men; but before were wicked profane Persons. Such is the Work of God by the Hands of poor Negroes: We have such Instances every Week from some Part of the Country or other. (4)

Whether this exemplary conversion really occurred or whether it represents merely a fantasy of empowerment, it nevertheless illustrates how prevalent was the expectation that the voice of Whitefield would, in the process of spectacular conversion, "discover itself in Multitudes" (Chauncy, *A Letter from a Gentleman* 12).

5. Coda: Uncontainability Limited

Whitefield offered his journals not as the mere record of a reiterated event, the conversion of sinners, but rather as the transcript of an epic quest (for opposers) and conquest (of opposers) conducted by an ever-enlarging hero whose growth was calculable in the number of adversaries overwhelmed and taken in. His sensitivity to the most pressing question of the revival—namely, how to sustain the religious fire once kindled—can be gauged in his sense of the importance not simply of a constantly resurrected opposition, but of one placed squarely in center stage. Whitefield made his relationship to the opposition the focus of his sermon in order to convert his audience from neutrality to partisanship, to dramatize his own rebirth, and to ensure a showing of his adversaries at the next performance. His strategic placement of the opposition at the conceptual center of the conversion experience reinforced his claims for its remarkably protean nature: manifesting itself somatically (as disease), socially (as a hostile corps of powerful and established natural men), psychologically (as his own or others' fear, anger, or indifference), and cosmically (as the machinations of Satan), the ubiquity of the opposition called for an equal effort at ubiquity on the part of the exemplary convert. As long as the opposition could be incrementally contained, on any of these fronts, its seeming irrepressibility simply confirmed the uncontainability of the continually enlarging self of the convert.

The hero's forward movement as well as his growth in grace, both synonymous with his narrative's continuation, if not precisely its development, could only be capped when the translation of adversaries into acolytes was complete: the hero was thus, in theory, uncontainable. The primary fact of the journals and the field sermons was not that of the originary conversion experience, reenacted for the edification of successive congregations on the itinerant's route, but rather the quality of uncontainability transferred to the "new man" in the process of conversion and the conditions it continually imposed upon him, in particular the duty or "gift" of public speech.

As the means of overcoming the opposition, the voice of the convert also served as the primary means, and thus as the signifier, of self-enlargement. For this reason, it is the voice of the convert as epic hero—a voice that continually insists upon its occupation of the boundary between the material and spiritual, the visible and invisible realms—that reveals uncontainability to be the dominant of his character. The voice of the convert, rather than his experience per se, constituted the prime object of his auditors' mimetic desire. The degree to which the manifest power of Whitefield's voice had been successfully appropriated by the acolyte could be verified to the extent that he or she transcended the limitations of a merely private existence and acceded to the public sphere by means of a voice inexorably rising, as if summoned by an external power, from out of a rigorously mandated silence.

If the instance cited above of the black servant delivering himself of Whitefield's words in order to deliver his master from sin confirms this transfer of vocal power, one must also notice who is emancipated at the conclusion of the slave's ringing and explicitly subversive address. The slave is invited to speak, but only to secure his master's liberation from his own enslavement to sin. The account thus suggests that, despite the black itinerant ministry to which Whitefield's own apparently gave rise as he traversed the British-American colonies, he and his followers envisioned a wholly different model of authentic selfhood for their black auditors than for their white.[26] The comparatively limited emancipation intended for black Christians limited not only Whitefield's claim to uncontainability but, inevitably, this enactment of it in the course of the conversion spectacle. This fatal limitation is clearly revealed in his journal account of his experience preaching to largely black audiences in the Bermudas from March through mid-June 1748 (qtd. in Gillies 165–67).

In the Bermudas, Whitefield confronted for the first time audiences composed mainly of enslaved blacks. He responded by seeking to control the reception of his sermon through a rigorous supervision of his principled practice of extemporaneous speech. To account for his uncharacteristic restraint, Whitefield described his black auditors' unexpected response to a sermon preached on the first of May. Aware of what the racial composition of his audience would be, Whitefield had endeavored to tailor his address to the peculiar limitations of his black auditors as he imagined them: "As the sermon was intended for the negroes, I gave the [whites] auditory warning, that my discourse would be chiefly directed to them, and that I should endeavour to imitate the example of *Elijah,* who when he was about to raise the child, contracted himself to its length" (qtd. in Gillies 165). The tactic of contraction appeared to work: Whitefield celebrated his own social acumen and rhetorical subtlety at the conclusion of his journal entry for 1 May, "I believe the Lord enabled me to discourse, as to touch the negroes, and yet not to give them the least umbrage to slight or behave imperiously to their masters" (qtd. in Gillies 165).

His confidence was shaken the following day when a group of black auditors informed him that they had disapproved of his sermon and would no longer attend: "They expected, they said, to hear me speak against their masters. Blessed be God, that I was directed not to say any thing, this first time, [about] the masters at all, though my text led me to it. It might have been of bad consequence, to tell [the masters] their duty, or charge them too roundly with the neglect of it, before their slaves" (qtd. in Gillies 166). Extrapolated from Matthew 10.16, the lesson Whitefield derived from this experience is, considering the principle of unrestricted speech that underlay his ministerial practice, remarkable: "If ever a minister in preaching, need the wisdom of the serpent to be joined with the harmlessness of the dove, it must be when discoursing to negroes," some of whose hearts, Whitefield opined, were "as black as their faces" (qtd. in Gillies 165, 166).[27]

As the expression of an evangelical strategy, Whitefield's concluding statement represents a reversal, however temporary, of the direction and energy of his ministerial practice, a fatal moment of prudence that undermines the integrity of his self-representation as an uncontainable force dedicated to realizing a universalist church.[28] In Bermuda, Whitefield confronted the limits of his own vision—he could not bring himself to contemplate the uncontainable enlargement of black Christians—and he was prepared to codify this lapse in his published "Prayer for a poor Negroe" (*Works* 4: 473–75). There Whitefield counseled black Americans to bless God for bringing them into "a christian country," to be content with their condition and eschew rebellion, and above all, to remain inoffensively speechless: "[K]eep the door of my lips," his addressee was directed to pray, "that I may not offend with my tongue" (*Works* 4: 474).

By condemning them to what he had elsewhere called "an awful silence," Whitefield betrayed his most fearful opponents to be the most destitute—and, by many accounts, the most faithful—of his constituents, black Christians. Powerless as they were, however, their status as exception to the promise that conversion would entail untrammeled self-enlargement ironically challenged the theological rationale of Whitefield's evangelism: for by definition, uncontainability could brook no exceptions. His fear of unleashing, in the cause of the spirit's emancipation, an oppositional force that he might prove incapable of containing ultimately led Whitefield to self-censorship as the necessary condition for constructing an image of the silenced black Christian required by his white constituency. If this image was disregarded by those free blacks in his audience who were able to seize the power of the voice and become religious exhorters in turn, its contours are clear in the evangelical literature, including Whitefield's journals, as that negative construct within which uncontainability was itself contained.

Notes

1. Most of Whitefield's sermons and letters are included in *The Works of the Reverend George Whitefield*. Other fruitful sources of Whitefield's pronouncements are the eighteenth- and nineteenth-century biographies by

Gillies and Tyerman. Modern biographies include Belden; Henry; and Stout, *Divine,* which provides an excellent reading of Whitefield as America's "first intercolonial hero" (xiv).

2.   On the publication history of Edwards's "A Faithful Narrative of Surprising Conversions," see Goen, *Jonathan Edwards* 32–46. For an excellent synopsis of the Great Awakening, see Heimert, Introduction. See also Bushman. Nissenbaum has compiled primary documents relating to events at Yale. Also of value are Tracy; Gaustad; and Lovejoy. Historians Butler (*Awash* and "Enthusiasm") and Hyerman (see esp. 182–204, 366–89) have recently challenged the scholarly consensus on the reformative power of the Great Awakening. For an excellent recent study of the democratizing effects of American popular religion in the post-Revolutionary period, see Hatch.

3.   The classic study of the relationship between the Great Awakening and the American Revolution is Heimert's *Religion,* a useful corrective to Anderson's *Imagined Communities* insofar as Anderson asserts the centrality of itinerancy to the development of Latin American national consciousness but gives printing primacy of place in the North American context. Stout's *New England* shares Heimert's premise of the centrality of evangelism to the formation of a Revolutionary ideology in colonial America. Also extremely useful for its emphasis on evangelical oratory and the beginnings of Revolutionary sentiment is Stout, "Religion." See also Goen, *Revivalism;* McLoughlin; and especially Lovejoy.

4.   Several of Whitefield's contemporaries testified to the extraordinary range of his voice, most famously Benjamin Franklin, who experienced a kind of conversion of his own upon hearing the Grand Itinerant preach. Against his earlier resolve, he found himself contributing generously to Whitefield's collection for his pet project, a Georgia orphanage, at the sermon's conclusion (Franklin 177, 179). On Whitefield and Franklin's relationship, see J. Williams. On Whitefield's astonishing "appropriation of new commercial techniques to publicize the revivals" (812), his uncanny appreciation of the importance of the press in creating a desire for the New Birth by advertising it as one would a commodity, see Lambert's indispensable article.

5.   The early history of this fragmentation is captured in a public letter written by the Rev. Theophilus Pickering to the Rev. Nathanael Rogers, Jr., in 1742. Rogers's oppositional behavior, according to Pickering, mimics Whitefield's own as described by an eyewitness in a 1737 issue of the *New England Weekly Journal* (Bushman 56–57, 22–23). Cf. Timothy Cutler's complaint in his 5 Dec. 1740 letter to the Bishop of London (Perry 346–47).

6.   On the establishment of the Log College, see Trinterud; Briggs 304–10; and Ahlstrom 270–73.

7.   According to Heimert, by the 1760s "the commitment to the Work of Redemption had translated even the ecumenical spirit into a New World nationalism" (*Religion* 142). Cf. Niebuhr's characterization of the Great Awakening as "our national conversion" (126); Goen, *Revivalism;* and Stout, *Divine,* on the association of the Whitefield phenomenon with the growth of nationalist sentiment in the colonies. Franklin's biographer, Carl

Van Doren, notes that Franklin "bec[ame] intercolonial" (138) directly following Whitefield's first visit to Philadelphia in 1739. Opponents of the revival tended to assume that Whitefield single-handedly created the class of lay exhorters. See, for example, Chauncy, who describes them as "the Preachers of Mr. *Whitefield*'s making" (*A Letter from a Gentleman* 15). See also the nineteenth-century historian Bacon's account (222). On undergraduates preaching, see Dexter 357. For a suggestion of the limits of female evangelism in this period, see Stein, "A Note."

8.   The self's abasement, that is, is neither the condition nor the premise of its exaltation since the terms "humble" and "exalted" suggest no temporal differentiation, as in the compensatory formulation that appears elsewhere in the journal, "the more thou art humbled now, the more thou shalt be exalted hereafter" (*Journals* 62).

9.   For an attempt to examine the grounds for popular hostility against Methodists, see Walsh.

10.   Whitefield did not discover the theatrical possibilities of conversion, hence its usefulness in the field of social control, nor was he the first to overcome his own social marginality to win celebrity by these means. See D. Williams, who notes that executions routinely attracted crowds of up to 6,000, with some accounts claiming up to 12,000, making them a close second, in terms of draw, to Whitefield's field sermons, and the first materialization of the crowd in America.

11.   Beginning in grammar school, Whitefield was chosen for his "good elocution and memory" to "make speeches before the corporation at their annual visitation," and, at about age 12, he even permitted his schoolmaster to dress him in girls' clothing for the corporation's entertainment. Among the many parts he prepared himself so assiduously to play, the ministerial role was apparently the only one that influenced his everyday behavior, such that "[p]art of the money I used to steal from my parent I gave to the poor, and some books I privately took from others, for which I have since restored fourfold, I remember were books of devotion" (*Journals* 29).

12.   For the historical association of players with vagabonds, see Barrish 238. Barrish's study is particularly suggestive in reference to Whitefield's own relationship to the theater. Cf. Stout, *Divine*.

13.   Cf. Trilling's analysis of the formation and evolution of what he identifies as a new, fundamentally histrionic type of personality that emerged in the late sixteenth and early seventeenth centuries.

14.   One might compare the epochal personality in this regard to Burke's definition of the "god-term" (25–27).

15.   Cf. Lotman's analysis of "khlestakovism" (after the Gogol character).

16.   The term "self-fashioning" derives, of course, from Greenblatt. Of all Greenblatt's Renaissance self-fashioners, Whitefield perhaps most resembles Tyndale, who could not obey Christ's exhortation "to do . . . good deeds secretly," and whose "whole self" was transformed into "*voice*" insofar as

his was "a life lived as a *project*," in Tyndale's case the project of translating the Bible into English (*Renaissance* 107). Greenblatt's affinity with the Soviet cultural semioticians, most prominently Ginzburg and Lotman, and particularly with their notion of a "poetics of everyday behavior," is suggested in his "Towards a Poetics of Culture."

17.   Weller points explicitly to Whitefield's "spiritual Pride" in the journals: "Nay, the Discourses of the blessed Jesus, *who spake as never Man spake,* fell far short of that Conviction and Force on the Minds of his Hearers, if Mr. *Whitefield* may be believed, which are boasted of in almost every Page of the Journals." Moreover, Whitefield's "*Acts* are already three or four times more voluminous than the History of all the Apostles of Jesus Christ" (18, 12).

18.   Gillies in particular was anxious to divorce Whitefield from any insinuation that his eloquence was the result of artfulness or his early involvement with the theater (3).

19.   Because this tautology was the real goal of evangelism, it is easy to understand why the evangelical movement posed such a threat to the social elite: to the degree that it succeeded, it would obliterate the differences that constituted both the social hierarchy and the structure of representation itself. As a representation of a particular relationship to God, evangelism thus carries within it the seeds of its own destruction, unless it dissembles the similitude of message, messenger, and receiver upon which it is ostensibly based (or at least toward which it is ostensibly moving). Such dissemblance is the crux of contemporary critiques of (tel)evangelism, but as Wills has shown, the charge of hypocrisy is meaningless to evangelicals, who do not consider their ministries compromised by it.

20.   John Marrant, a black freeman who was converted by Whitefield in South Carolina as a teenager, and who himself became an itinerant preacher in Nova Scotia (after suffering captivity at the hands of the Cherokee and impressment into the British Navy), also characterized himself as having "no continuing city" (180). See the extraordinary (ventriloquized) "A Narrative of the Lord's Wonderful Dealings with John Marrant" (Aldridge).

21.   See also *Works* 2: 76.

22.   Compare the outrageousness of Whitefield's enactment and later account of the Joshua story to Edwards's conventional reading of it:

> The destruction of the city of Jericho is evidently, in all its circumstances, intended by God as a great type of the overthrow of Satan's kingdom; the priests blowing with trumpets at that time, represents ministers preaching the Gospel; the people compassed the city seven days, the priests blowing the trumpets; but when the day was come that the walls of the city were to fall, the priests were more frequent and abundant in blowing their trumpets. (*Some Thoughts* 398)

23.   In his initial letter of invitation to Whitefield, even Edwards, who later had reservations about the Grand Itinerant's techniques, expresses his hope that Whitefield will "rise to a greater height, and extend further and further, with an irresistable Power bearing down all opposition! and may the Gates of Hell never be able to prevail against you!" (Abelove 488).

24. For an eyewitness account of Whitefield's death, given by one Richard Smith, who accompanied the Grand Itinerant on his last American tour, see Gillies 272–74. See also Stiles's Franklinesque challenge to Jonathan Parson's account of the number of mourners attending the funeral, based on a calculation of the square footage of Parson's church (79–80). On the decades-long obsession with viewing and handling Whitefield's remains, see Butler, *Awash* 188.

25. Seward, Whitefield's devotee and the one whom Lambert describes as his "press agent" (817), relates in his journal a suspiciously similar incident in Philadelphia (7–8).

26. On Whitefield's contradictory pronouncements on the subject of slavery due to his overriding fear of blacks, see Stein, "George Whitefield." Cf. Stout's claim that the Grand Itinerant supplied black Christians "with an evangelical vocabulary they later adapted to their own purposes" (*Divine* 197). See also Jackson.

27. Whitefield's idiosyncratic use of Matthew 10.16 is underscored by Edwards's more conventional invocation of the passage to caution friends of the New Light movement against providing detractors with grounds for complaint (see "Distinguishing" 277).

28. Interestingly, it was immediately after his visit to the Bermudas en route to England that Whitefield undertook to edit his journals so that he might "have a new edition before I see *America*," and bemoans in a letter to a supporter his habit of verbal impetuosity, which only stirred up "needless opposition": "I frequently wrote and spoke in my own spirit, when I thought I was writing and speaking by the assistance of the Spirit of God. I have likewise too much made inward impressions my rule of acting, and too soon and too explicitly published what had been better kept in longer, or told after my death" (*Works* 2: 143–45).

Works Cited

Abelove, Henry. "Jonathan Edwards's Letter of Invitation to George Whitefield." *William and Mary Quarterly* 3rd ser. 29 (1972): 487–89.

Ahlstrom, Sydney E. *A Religious History of the American People.* New Haven: Yale UP, 1972.

Aldridge, Rev. Mr. "A Narrative of the Lord's Wonderful Dealings with John Marrant . . . Taken Down from His Own Relation, Arranged, Corrected, and Published by the Rev. Mr. Aldridge." *Held Captive by Indians: Selected Narratives, 1642–1836.* Ed. Richard Van Der Beets. Knoxville: U of Tennessee P, 1973. 177–201.

Anderson, Benedict. *Imagined Communities: Reflections on the Origin and Spread of Nationalism.* 2nd ed. London: Verso, 1983.

Bacon, Leonard. *Thirteen Historical Discourses.* New Haven, 1839.

Barrish, Jonas. *The Antitheatrical Prejudice.* Berkeley: U of California P, 1981.

Belden, Albert D. *George Whitefield, the Awakener: A Modern Study of the Evangelical Revival.* New York: Macmillan, 1953.

Bell, Rudolph M. *Holy Anorexia.* Chicago: U of Chicago P, 1985.

Bercovitch, Sacvan. *The Puritan Origins of the American Self.* New Haven: Yale UP, 1975.

Briggs, Charles Augustus. *American Presbyterianism, Its Origins and Early History.* New York, 1885.

Burke, Kenneth. *The Rhetoric of Religion: Studies in Logology.* Berkeley: U of California P, 1970.

Bushman, Richard L., ed. *The Great Awakening: Documents on the Revival of Religion, 1740–1745.* Chapel Hill: U of North Carolina P, 1989.

Butler, Jon. *Awash in a Sea of Faith: Christianizing the American People.* Cambridge: Harvard UP, 1990.

———. "Enthusiasm Described and Decried: The Great Awakening as Interpretative Fiction." *Journal of American History* 69 (1982): 314–22.

Chauncy, Charles. *A Letter from a Gentleman in Boston, to Mr. George Wishart . . . Concerning the State of Religion in New England.* Edinburgh, 1742.

———. *A Letter to the Reverend Mr. George Whitefield.* Boston, 1745.

Crawford, Michael J. "The Spiritual Travels of Nathan Cole." *William and Mary Quarterly* 3rd ser. 33 (1976): 92–126.

Dexter, Franklin B., ed. *Documentary History of Yale University under the Original Charter of the Collegiate School of Connecticut, 1701–1745.* New Haven: Yale UP, 1916.

Edwards, Jonathan. "The Distinguishing Marks of a Work of the Spirit of God." Goen, *Jonathan Edwards* 32–46.

———. *Some Thoughts Concerning the Present Revival of Religion in New England.* Goen, *Jonathan Edwards* 290–520.

Franklin, Benjamin. *The Autobiography of Benjamin Franklin.* Ed. Leonard W. Labaree et al. New Haven: Yale UP, 1964.

Freccero, John. "Logology: Burke on St. Augustine." *Representing Kenneth Burke.* Ed. Hayden White and Margaret Brose. Baltimore: Johns Hopkins UP, 1982. 52–67.

Garden, Alexander. *Six Letters to the Reverend Mr. George Whitefield.* 2nd ed. Boston, 1740.

Gaustad, Edwin S. *The Great Awakening in New England.* New York: n.p., 1957.

Gillies, Rev. John. *Memoirs of the Life of George Whitefield, M.A.* 1772. New Haven, 1834.

Ginzburg, Lydia. *On Psychological Prose.* Trans. and ed. Judson Rosengrant. Princeton: Princeton UP, 1991.

Goen, C. C., ed. *Jonathan Edwards: The Great Awakening.* New Haven: Yale UP, 1972.

Goen, C. C. *Revivalism and Separatism in New England, 1740–1800:*

Strict Congregationalists and Separate Baptists in the Great Awakening. New Haven: Yale UP, 1969.

Greenblatt, Stephen. *Renaissance Self-Fashioning: From More to Shakespeare.* Chicago: U of Chicago P, 1980.

———. "Towards a Poetics of Culture." *Learning to Curse: Essays in Modern Culture.* New York: Routledge, 1990. 146–60.

Hatch, Nathan O. *The Democratization of American Christianity.* New Haven: Yale UP, 1989.

Heimert, Alan. Introduction. *The Great Awakening: Documents Illustrating the Crisis and Its Consequences.* Ed. Alan Heimert and Perry Miller. Indianapolis: Bobbs, 1967. xiii–lx.

———. *Religion and the American Mind, from the Great Awakening to the Revolution.* Cambridge: Harvard UP, 1966.

Henry, Stuart C. *George Whitefield, Wayfaring Witness.* New York: Abingdon, 1957.

Hyerman, Christine Leigh. *Commerce and Culture: The Maritime Communities of Colonial Massachusetts, 1690–1750.* New York: Norton, 1984.

Jackson, Harvey H. "Hugh Bryan and the Evangelical Movement in Colonial South Carolina." *William and Mary Quarterly* 3rd ser. 43 (1986): 594–614.

Lambert, Frank. " 'Pedlar of Divinity': George Whitefield and the Great Awakening, 1737–1745." *Journal of American History* 77 (1990): 812–37.

Lovejoy, David. *Religious Enthusiasm in the New World: Heresy to Revolution.* Cambridge: Harvard UP, 1985.

Lotman, Iuri M. "Concerning Khlestakov." *The Semiotics of Russian Cultural History: Essays.* Ed. Alexander D. Nakhimovsky and Alice Stone Nakhimovsky. Ithaca: Cornell UP, 1985. 150–87.

McLoughlin, William G. *The Baptists and the Separation of Church and State.* Cambridge: Harvard UP, 1971. Vol. 1 of *New England Dissent, 1630–1833.* 2 vols. 1971.

Niebuhr, H. Richard. *The Kingdom of God in America.* 1937. New York: Harper, 1959.

Nissenbaum, Stephen. *The Great Awakening at Yale College.* Belmont, CA: Wadsworth, 1972.

Perry, William, ed. *Massachusetts.* Hartford, CT, 1873. Vol. 3 of *Historical Collections Relating to the American Colonial Church.* 5 vols. 1870–78.

"A Remarkable Account of a Reformation among Some Gentlemen, at Boston in New England; . . . " *Weekly History* [London] 17 Oct. 1741: 3–4.

"A Report on Whitefield in New York: *The New England Weekly Journal,* 1739." Bushman 22–23.

Seward, William. *Journal of a Voyage from Savannah to Philadelphia, and from Philadelphia to England.* London, 1740.

Stein, Stephen J. "George Whitefield on Slavery: Some New Evidence." *Church History* 42.2 (1973): 243–57.

———. "A Note on Anne Dutton." *Church History* 44.4 (1975): 485–91.

Stiles, Ezra. *The Literary Diary of Ezra Stiles.* Ed. Franklin B. Dexter. Vol. 1. New York: Scribner's, 1901. 3 vols.

Stout, Harry S. *The Divine Dramatist: George Whitefield and the Rise of Modern Evangelicalism.* Grand Rapids: Eerdmans, 1991.

————. *The New England Soul: Preaching and Religious Culture in Colonial New England.* New York: Oxford UP, 1986.

————. "Religion, Communications, and the Ideological Origins of the American Revolution." *William and Mary Quarterly* 3rd ser. 34 (1977): 519–41.

Stout, Harry S., and Peter Onuf. "James Davenport and the Great Awakening in New London." *Journal of American History* 70 (1983): 556–78.

Tracy, Joseph. *The Great Awakening: A History of the Revival of Religion in the Time of Edwards and Whitefield.* Boston, 1842.

Trilling, Lionel. *Sincerity and Authenticity.* Cambridge: Harvard UP, 1971.

Trinterud, Leonard. *The Forming of an American Tradition: A Re-examination of Colonial Presbyterianism.* Philadelphia: n.p., 1949.

Tyerman, Rev. Luke. *The Life of the Rev. George Whitefield in Two Volumes.* 2nd ed. London, 1890.

Van Doren, Carl. *Benjamin Franklin.* 1938. New York: Penguin, 1991.

Walsh, John. "Methodism and the Mob in the Eighteenth Century." *Popular Belief and Practice.* Ed. G. J. Cuming and Derek Baker. Cambridge: Cambridge UP, 1972. 213–27.

Weller, Samuel. *The Trial of Mr. Whitefield's Spirit.* Boston, 1741.

Whitefield, George. *George Whitefield's Journals (1737–1741), to Which Is Prefixed His "Short Account" (1746) and "Further Account" (1747).* Ed. William Wale. Gainesville: Scholars' Facsimiles and Reprints, 1969.

————. *The Works of the Reverend George Whitefield.* 6 vols. London, 1771.

Williams, Daniel E. "'Behold a Tragic Scene Strangely Changed into a Theater of Mercy': The Structure and Significance of Criminal Conversion Narratives in Early New England." *American Quarterly* 38 (1986): 825–47.

Williams, John R. "The Strange Case of Dr. Franklin and Mr. Whitefield." *Pennsylvania Magazine of History and Biography* 102.4 (1978): 399–421.

Wills, Garry. "The Phallic Pulpit." *New York Review of Books* 21 Dec. 1989: 20–26.

What's Art Got to Do with It? The Status of the Subject of the Humanities in the Age of Cultural Studies

Charles Bernstein

The gradual shift from literary studies to cultural and multicultural studies is probably the most useful change to have occurred within the American academy in the past decade. The literary studies approach to the humanities tended to make a clear-cut distinction between works of art and works of mass or popular culture. Works of art were the primary field of study for the critic, whose secondary role was to explicate or illuminate these art objects. Yet it is difficult to provide a rule for distinguishing great art from cultural artifact, and the ideological biases of much of the prevailing literary and art connoisseurship have served literary studies poorly. In contrast, the cultural studies approach seems both more reasonable and more malleable. We start not with art and its others but with a variety of signifying practices. The field of possible attention is vast and might just as well include film comedies of the thirties as Dickens's novels, Kewpie dolls as much as Picassos, although, for practical purposes, the focus of any given study will be narrowed.

The shift to poststructuralist cultural studies has been precipitated by an intriguing variety of frames of interpretation—theoretical, historical, psychological, and sociological—and within each of these frames there are a number of distinct, and competing, methodologies. The present crisis of cultural studies results from the seeming autonomy of the frames of interpretation from what they are to interpret; we have less objects of study than what Stanley Fish calls "interpretive communities." What is to be interpreted is by no means secure, nor are the objects of interpretation necessarily of any determining significance. This is a somewhat awkward, even anxious situation. But it is not fundamentally different from the methodological approach of much modernist and contemporary art, where forms of interpretation constitute the subject.

1

In large measure the controversy in the national media over the political crisis of higher education—whether characterized in terms of "political correctness," the canon, multiculturalism, or the ascent of theory—can be attributed to the shift from literary to cultural studies. While I am troubled by aspects of the cultural studies model, my own disagreements have little in common with the chorus of self-described liberals and conservatives who see in cultural studies the loss of "disinterested" scholarship and common cultural standards. The vehemence of the attacks on cultural and new historical studies has left too little room for a critique of the ways in which cultural studies continues to perpetuate a deterministic or professional rather than rhetorical or poetic approach to its subjects. This left-libertarian or aesthetic critique of cultural studies becomes almost impossible to hear amidst the mischaracterizations of its goals that seem mischievously aimed at preventing any thoughtful discussion of the issues. As in national politics, the Right has been able to define the terms of the debate. If the naysayers better understood the issues, they might find they have little to fear from new developments in the literary academy and that, indeed, cultural and multicultural studies offer a revitalized version of the traditional humanities, which have suffered from near asphyxiation by means of the antidemocratic arguments for the received authority of a narrow band of cultural arbiters. Far from challenging the legitimating process of the university, the cultural studies movement actually extends this process in ways that are largely consonant with a tradition that comes to us in fits and starts from the Enlightenment's attack on Scholasticism. Indeed, cultural studies extends the principles of critical self-reflection and disinterested observation in ways that actively work to preserve existing cultural values. For the exponents of cultural and multicultural studies represent mainstream American conceptions of value and practice.

In this light, the abusive series of attacks in the media can be understood in the first instance as anti-intellectual and in the second, when carried out by scholars, as a form of intellectual self-hatred. By speaking of intellectual self-hatred I mean to carry over Sander Gilman's arguments in *Jewish Self-Hatred*. The intellectual imagines that there is a hidden language of truth from which she or he is barred by reliance on the slippery and partial slopes of metaphoric language. In this fantasy, intellectuals, like Jews, are exiled from a deeper connection to the world and so denounce their own language, the only language that they know or can speak. Self-hating intellectuals internalize the anti-intellectuals' conception of their coworkers as professional ciphers, unmoored from the values of the "larger" society. By internalizing the larger community's most negative stereotype of their activity, self-hating intellectuals become the most vocal critics of the relativism and social anarchy that they testify is the true message of "theory." For who could know better the dangers of theory than one who has witnessed its dark secret or its corrosive powers? For the self-hating intellectual, the hidden language of reason is nihilism.

By internalizing the larger community's most negative stereotype of their activity, self-hating intellectuals become the most vocal critics of the relativism and social anarchy that they testify is the true message of "theory."

What, for example, could be more disorienting than casting Stanley Fish as a radical? Fish's defense of professionalization is the model of an enlightened, pragmatic approach to the humanities. He is witty and ingenious in his critiques of any attempt to give special moral weight or ideological force to one theoretical position rather than another. While that may undercut the Romantic humanism that gives a self-righteous tone or hubris to so many traditional professors of English literature, Fish's antifoundationalism is rooted in the values of the profession of which he is a part. Moreover, he insists on politesse, against the authoritarian demagoguery that tends to undermine the values of consensus and reason in an academic setting.

Fish's position is aimed at preserving and respecting institutional memory; it assures continuities and the representation of a variety of viewpoints in any dispute. That is, Fish's antifoundationalism is a moderate and centrist position—no more radical than the democratic principles upon which it is based. It is a measure of the corrosiveness of racism and misogyny that his position favoring the inclusion of African Americans and women in determining curricular policy is so routinely caricatured as extreme.

My own misgivings about Fish's position take an entirely different direction, since I find his professionalization of discourse undermines the possibility of any trenchant critique of canonical values or indeed of the institutionalized rationality that Fish enacts. Fish's system suffers from being a self-enclosed artifact, unable to confront its own, inevitable positionality. It represents the professionalization of professionalization and precludes the aestheticizing of its own values, insofar as such aestheticizing might ground judgments outside the context of a profession, holding one's judgments to a continual testing of and in the world.

2

Many of the welcome changes in the humanities curriculum reflect not revaluations of the role of high or canonical culture but shifts in the representation of various groups in determining what these canonical works should be. The Arnoldian criterion of touchstone works of a culture simply has been applied to a greater number of contexts, just as the Jeffersonian conception of democracy has at times been applied to a greater number of constituencies. The mechanism of discrimination between canonical and noncanonical works is not dismantled but rather extended to previously uncovered areas. Institutionalized multiculturalism represents the culmination of Arnoldian principles of distinction; its great failure lies in its tacit acceptance of the concept of touchstone or representative works. To be sure, institutionalized multiculturalism represents a necessary revision of the concept of representation. In this newer context, what is represented by a work is not, at least in the first place, the culture understood as a homogenous whole. But an initial recognition of ethnic origin often gives way to a supervening program of cultural recuperation, where works are chosen because they represent ennobling voices of their subculture, voices that enter into the great conversation of universal human values, as proponents of the Great Books used to put it. Houston Baker, in *Modernism and the Harlem Renaissance,* makes an eloquent case for something like this strategy when he argues for the mask of mastering form over the guerrilla tactic of deforming mastery. The uncertain success of this strategy is represented by the pride of place given, in such textbooks as the *Norton Anthology of Modern Poetry,* to the sonnets of Countee Cullen and Claude McKay and the exclusion in the same anthologies of the dialect and vernacular poems of Paul Laurence Dunbar, James Weldon Johnson, and Sterling Brown, which, however, can be found in the new multicultural *Heath Anthology of American Poetry.*

Despite the fact that the Heath anthology does a better job of "representing" the touchstones of American culture than Norton, I see no radical conceptual difference between the two. Both have the primary effect of taking a very heterogenous field and domesticating it. Both represent literature in measured doses, uniform typography, and leveling head- and footnotes—making the poetry the subject of its frame rather than presenting poetry itself as a contest—a conflict—of frames.

One thing the Norton modern poetry anthologies have never done is to represent white or European culture. Yet this point is too rarely acknowledged because of a confusion as to what constitutes "high" or canonical culture in America, a situation abetted by the fact that many of the defenders of a putative "high" culture imagine this culture to exist solely in the past—or act as if it were in the past.

The cultural canon of the Norton anthology is as aggressively anti–"high" cultural as the Heath anthology. As a matter of policy, the Norton anthology systematically excludes the aesthetically radical innovations of European and American art in preference for a so-called middlebrow or suburban poetry that tends to be anti-European and is often antiaesthetic. Within this deaestheticizing ideology, it is far easier to include token ethnic representation, as the *Norton Anthology of Modern Poetry* does in its most recent version, than to include works, including those written by historically underrepresented groups, that undermine the formally complacent, content-focused biases of official verse culture.

It turns out that those most likely to defend the importance of great art are themselves the major perpetrators of a disastrous lowering of standards. Indeed, it's a wild irony to see the *New York Times* run article after article debunking the new university barbarians for abandoning the great works of our cultural heritage, when in its own book supplement it primarily promotes literary works that make no claims on the most resonant cultural traditions of Europe or America. It would scarcely be an exaggeration to say that of the 100 most formally, theoretically, intellectually, prosodically, or politically challenging works of or about poetry published in the last 10 years, the *New York Times* has reviewed less than five percent. The same could be said for the *New York Review of Books,* but also for every other highly visible, nationally distributed newspaper or magazine. In the defense of the mediocre, left journals like the *Nation* and right journals like the *New Criterion* compete with each other only in their scrambling to promote the same conventional poetic values. (See, for example, an article in a recent issue of the *Nation,* by its former literary editor, applauding a defense of the "middlebrow" in the *New Republic*; or the ongoing efforts by the *Nation*'s theater critic to uphold the vapid in literature and art against all comers.)

"High," "middle," "low"—there are no fixed meanings for these terms, and I mean to use them against themselves. I want to suggest that a collapsing of the low and the high against the middle is a feature not just of cultural studies but also of significant directions within twentieth-century philosophy and poetry. In philosophy, this is most explicitly signaled by the "quest for the ordinary," in Stanley Cavell's phrase, a quest related to the preoccupation with the vernacular, dialect, the everyday, and the common in poetry. High and low are also literally collapsed when elements from popular or regional or "other" (for example, tribal) cultures are collaged into poems or paintings—a feature some have argued is a hallmark of postwar modernisms but whose roots go back much earlier and, indeed, suggest a model for cultural studies in modernist collage and appropriation. Finally, the insistence of many artists, contemporary and modern, on the taboo, the vulgar, and the mean also represents an alliance of the high and the low against a self-defining middle. It is this direction that has caused the greatest fury, with attacks on the National Endowment for the Arts being the most visible battleground. Those concerned with the fate of cultural, multicultural, and poststructuralist studies need to join artists in resisting these attacks—which have targeted gay and feminist performance artists—as passionately as they would attacks on academic freedom, which they closely resemble.

3

We're all middle class now, or it is as if the culture inscribes this allegiance to middle-class values as a psychic tax on consumer purchases. As with all regressive taxes, this one hits those with less than middle incomes the hardest and is easily absorbed by the wealthy. Which is to say, it is the right to define the "middle" that is being contested by the Left, Right, and Center. But earning this right requires the rejection of all the highs and lows—the obscure, the peripheral or marginal or minor, the avant-garde, the complex, the eccentric, the dark, the distasteful, the ugly, the unassimilable, the erotic, the repulsive, the formally unsettling. From the populist perspective, such work may be discounted as elitist or regressive or both; from the defenders of transcendental literary values, such work is attacked as corrosive. Moreover, the contest for the middle is less something that pits high culture against low culture than it is a struggle within "high" and "popular" culture: Kathy Acker versus James Merrill, Vanilla Ice versus Linton Kwesi Johnson, *The Cosby Show* versus *The Simpsons*.

4

Just because something is neglected is sufficient reason to consider it.

5

Is there a special status of high art that should be accorded our most respected poets and novelists and denied Paul Rubens or Peter Straub or Jackie Mason? Are these writers any more deserving of a place in the classroom than *Pee-Wee's Playhouse* or *Mystery* or *The World According to Jackie Mason*? On the contrary, these three works are more interesting and more worthy of close reading than many of the recent winners of the Pulitzer Prize or National Book Award. If the prizewinners are the contemporary case for high culture, then there can be no question that those who prefer to study cultural and social texts are probably right. There's more innovation and more cultural acumen in any episode of *Ren and Stimpy* than in any of the books of our last trio of national poet laureates.

Our worst examples, foisted on us by the cultural orthodontics of official literary culture, serve us badly. We keep thinking that what is canonized as high art is what art is all about—but this whitewash of our literary and aesthetic histories represses what indeed is the lasting legacy of even white, Eurocentric male artists, much less artists of different origins and, perhaps more useful to say, different destinations. In the great shell game of art in the university, the "art" has too often disappeared, replaced by administered culture. And administered art may be no better than no art, since it's the administration that is doing most of the signifying.

6

What, then, accounts for the complacently narrow range of styles and tone in the official verse culture of the postwar period? Perhaps this too can be understood as a manifestation of intellectual self-hatred. Professional anti-intellectualism plays itself out in a particularly uninhibited form in the promoting of works of poetry that espouse a distaste for the intellectual and rhetorical nature of writing—poems that insist on affiliation with innocuous abstractions like the "universal human spirit" while denying their implication in the material forms in which particular human spirits actually might appear. Ironically, it is such nostalgic values, fundamentally aversive to a contemporary engagement with the poetic, that those who profess both literary and cultural studies too often ascribe to poetry as such.

The products of official verse culture are no more interesting or valuable than the products of Madison Avenue. (What would be the state of film studies if it were confined to Oscar nominees?) Indeed, poetry can also be a form of cultural studies that incorporates reading the products of Madison Avenue; call it, Social Expressionism. Yet the university as a professional environment remains hostile to this type of approach both in its creative-writing programs and in its normalizing writing practices.

There is no art, only signifying practices. Or rather, who's to say what's just a signifying practice and what a work of art? Once the fixed points of difference are undermined, there can be no rule to make such distinctions. But it doesn't follow from this that distinctions cannot be made in particular contexts. Of course, if poetry is above the fray of competing social discourses, then its special status is secure. But there is no Poetry, only poetries. The patchwork quilt of works I have in mind insists on its reflectiveness as a means of refracting the pull of commodification or, to put it more historically, zeitgeistization. The works of social expressionism—whether by Bruce Andrews or Hannah Weiner, Ron Silliman or William Burroughs—are neither the unreflected products of their period nor the lyric expression of individual selves. Rather, the social field itself is expressed, in the sense of brought into view, represented by means of interpretation and interpenetration.

7

The university environment is not just nonpoetic, which would be unexceptional, but antipoetic. And this situation has remained constant as we have moved from literary studies to the more sociologically and psychoanalytically deterministic approaches to cultural studies. At the same time, the university is perhaps the only one among many antipoetic and antiphilosophic American institutions that will entertain its antipathy to the poetic and the philosophic as a significant problem, and it is this approach that I think becomes more possible in the age of cultural studies.

Within the academic environment, thought tends to be rationalized—subject to examination, paraphrase, repetition, mechanization, reduction. It is treated: contained and stabilized. And what is lost in this treatment is the irregular, the nonquantifiable, the nonstandard or nonstandardizable, the erratic, the inchoate. (Is it just a mood or sensibility I'm talking about, and if that's it, can mood be professionalized?)

Poetry is turbulent thought, at least that's what I want from it, what I want to say about it just here, just now (and maybe not in some other context). It leaves things unsettled, unresolved—leaves you knowing less than you did when you started.

Here, then, is my thesis: There is a fear of the inchoate processes of turbulent thought (poetic or philosophic) that takes the form of resistance and paranoia. A wall (part symbolic, part imaginary) is constructed against the sheer surplus of interpretable aspects of any subject. You fix upon one among many possible frames, screens, screams, and stay fixed on that mode monomaniacally. Such frame fixation is intensified by the fetishizing of dispassionate evaluation not as a critical method but as a marker of professional competence and a means of enforcing a system of ranking.

In theory, the proliferation of frames of interpretation (feminist, psychoanalytic, grammatologic, economic, sociologic, Romantic, historical materialist, New Critical, reader-response, canonic, periodic) is a positive development. In practice, the incommensurability among these frames has led to a balkanization of theory. The normalizing tendency, resisted by some of the most resourceful practitioners of cultural studies, is to elect one interpretive mode and to apply it, cookie-cutter-like, to any given phenomenon. On the one hand, this can be defended on scientific or religious grounds and on the other hand, as a form not of faith or positivism but of specialization.

8

To say that the literary academy is antipoetic is not to say that poets or literary artists are the sole repository of the poetic. This would be to split the aesthetic and philosophic from other forms of cultural activity when it is just this splitting—splintering—that is the problem. The poetic is not confined to poetry but rather is embedded in all our activities as critics, teachers, researchers, and writers, not to mention citizens. When we use figurative language, which is just about whenever we use language at all, we are entangled in the poetic realm. Whenever we choose one metaphoric or trope-ic system of interpretation we make aesthetic choices, moral judgments. Poetry is too important to be left to poets, just in the way that politics is too important to be left to politicians or that education is too important to be left to educators; though poets, politicians, and educators may exercise a valuable function when they elucidate how poetry, politics, and learning can be hyperactivated in everyday life.

Our political and academic culture of imposed solutions at the expense of open-ended explorations, of fixed or schematic or uniform interpretive mechanisms and political platforms versus multiple, shifting, context-sensitive interventions, splits off the "bad" poetic from "good" rigor and critical distantiation. Such splitting eclipses reason in its uncontained denial. Out of fear of the Dark, we turn our back to the lights we have at hand, in hand.

9

With justification, we have removed poetry—the "literary"—from any privileged status as an object of study but have not enlisted the poetic as an allied interpretive activity. Because of the lingering hold of reductive rationalism, we have administered to art the one-two punch: neither valuing it, Romantically, for itself nor valuing it for its critical and cognitive function.

My point is not to relegate criticism or literary theory to secondary status. I agree with Fish and others that the new interpretive approaches change the objects of study. Rather, I am insisting that art not be reduced to secondary status, the "object" of critical projection, but understood as an irreplaceable method of interpreting culture, including other artworks— "poetry as discourse," in Antony Easthope's useful formulation.

The poetic—the aesthetic—the philosophic—the rhetorical: these intertwined figures dissolve into the art of everyday life, the multiple and particular decisions and revisions, recognitions and intuitions, that make up—constitute—our experiences of and in the world. The poetic is not simply another frame of interpretation to be laid down next to the psycholinguistic and sociohistorical. The poetic is both a hypoframe, inhering within each frame of interpretation, and a hyperframe, a practice of moving from frame to frame.

Such hypertextuality offers not a theory of frames—a supervening or hypotactic ordering principle—but an art of transition through and among frames. Call it the art of parataxis, where the elements set side by side are critical methods rather than images or ideas: an art of practice, which provides not answers but paths of reading and provisional connections among these paths. The alternative to frame fixation is context sensitivity; that is, allowing different contexts to suggest different interpretative approaches while at the same time flipping among several frames or, at the least, acknowledging the provisionality of any single-frame approach. The poetic is not a master frame, able to reconcile incommensurable approaches. Rather, poetry has its expertise in encompassing incommensurable elements without getting locked into any one of them; this, anyway, is a strain of poetry that goes back to Blake and Heraclitus and forward to many writers—poets and critics, scholars and theorists—in our own time.

10

It is not theory that has supplanted criticism or art but rather an axiometric, solution-focused theory that marks a continuity from literary to cultural studies, over and against the heterogenous traditions of critical theory and aesthetic practice associated with such antipositivist writers as Roland Barthes and Stanley Cavell, Erving Goffman and Robert Creeley, Michel de Certeau and Bernadette Mayer, Raymond Federman and John Ashbery, James Clifford and Luce Irigaray, Guy Debord and Lyn Hejinian, Jackson Mac Low and Paul Feyerabend; *add your name here.*

Of course, it is possible for any writer's work to be turned from practice to doctrine, and surely this is what has happened to the work of many of the governing Proper Names of structuralist and poststructuralist theory. It is not surprising that literary professionals might prefer answers to questions, explications to evocations, doctrine to introspection, probity to pleasure. But this system of preferences and inclinations, this habitat of professionalism, in Pierre Bourdieu's sense, is untheorized, uncritical. The habitat of professionalism marks not a substantive position but a self-justifying apparatus of control. While one of the defining axioms of cultural studies is the death of the author, the authors of cultural studies seem to exempt themselves from the full effect of this theory, much the way a queen might be exempted from her own decrees. The theory death of the author seems to apply only to other people's authors.

If we are to understand, following Bourdieu, that the value of a work of art is determined by the same system of discriminations—class-based dispositions or tastes—that determines the differential value of styles of furniture or dresses or table manners, then why not apply this to Bourdieu's *Distinction: A Social Critique of the Judgment of Taste*? Why not demystify the social scientific claim for his theory and see his book as a commodity whose status is determined by its role in the professional habitat to which he belongs? On such a sociometric reading, on what basis do we make a distinction between Bourdieu's empirical analysis and that found in consumer surveys in *Elle* or *Ladies Home Journal*? Put another way, Is Fredric Jameson's writing on postmodernism a symptom of postindustrial capitalism?

For those who wish to model cultural and New Historical and psychoanalytic studies on the social sciences, these questions will seem merely silly. It is literary authors who are the product of their period, while social scientists are able to maintain their authority and, not unimportantly, their status as authors and professors, because their methods immunize them from becoming subjects of the historical forces within which they operate.

11

My method immunizes me against nothing, accelerating my subjection to the multivectoral forces I am periodically digested by. My signifying behavior is eclipsed by the semiotic maelstrom I feel myself falling, slipping, tumbling, and twirling into. The only distance I know the one from *me* to *you*; yet it's enough to ground me in the runes of what I would otherwise imagine could be my possession. For there is nothing other than this grounding in "communities of discourse," a language play of hide and seek. And this makes me count my judgment, learn what making judgment is.

12

Signifying practices have only art from which to copy.

13

The idea that a statistical or objectifying orientation, or else a tone of disinterested probity, raises criticism or theory above the level of cultural artifact is profoundly ahistorical; nor is there any reason to suppose that this has changed in the age of cultural studies. Art and critical writing can be sites of social and aesthetic resistance. Yet both share the tendency to conformism and complacency. Typical professional criticism, like the dominant forms of verse and visual arts, reifies more than resists. Against its most advanced theory, such writing retains the illusions of voice and its authority, in blissless compliance with received standards. Its authors are not so much dead as operating on automatic pilot, and it is as if cries to wake them are jammed by the control towers.

This is not an unregulated process. Norms are strictly enforced by a system of hazards and penalties for those who drift outside the narrow stylistic confines of official critical discourse. And what justifies this monologic, tone-jammed prose? Not the intrinsic virtues of the style, since the threats of being unmarketable or unpublishable are internally enforced professional criteria, part of a system of self-regulation, in Foucault's sense, that gains its legitimacy by being able to enforce a distinction between acceptable and unacceptable discursive manners. The need for discipline preexists the particular distinction that gives content to the discipline. Thus the poetic as a negative space is necessary to give disciplinarity to disinterested scholarship or rigorous theory.

Research and analysis can exist independent of the forms in which they are represented but cannot, finally, remain unaffected by them. The governing principle of the plain style of much critical prose is that it should be as neutral as possible, that it should not call attention to itself. Untidy thoughts and facts must be made to conform to this "anti"rhetoric, if not by the author then by the interventionist editorial practices of professional journals that enforce mood and tone control as if a loose sentence were a case of intemperance or the conventions of grammar and style were hieratic laws, not matters of agreement and disagreement.

It is always fair to ask of a mode of writing, "What interests does it serve?" Are there studies that demonstrate that the currently enforced dissertation styles make better teachers? Do they increase interest on the part of readers in their subjects? Are they the only way to encourage the depth of detailed knowledge of a particular subject or period that remains one of the overriding values of scholarship? Are they more a rite of initiation into a profession than a mark of an active engagement with a culture?

14

Is prose justified? Or aren't you the kind that tells? That's no prose that's my default. Default is in our sorrow not our swells.

I am writing this with a fountain pen on a yellow legal pad, lying down on a couch, the pad propped up by my knee. I resist sitting down at a machine on a desk; I want to write from a more comfortable position. I enjoy writing more this way.

Does not knowing the relevance of this factor argue that I should leave it out? What kind of writing results from suppressing all the elements that can't be justified? My most fruitful thoughts at first seem unfounded, foundering; if not elusive, then wildly speculative. I like to follow the course of such thoughts even as I am taken to more and more improbable conclusions. In my court of writing, I have loose rules of evidence. If a phrase occurs to me and I don't see the pertinence, I know better than to abandon course. Perhaps some useful turning is at hand. Rather than discount what may not at first appear to fit my theme, and risk losing a new and more resonant address, I hold a thought relevant until proven otherwise, give the benefit to what I doubt, pursuing a flicker in preference to reiterating what I already knew.

The shortest distance between two points is a digression. I hold for a wandering thought just that I may stumble upon something worthy of report. Montaigne is the most typical writer in all of Western prose.

15

The idea is to put the shoe on the other foot—evaluate the evaluators, historicize the historicizers, decode the decoders, critique the critics, rebuke the rebukers, debunk the debunkers, categorize the categorizers, schmooze the schmoozers, level the levelers, revel with the revelers.

Put the shoe on the other foot and tear it.

16

"There's a lot of anger there, Charles. You really need to work it out."

"You've got a million crackpot theories; I only wish one of them would pan out." (As if writing were prospecting for the pleated gold at the end of the theory rainbow.)

17

I suppose the only thing I count as an absolute moral virtue is learning difficulties, disorientation, and lexical hindrances. When I hear people talking about scanning lines, I assume they're referring to the security guards at grocery checkouts. Not that I don't admire scrupulous accuracy and competence; I just happen to prefer the company of small businesspersons.

But seriously, you can't go wrong if your attitude is bad from the start. You've got nowhere to go but up. Virtue is easier to strive for than to hold onto.

18

A friend of my daughter just got into the school for the gifted and talented, but she was confused and wanted me to tell her if she was gifted or talented. I always wanted to be gifted but evidently didn't have the talent for it. Anyway, my philosophy of education is—don't take gifts, but don't pay retail either.

Yet many of my friends in the university are conflicted—are they artists or scholars, teachers or writers—as if you aren't one by virtue of the other. That's what virtue is all about.

Or consider the professor who was always distracted at his seminars because, he said, they were taking him from his work. My teaching also keeps me from my work, which is teaching.

But while I love Art, I wouldn't want to marry her.

Or have you heard the one about the person who was half critic and half artist. What she can't objectify, she appropriates.

Behind every successful artist is a New Historian who says it's all just a symptom. Behind every successful New His-

torian is an artist who says you forgot to mention my work—
and, boy, is it symptomatic!

I've never met an artist who felt she or he was getting
enough attention. Prizes, books on the work, multiyear grants.
"But still, did you see the fifth sentence of that review where it
says 'possibly the greatest'?" Or: "Did you see the index to
that book on the twentieth century?—no mention of my name."
Scholars, in contrast, seem surprised if you've ever read a
paragraph of theirs. "What? You saw that article? I didn't realize anybody read that journal." "What? You read my book? But
it was just published eight years ago, and I didn't realize your
research took you so far afield to read about the decline of
modern civilization."

19

One can learn as much about a profession by dwelling on
what it frowns upon as on what it prizes. Our professionalism
encourages us to act as administrators of culture rather than
participants, collaborators, or partisans enthralled with our
subjects. Yet this very professionalism can preclude perspective on our own absorption in the fictions of critical distance.
The problem with the normalizing critical writing practices of
the humanities is not that they are too theoretical but that they
are not theoretical enough—they fail to theorize themselves or
to keep pace with their own theories.

Our professionalism encourages us to act as administrators of culture rather than participants, collaborators, or partisans enthralled with our subjects.

For models for the new writing the age demands, North
American literary and cultural critics, essayists, and historians
have turned to the radical literary arts of this century producing
a startling range of prose forms.[1] No doubt the range of writing
I'm thinking about here collapses conventional distinctions
among scholarly, popular, and general interest prose; but in an
age of cultural studies, such segmentation will not hold. The
space of prose is an operating environment that embeds genres
within genres. Nor does one have to choose between fiction
and story, for there are the stories of our searches and research-
es. The art of the essay; but also the essay as art.

For prose can sing. It can swim against the remorseless
tide of axiomatizing and tone-lock. But that requires that as
writers we listen to the sounds that we make with our words;
that we own the shapes our paragraphs declare as they crash
into one another or erode each other's edges; that we hear both
the studied and the studying as always art, music, the movement
of ideas through measures and measuring, shifted and shifting

tempos and modulations. This is the promise of a writing-conscious cultural studies as much as of a proactive poetics.

The test of the new poststructuralists will be whether we will change the prevailing institutionalized infatuation with triumphalist specialization, neoscientific prose, and all shape and manner of standardization, from tests to course designs. Will we apply our theories of ambiguity, provisionality, and the nomadic not just to reinterpreting the power dynamics of centuries no doubt prematurely consigned to history, but also to our own workplace and its administrative and professional apparatuses?

20

Of course, poetry and fiction are institutionalized in university creative-writing programs. But for the most part such programs do little to further social expressionism in poetry or cultural activism in criticism. Too often creative-writing programs lock themselves into counterproductive antagonism with English departments, especially with the new literary theory, fearing philosophy will compromise the intuitive and emotional capacity on which a poet must rely in fabricating her or his voice.

It doesn't have to be this way. Creative-writing programs could be transformed into university centers for the art of writing, specializing in research and development into the social and aesthetic dimensions of writing. At the same time, literature classes could be transformed from a knowledge-acquisition approach to creative-reading workshops, replacing tests with poetic response in the form of free-form journals, poems, and literary imitations.

I don't teach Literature, I teach poetry-as-a-second-language, or PSL—People in Solidarity with Language. That means I try to immerse the workshop (formerly class) in poetic forms, poetic sounds, and poetic logics. Tapes of poets reading their own work are indispensable, since there is no way to fully explain sound values; it would be as if you tried to teach music only from scores. Poetry readings, along with regular visits by literary artists to graduate and undergraduate classes, can be catalytic, offering an entirely different context for poems than books and anthologies, one immensely more immediate and performative.

PSL isn't focused on just the big nouns; its immersion is into the wide and varied syntax of poetic practice, from popular and folk and novelty to conventional to radically innovative (a project it shares with cultural and multicultural studies). There's nothing like juxtaposing Robert Service's "The Shooting of Dan McGrew" with T. S. Eliot's "Prufrock," or Melvin Tolson with Lorine Neidecker, or Laura Riding with John Masefield. And the fact that no anthology represents this conflict and context of poetries is all the better, since it helps to dispel any notion that poetry is a single activity with a unified purpose. (Eliot is the only one of these six poets in either the *Norton Anthology of Modern Poetry* or the Heath anthologies.)

PSL immersion need not be confined to twentieth-century literature, for one can read poems through other poems as much as through more traditional critical methodologies. I can't help reading the poems of the past with the benefit of the many new critical approaches of the present, but neither can I read these older poems without having my reading altered by the poetry of the present. I understand Wordsworth better because I've read *Flow Chart*. I'm convinced William Cowper read J. H. Prynne before writing *The Task*. And I'm more likely to give a Jabesian reading of Heine than a Kristevan one.

21

Finally, let me turn to one of the most pressing issues facing the university in the 1990s: PC. I believe that PC is crucial for a writer—personal cappuccino. Of the three types—the Italian hand-pump style, the German electric, and the American pump or press—all have much to offer.

Notes

Presented as the keynote speech at the annual spring convention of the Northeast Modern Language Association, 3 April 1992, in Buffalo.

1.   To mention just those from the last few years: the dialogues of Jerome McGann, the use of typographic and visual elements as integral to both the critical analysis and mode of argument in Trinh T. Minh-ha's *Woman, Native, Other,* Art Spiegelman's *Maus,* Avital Ronell's *The Telephone Book,* and Johanna Drucker's *Simulant Portrait*; the insistence on the autobiographical in the recent talk essays of David Antin, Samuel R. Delany's *The Motion of Light in Water,* and Nancy K. Miller's *Getting Personal*; the politically and performatively charged essays of Kofi Natambu; the pataphysically playful, detail-centered sixteenth- and seventeenth-century textual criticism of Randall McLeod; the new historiography of Susan Howe's *The Birth-mark: Unsettling the Wilderness in American Literary History*; the

improvisatory prose of Amiri Baraka; the essays-in-film of Yvonne Rainer; the exuberant championing of nonstandard poetries as part of a context of visual and popular culture in Cary Nelson's *Repression and Recovery* and Marjorie Perloff's *The Futurist Moment, Poetic License,* and *Radical Artifice*; the reworking of biography and autobiography as oral history in Quincy Troupe's rethinking of the vernacular in *Miles, The Autobiography* and Peter Brazeau's earlier book on Wallace Stevens, *Parts of a World*; Dennis Tedlock's continuing explorations of oral and performative modes of interpretation and translation; Larry McCaffery's championing of the interview and other metafictional critical forms; the glorious speculative flights of Nick Piombino in *Boundary of Blur* or Steve McCaffery in *North of Intention* or in Christopher Dewdney's natural history as sci-fi; the intertwining of poetry and philosophy in Linda Reinfeld's *Language Poetry: Writing as Rescue*; the hypertextual investigations of Michael Joyce and Jay Boltner and the electronic format of the new electronic-mail magazine *Postmodern Culture*; and such marvelous reworkings of the essay form as Larry Eigner's *Areas/Lights/Heights,* Nathaniel Mackey's *Bedouin Hornbook,* Madeline Gins's (forthcoming) *Helen Keller or Arakawa,* James Sherry's *Our Nuclear Heritage,* Nicole Brossard's *Picture Theory,* and Leslie Scalapino's *How Phenomena Appear to Unfold.*